MW00490952

Dispute resolution in China

In recent years, the Chinese legal system on civil litigation, arbitration, and mediation, including the respective laws, regulations, and legal institutions, has undergone many changes. Offering a detailed examination of the elements in the Chinese legal system and the relevant reforms to civil litigation, arbitration, mediation, and hybrid dispute resolution, this book provides a comprehensive study of the civil and commercial dispute resolution landscape in China today. It situates these developments within a unique hybrid of empirical, contextual, and comparative analytical framework, while providing roadmap for productive reforms in future.

This book argues that, rather than being a legal project, China's civil dispute resolution system is essentially a social development project and that the system is constrained by China's political imperatives, which distinguishes the Chinese approach to civil justice reform from contemporary civil justice movements elsewhere. Commercial arbitration in China today being comparatively less political in nature, its reform has been more driven by market-oriented considerations and shaped by socio-economic forces. By contrast, civil litigation and mediation being more instrumentalist in nature, their reform is socio-politically embedded and subject to the Chinese government's social and political objectives. This book will be essential reading and invaluable reference tool for scholars with a focus on comparative Chinese law, dispute resolution, and broader economic and political dimensions of dispute resolution development in China.

Weixia Gu is an Associate Professor at the University of Hong Kong (HKU), Faculty of Law, and a Co-Chair of the American Society of International Law Asia-Pacific Interest Group, where she specializes in arbitration and dispute resolution (both international and domestic) and private international law, with a focus on China. She is the author and editor of over 60 books, book chapters, and journal articles. Her works have appeared in leading comparative and international law journals in the East and West, and her scholarship has been cited by the US Court of Appeals Eleventh Circuit, US Texas Supreme Court, and Singapore Law Gazette. She is the recipient of HKU's Outstanding Young Researcher Award in 2018.

Dispute resolution in China

Litigation, arbitration, mediation, and their interactions

Weixia Gu

LONDON AND NEW YORK

First published 2021
by Routledge
2 Park Square, Milton Park, Abingdon, Oxon OX14 4RN

and by Routledge
52 Vanderbilt Avenue, New York, NY 10017

Routledge is an imprint of the Taylor & Francis Group, an informa business

British Library Cataloguing-in-Publication Data
A catalogue record for this book is available from the British Library

Library of Congress Cataloging-in-Publication Data
A catalog record has been requested for this book

ISBN: 978-1-138-82359-4 (hbk)
ISBN: 978-1-315-74197-0 (ebk)

Typeset in Times New Roman
by KnowledgeWorks Global Ltd.

Contents

Charts

Tables

Acknowledgments

Dispute Resolution in China represents the fruits of my research efforts in this field in the past few years. It seeks to provide comprehensive insights into the contemporary situation of the entire civil dispute resolution landscape (civil litigation, arbitration, mediation, and hybrid dispute resolution systems arising out of their interactions) and its reform, through empirical, contextual, comparative, and law and development studies. In the process of writing this book, many institutions and people have helped me and should be acknowledged.

I would like to first thank the support from my home institution, Faculty of Law of the University of Hong Kong. Sincere thanks are due to our Dean Hualing Fu, Associate Dean for Research Simon Young and Department Head Yun Zhao, who have provided me with a supportive research environment, and have given their full support throughout the organizing and progress of this book.

Many scholars have helped me with this book project. Albert Chen has always encouraged me to write a book on China's dispute resolution and has commented on different parts of the draft manuscript. Michael Palmer has read through all the draft chapters and contributed his expertise and insights which have improved the book. Xin He has read a substantial portion of the draft manuscript and offered valuable comments to improve the book's methodologies and arguments. Anselmo Reyes has guided me a great deal on international dispute resolution developments and contributed his distinctive perspective as an international judge. Xiao Cheng has been a working dictionary of China's civil laws in the course of my writing. Margaret Woo has invited me to join the Max-Planck Institute Luxembourg for Procedure Law's global project on "Comparative Procedural Law and Justice," at which I engaged with global comparative procedural law scholars. I have also had the privilege and pleasure to co-chair the American Society of International Law's Asia-Pacific Interest Group, first with Pasha Hsieh, and then with Matthew Erie, from where I gained much inspiration on China's law and development. I am also grateful for the anonymous reviewers of this book manuscript who provided extremely valuable peer review input at the early stage of the project and offered incisive recommendations throughout the writing process.

I am also indebted to many scholars in the communities of Chinese law and development as well as contemporary dispute resolution reform (civil justice reform), in China, Asia, and overseas who have kindly shared with me their thoughts about and insights into the contexts, paths and models of China's dispute resolution reforms. Their engagements with the arguments made in this book at various stages have pushed me to be more attentive to issues that would otherwise have been overlooked. Space does not allow me to record a full list of their names here.

The research for this book project would not have been possible without the generous financial support by the General Research Fund (GRF) Scheme of the Hong Kong Government Research Grants Council for the three dispute resolution projects (Project Codes: HKU 17617416, 17602218, and 17609419). The research has also been supported by the Outstanding Young Researcher Award (OYRA) Scheme of the University of Hong Kong. The research grants have enabled me to reduce some teaching and administrative duties so that I could have concentrated time for thinking and writing. The grants have further enabled me to compile empirical statistics, employ research assistants, conduct research trip investigations, and talk to domestic and overseas experts on the possible penetrating factors (economic, political, societal, cultural, and international civil justice movements) that have impacted on dispute resolution systems and reforms in China.

Special thanks go to an excellent team of research assistants including Wilson Lui, Herman Wan, Yi Tang, Jack Lau, Antonia Ma, and Edith Yim, all of whom provided invaluable research assistance and technical support at different stages of my writing. They have been indispensable to this book project. Yi has demonstrated capable skills in making some of the empirical tables and charts. Wilson and Herman have provided unceasing assistance in checking the styles and citations throughout the book at the final stage. Their perfect sense of responsibility and professionalism has impressed me immensely.

Siobhan Poole Joanna Hardern, and Chloe James, law editors at Routledge, are acknowledged for expertly guiding me in getting the manuscript to press and overseeing the publication of this book.

Two book chapters draw on some of my previous studies on dispute resolution in China, but they have been substantially rewritten and updated to fit into the empirical, contextual, and comparative analyses, as well as the law and development framework of this book. The discussion in Chapter 4 drew from studies in a previous book chapter entitled "China's Arbitration Modernisation under Judicial Efforts and Marketisation Waves," in *The Developing World of Arbitration: A Comparative Study of Arbitration Reform in the Asia Pacific*, eds. Anselmo Reyes and Weixia Gu (Oxford: Hart Publishing, 2018), 17–38. Chapter 8 drew from studies in a previous article entitled "When Local Meets International: Mediation Combined with Arbitration in China and Its Prospective Reform in a Comparative Context," *The Journal of Comparative Law* 10, no. 2 (2016): 84–105.

Finally, I must record my deepest gratitude to my family—my parents, my husband, and above all, my three boys. The writing of this book would have been impossible without their understanding and unswerving support. My parents have always encouraged me to be a good scholar. My father has, in particular, encouraged me to be mindful of law reforms. My husband has been consistently supportive of my professional endeavors. This book is especially dedicated to my three boys, whose ages range from five to nine. The final stage of this book project was completed in the days when the COVID-19 pandemic had been rampant throughout the world. In the most difficult lockdown days, I had to shoulder heavier family commitments and take care of the children's homeschooling. My two younger sons, Lawrence and Lucas, always brought joy to me by drawing cute heroes. Their optimism and cheerfulness have "trained" me to budget time well. My eldest son, Victor, has been working diligently on his homeschooling via Zoom classes and assignments despite the pandemic. Victor is my sunshine and he has been curiously checking how many pages I have been writing on a frequent basis. His industriousness and curiosity have "pushed" me forward even in those most difficult times.

All that is positive in this book reflects the support and generosity of my family, colleagues, and friends. All errors and omissions are my own.

List of abbreviations

1991 CPL	The 1991 Civil Procedure Law
1998 SPC Provisions	The 1998 SPC Provisions on Issues Relating to the Reform of the Mode of Adjudication of Civil and Economic Cases
2001 SPC Provisions	The 2001 SPC Provisions on Evidence in Civil Litigation
2002 Interpretation	The 2002 SPC Judicial Interpretation Regarding Some Provisions on Trying Civil Cases Involving the People's Mediation Agreements
2004 SPC Draft Provisions	The 2004 Draft Provisions of the 2006 SPC Interpretation
2004 SPC Interpretation on Mediation	SPC Rules on Several Problems Concerning Civil Mediation Work in the People's Courts
2006 SPC Interpretation	The 2006 Interpretation Concerning the Implementation of the Arbitration Law
2007 CPL/first amendment	The 2007 Civil Procedure Law
2007 Opinion	Several Opinions on Further Increasing the Positive Role of Mediation (in Litigation) in Constructing Socialism and a Harmonious Society
2012 CPL/second amendment	The 2012 Civil Procedure Law
2012 Rules	The 2012 CIETAC revised Arbitration Rules
2013 Notice	SPC Notice on Certain Issues Relating to Correct Handling of Judicial Review of Arbitration Matters

2014 EPL	The 2014 Environmental Protection Law
2014 Party Decision	The 2014 Party Central Committee Decision concerning Some Major Questions in Comprehensively Promoting Governance of The Country According to Law
2015 CIETAC Rules	The 2015 CIETAC International Investment Arbitration Rules
2015 Reply	Zuigaoyuan jiu maozhongwei Huanan fenhui, Shanghai fenhui tiaokuan anjian de guanxia ji caijue de sifa jiandu shensha wenti zuochu pifu 最高院就贸仲委华南分会、上海分会条款案件的管辖及裁决的司法监督审查问题作出批复
2015 SPC EPICL Opinion	The SPC Opinion on Environmental Public Interest Civil Litigation
2016 ADR Opinion	Zuigao renmin fayuan guanyu jinyibu shenhua duoyuanhua jiufen jiejue jizhi gaige de yijian最高人民法院关于人民法院进一步深化多元化纠纷解决机制改革的意见
2016 CPIL Opinion	The 2016 SPC Opinion of the Consumer Public Interest Litigation
2016 FTZ Opinion	Opinions of the Supreme People's Court on Providing Judicial Safeguard to the Construction of Free Trade Zones
2017 CPL/third amendment	The 2017 Civil Procedure Law
2017 SPC Provisions on Arbitration Review	SPC Provision on Several Issues Relating to the Judicial Review over Arbitration
2017 SPC Provisions on Pre-reporting	SPC Provision on Cases Relating to the Pre-Reporting System of Arbitration

2018 SPC Provisions on Award Enforcement	SPC Provision on Several Issues Relating to the Enforcement of Arbitral Awards
2019 BAC Rules	The 2019 BAC Rules
2019 SCIA Rules ACFTU	The All-China Federation of Trade Unions
ACLA	The All-China Lawyers Association
ADR	Alternative dispute resolution
AL	Arbitration Law
AMA Protocol	Arb-Med-Arb Protocol
Annual Report	Annual Report on International Commercial Arbitration in China
BAC	Beijing Arbitration Commission
BRI	Belt and Road Initiative
BRI Mechanism and Institutions Opinion	Opinion Concerning the Establishment of the Belt And Road International Commercial Dispute Resolution Mechanism and Institutions
CAA	The China Arbitration Association
Castel	Reply of the SPC to Application of Castel Electronics Pty Ltd for Recognition and Enforcement of a Foreign Arbitral Award [2013] Min Si Ta Zi No. 46
CCA	The China Consumers' Association
CCIC	The China Chamber of International Commerce
CCPIT	The China Council for the Promotion of International Trade
CIArb	The Chartered Institute of Arbitrators
CICC	The Chinese International Commercial Court

CICC One-Stop Institution Notice	Notice of the Supreme People's Court on Inclusion of the First Group of International Commercial Arbitration and Mediation Institutions in the "One-Stop" Diversified International Commercial Dispute Resolution Mechanism
CICC Provisions	The Provisions on Several Issues Concerning the Establishment of the International Commercial Court
CIETAC	The China International Economic and Trade Arbitration Commission
CIETAC split	The Shenzhen and Shanghai sub-commissions claiming independence from CIETAC
CJR	The Civil Justice Reform
CMAC	The China Maritime Arbitration Commission
CPL	The Civil Procedure Law
CPR	The Civil Procedural Rules
DHDR	Diversified Harmonious Dispute Resolution
FDI	Foreign direct investment
FIE	Foreign investment enterprise
FTZ	Free Trade Zone
GAC	The Guangzhou Arbitration Commission
GBA	Great Bay Area
Golden Landmark	*Siemens International Trading (Shanghai) Co Ltd v Shanghai Golden Landmark Co Ltd* [2013] Hu Yi Zhong Min Ren (Wai Zhong) Zi No. 2
HAC	The Hangzhou Arbitration Commission
HKIAC	The Hong Kong International Arbitration Centre
HPC	Higher people's court
Hu–Wen administration	The Hu Jintao–Wen Jiabo administration
ICC	The International Chamber of Commerce

ICEC	The CICC International Commercial Experts Committee
IPC	Intermediate people's court
IPR courts	Intellectual property right courts
Jinan Court	The Jinan People's Intermediate Court
JV	joint venture
LDMAL	The Labor Dispute Mediation and Arbitration Law
LDMC	Labor dispute mediation committee
Luck Treat	*Luck Treat Limited v Zhong Yuan Cheng Commercial Investment Holdings* [2019] Zui Gao Fa Min Te No. 1
Model Law	The United Nations Commission on International Trade Law Model Law on International Commercial Arbitration
NDRC	National Development and Reform Commission
New York Convention	The Convention on The Recognition and Enforcement of Foreign Arbitral Awards
NGO	Non-governmental organizations
NPC	The National People's Congress
NPCSC	The National People's Congress Standing Committee
OFDI	Outward foreign direct investment
PMC	People's Mediation Committee
PML	The People's Mediation Law
RHC	Hong Kong Rules of the High Court
SAC	The Shanghai Arbitration Commission
Sanlu Incident	The 2008 Sanlu tainted milk incident
SCIA	Shenzhen Court of International Arbitration
SCIA UNCITRAL Guidelines	Guidelines for the Administration of Arbitration under the UNCITRAL Arbitration Rules

SCIETAC	South China International Economic and Trade Arbitration Commission
SCMC	Shanghai Commercial Mediation Center
Shanghai Court	The Shanghai No.1 Intermediate People's Court
SHIAC	The Shanghai International Arbitration Center
SIAC	The Singapore International Arbitration Center
SIETAC	Shanghai International Economic and Trade Arbitration Commission
Singapore Mediation Convention	The United Nations Convention on International Settlement Agreements Resulting from Mediation
SOE	State-owned enterprise
SPC	The Supreme People's Court
SPFTZ	The Shanghai (Pudong) Pilot Free Trade Zone
STA	Share transfer agreement
Starr Investments	*Starr Investments Cayman II Inc v Fujian Zongheng MediaExpress Technology Inc, Fujian Fenzhong Media Inc, Zheng Cheng* [2014] Rong Zhi Jian Zi No. 51
TLL	The Tort Liability Law
UNCITRAL	The United Nations Commission on International Trade Law
WAC	The Wuhan Arbitration Commission
WEAC	The Wenzhou Arbitration Commission
WFOE	Wholly foreign owned enterprise
White Book	The Environmental Adjudication White Book
XAC	The Xi'an Arbitration Commission
Yongning	*Hemofarm DD et al v Jinan Yongning Pharmaceutical Co Ltd*, Reply of the SPC Concerning the Request for Refusal to Recognize and Enforce the Arbitral Award of the International Court of Arbitration of ICC [2009] Min Si Ta Zi No. 11

Part I

Background of dispute resolution in China

1 Introduction to dispute resolution in China

1 Scope and subject

To date, most legal studies on contemporary China, particularly in the English-language literature, have focused on substantive Chinese laws (both public and private laws) and their reforms, particularly in the context of China's booming economy and its development of rule of law. Less attention has been given to the burgeoning disputes brought about in China by the economic boom and societal changes. This includes how the regulatory and institutional landscape of dispute resolution has developed in China, how it responds to the country's socio-economic, socio-political, and socio-legal transformation, as well as how reforms on procedural law would impact on the rule of law development.

There are multiple means of dispute resolution in China, ranging from formal court adjudication, alternative dispute resolution ("ADR") methods of arbitration[1] and mediation, to the means with more Chinese character-istics such as petitions (or "letters and visits"), and in some extreme cases, protests in the streets.[2] In the rapidly expanding dispute resolution commu-nity in China, three major means have developed rapidly in the resolution of civil and commercial disputes. They are: (1) civil litigation (including com-mercial litigation), (2) commercial arbitration, and (3) civil mediation (both judicial and extra-judicial).

With respect to the division between civil and commercial disputes, in the past, China has never made a clear distinction between its various branches

---

1 Views as to whether arbitration is a form of ADR are divided among Chinese academics. Fan Yu, leading expert on ADR in China, argues that ADR includes any alternatives to litigation that resolve disputes, and hence, arbitration is a form of ADR. On the other hand, the China Chamber of International Commerce ("CCIC") holds that arbitration is not a form of ADR. To the CCIC, ADR only includes means of dispute resolution other than arbitration and litigation. See Gu Weixia, "Looking at Arbitration through A Comparative Lens: General Principles and Specific Issues," *The Journal of Comparative Law* 13, no. 2 (2018): 168.
2 Randall Peerenboom and He Xin, "Dispute Resolution in China: Patterns, Causes, and Prognosis," *University of Pennsylvania East Asia Law Review* 1, no. 4 (2009): 1–61.

of civil laws. Albert Chen, a leading Chinese law expert from a comparative law perspective, commented that civil and commercial matters did not come into the forefront of discussion until only several decades ago.[3] The relevant Chinese legislation, such as China's Civil Code most recently passed in 2020,[4] is equally applied to both civil or commercial matters in China.[5] Commercial matters are not defined or discussed in the Civil Procedure Law either. China's development of the market economy has contributed to the development of the concept of commercial law which closely relates to civil law practices in China, and there is a consensus among academics and practitioners that there is a fusion between civil and commercial law.[6] It is for this reason that there is only one Civil Procedure Law in China, governing both civil litigation and commercial litigation in the Chinese courts, rather than a separate code of litigation for commercial lawsuits. Article 3 of the Civil Procedure Law discusses the scope of civil actions. It states that the Civil Procedure Law "[applies] to civil actions accepted by a people's court regarding property or personal relationships between citizens, legal persons, and other organisations,"[7] while actions with respect to governmental bodies are precluded. While mediation could be applied to both civil and commercial disputes, arbitration, as under the current version of the China Arbitration Law, applies only to commercial disputes and is largely considered a means of commercial dispute resolution.[8]

The Chinese dispute resolution landscape[9] could be described as analogous to a dynamic ecology. It consists of three primary (and established) civil and commercial dispute resolution systems in China (the systems of civil litigation,[10] arbitration,[11] and mediation),[12] each having its own set of institutions and procedural rules, and in the meantime interacting with one another. As such, there are many "interactions" arising out of this

---

3 Chen Albert H.Y., *An Introduction to the Legal System of the People's Republic of China*, 5th ed. (Hong Kong: LexisNexis, 2019), 314.

4 Zhonghua Renmin Gongheguo Minfa Dian (中华人民共和国民法典) [Civil Code of the People's Republic of China] promulgated by the National People's Congress, May 28, 2020, effective January 1, 2021), http://www.npc.gov.cn/npc/c30834/202006/75ba6483b8344591abd07917e1d25cc8.shtml.

5 Ibid., art. 2.

6 Chen, *An Introduction to the Legal System of the People's Republic of China*, 317.

7 Minshi Susong Fa (民事诉讼法) [Civil Procedure Law] (promulgated by the National People's Congress Standing Committee, June 27, 2017, effective July 1, 2017), arts. 3, http://en.pkulaw.cn/display.aspx?id=6d9ce94e57cee7afbdfb&lib=law.

8 Zhongcai Fa (仲裁法) [Arbitration Law] (promulgated by the Standing Committee of the National People's Congress, August 31, 1994, effective September 1, 1995), arts. 2–3, http://www.npc.gov.cn/wxzl/wxzl/2000-12/05/content_4624.htm.

9 The term "landscape" is inspired by Marc Galanter. See Marc Galanter, "Reading the Landscape of Disputes: What We Know and Don't Know (and Think We Know) about Our Allegedly Contentious and Litigious Society," *UCLA Law Review* 31, no. 1 (1983): 12.

10 See discussions in Chapter 3.

11 See discussions in Chapter 4.

12 See discussions in Chapter 5.

ecology—the interactions among different institutions, procedures, and individual systems—thus creating "hybrid" (and emerging) civil dispute resolution systems, such as the judicial mediation system,[13] the system of judicial enforcement of arbitration,[14] and med-arb where mediation is combined with arbitration.[15] This book also examines these hybrid mechanisms and their growing importance, which has either been ignored or not sufficiently addressed in the existing literature.

In sum, this book studies the three primary civil and commercial dispute resolution systems and their associated hybrid dispute resolution systems, which are collectively referred to as "civil dispute resolution" in this book. For ease of reference, throughout the book, the term "dispute resolution in China" is intended to refer to "civil dispute resolution in China," and the two terms are used interchangeably.

2 Engagement of literature and empirical evidence

The civil dispute resolution landscape in China is concerned with the civil procedures and associated legal institutions that design and implement the civil procedures and hybrid civil procedures. Procedurally, it refers to the procedural laws that deal with specific areas of civil, commercial, or private rights (i.e., procedures of civil litigation, arbitration, and mediation). These laws include the Civil Procedure Law, the Arbitration Law, the People's Mediation Law, and regulatory documents that govern judicial mediation, judicial enforcement of arbitration, and mediation combined with arbitration. Institutionally, civil dispute resolution landscape refers to the specific legal institutions where parties turn to for filing legal actions to enforce their civil, commercial, or private rights, including the institutional design of the people's courts (in particular, their civil and commercial tribunals), arbitration commissions, and mediation committees.

In the past decade, many changes have taken place in the regimes for civil dispute resolution in China, such as their respective legal institutions, procedural laws and regulations. These include, for example, publication of the five Reform Outlines of the People's Courts (1998–2023);[16] amendments to the Civil Procedure Law in 2007, 2012, and 2017, respectively;[17] internal split of China's flagship arbitration institution, the China International Economic and Trade Arbitration Commission ("CIETAC"), in 2013;[18] formation of the Chinese arbitration market[19] and flourishing

---

13 See discussions in Chapter 6.
14 See discussions in Chapter 7.
15 See discussions in Chapter 8.
16 See discussions in Chapter 2.
17 See discussions in Chapter 3.
18 See discussions in Chapter 4.
19 Ibid.

of several leading locally based Chinese arbitration commissions in the 2010s;[20] promulgation of the People's Mediation Law and Labor Dispute Arbitration and Mediation Law in the first decade of this century;[21] as well as the establishment of the China International Commercial Court and promotion of the "One-Stop" Multi-tiered (Hybrid) Dispute Resolution Platform in 2018.[22]

A significant body of literature on the laws of civil dispute resolution regime in China is technical and promotional.[23] Many authors also practice as litigators, arbitrators, or mediators. Scholarship on civil dispute resolution frequently grows out of the legal practice. Updated analytical works in the field are still scarce. Even on the practical side, there is a lack of empirical work such as studies on to what extent the civil dispute resolution systems are actually utilized and how they are utilized. This book robustly seeks to improve upon this tradition of scholarship.

First, it will bring the literature on civil dispute resolution in China up to date. This book offers a most recent and comprehensive status quo analysis of the legal systems and developments in the field, particularly those of the late 2000s and throughout the 2010s, such as their respective regulatory design, legal and institutional framework, and reform. Existing analytical literature has either focused on one particular area of the civil dispute resolution regimes or has failed to cover the most recent developments in the late 2000s and the 2010s. Among the analytical works on civil dispute resolution in China, the most recent is Hualing Fu and Michael Palmer's co-edited book in 2017, *Mediation in Contemporary China: Continuity and Change*.[24] But the book is focused on mediation, with limited coverage on civil litigation and arbitration. Another recent and influential work is Margaret Woo and Mary Gallagher's co-edited book in 2011, *Chinese Justice: Civil Dispute Resolution in Contemporary China*.[25] The book focused on Chinese courts and civil litigation, with little coverage on mediation, and none on arbitration. Randall Peerenboom and Xin He's co-authored article, *Dispute Resolution in China: Patterns, Causes, and Prognosis*, though with a more comprehensive coverage in

---

20 Such as the Beijing Arbitration Commission (BAC) in Beijing, and the post-CIETAC-split Shenzhen Court of International Arbitration (SCIA) in Shenzhen. See discussions in Chapters 4 and 8.

21 See discussions in Chapter 5.

22 See discussions in Chapter 8.

23 See, for example, Michael Moser, ed., *Dispute Resolution in China*, 2nd ed. (New York: Juris Publishing, 2020); Michael Moser, ed., *Business Disputes in China*, 3rd ed. (New York: Juris Publishing, 2011); Tao Jingzhou, *Arbitration Law and Practice in China*, 3rd ed. (The Hague: Kluwer Law International, 2012).

24 Fu Hualing and Michael Palmer, eds., *Mediation in Contemporary China: Continuity and Change* (London: Wildy, Simmonds & Hill Publishing, 2017).

25 Margaret Y. K. Woo and Mary E. Gallagher, *Chinese Justice: Civil Dispute Resolution in Contemporary China* (Cambridge: Cambridge University Press, 2011).

scope, was published more than a decade ago and did not address the law and development in the 2010s.[26]

Second, this book engages in intellectually stimulating dialogue with leading scholars in the Chinese civil dispute resolution field both at home and abroad. For example, on Chinese civil litigation, Yulin Fu, a leading Chinese domestic scholar on the topic, argued that the landscape of civil litigation requires not only the revamp of the civil procedural laws, but also effective reforms of the Chinese courts institutionally.[27] Kwai Hang Ng and Xin He, authors of the leading empirical work on Chinese courts, argued that the Chinese court system is still more a political regime than a separate professional institution.[28] Margaret Woo, one of the leading scholars on Chinese civil procedure in the West, observed the inevitable rise of collective actions amid the socio-economic transformation in China. She argued that the introduction of public interest litigation only resolved the issue of standing to sue, and the Chinese courts are still very cautious about the development of capacity building in the civil society that may potentially threaten the courts' politically instrumental roles.[29] Xianchu Zhang shared a similar view that China's civil procedural law reform is essentially a reform with political agendas.[30] In Hualing Fu and Michael Palmer's treatise on Chinese mediation, they pointed out that disputes in China are regarded as undermining social stability; informal and extra-legal measures including both judicial and extra-judicial mediation are extensively used and politicized.[31] Hualing Fu, one of the most influential minds on the Chinese legal system, further pointed out that judicial mediation carried out by Chinese courts is a distinctive feature of the Chinese civil justice system and is largely driven by political considerations.[32] Carl Minzner worried about the massive mediation campaign in China as a "turn against law."[33] As Yulin Fu and Randall Peerenboom further argued, in the case of China, given the courts' inability

---

26 Peerenboom and He, "Dispute Resolution in China."

27 Fu Yulin, "Zou xiang xiandaihua de minshi susong chengshi" 走向现代化的民事訴訟程式, (presentation, Hong Kong, October 26, 2015).

28 Ng Kwai Hang and He Xin, *Embedded Courts: Judicial Decision-Making in China* (Cambridge: Cambridge University Press, 2017), Chapters 1 and 4.

29 Margaret Woo, "The Dynamism of China's Civil Litigation System," in *The Dynamism of Civil Procedure—Global Trends and Developments*, eds. Colin B. Picker and Guy I. Seidman (New York: Springer, 2016), 151.

30 Zhang Xianchu, "Civil Justice Reform with Political Agendas," in *The Development of the Chinese Legal System: Change and Challenges*, ed. Yu Guanghua (Oxford: Routledge, 2011), 253–271.

31 Fu and Palmer, *Mediation in Contemporary China*, 4.

32 Ibid. See also Fu Hualing and Richard Cullen, "From Mediatory to Adjudicatory Justice: The Limits of Civil Justice Reform in China," in *Chinese Justice: Civil Dispute Revolution in China*, eds. Margaret Woo and Mary Gallagher (Cambridge: Cambridge University Press, 2011), 25–57.

33 Carl Minzner, "China's Turn Against Law," *American Journal of Comparative Law* 59, no. 4 (2011): 963.

to provide an effective remedy in some socio-economic cases, access to civil justice is necessarily limited.[34] This book will engage with all the above analytical works and other arguments to examine whether civil dispute resolution in China is politicized and how access to civil justice is limited. At the same time, since none of the existing literature by leading civil dispute resolution scholars has covered Chinese arbitration in much length, this book will fill in this gap.

Third, there are comparative studies such as frequent references to the global civil dispute resolution systems and to points of difference and distinctiveness in China's approach to civil dispute resolution in the chapters of this book on each individual dispute resolution system. The concluding chapter will further refer to contemporary civil justice movements elsewhere in the world so as to provide a comparative framework for thinking about the likely trajectories of civil justice reform in China in the years to come. For example, the United Kingdom is one of the first contemporary movers for civil justice reform in the common law world which encouraged the use of ADR and settlement in civil trials.[35] The ADR movement and the rise of civil mediation have been features of other established jurisdictions in both the East (such as Japan, Hong Kong, and Singapore)[36] and the West (such as the United States).[37] The civil dispute resolution systems and civil justice reforms of these jurisdictions are discussed in this book, so as to suggest comparative insights that China might gain from their experience.

Fourth, this book reflects analytically upon China's civil dispute resolution from a law and development perspective in terms of its ability to adapt, and respond to, new contexts of the Chinese economic and political transitions as well as the new composition of the Chinese society; it also offers a rigorous analysis of the reform patterns and process. Details of the law and development perspective as a special feature of the analytical framework in this book will be further explained in the subsequent section.

Moreover, this book engages with the empirical evidence in great detail and contributes to the literature by examining empirical aspects of the entire civil dispute resolution landscape in contemporary China. It studies the extent to which various means of civil dispute resolution have been developed and adopted in practice in China in the most recent decade and provides detailed statistical insights.

---

34 Fu Yulin and Randall Peerenboom, "A New Analytical Framework for Understanding and Promoting Judicial Independence in China," in *Judicial Independence in China: Lessons for Global Rule of Law Promotion*, ed. Randall Peerenboom (Cambridge: Cambridge University Press, 2010), 115.

35 See discussions in Section 3.1 of Chapter 9.

36 See discussions in Section 5.1 of Chapter 5 and Section 3.1 of Chapter 9.

37 See discussions in Section 5.2 of Chapter 5, Section 6 of Chapter 6, and Section 3.1 of Chapter 9.

First, on primary (and established) civil dispute resolution systems (such as civil litigation, arbitration, and mediation), it intends to empirically explore whether legalization and formalization (such as legislative enactment or amendment) have brought about significant increases in the caseload and handling institutions of the relevant dispute resolution system to enhance access to justice. Second, on hybrid (and emerging) civil dispute resolution systems (such as judicial mediation, judicial enforcement of arbitration, and mediation combined with arbitration), it seeks to empirically test whether a particular hybrid dispute resolution means has been widely adopted in resolving civil and commercial disputes in China and whether reform is necessary. To achieve these research outcomes, this book examines all relevant Chinese legal research databases in the civil dispute resolution field[38] to compile empirical statistical tables, charts, figures, and trends. At the time when the book manuscript was completed, the 2019 data had not been published yet. This book thus focuses on empirical evidence in the most recent decade covering the period from 2009 to 2018.

3 Law and development studies

Seidman argues that dispute resolution mechanisms, particularly civil procedures, form the basis of social structures. Civil dispute resolution is often linked with the study of the civil procedural system and civil justice reform and presents an interesting case study of law and development.[39]

The development of the civil dispute resolution system is a microcosm of the overall legal developments in China. Scholars have described legal reforms in China in both the horizontal dimension of transplanting and subsequently adapting legal principles and practices from foreign jurisdictions, and in the vertical dimension of domestic top-down and bottom-up reforms.[40] Previous works have traditionally framed the debate in terms of whether Chinese economic growth has occurred because of, or in spite

---

38 These databases include Chinese Supreme People's Court Annual Report (中国最高人民法院年度工作报告), China Law Yearbook (中国法律年鉴), China Statistical Yearbook (中国统计年鉴), China Labor Statistics Yearbook (中国劳动统计年鉴), China's Environmental Adjudication White Book (中国环境资源审判白皮书), Annual Report on International Commercial Arbitration in China (中国国际商事仲裁年度报告), Chinalawinfo (北大法律信息网), and arbitration statistics compiled by Chinese leading arbitration institutions.

39 Guy I. Seidman, "Comparative Civil Procedure," in *The Dynamism of Civil Procedure— Global Trends and Developments*, eds. Colin B. Picker and Guy I. Seidman (New York: Springer, 2016), 3–5.

40 Randall Peerenboom, "What Have We Learned about Law and Development? Describing, Predicting, and Assessing Legal Reforms in China," *Michigan Journal of International Law* 27, no. 3 (2006): 824.

of, the development of formal legal structures in China or their deficiencies.[41] However, few of these studies have focused on civil procedures, and the underlying broader contextual developments (e.g., from socio-economic and socio-political angles) that have influenced the civil procedural reform. For example, China's civil procedures and their respective legal institutions have undergone many changes in the most recent decade, due to both the need for inbound[42] and outbound economic development,[43] an increasing demand by China's internal rule-of-law progress,[44] as well as the external pressure by the international civil justice movement for enhancement of due process and access to civil justice in China.[45]

3.1 Reform context analyses

A first feature of the law and development study that this book contributes to the literature is the contextual analyses.

Ng and He have argued that the social science context is an essential feature for an understanding of the Chinese dispute resolution regime.[46] The dispute resolution systems do not develop in isolation, but they adapt, and respond to, changes to the broader Chinese socio-economic, socio-political, and socio-legal contexts. In the rapidly changing society of China, it is inadequate to understand the developments of the civil litigation, arbitration, mediation systems and their hybrid systems as mere amendments to laws and regulations, and updates in legal practices. There are multiple social science penetrating factors such as China's economic, political, societal, administrative, and cultural conditions and changes. The contextual analyses help to provide more comprehensive insights into and objective knowledge of the contemporary Chinese civil dispute resolution regime. On the one hand, these penetrating factors bring about, or restrict, the direction of dispute resolution policy reform, the application of dispute resolution laws and regulations, and the way by which social agents utilize the dispute resolution systems. On the other hand, as Woo and Gallagher pointed out, the dispute resolution system itself is a driver for social change. It can reinforce existing structures

---

41 Donald Clarke, "Economic Development and the Rights Hypothesis: The China Problem," *American Journal of Comparative Law* 51, no. 1 (2003): 89; Tom Ginsberg, "Does Law Matter for Economic Development? Evidence from East Asia," *Law and Society Review* 34, no. 3 (2000): 826–856.
42 Inbound economic development refers to the further marketization waves within China.
43 Outbound economic development refers to China's outgoing investment moves such as the Belt and Road Initiative. See discussions in Chapters 4, 7, and 8.
44 See, for example, since Chinese President Xi Jinping took up the office, judicial reform has been reconsidered in light of Xi's rule of law. Judicial mediation is no longer prioritized but has been treated more cautiously. See discussions in Chapters 2 and 6.
45 For example, med-arb reform has been much pushed by the international due process pressure. See discussions in Chapter 8.
46 Ng and He, *Embedded Courts*, 17–28.

or adapt or reinterpret existing rules.[47] As such, reciprocally, the Chinese dispute resolution system is also capable of shaping China's socio-economic and socio-political contextual environment. This book will speak to the literature by engaging a social-science-wise contextual analysis of the law and development of civil dispute resolution institutions and procedures, and reflecting analytically upon them as forms of societal transformers.[48] It thus contributes to the rapidly growing literature that concerns the social science analyses of Chinese law from the civil dispute resolution perspective.

The contextual analyses also draw insights from the disparities among different Chinese regions. Although China employs a unitary regulatory style at the central state level, it is important to appreciate that different regions of China face unique socio-economic issues that shape how their civil dispute resolution mechanisms are reformed and utilized to resolve civil and commercial disputes. As we will see, cities in the economically developed regions of China have developed better legal infrastructures with more sophisticated and mature legal systems, while dispute resolution developments in the hinterland and the western part of China are relatively limited. Thus, economically better-developed areas in China, such as coastal cities and special economic zones, are more likely to welcome foreign trade and investment and consider themselves as "legal hubs."[49] The development of the courts and arbitration infrastructures in these jurisdictions and their willingness to embrace more innovations when making juridical and arbitral decisions are vivid examples.[50]

3.2 Reform pattern analyses

A second feature which this book contributes is our understanding of the uniqueness of the reform patterns in civil justice in China.

China's civil dispute resolution system is highly dynamic, yet restrained by the state. This controlled dynamism has led to the hybrid reform patterns of "both top-down and bottom-up" approaches to civil procedural reform. Reforms are often initiated by grievances of the civil society (through civil litigation and mediation)[51] and of the market (through arbitration),[52] when conflicts could not be properly dealt with by existing procedural mechanisms. This prompts a demand for reform from the bottom. In return, the

---

47 Margaret Y. K. Woo and Mary E. Gallagher, "Introduction," in *Chinese Justice: Civil Dispute Resolution in Contemporary China*, eds. Margaret Y. K. Woo and Mary E. Gallagher (New York: Cambridge University Press, 2011), 3.

48 See discussions in Chapters 3–8 on the sections entitled "Development Analyses."

49 Matthew Erie, "The New Legal Hubs: The Emergent Landscape of International Commercial Dispute Resolution," *Virginia Journal of International Law* 59, no. 3 (2020), 225–298.

50 See discussions in Chapters 2, 4, 6, and 7.

51 See discussions in Chapters 3 and 5.

52 See discussions in Chapter 4.

state implements a top-down regulatory response to address bottom-up demands by way of reform means which are exclusive to the state power.

Top-down responses can take various forms, mostly legislative (first type) or judicial (second type). The most direct way for the state to respond to civil and commercial conflicts in the society is to introduce new, or to amend existing, legislation through the National People's Congress ("NPC") or its Standing Committee ("NPCSC"). As the legislative organ at the central level, the NPC and NPCSC enjoy national legislative power for "basic systems of civil procedure such as litigation and arbitration," among other areas.[53] The amendment of China's Civil Procedure Law[54] and the promulgation of the People's Mediation Law[55] both belong to this first type of top-down response.

Top-down response in the form of extensive legislative power is not always invoked. As we will see in the development path of China's arbitration system and its related hybrid systems such as judicial review over arbitration and mediation combined with arbitration, formal legislation is easily outdated and often insufficient. Instead, judicial interpretations by the Supreme People's Court ("SPC") are made to either fill in the gap (where there is a legal vacuum), or to align with international standards (where the legislative pace has been too slow and there are outdated legislative provisions which harm China's economic interests). These judicial interpretations have a quasi-legislative effect and are binding on all Chinese courts.[56] In the area of arbitration and its related hybrid dispute resolution which are more closely related to development arising from inbound and outbound economic transactions, judicial interpretations have become the primary and more flexible means for the state to proactively respond to new arbitration developments in the interests of China's investment environment and the market in general. As such, top-down responses in the landscape of arbitration[57] are provided mostly by this second type of response, that is, in the judicial form.

Sometimes, top-down reforms do not adequately address the issues in the society at the bottom, or may inadvertently create new conflicts that require new top-down reforms to redress. When the state fails to remedy, or decides against remedying these issues, the ball is then passed back to the society and the market to push for alternatives or other initiatives. The unique development path of China's arbitration system where hundreds of Chinese arbitration commissions form the institutional arbitration market and compete for cases and quality development both among themselves

---

53 Lifa Fa (立法法) [Legislation Law] (promulgated by the National People's Congress, March 15, 2015, effective March 15, 2015), art. 8, http://en.pkulaw.cn/display. aspx?cgid=9073d435178b9633bdfb&lib=law.
54 See discussions in Chapter 3.
55 See discussions in Chapter 5.
56 See discussions in Section 2.1 of Chapter 2.
57 See discussions in Chapters 4, 7, and 8.

and with international arbitration market players is an example where bottom-up actors have pushed for other alternatives.[58] This book will examine all these reform patterns and recent development dynamics in China's civil dispute resolution landscape, which have not been fully covered by the existing scholarship.

3.3 Reform process analyses

A third feature is the lack of central planning by the Chinese state—planning that might otherwise dictate the direction of the overall development of the dispute resolution landscape.

Although the state offers regulation and control, Chinese dispute resolution is also shaped by other factors: the market in general, the social issues (sometimes unforeseen by the state), and the general political milieu. Even in areas of civil justice reform where the state wishes to push forward (as seen in the five rounds of court reform), the state has so far failed to set out and ultimately carry out a holistic, coherent, and methodical scheme that accounts for all existing forms of civil dispute resolution procedures and their pertinent institutions, though recent judicial policies have tried to engage civil litigation, arbitration, and mediation in building a multi-tiered dispute resolution platform.[59]

The rapid industrialization and urbanization developments in the 2000s, for instance, have created unforeseen social costs, which required the state to constantly create ad hoc solutions to resolve civil mass disputes such as those related to the community, environment, and labor. The Chinese state is less prepared to review the shortcomings of the civil justice system from the macroscopic level. The piecemeal, fragmented, and politicized development of the civil mediation regime in China (judicial versus extra-judicial; general versus special) is one of the consequences.[60]

4 Aims of this book

This book examines the laws of and developments in the Chinese civil dispute resolution system over the past two decades, particularly the most recent decade.

As discussed previously, few of the existing studies have offered empirical insights into the civil dispute resolution regime in China, examined their broader socio-economic and socio-political contexts, looked into their interactions, analyzed their "law and development" uniqueness, and thought about comparative prospects of China's civil justice reform in the future. This book will fill in all these gaps.

---

58 See discussions in Chapters 4 and 8.
59 See discussions in Chapter 6, in particular, Section 3.2.
60 See discussions in Chapters 5 and 6.

A first and direct aim is to bring the literature up to date, and this book offers a most recent legal status quo account of the Chinese civil dispute resolution landscape. Moreover, this book engages with the empirical evidence comprehensively. It examines the empirical side of the entire Chinese civil dispute resolution landscape in the last decade, such as how a particular dispute resolution system has developed and been practiced.

The second, third, and fourth aims are all related to law and development studies of the reform.

The second aim of this book is to present social science contextual analyses, and to probe into the wider socio-economic, socio-political, and other penetrating factors that have driven or restricted the reform of the civil dispute resolution systems and examine how they have done so.

Related to the second aim, the third and fourth aims are to study the reform patterns (whether top-down, bottom-up, or a hybrid) and reform processes (whether holistic or fragmented). Despite the familiar labels of civil procedures and civil justice reforms that other jurisdictions in the world might adopt, the patterns and process of the reform in civil litigation, arbitration, and mediation systems in China have evolved distinctively to adapt and respond to the unique Chinese socio-economic and socio-political contexts from which these systems have developed.

As the title of the book further indicates, the topics studied in this book also extend to "interactions" of different civil dispute resolution systems. Hence, the above aims are equally applied to study the hybrid civil dispute resolution systems in China, namely the issues that arise when institutions and procedures of civil litigation, arbitration, and mediation are blended and juxtaposed. As with the above aims, this book also examines the empirical status quo, the "law and development" uniqueness such as the reform contexts, patterns, and processes of the hybrid systems.

Lastly, this book aims to provide a comparative framework for thinking about likely trajectories of civil justice reform in China in the future. This book places the law and development of Chinese civil dispute resolution in the context of the wider international shifts of global civil justice movements. The book will refer to contemporary civil dispute resolution systems and reforms elsewhere to suggest comparative insights that China may gain from their experience.

5 An overview of this book

Structurally, this book is organized into four parts.

Part I is composed of two chapters and provides a macroscopic introduction to the book.

Chapter 1 provides the background to the study of civil dispute resolution in China. It introduces and explains the scope, subject, methodology, features, aims, overview, and structure of the book.

Chapter 2 studies the Chinese judiciary, the people's courts ("courts"), and how they are involved in the various civil dispute resolution systems in China. At the institutional level, the courts are highly intertwined with the civil procedures. The courts are the sole platform in China to conduct civil litigation and enforce civil judgments.[61] The courts also exercise supportive and supervisory powers over arbitration[62] and mediation proceedings.[63] The courts cross paths with the laws of and developments in those various civil dispute resolution mechanisms in China. Over the past two decades, to improve the judicial infrastructure and enhance access to justice, the SPC has published five court reform plans (1998–2023). Chapter 2 discusses the structure, size, function, perception, and reform of the Chinese courts and lays an institutional foundation for the subsequent discussion on specific civil procedures and their reforms.

Part II consists of three chapters, with each exploring the laws of and developments in one of the primary civil dispute resolution systems in China—civil litigation (Chapter 3), arbitration (Chapter 4), and mediation (Chapter 5)—using a law and development approach.

Each of the chapters in Part II follows more or less similar themes and research questions. Each chapter first empirically assesses how a particular civil dispute resolution system is actually utilized in China in the most recent decade by studying the empirical statistical evidence. It then explains the regulatory background (legislative and institutional) that shapes the current system. Afterwards, it explains the reform, both legislative and institutional (other than those institutional reforms of the courts which have been examined in Chapter 2), that have taken place in the past decade, through a law and development study. In conducting the development analyses, two main research questions are examined. On the one hand, what are the penetrating factors (political, economic, social, cultural, etc.) that have influenced (driven or constrained) the reform? On the other hand, what are the patterns of reform (top-down, bottom-up, or a hybrid)? Finally, each chapter proposes a direction for future reform and analyzes the likely challenges. This standardized format is intended to enhance the readers' comparative, contextual, and developmental understanding of the achievements and setbacks of the three major civil dispute resolution systems in the most recent decade in China. A synopsis of the three-component chapters under investigation by Part II of the book is set out as follows.

Chapter 3 concerns the civil litigation system in China. Recent years have seen rising numbers of consumer and environmental class actions in the civil litigation arena, and these bottom-up disputes prompted the revision of China's Civil Procedure Law in 2012 to include a new cause of action, namely

---

61 See discussions in Chapter 3.
62 See discussions in Chapters 4 and 7.
63 See discussions in Chapters 3, 5, and 6.

"public interest litigation." The reforms were shaped by the socio-economic and socio-political contexts of China. The institutional recognition of public interest litigation, particularly those involving devastating product liability and environment pollution cases, is, on the one hand, informed by the socio-political climate of promoting social harmony and social pluralism, and on the other hand, serves as an answer to the societal dissatisfaction. The development has presented a clear case of top-down responses to bottom-up demands by way of legislative amendment and presents a case study of evolution toward a more litigious Chinese society.

Chapter 4 looks into the arbitration system in China. The Chinese path to arbitration design and reform relies very much on control from the top (such as the "institutional arbitration monopoly"). But, at the same time, the system depends on competition for cases among hundreds of Chinese arbitration commissions to make arbitration an attractive option for dispute resolution from the bottom (such as the "institutional arbitration market"). As a stark contrast with civil litigation and mediation, there have not been recent revisions of China's Arbitration Law.[64] The progressive stance taken by the state toward arbitration has synthesized a unique socio-economic dynamic, with a top-down controlling element, while at the same time being reliant on and even accommodative of a Chinese arbitration market and vigorous bottom-up competition, with the dramatic CIETAC split in 2013 being the climax.

Chapter 5 analyzes the mediation regime in China. Contemporary mediation development in China, though rooted in Chinese cultural legacy, is a scattered regime (expressed in many different types, forms, and initiatives). Among the many extra-judicial types of Chinese mediation, people's mediation and labor mediation stand out as two mainstream and legalized Chinese mediation systems for resolving domestic civil disputes. Despite the increasing institutionalization and formalization in the past decade, people's mediation and labor mediation have been instrumentalist in nature, used more to prevent the expression of disagreements than to deal with the socio-economic conflicts. The Chinese path to mediation development, though led from the top, is a checkered one, restricted by socio-political policy orientations.

Part III of the book again consists of three chapters and turns to the interactions between litigation, arbitration, mediation, and the hybrid civil dispute resolution systems—judicial mediation as interaction between civil litigation and mediation (Chapter 6), judicial enforcement of arbitration as interaction between civil litigation and arbitration (Chapter 7), and med-arb as interaction between arbitration and mediation (Chapter 8).

Although the topics covered are unique to each of the hybrid dispute resolution systems, Part III, as with Part II, also follows more or less similar

---

64 Although the Civil Procedure Law as amended in 2012 added several provisions on arbitration, it was not significant.

themes and research questions in the component chapters. The research questions which Part III puts forward across all the three chapters are as follows. It first empirically tests whether a particular hybrid dispute resolution mechanism is widely used in China and how it is used. It then explains to what extent they are regulated. Afterwards, it analyzes the reform to penetrate the contextual factors that have driven or constrained the reform and probes into the development trajectory (patterns of reform), before each chapter concludes with the prospective challenges for future development. A synopsis of the three-component chapters under investigation by Part III of the book is set out as follows.

Chapter 6 investigates judicial mediation in China. The development of judicial mediation has shown itself to be much politicized—particularly so during the Third Five-Year Court Reform Outline (2009–2013). However, in spite of the fluctuations in judicial policy, legislatively, China has always displayed inclination, and perhaps favoritism, toward mediation, as China values social stability over the rule of law. The role of mediation within the civil procedure system in China has remained prominent throughout, but its scale has been decreased since the period of the highly politicized and prioritized approach in the late 2000s and early 2010s, moving toward a more nuanced approach after 2013. The precaution in mediatory justice is a typical case study on the importance of rebalancing the rule of law in the context of China's economic and societal transitions.

Chapter 7 examines judicial review over arbitration in China. In its dual role as China's Supreme Court and a de facto rule-maker, the SPC has published an impressive body of judicial interpretations to recognize the importance of being arbitration-friendly. The pace has been especially quickened in the past couple of years as China is required to deal with dispute resolution needs arising from the development of the Free Trade Zone and the Belt and Road Initiative. Chinese lower level courts, especially those in the economically developed regions, have also been proactive in supporting arbitration in some of the most controversial cases. Those liberal rulings provide helpful clarification on issues of public policy, foreign institutional arbitrations seated in China, as well as granting limited recognition to *ad hoc* arbitration in China's Free Trade Zones.

Chapter 8 explores the med-arb system in China. Due to the legislative vacuum, med-arb practices in China are highly disparate and have been challenged by international due process standards when arbitral awards following Chinese med-arb procedures seek enforcement outside China. Recent reforms on med-arb are, on the one hand, propelled by regulatory competition among China's leading arbitration commissions, and on the other hand, driven by the SPC's promotion efforts as med-arb is increasingly applied in cross-border contexts in the Belt and Road arbitration market. The reform of med-arb is increasingly important to China's rule of law and internationalization, as it is a much relied-on commercial dispute resolution mechanism in a jurisdiction without an established due process tradition, yet, with a booming economy and burgeoning commercial disputes, both domestically and in cross-border contexts.

The similar themes and research queries in Parts II and III are designed to help readers to engage in a comparative understanding of the law and development of the three civil dispute resolution systems and the three hybrid civil dispute resolution systems that form the subject of this book. In the meantime, the format is not intended to be too detailed to amount to a microscopic description of each dispute resolution system or hybrid dispute resolution system. In short, the emphasis is on the development context, trajectory, and reform path of each individual dispute resolution or hybrid dispute resolution system.

Part IV (Chapter 9) finally concludes the entire book. It reflects on the uniqueness, promises, and pitfalls of the Chinese civil dispute resolution landscape, and predicts the prospects of China's civil justice reform in the future.

Bibliography

Chen, Albert H.Y. *An Introduction to the Legal System of the People's Republic of China*, 5th ed. Hong Kong: LexisNexis, 2019.

Clarke, Donald. "Economic Development and the Rights Hypothesis: The China Problem." *American Journal of Comparative Law* 51, no. 1 (2003): 89–111.

Erie, Matthew. "The New Legal Hubs: The Emergent Landscape of International Commercial Dispute Resolution." *Virginia Journal of International Law* 59, no. 3 (2020): 225–298.

Fu, Hualing and Michael Palmer, eds. *Mediation in Contemporary China: Continuity and Change*. London: Wildy, Simmonds & Hill Publishing, 2017.

Fu, Hualing and Richard Cullen. "From Mediatory to Adjudicatory Justice: The Limits of Civil Justice Reform in China." In *Chinese Justice: Civil Dispute Resolution in Contemporary China*, edited by Margaret Woo and Mary Gallagher, 25–57. Cambridge: Cambridge University Press, 2011.

Fu, Yulin. "Zou xiang xiandaihua de minshi susong chengshi" 走向现代化的民事诉讼程式. Presentation, Hong Kong, October 26, 2015.

Fu, Yulin and Randall Peerenboom. "A New Analytical Framework for Understanding and Promoting Judicial Independence in China." In *Judicial Independence in China: Lessons for Global Rule of Law Promotion*, edited by Randall Peerenboom, 95–133. Cambridge: Cambridge University Press, 2010.

Galanter, Marc. "Reading the Landscape of Disputes: What We Know and Don't Know (and Think We Know) About Our Allegedly Contentious and Litigious Society." *UCLA Law Review* 31, no. 1 (1983): 4–71.

Ginsberg, Tom. "Does Law Matter for Economic Development? Evidence from East Asia." *Law and Society Review* 34, no. 3 (2000): 826–856.

Gu, Weixia. "Looking at Arbitration through a Comparative Lens: General Principles and Specific Issues." *The Journal of Comparative Law* 13, no. 2 (2018): 164–188.

Lifa Fa (立法法) [Legislation Law] (promulgated by the National People's Congress, March 15, 2015, effective March 15, 2015). http://en.pkulaw.cn/display.aspx?cgid=9073d435178b9633bdfb&lib=law.

Minshi Susong Fa (民事诉讼法) [Civil Procedure Law] (promulgated by the National People's Congress Standing Committee, June 27, 2017, effective July 1, 2017). http://en.pkulaw.cn/display.aspx?id=6d9ce94e57cee7afbdfb&lib=law.

Minzner, Carl. "China's Turn Against Law." *American Journal of Comparative Law* 59, no. 4 (2011): 935–984.

Moser, Michael, ed. *Business Disputes in China*, 3rd ed. New York: Juris Publishing, 2011.

Moser, Michael, ed. *Dispute Resolution in China*, 2nd ed. New York: Juris Publishing, 2020.

Ng, Kwai Hang and He Xin, *Embedded Courts: Judicial Decision-Making in China*. Cambridge: Cambridge University Press, 2017.

Peerenboom, Randall. "What Have We Learned About Law and Development? Describing, Predicting, and Assessing Legal Reforms in China." *Michigan Journal of International Law* 27, no. 3 (2006): 824–871.

Peerenboom, Randall and He Xin, "Dispute Resolution in China: Patterns, Causes, and Prognosis," *University of Pennsylvania East Asia Law Review* 1, no. 4 (2009): 1–61.

Seidman, Guy I. "Comparative Civil Procedure." In *The Dynamism of Civil Procedure—Global Trends and Developments*, edited by Colin B. Picker and Guy I. Seidman, 3–17. New York: Springer, 2016.

Tao, Jingzhou. *Arbitration Law and Practice in China*, 3rd ed. The Hague: Kluwer Law International, 2012.

Woo, Margaret. "The Dynamism of China's Civil Litigation System." In *The Dynamism of Civil Procedure—Global Trends and Developments*, edited by Colin B. Picker and Guy I. Seidman, 141–153. New York: Springer, 2016.

Woo, Margaret Y. K. and Mary E. Gallagher. *Chinese Justice: Civil Dispute Resolution in Contemporary China*. Cambridge: Cambridge University Press, 2011.

Woo, Margaret Y. K. and Mary E. Gallagher. "Introduction." In *Chinese Justice: Civil Dispute Resolution in Contemporary China*, edited by Margaret Y. K. Woo and Mary E. Gallagher, 1–24. New York: Cambridge University Press, 2011.

Zhang, Xianchu. "Civil Justice Reform with Political Agendas." In *The Development of the Chinese Legal System: Change and Challenges*, edited by Yu Guanghua, 253–271. Oxford: Routledge, 2011.

Zhongcai Fa (仲裁法) [Arbitration Law] (promulgated by the Standing Committee of the National People's Congress, August 31, 1994, effective September 1, 1995). http://www.npc.gov.cn/wxzl/wxzl/2000-12/05/content_4624.htm.

Zhonghua Renmin Gongheguo Min Fadian (中华人民共和国民法典) [Civil Code of the People's Republic of China] promulgated by the National People's Congress, May 28, 2020, effective January 1, 2021). http://www.npc.gov.cn/npc/c30834/202006/75ba6483b8344591abd07917e1d25cc8.shtml.

2 Courts and dispute resolution

1 Introduction

There is an increasing recognition of the importance and multi-faceted roles that courts play in global dispute resolution transformations.[1] China's court system offers an interesting case study from the Chinese perspective. In this chapter, we examine the Chinese courts in order to lay an institutionally contextual basis for analyzing the procedural reforms of civil litigation, arbitration, and mediation that cross paths with the courts in subsequent chapters. Apart from giving an updated analytical and empirical account of the profile of the Chinese courts (structure, size, function, perception, etc.), this chapter examines, in particular, the five rounds of the court reform plans (from 1999 to 2023) that aim to improve the integrity and quality of the Chinese courts under the rule of law agenda. As the fifth round of the court reform plan (2019–2023) was very recently promulgated, the emphasis will be on the first four rounds. This chapter further suggests that developments in the Chinese courts are undermined by the sometimes-conflicting goals of justice, the different vision of the leadership in the Supreme People's Court ("SPC"), as well as China's unique contextual factors such as political orientation, economic development, and social stability.

2 Contemporary Chinese courts

The following discussion presents an analytical study of the contemporary Chinese courts. This includes their structure, size, function, role, and perception, as well as judicial independence, in order to provide an institutional background of the courts that interact with various civil procedures.

---

1 Michael Palmer and Simon Roberts, *Dispute Processes: ADR and the Primary Forms of Decision-Making* (Cambridge: Cambridge University Press, 2020), Chapter 8.

2.1 Structure

The traditional theory of the Chinese courts has been that the courts are "weapons" of the people's democratic dictatorship. However, as the socialist market economy became a larger part of the state policy, the Chinese government has increasingly stressed the courts' role as a contributor to economic construction. In the early days of judicial development in the late 1990s, norms such as judicial professionalism, procedural justice, and court efficiency were promoted by the leadership of the SPC. In recent years, the courts have been regarded as instruments of the state to promote both economic development and social harmony.[2]

The Chinese court system is structured into four levels that correspond to the administrative hierarchy in China. In addition to specialist courts, basic people's courts are situated at the district or county level, intermediate people's courts at the city or prefecture level within provinces, high people's courts at the provincial level, and the SPC at the national level.

Civil litigation in China follows the principle of "two trials to conclude a case" (one trial at first instance and one trial on appeal, also known as *liangshen zhongshen zhi* 两审终审制). Civil and commercial cases in the Chinese courts are usually heard before a collegiate bench of three judges, except for simple ones that may be heard before a single judge. The basic-level people's courts process the great majority of disputes tried at first instance. The city-level intermediate people's courts have appellate jurisdiction over civil and commercial disputes on appeal from the basic-level courts, as well as original jurisdiction over important foreign-related civil and commercial disputes. The provincial-level high people's courts hear appeals from the intermediate courts and try first instance cases considered to be of provincial significance. The national-level SPC exercises original as well as appellate jurisdiction in important cases at the national level.

In addition to adjudication, the SPC exercises an important quasi-legislative power by issuing judicial interpretations.[3] These interpretations fill lacunae in the implementation of laws in judicial practice and have a binding effect on all the Chinese courts. Cases and judicial precedents in China are not formally recognized as sources of law, but some judicial decisions of the courts, particularly those of the provincial and national levels,

---

2 Chen Albert H.Y., *An Introduction to the Legal System of the People's Republic of China*, 4th ed. (Hong Kong: LexisNexis, 2011), 166.

3 Renmin Fayuan Zuzhi Fa (人民法院组织法) [Organic Law of People's Courts] (amended on 26 October 2018), art. 18, http://www.npc.gov.cn/zgrdw/npc/xinwen/2018-10/26/content_2064483.htm. However, the scope of SPC's interpretative power is not clearly defined between *interpreting law* and *making law* although there may be a literal distinction that legislation is the act of making a law, while interpretation is the art or process of ascertaining the meaning of existing laws.

may be persuasive or even binding in practice. Decisions published in the SPC Gazette are considered to be authoritative, and in practice, precedents of the SPC are binding on lower courts. Since 2011, the SPC has introduced a "Guiding Case" system to publish model judgments on civil and criminal cases on its website. These judgments are expected to act as (1) guides for lower courts in ruling on issues of similar types and (2) style guides for writing judicial decisions by Chinese judges. Zhang of the Peking University Law School, a leading authority in the field, argued that the guiding cases published should be binding among all the Chinese courts, at least on cases with the same fact patterns.[4] In recent years, a growing number of Chinese court judgments have been published on websites in order to promote more analytical writing.

2.2 Size

With respect to the size of the Chinese courts, as at the end of 2015, based on the SPC's calculation, there were 32 provincial-level high people's courts,[5] 413 city-level intermediate people's courts and specialized courts, and 3,129 district- or county-level primary people's courts (also knowns as "basic people's courts").[6] In 2014, the SPC introduced the circuit court system to handle major civil and administrative lawsuits across multi-provincial jurisdictions that the circuit court covers. The circuit courts are permanent bodies of the SPC and their judgments enjoy the same effect as an SPC judgment.[7] So far, the SPC has established six circuit courts throughout China.[8]

In recent years, the SPC quickened its pace in establishing specialized courts. Traditional specialized courts include the ten intermediate-court-level maritime courts located in Chinese coastal cities. Since 2014, three intermediate-court-level specialized intellectual property right courts ("IPR courts") have been established in Beijing, Shanghai, and Guangzhou.[9] In 2018, China's first intermediate-court-level financial court

---

4   Zhang Qi 张骐, *Zhongguo sifa xianli yu anli zhidao zhidu yanjiu* 中国司法先例与案例指导制度研究 (Beijing: Peking University Press, 2016).

5   This figure also includes one Military Court directly under the SPC.

6   The Supreme People's Court of the People's Republic of China, *The Supreme People's Court of the People's Republic of China*, accessed July 29, 2020, http://www.court.gov.cn/style/system/files/spc_en_cn.pdf.

7   Renmin Fayuan Zuzhi Fa (人民法院组织法) [Organic Law of People's Courts] (promulgated by the Standing Committee of the National People's Congress, October 26, 2018, effective January 1, 2019), art. 19, http://www.lawinfochina.com/display.aspx?id=29192&lib=law.

8   All the six circuit courts could be seen from the SPC's official website at "Organization," The Supreme People's Court of the People's Republic of China, accessed July 29, 2020, http://english.court.gov.cn/organization.html.

9   A brief introduction of the first IPR Court, the Beijing IPR Court is at "Home," Beijing Intellectual Property Court, accessed July 29, 2020, http://bjzcfy.chinacourt.gov.cn/index.shtml.

was established in Shanghai.[10] Among the basic-level courts, there are three specialized internet courts recently established in Hangzhou, Beijing, and Guangzhou in the late 2010s to consolidate the adjudication of first instance cases relating to internet- and e-commerce disputes in the three cities.[11] Grassroots-level judges serving on the basic-level courts are recognized as the forerunners of Chinese judicial practices.

As to the numbers of Chinese judges, as at the end of 2015, there were approximately 211,000 judges in China, with around 7,000 serving in the high people's courts, 40,000 in the intermediate people's courts, and 164,000 in the primary people's courts.[12] More recently, due to the reform of the judge quota system,[13] the number of Chinese judges were reduced dramatically. By the end of 2017, there were around 120,000 judges in China.[14]

In terms of caseload, in 2018, the SPC handled 34,794 cases and concluded 31,883 cases, amounting to a year-on-year increase of 22.1% and 23.5%, respectively. During 2018, all the lower-level Chinese courts handled a total of 28 million cases, increased by 8.8% from the previous year.[15] From 2013 to 2017, the SPC handled a total of 82,383 cases (an increase of 60.6% over the previous five-year period), and all the lower-level courts nationwide handled approximately 88.97 million cases (an increase of 58.6% over the previous five years).[16] A summary of the caseload of the Chinese courts in recent years and the trend development is set as Table 2.1 and Chart 2.1.[17]

2.3 Judicial independence

Contemporary scholarship on the Chinese legal system classifies judicial independence into two categories: *institutional independence* of the judiciary as a whole (the "thinner" version of judicial independence); and *independent*

---

10 A brief introduction of the Shanghai Financial Court is at "Dazao guoji jinyong jiufen jiejue youxuan di – Shanghai jinyong fayuan chengli yizhounian jishi" 打造国际金融纠纷解决优选地—上海金融法院成立一周年纪实, *Renmin fayuan bao* 人民法院报, August 20, 2019, http://www.court.gov.cn/zixun-xiangqing-177832.html.

11 "Zengshe Jing Guang 'hulianwang fayuan' huanjie wangluo jiufen susong nan" 增设京广"互联网法院"缓解网络纠纷诉讼难, *Xinlang sifa* 新浪司法, September 4, 2018, http://news.sina.com.cn/sf/news/fzrd/2018-09-04/doc-ihiixyeu3072377.shtml.

12 The Supreme People's Court of the People's Republic of China, *The Supreme People's Court of the People's Republic of China*.

13 See Section 3.4 of this chapter for discussions on the Fourth Five-Year Reform Outline (2014–2018).

14 "Faguan yuangezhi gaige zai quanguo luoshi 9 wan faguan bei dangzai menwai" 法官员额制改革在全国落实 9万法官被挡在门外, *Zhongguo xinwen wang* 中国新闻网, July 5, 2017, http://www.chinanews.com/gn/2017/07-05/8269363.shtml.

15 Zhou Qiang 周强, *Zuigao renmin fayuan gongzuo baogao* 最高人民法院工作报告, March 12, 2019, http://www.court.gov.cn/zixun-xiangqing-146802.html.

16 Zhou Qiang 周强, *Zuigao renmin fayuan gongzuo baogao* 最高人民法院工作报告, March 12, 2017, http://www.court.gov.cn/zixun-xiangqing-82602.html.

17 Zhou Qiang 周强, *Zuigao renmin fayuan gongzuo baogao* 最高人民法院工作报告 (2014–2019), covering the period of 2013 to 2018.

Table 2.1 Caseload of Chinese courts (2013–2018)

Year	Caseload of SPC	Caseload of Chinese lower level courts combined
2013	11,016	14,217,000
2014	11,210	15,651,000
2015	15,985	19,511,000
2016	22,742	23,030,000
2017	21,430	16,558,000
2018	34,794	28,000,000

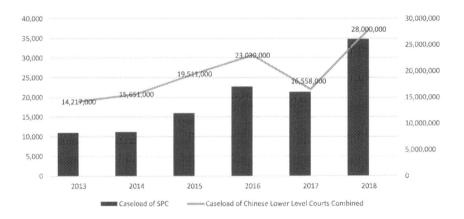

Chart 2.1 Caseload of Chinese courts (2013–2018)

decision-making by individual judges (the "thicker" version of judicial independence).[18] Institutional independence requires the courts to be adequately funded, so that they function free from governmental influence. Independent decision-making requires the judges' terms of office to be secured and their appointment depoliticized, so that judges can perform impartially.

Both the Constitution and Organic Law of the People's Courts provide that Chinese courts have the right to be free from external interference in their work.[19] However, the laws further require that individual courts at different levels must be administratively and institutionally accountable to the people's congresses of the corresponding level.[20] Courts are also subject to dual

18 See, for example, Randall Peerenboom, *China's Long March Toward Rule of Law* (Cambridge: Cambridge University Press, 2002), 288–290.
19 Zhonghua Renmin Gongheguo Xian Fa (中华人民共和国宪法) [Constitution of the People's Republic of China] (promulgated by the National People's Congress, March 11, 2018, effective March 11, 2018), art. 126, http://en.pkulaw.cn/display.aspx?cgid=311950&lib=law; Organic Law of the People's Courts, art. 4.
20 Constitution, art. 128.

leadership. They receive political supervision from the Party Committee (*dangwei* 党委) within the particular court and the Party Political and Legal Committee (*zhengfawei* 政法委) outside the court (known as "horizontal supervision"). In the meantime, their decisions and court judgments are scrutinized professionally by people's courts at higher levels on the basis of judiciary hierarchy (known as "vertical scrutiny"). This stands in sharp contrast with the understanding of collective independence in Western legal theory and rule of law ideology where individual courts enjoy functional independence and individual judges enjoy independent decision-making. As such, the Chinese courts as a whole appear to enjoy institutional independence, although individual courts and individual judges do not.

The independence of local people's courts in China is further undermined by their source of funding. The courts in China are financed by governments at the same administrative level. While the SPC supervises the adjudicative work of all other people's courts, it has no power over their budget. Local judiciaries are dependent on local governments for salaries and housing allowances. Since local governments need to support themselves (including local courts) through local taxes, fees, and charges collected from local businesses, the courts are incentivized to favor local businesses. By the same token, a locally subsidized court may be subject to local criticism if its rulings hamper local economic interests, and the court might become financially disadvantaged.

The courts' financial reliance on local governments has not only encouraged local favoritism, but also creates unbalanced development of local people's courts across the country. The court system in the coastal areas of China is overall better developed than their rural counterparts, as the economy in coastal areas is more developed and the governments' administrations are more liberal. The combination of areas with well-developed and poorly developed economies, and of areas with mature judicial infrastructures and systems and developing ones, presents serious challenges to the Chinese court reform and civil justice reform as a whole.

The thicker version with respect to judicial independence, that is, independent decision-making by Chinese judges, is another thorny issue. Individual judges, by and large, do not have the right to decide cases on their own. Judges at all levels of people's courts, apart from their judicial ranks, are further divided into different administrative levels; that is, the President of the Court (*yuanzhang* 院长), the Vice Presidents (*fuyuanzhang* 副院长), and the Division Heads of the Chambers (*tingzhang* 庭长).[21] The people's congresses at different levels decide on the appointment of the court presidents, and the presidents then decide on the appointment of the vice presidents and division heads. In cases heard by a panel of three judges, the presidents or division heads will determine which judge will act as the chair

---

21 Organic Law of the People's Courts, arts. 40–43.

of the panel, and they may further review the panel's decision(s) if they deem necessary. In turn, collegiate panels are often required under the court's internal rules to obtain the approval of the division heads, the vice presidents, the president and the court's Adjudicative Committee (*shenpan wei-yuanhui* 审判委员会) before they render their judgments. The Adjudicative Committee is the highest adjudicative body inside the court, established with the function to guide the handling of difficult cases received by the court. The committee is composed of the Party Secretary, the President, the Vice Presidents and the Division Heads of the court concerned. By submitting his/her tentative decisions to the Adjudicative Committee for approval, a judge in China is obliged to obey rank, instead of reason, and becomes little more than a bureaucratic clerk.[22] The administrative rank of the judges is important in determining the final outcome of the case, and the decision-making of individual judges is controlled indirectly through these administrative means.

Outside the court, local governments and the Party Committee may further influence judicial decisions on significant cases, and on the appointment, promotion, and removal of local judges. The Party Committee exerts tremendous influence at all levels of the court system. As discussed earlier in this chapter, the local people's congress has the power to appoint the president of the relevant local court, and the president will then nominate the other judges. However, in reality, the local Party committee often selects judges, and the people's congress more often ratifies such selection. The judges serving on the Adjudicative Committee of each court wield considerable power in determining the outcome of controversial cases. Once appointed, judges rely on salaries and housing benefits provided by the municipal government. Moreover, when appointing and promoting judges, the local political and administrative regime evaluates them in terms of obedience to its policies.[23] Hence, in cases where local business interests are at stake, local judges are incentivized to render judgments favorable to those businesses, as judges know that they will continue to be promoted if their judgments safeguard the court's financial position. Such personal dependence has been resulted from the institutional dependence of the individual local people's court, the combination of which have subjected the Chinese local judiciary to local politics and administration. Judicial interventions in adjudication and enforcement follow as a natural result.

The SPC is aware of these issues and has openly criticized local protectionism. Zhang argues that, since 2007, the SPC could be viewed as

22 Stéphanie Balme, "Local Courts in Western China: The Quest for Independence and Dignity," in *Judicial Independence in China: Lessons for Global Rule of Law Promotion*, ed. Randall Peerenboom (New York: Cambridge University Press, 2010), 169.

23 Li Yuwen, "Court Reformation in China: Problems, Progress and Prospects," in *Implementation of Law in the People's Republic of China*, eds. Chen Jianfu, Li Yuwen and Jan Michiel Otto (The Hague: Kluwer Law International, 2002), 63.

pragmatically strengthening the Chinese judiciary's overall socio-political status.[24] Finder further argues that the SPC, within the boundaries of what is politically achievable, is taking concrete steps to expand the judicial transparency and considers international indicators when doing so.[25]

Although there have been considerable improvements in general judicial enforcement, the improvements are less significant if we separate the judicial enforcement records by different localities. The problem lies in the ability of local judicial powers to deviate from their central supervisors to pursue local economic interests, in spite of the highly centralized and unitary system in which the SPC supervises all Chinese courts at lower levels. Leading experts in the field earlier commented that the Chinese courts could be more dependent upon the local governments due to a gradual administrative decentralization that is taking place since China's accession to the World Trade Organization ("WTO").[26] This decentralization process in the course of pursuing economic reforms may have fueled local judicial efforts to implement the national rules according to their own needs.[27] Thus, even though local judges might understand the SPC's reformist approach, they may not be able to implement it where a local interest must be protected.

2.4 Role in the society

In contrast to the Maoist era, when economic and social disputes were resolved through mediation or by executive organs, nowadays, people have increasingly turned to the courts for remedies. The ever-increasing volume of the litigation in the courts testifies to the rising consciousness among Chinese citizens of the law and of their rights under the law.

Over the years, the jurisdiction of the courts has expanded, and citizens and their lawyers have increasingly turned to the courts as the "fora for the airing of rights-based grievances."[28] The Chinese judiciary is being asked to play a larger and more crucial role than that in the past. Cases involving class actions, discrimination claims, and environmental protection have been brought before the courts. In the meantime, public interest litigation as a phenomenon has arisen in China.[29] There are signs that lawyers are filing

---

24 Zhang Taisu, "The Pragmatic Court: Reinterpreting the Supreme People's Court of China," *Columbia Journal of Asian Law* 25, no. 1 (2012): 1–61.
25 Susan Finder, "China's Translucent Judicial Transparency," in *Transparency Challenges Facing China*, eds. Fu Hualing, Michael Palmer and Zhang Xianchu (London: Wildy, Simmonds & Hill Publishing, 2019).
26 Pitman B. Potter, "Legal Reform in China: Institutions, Culture, and Selective Adaptation," *Law & Social Inquiry* 29, no. 2 (2004): 473.
27 He Xin, "A Tale of Two Chinese Cities: Economic Development and Contract Enforcement," *Journal of Law and Society* 39, no. 3 (2012): 384–409.
28 Benjamin Liebman, "China's Courts: Restricted Reform," *China Quarterly* 191, no. 1 (2007): 620.
29 See discussions in Chapter 3.

lawsuits against influential corporations for causing environmental pollution and applying for judicial review against powerful government departments. Scholars are of the view that despite its antagonistic stance toward cases involving critical and radical lawyering, the government is tolerant of moderate public interest litigation.[30] As such, although the Chinese law does not formally allow representative litigation, the most recent amendment to the Civil Procedure Law, as will be analyzed in detail in Chapter 3, has provided for public interest litigation and developed rules to extend standing to non-governmental organizations to litigate in mass torts such as product liability and environmental pollution disputes.[31] Such litigation has sometimes served to promote policy or legal changes, primarily because of the media and public attention generated by these cases.

With Xiao Yang as the then Chief Justice (1998–2008), courts were more receptive to activist lawsuits. However, when Wang Shengjun took up the office (2008–2013), more constraints were placed on legal activism and public interest litigation. Both the Party leadership and the courts themselves set limits on the role of the courts in this regard, and a leading scholar even identifies a trend or logic of "dejudicialization" in cases that are too politically sensitive or socially controversial for the courts to cope with.[32] For example, in the "Sanlu tainted milk" case in 2009, the Central Government decided to settle the case by compensating the children on a one-off basis, thus preventing the courts from exercising their adjudicating power. After claims were filed against Sanlu, the people's courts refused to accept the actions, delaying it for more than six months, until Sanlu was declared bankrupt and was subsequently taken over by a dairy producer with state-controlling interests. The SPC expressed that courts would not support all the filed claims as it would be more appropriate to use administrative measures to resolve the crisis.[33] When Zhou Qiang assumed the position of the President of the SPC to head the Chinese courts (2013–now), the overall role of the courts has revealed more dynamism. For example, the 2012 and 2017 amendments to the Civil Procedure Law on the availability and expansion of public interest litigation to bodies which do not have a direct interest in

---

30 Fu Hualing and Richard Cullen, "The Development of Public Interest Litigation in China," in *Public Interest Litigation in Asia*, eds. Yap Po Jen and Lau Holning (New York: Routledge, 2010), 1–29.

31 See discussions in Chapter 3.

32 This means that the courts may not have the capacity to deal with or may not be the appropriate forum for handling such cases. See Randall Peerenboom, "More Law, Less Courts: Legalized Governance, Judicialization, and Dejudicialization in China," in *Administrative Law and Governance in Asia: Comparative Perspectives*, eds. Tom Ginsburg and Chen Albert H.Y. (London: Routledge, 2009), 175–202.

33 Zhang Xianchu, "Civil Justice Reform with Political Agendas," in *The Development of the Chinese Legal System: Change and Challenges*, ed. Guanghua Yu (Oxford: Routledge, 2011), 265. See detailed discussions in Section 4.1 of Chapter 3.

a case[34] is one aspect where China is striving to fulfil multiple policy goals, such as offering an outlet for discontent, whilst also maintaining a tight level of control over the operation of such mechanisms.[35]

In this regard, the role of the courts in the Chinese society, although being much more important than before in achieving societal justice, is still limited and undermined by political orientations.

2.5 Perception evaluation

There are studies suggesting that despite the positive general perception of and support for the Chinese courts, with non-users bearing "vague but benevolent notions of the judicial system and its effectiveness,"[36] the minute number of people who have first-hand experience with the system view it negatively.[37] Although economic development serves as a factor that improves popular perceptions of official justice, the practical effect of the judiciary and its recent court reform does not seem to be well appreciated by the society. Judicial incompetence and corruption remain major concerns of the general Chinese public. Even more worrying are those extreme cases where dissatisfied losing parties in "corrupted" civil cases have attacked the people's courts, reflecting discontentment with the imbalance of power in the system.[38]

The Working Report of the SPC, an important indicator of public satisfaction with the court system and judicial work, has in recent years reflected low satisfaction, and it was only in 2010 that the satisfaction rate was slightly improved.[39] In particular, personal experiences with the courts are assessed far more negatively in rural China than in big urban cities such as Beijing or Shanghai.[40] However, since the people with personal experience constituted a small percentage of the population, their

---

34 See detailed discussions in Chapter 3.

35 Kristie Thomas, "Dynamism in China's Civil Procedure Law: Civil Justice with Chinese Characteristics," in *The Dynamism of Civil Procedure—Global Trends and Developments*, eds. Colin B. Picker and Guy I. Seidman (New York: Springer, 2016), 137.

36 Mary E. Gallagher and Yuhua Wang, "Users and Non-Users: Legal Experience and Its Effect on Legal Consciousness," in *Chinese Justice: Civil Dispute Resolution in Contemporary China*, eds. Mary E. Gallagher and Margaret Y.K. Woo (Cambridge: Cambridge University Press, 2011), 204.

37 Ethan Michelson and Benjamin L. Read, "Public Attitudes toward Official Justice in Beijing and Rural China," in *Chinese Justice: Civil Dispute Resolution in Contemporary China*, eds. Mary E. Gallagher and Margaret Y. K. Woo (Cambridge: Cambridge University Press, 2011), 170.

38 Zhang, "Civil Justice Reform with Political Agendas," 256.

39 Wang Shengjun 王胜俊, *Zuigao renmin fayuan gongzuo baogao* 最高人民法院工作报告, March 11, 2010, http://www.gov.cn/test/2012-11/13/content_2264068.htm.

40 Michelson and Read, "Public Attitudes toward Official Justice in Beijing and Rural China," 178.

evaluation may only have a trivial impact on the public perception of the judiciary's performance. On the other hand, some studies pointed out that older, urban disputants employed in the state sector are more likely to feel disillusioned and powerless, whereas younger, rural disputants employed in the private sector are more likely to have positive evaluations of their judicial experience and to view the judicial system as capable of protecting rights.[41] While the older generation would petition before, during and after the civil proceedings and view the judicial system as a last resort, disputants in the younger age group tended to take their cases directly to the court.[42] One possible explanation is that the state sector is more intertwined with the government, as well as the political and administrative powers. Hence, corruption is more likely to take place when the court has to protect state interests and social stability.

A disconcerting issue suggested in various studies about perception evaluations of the Chinese courts is that some people fail to distinguish between substantive (distributive) and procedural justice.[43] When some people conflate procedural justice and distributive justice, they are more concerned about substantive outcomes than the fairness of the procedures that lead to those outcomes. This diversion of attention contributes to the disappointment of some people and their negative assessment of justice.[44] Accordingly, people in the older generation tend to judge the experience based on distributive outcomes. Even when the law is applied correctly and fairly, procedural matters that obstruct a desired outcome would be considered illegitimate.[45] It has been suggested in some studies that only when people start defining the quality of their experiences in terms of procedural fairness will objective improvements in procedures positively improve experience-based assessments of official justice in China.[46]

3 Five rounds of court reform

Since 1999, the SPC has initiated five rounds of court reform in the form of consecutive Five-Year Reform Outlines of the People's Courts. The first two rounds (1999–2008) were carried out under the auspices of the then SPC leader Xiao Yang's ideology of modernizing the Chinese courts both institutionally and procedurally, with "justice" and "efficiency" as the twin pillars of reform. With the change of the SPC leadership to Wang Shengjun in

41 Gallagher and Wang, "Users and Non-Users," 206.
42 Ibid., 225–230.
43 Michelson and Read, "Public Attitudes toward Official Justice in Beijing and Rural China," 171.
44 Ibid.
45 Gallagher and Wang, "Users and Non-Users," 232.
46 Michelson and Read, "Public Attitudes toward Official Justice in Beijing and Rural China," 197.

2008, the third round (2009–2013) saw a retreat from judicial professionalism toward judicial populism and judicial instrumentalism for constructing a "harmonious society." With Zhou Qiang taking the SPC presidency in 2013, the fourth round of the reform (2014–2018) aimed to revert back to judicial professionalism from the overemphasis of judicial populism. The current fifth round (2019–2023) seems to re-emphasize the full-scale leadership by the Chinese Communist Party (the "Party") over the Chinese judicial work. As the fifth round of the court reform was only very recently published (in 2019), the analytical emphasis will be put on the first four rounds of the reform. The analyses below are also intended to provide an institutionally contextual background for analyses of the procedural reforms of court-based civil dispute resolutions in China (such as civil litigation, judicial mediation) in subsequent chapters.

3.1 The first five-year reform outline (1999–2003)

Promulgated by the SPC in October 1999, as the first of the five-year court reform series, it is more often referred to as the "First Five-Year Reform Outline" in the literature, detailing reforms between 1999 and 2003.[47]

The cruxes of the first Five-Year Reform Outline were first, to elevate the quality of judges by introducing a less politicized judge selection system called the "national judicial exam",[48] and second, to enhance efficiency in the judicial justice, with emphasis on procedural justice and the transition from judge-centric to party-centric justice. In particular, the reform focused on promoting court efficiency given the increase in court cases in large coastal cities, which accompanied China's rapid economic development and urbanization in the 1990s and resulted in pressure on Chinese judges to dispose cases quickly based on formal rules.

Prior to the enactment of the Judges' Law in 1995, judges in China were treated as cadres of the state. The promulgation of the Judges' Law has promoted the professionalization of the Chinese judges. The minimum eligibility criteria set out in the Judges' Law as amended in 2001 required new judges to pass a unified national judicial exam,[49] and to have one to

---

47 Supreme People's Court, *Outline of the Five-Year Reform of the People's Court (1999–2003)*, October 20, 1999, http://www.iolaw.org.cn/web/special/2015/new.aspx?id=44911.

48 Ibid., art. 32.

49 The "National Judicial Exam" (国家司法考试) is intended for all prospective judges, prosecutors and lawyers. Faguan Fa (法官法) [Judges' Law] (promulgated by the Standing Committee of the National People's Congress, on February 28, 1995, amended in June 30, 2001), arts. 12, 51, http://www.gov.cn/banshi/2005-05/26/content_1026.htm. In 2018, the National Judicial Exam is further renamed to "National Unified Legal Profession Exam" (国家统一法律职业考试), for all intending legal professionals in China. The scope goes beyond judges, prosecutors and lawyers to include legal professionals such as arbitrators, in-house counsels, and legal administrators.

three years of working experience in a Chinese court after obtaining a law or a non-law degree.[50] The required years of work experience depend on the degree held by the candidate and the level of the court to which he or she is being appointed. For instance, with at least two years of work experience, a holder of a doctoral degree in a non-law specialization who is equipped with professional legal knowledge can be appointed judge of a provincial high people's court, in which the candidate is assumed to possess professional legal knowledge. Existing judges without a law degree who were appointed before the implementation of the Judges' Law are to be trained at central or local judges' colleges.[51] This requirement ensures that even judges previously appointed based on their political background as opposed to legal professional background would be qualified for their positions.

In order to enhance procedural justice, the SPC issued a series of civil procedural rules during the 1990s and 2000s to facilitate court procedures. On the transition to party-centric justice, new evidence rules in 2002 were enacted to solve problems that had not been considered in the 1991 Civil Procedure Law, such as shifting the burden of fact finding to the parties, and abolishing pre-trial investigations. Other changes included imposing time limits on the delivery of judgment, and enacting rules to combat corruption. For example, judges were asked to deliver prompt in-court decisions after the case hearing, and must complete the case within one year of the hearing (in addition to the three- and six-month time limits imposed on summary and normal procedures, respectively). Moreover, judges were banned from making ex parte contacts with parties and their lawyers, a practice that had been prevalent in China's judicial practice, particularly in judicial mediation. These changes resulted in a decline of mediation from the mid-1990s to mid-2000s.[52] As a result, there were attempts by Chinese authorities to reverse the declining trend of mediation through restoring to people's mediation committees.[53]

3.2 The second five-year reform outline (2004–2008)

In October 2004, the SPC promulgated the Second Five-Year Reform Outline of the People's Court.[54] The second round of court reform set bolder reform goals and laid out no fewer than 50 objectives for upgrading the

50 Ibid., art. 9.
51 Ibid., art. 9(6) para. 2.
52 See discussions in Chapters 5 and 6.
53 See discussions in Chapters 5 and 6. See also Carl Minzner, "China's Turn Against Law," *American Journal of Comparative Law* 59, no. 4 (2011): 945; Aaron Halegua, "Reforming the People's Mediation System in Urban China," *Hong Kong Law Journal* 35, no. 1 (2005): 747–750.
54 Supreme People's Court, Outline of the Second Five-Year Reform of the People's Court (2004–2008), October 26, 2005, https://www.cecc.gov/resources/legal-provisions/second-five-year-reform-program-for-the-peoples-courts-2004-2008-cecc#body-chinese.

Chinese court system. As a whole, the reform provisions demonstrated a cautious awareness of the importance of greater professionalism, independence, and integrity of the judiciary. In the meantime, the provisions aimed to reduce local protectionism and stamp out corruption while acknowledging the leadership of the Party and supervision of the courts by people's congresses at each corresponding level.[55]

On collective independence, to reduce the local courts' dependence on the local governments, the SPC wished to explore the feasibility of establishment of a "guaranteed financing" system for local courts by inserting the operational costs of the courts into the budgets of the central and provincial governments.[56] Perhaps the Second Five-Year Reform Outline's boldest proposal was to loosen the grip of local power holders on personnel matters over local courts. Within a certain geographic area, the SPC called for the implementation of a system of "uniform recruitment" and "uniform assignment" of local judges in basic and intermediate courts by upper level people's courts.[57]

On enhancing judicial professionalism, apart from passing the unified national judicial exam, opportunities for overseas legal training for judges had become popular in the second round of court reform. For example, in response to China's accession to the WTO, legal education opportunities in the area of international business law, particularly international commercial transactions, had begun to be offered in China. From 1999 to 2008, more than 500 provincial-court-level and intermediate-court-level judges graduated from the Tsinghua–Temple International Business Law LLM program sponsored by the SPC.[58] Local judges from courts in the coastal areas may have more opportunities to study abroad, due to the more developed economies and more liberal administration of those areas. This supports the finding of better enforcement rates regarding both civil and commercial judgments as well as arbitral awards in coastal cities' courts.[59]

Despite the bold objectives to cultivate the Chinese judiciary's professionalism, the Second Five-Year Reform Outline was not faced without criticism. On the implementation of the Outline, critics argued that the formal laws and legal institutions introduced that might have satisfied urban users and elites completely failed to harmonize with the practical realities in China's rural areas.[60] More ideological criticisms suggested that Chinese

---

55 Ibid., art. 7.
56 Ibid., art. 48.
57 Ibid., art. 37.
58 Huang Ying (judge from the Shanghai Higher People's Court who participated in the Tsinghua–Temple LLM program in 2001), discussion with the author.
59 Mei Ying Gechlik, "Judicial Reform in China: Lessons from Shanghai," *Columbia Journal of Asian Law* 19, no. 1 (2005–2006): 122–132.
60 Minzner, "China's Turn Against Law," 947.

courts and judicial personnel had departed from their populist roots as they had been led astray under the corrosive influence of Western legal concepts.[61]

Toward the end of the Second Five-Year Reform Outline, it was increasingly clear that the objectives set out could not be achieved. The concept of "harmonious society" was promoted in 2006 as a state policy under the then Chinese leader, Hu Jintao, which resulted in a nationwide "mediation campaign" and a resurge of judicial mediation in the Chinse courtroom.[62] The guaranteed financing system had not been established by the end of the second round of court reform, and has yet to be implemented more than ten years thereafter.

3.3 The third five-year reform outline (2009–2013)

The Third Five-Year Reform Outline,[63] promulgated in March 2009, marked a departure from the previous professionalism-building direction of reform to judicial populism, and had regard for the politics in the daily adjudication work. The shift in judicial policy was not unexpected.

With a sudden surge in the number of petitions to the central authorities in Beijing in the early 2000s due to litigants' dissatisfaction with the court decisions, the earlier judicial reforms became a scapegoat.[64] Discontent was no longer contained within the courts but was petitioned to administrative organs, rendering it more visible to the Party. The Party attributed these societal angers to the courts' failure in the past two rounds of court reform plans to contribute to a harmonious society, which the Party perceived to be harmful to its regime legitimacy. In tandem with the rise of social conflicts that came as a by-product of too-rapid economic growth, the Party believed that professionalization of the courts, which stressed adherence to formal laws and procedures, had hindered the courts in performing their political duty as a "major contributor" to the maintenance of a harmonious social order.[65]

---

61 Ibid.
62 See discussions in Chapters 5 and 6. See generally Central Committee of the Communist Party of China, *Zhonggong Zhongyang guanyu goujian shehuizhuyi hexieshehui ruogan zhongda wenti de jueding* 中共中央关于构建社会主义和谐社会若干重大问题的决定, October 11, 2006, http://www.gov.cn/gongbao/content/2006/content_453176.htm; Maureen Fan, "China's Party Leadership Declares New Priority: 'Harmonious Society'," *Washington Post*, October 12, 2006.
63 Supreme People's Court, *Outline of the Third Five-Year Reform of the People's Courts (2009–2013)*, March 17, 2009, http://www.lawinfochina.com/display.aspx?lib=law&id=7380&CGid=.
64 Fu Hualing and Richard Cullen, "From Mediatory to Adjudicatory Justice: The Limits of Civil Justice Reform in China," in *Chinese Justice: Civil Dispute Revolution in China*, eds. Margaret Y.K. Woo and Mary E. Gallagher (Cambridge: Cambridge University Press, 2011), 44–45.
65 Ibid., 46.

After Wang Shengjun assumed the presidency of the SPC in late 2008, the SPC responded to the aforementioned political demands by incorporating the new ideologies of the Party—namely, the "Three Supremes"[66] and the "socialist rule of law"[67]—into the Third Five-Year Reform Outline. Wang emphasized the duty of the courts to serve goals and policies as determined by the Party and to account for the circumstances of the society. In other words, the courts must have regard for the "mass line,"[68] which refers to the "adjudication for the people." As the mass line required the courts to account for the Party leadership, socio-economic and socio-political conditions when rendering judicial decisions, as opposed to strictly applying legal rules, judicial decision-making became more "outcome-oriented" rather than "process-oriented."

With the "mass line" referring to the "adjudication for the people," the third round of court reform encouraged, and even prioritized, the use of judicial mediation to manipulate the influence of the Party leadership, socio-economic and socio-political conditions in decision-making processes.[69] Some commentators opined that this court reform would help facilitate social harmony and reflect transitional justice, while many others argued that the plan was characterized by its "cautiousness" rather than touching on systemic issues under the Party leadership.[70]

This reversal in the policy of court reform and the stress placed on a more socialist direction could also be analyzed from the perspective of the personal background of the leaders of the Chinese judiciary. When China acceded to the WTO in 2001, most, if not all, of the presidents of the provincial-level high courts had a formal, systematic legal education background.[71] The then Chief Justice and President of the SPC, Xiao Yang, had received both a university-level legal education and practical qualifications in law. His successor, Wang Shengjun, had neither formal legal education nor judicial experience. Wang, who was previously an official from the Party Central Political Legal Committee, was appointed on the basis of his political and administrative background. Similar to Wang's appointment, the newly appointed presidents of some provincial high courts also took office

---

66 The "Three Supremes" is a school of thought advocated by the Party during Hu Jintao's leadership, which involves three layers of meaning: the supremacy of the work of the Party, the supremacy of people's interests, and the supremacy of the Constitution and laws. See the speech by Wang Shengjun on the correlation between the then new round of judicial reform and the "Three Supremes" theory advanced by Hu Jintao, available at http://news.xinhuanet.com/legal/2008-06/23/content_8420938.htm.

67 Wang Shengjun, *Working Report of the Supreme People's Court (2009)*, March 17, 2009.

68 Ibid.

69 Ibid.

70 See Qin Xudong, "Judicial Reform: A New Round," *Caijing Magazine*, January 24, 2009.

71 Jerome Cohen, "Body Blows for the Judiciary," *South China Morning Post*, October 18, 2008, http://www.scmp.com/article/656696/body-blow-judiciary.

without any formal legal training.[72] This change in the judicial leadership suggests an uprise in political pressure over the judiciary that conflicts with the professionalism-oriented judicial appointment.[73]

Apart from the change in the leadership background, the change in the direction of the reform also reflected the change of the Party's policy on the judiciary. On 28 November 2008, the Party Central Committee Politburo issued its Opinions on Deepening the Reform of the Judicial System and its Working Mechanisms.[74] This document did not respond to increasing demands for major systemic reforms raised by the previous two rounds of the court reform plans, such as the reform of the court financing system and the judge selection and appointment system. Instead, the Party's central-level document placed a greater deal of emphasis on "Chinese characteristics" and "national conditions" in combination with the "popularization of law."[75] Under these overarching themes, the tasks of the judicial reform as set out by the Party agenda were to optimize the distribution of judicial functions and powers, balance the strict execution of criminal law with clemency in certain situations, ensure a healthy budget for the people's courts, stress the function of judicial service, achieve flexibility, and ensure social stability and predictability.[76] In a sense, the development of the Chinese courts closely followed and consolidated the Party's "Three Supremes."

3.4 The fourth five-year reform outline (2014–2018)

The SPC issued its Fourth Five-Year Reform Outline in July 2014.[77] The assumption of power by Xi Jinping in late 2012 started to shift the focus from the highly politicized reform back to the rule of law.[78] To echo Xi's move, Zhou Qiang, the first Chief Justice trained in law in the post-cultural-revolution era, was appointed to the President of the SPC in 2013. In context of the political reorientation, the plan of the fourth round of court reform put forward quite a few major changes.

---

72 Zhang, "The Pragmatic Court," 25.
73 Jerome Alan Cohen, "The PRC Legal System at Sixty," *East Asia Forum*, October 1, 2009, https://www.eastasiaforum.org/2009/10/01/the-prc-legal-system-at-sixty/.
74 A detailed report of the Opinions of the CCP is available at the China Legal Information Website, www.law-star.com/zt/zt0216/index.htm. The new trend of judicial reform and its failure to respond to systematic issues raised by the two previous rounds of court reform sparked wide-ranging discussions by legal academics and practitioners on that same website in 2009.
75 Ibid.
76 Ibid.
77 Supreme People's Court, *Zuigao renmin fayuan fabu "siwu gaige gangyao"* 最高人民法院发布"四五改革纲要," July 10, 2014, http://www.court.gov.cn/zixun-xiangqing-8168.html.
78 The Central Committee of the Communist Party of China, *Decision of the CPC Central Committee on Major Issues Pertaining to Comprehensively Promoting the Rule of Law*, October 23, 2014.

One of the principal tasks was to reform the judicial profession. The introduction of the Judge Quota System (*yuan'e zhi* 员额制) was designed to implement a specialized personnel management system for judges as different from that of ordinary civil servants, and to retrieve judicial professionalism and elitism that had been pushed in the first two rounds of court reform. It divides court personnel into three types: (1) judges, (2) judicial assistants, and (3) judicial administrative personnel. The judge qualification is then only reserved to type (1), and removes the remaining two types of personnel from the original judge group, that is, those who do not engage in case trials, or those who engage in case trials but do not have the competency to hear cases.[79] As such, except for judges who are admitted in the Judge Quota system (*ru'e* 入额), law assistants, law clerks and officers for judgment enforcement are all listed as judicial assistants; and the remaining others are listed as judicial administrative staff.

The SPC further required each individual court to determine the number of its judges under the Judge Quota system based on the economic and social development, the population, the caseload in their jurisdiction, as well as the court level, the court size, the court workload, etc.[80] However, in practice, how to determine the number of judges in each court has become a problem. Although the SPC lists the elements for consideration, how to accurately calculate the number based on these elements is left to local courts to explore. It has also stimulated many Chinese scholars to propose various programs.[81] The Shanghai Higher People's Court took the lead in adjusting the proportion of judges. Specifically, it required courts in Shanghai to have 33% of judges, 52% of judicial assistants, and 15% of judicial administrative staff.[82] Since then, most Chinese courts have determined the proportion of their court staff. According to the 2018 SPC's Annual Report, the number of judges nationwide dropped from 211,990 to 120,138, down by 43%.[83]

To address the existing administrative problems, another principal task of the reform focused on the power transfer to provincial-level governments over finances and personnel matters in basic-level courts, which are

79 Wang Shirong 汪世荣, "Faguan yuan'e zhidu luodi dui sifa neibu guanli jizhi jianshe yiyi zhongda" 法官员额制度落地对司法内部管理机制建设意义重大, *Renmin fayuan bao* 人民法院报, July 8, 2017, https://www.chinacourt.org/article/detail/2017/07/id/2916592.shtml.
80 Supreme People's Court, *Zuigao renmin fayuan fabu "siwu gaige gangyao."*
81 Chen Ruihua 陈瑞华, "Faguan yuan'e zhi gaige de lilun fansi" 法官员额制改革的理论反思, *The Jurist* 法学家 no. 3 (2018): 1–14.
82 Shanghaishi Renmin Zhengfu 上海市人民政府, *Shanghai sifa tizhi gaige* 上海司法体制改革, May 19, 2017, http://www.shanghai.gov.cn/nw2/nw2314/nw24651/nw42131/nw42135/u21awl230816.html.
83 Zhou Qiang 周强, *Zuigao renmin fayuan gongzuo baogao* 最高人民法院工作报告, March 9, 2018, http://www.court.gov.cn/zixun-xiangqing-87832.html.

currently held by local governments and people's congresses corresponding to the level of the basic courts, but whether this is of furtherance of the "guaranteed financing" proposed in the second round of court reform remains unknown.[84] Structurally, the fourth round of court reform introduced the circuit court system to separate the judicial jurisdiction from the administrative jurisdiction.[85] As previously discussed, the SPC has since established six circuit courts.[86]

In addition to de-administratization, a highlighting feature of the fourth round of the reform was to enhance the transparency of the Chinese courts. The reform sought to do so by making the trial procedure more open, providing for real time broadcasts of hearings, improving access to judicial information, and developing a judgment database. Correspondingly, the SPC established the China Judicial Process Information Online,[87] the China Trials Online,[88] the China Judgments Online,[89] and the China Enforcement Information Online.[90]

In order to enhance procedural justice, the Fourth Five-Year Reform Outline responded to some of the international calls of rule of law and took a more nuanced approach between adjudicatory justice and mediatory justice. Fu and Palmer have acutely pointed out that Zhou Qiang's appointment and his personal background would be a clear indication of re-embracing judicial formalism such that judicial mediation would no longer receive the same priority it once did in the third round of court reform.[91] The SPC now required a more prudential attitude toward the adoption of judicial mediation in the Chinese courts. It confirmed that the policy of the Chinese litigation system should center on adjudication and proposed the improvement of the rules of proof in civil proceedings. It further proposed the creation of a more diversified dispute resolution mechanism so that disputants could be offered a choice of processes.[92] In association with the move to diversify

---

84 Supreme People's Court, *Zuigao renmin fayuan fabu "siwu gaige gangyao."*

85 Ibid.

86 All the six circuit courts could be glanced at SPC's official website. See "Organization," The Supreme People's Court of the People's Republic of China, accessed July 29, 2020, http://english.court.gov.cn/organization.html.

87 "Home," *Zhongguo shenpan liucheng xinxi gongkai wang*中国审判流程信息公开网, accessed July 29, 2020, https://splcgk.court.gov.cn/gzfwwww/.

88 "Home," *Zhongguo tingshen gongkai wang* 中国庭审公开网, accessed July 29, 2020, http://tingshen.court.gov.cn/.

89 "Home," *Zhongguo caipan wenshu wang* 中国裁判文书网, accessed July 29, 2020, http://wenshu.court.gov.cn/.

90 "Home," *Zhongguo zhixing xinxi gongkai wang* 中国执行信息公开网, accessed July 29, 2020, http://zxgk.court.gov.cn/.

91 Fu Hualing and Michael Palmer, *Mediation in Contemporary China: Continuity and Change* (London: Wildy, Simmonds & Hill Publishing, 2017).

92 See discussions in Section 3.2 of Chapter 6.

dispute resolution, in 2016, the SPC published the Opinions on Further Revolution of the ADR System.[93]

As with previous rounds of court reform, the fourth round of court reform is not free from political pressures. Scholars have argued that nothing in the reform has aimed at diminishing the Party's control over the courts. One example would be the provincial committees being set up to select judges. Although the committees would select judges based on professionalism, there is still a political dimension since the committees would also include officials responsible for maintaining the Party's discipline by reviewing potential candidates on their "political quality, integrity, and self-discipline."[94]

On the technical side, the fourth round of the reform has also had serious problems in implementation. China has been facing a litigation explosion for the past four decades. The caseload rose from 610,000 in 1978 to 28,000,000 in 2018, increased by nearly 46 times.[95] However, the strict implementation of the Judge Quota system has led to a significant reduction in the number of Chinese judges. As previously mentioned, by the end of 2017, the number of Chinese judges dropped from 211,990 to 120,138, leaving 90,000 former judges behind.[96] In the meantime, the number of judicial assistants has not increased simultaneously, and other measures to help judges reduce their workload have not been implemented in parallel. With the litigation explosion and the insufficiency in the number of judges appearing simultaneously, many judges have been overworking and are on the verge of collapse. The excessive workload of the Chinese judges has become one of the major topics in the Chinese judicial community these days.[97] Cases are backlogged which have caused dissatisfaction among the parties. In the meantime, it has also adversely affected the physical health and family life of the Chinese judges. As a result, many judges have chosen to resign and leave. The resignation of judges from courts and the judicial brain drain in economically developed Chinese regions such as Beijing, Shanghai, and Guangdong have been significantly more serious these years.[98]

93 "Zuigao renmin fayuan guanyu renmin fayuan jinyibu Shenhua duoyuanhua jiufen jiejue jizhi gaige de yijian" 最高人民法院关于人民法院进一步深化多元化纠纷解决机制改革的意见, *Renmin fayuan bao* 人民法院报, January 8, 2017, https://www.chinacourt.org/article/detail/2017/01/id/2509588.shtml.

94 Wei Lisi, "Inside China: Judicial and Legal Reform in the People's Republic," *International Judicial Monitor* (Washington DC: International Judicial Academy, 2015).

95 "Shige shuze, goule 2018 Renmin Fayuan gaimao" 十个数字, 勾勒 2018 年人民法院概貌, *Tengxun Wang* 腾讯网, https://new.qq.com/omn/20190312/20190312A0C5TU.html.

96 Zhou Qiang 周强, *Zuigao renmin fayuan gongzuo baogao* 最高人民法院工作报告, March 9, 2018.

97 Zu Xianhai 祖先海, "Jiceng faguan gongzuoliang taida" 基层法官工作量太大, *Renmin Fayuan Bao* 人民法院报, March 12, 2016, http://rmfyb.chinacourt.org/paper/html/2016-03/12/content_109341.htm?div=-1.

98 Zhang Zhiquan 张智全, "Jiceng faguan liushi de duochong lixing sikao" 基层法官流失的多重理性思考, *Zhongguo Fayuan Wang* 中国法院网, May 19, 2014, https://www.chinacourt.org/article/detail/2014/05/id/1297649.shtml.

3.5 *The fifth five-year reform outline (2019–2023)*

In February 2019, the SPC published its Fifth Five-Year Reform Outline.[99] Compared to the fourth round, the fifth round of the court reform plan appears more politically heightened and technically conservative.

Even though every five-year court reform plan reiterates the Party leadership, the fifth round spares no efforts to emphasize and concretize political correctness. Adhering to the correct political direction has become the overriding basic principle.[100] Ensuring the Party leadership over the judicial reform in all aspects and throughout the whole process is the general objective.[101] What is more, the first major task in the fifth round of court reform is to reinforce the mechanism of the people's courts insisting on the Party leadership.[102] Before this, ensuring the Party leadership has never become a concrete task of the court reform; instead, it just emerged at the beginning of the court reform plan as a house-keeping matter, symbolically representing the guiding ideology of the reforms.

Technically, the current fifth round of court reform does not propose a package of reform items to improve the judicial infrastructure than those already envisaged by the previous rounds, in particular, the fourth round; rather, it put emphasis on perfecting (*jianquan* 健全; *wanshan* 完善) the existing systems,[103] yet carefully reflecting the political orientation of the reform. For example, in terms of perfecting the selection and evaluation of judges, the fifth round requires viewing the political standard as the first criterion, before moving on to the previous requirements in promoting the standardization, specialization and professionalization of the judicial personnel.[104]

It is noteworthy to recall the Party Central Committee Politburo's Decision on Some Major Issues Concerning Comprehensively Deepening the Reform in China several years earlier, in which President Xi Jinping still described the Chinese judiciary as an important component of the Chinese political system.[105] Hence, any significant meaningful reforms would still be under the parameters set out by the Party. With the mounting pressure of

---

99 "Zuigaofa fabu Renmin Fayuan Wu Wu gaige gangyao" 最高法发布人民法院五五改革纲要, *Xinhua Wang* 新华网, February 27, 2019, http://www.xinhuanet.com/legal/2019-02/27/c_1124169476.htm.

100 Ibid., part 1(2).

101 Ibid., part 1(3).

102 Ibid., part 2(1).

103 Ibid. Out of the ten tasks raised in the fifth round of court reform, nine uses the term "perfecting the system" as their headings.

104 Ibid., part 2(1)(4).

105 "Explanatory Notes for the 'Decision of the Central Committee of the Communist Party of China on Some Major Issues Concerning Comprehensively Deepening the Reform'," *China.org.cn*, January 16, 2014, http://www.china.org.cn/china/third_plenary_session/2014-01/16/content_31210122.htm.

carrying out an actual political reform, the authority responds with a politically prudent and professionally reactionary judicial reform.

3.6 Reflection on court reform

In spite of the efforts devoted to the court reform, practical effects of the reform either did not take the predicted form (such as the "guaranteed financing" in the second round) or was met with implementation problems (such as the Judge Quota system in the fourth round). At the beginning of the reforms, the SPC aimed at promoting the integrity and quality of the judiciary. By allowing greater independence and giving more professional prestige to Chinese courts and judges, it was expected to generate increased judicial credibility and accountability. Despite this, so far, neither the "guaranteed financing" of the courts nor that of "uniform recruitment" of lower level court judges has been comprehensively achieved throughout China. These systematic issues have been enthusiastically emphasized in the first two rounds of court reform (1999–2008), completely ignored at the third round of court reform (2009–2013), resurfaced for some attention in the fourth round of court reform (2014–2018), and retreated to political sensitiveness in the fifth round of court reform (2019–2023). Meanwhile, the reforms have failed to address judicial corruption, which remained one of the major concerns by the people in China.

Insiders will know that these changes in court reform policy actually reflected the tensions and struggles present in the political reform. It also ties in well with an earlier observation by Cohen. He insightfully pointed out that the political status quo in China does not allow rapid expansion of judicial power, especially when such an expansion might threaten the primacy of administrative power.[106] This explains the checkered path of Chinese court reform during political and social transitions, as the court reform has been largely dependent on the country's further political and administrative liberalization. Therefore, more ground-breaking changes need to take place to empower the courts and individual judges in the decision-making process. And the success of the reform of the courts can only be tested according to its actual degree of implementation in practice.

4 Courts and civil dispute resolution

The following discussion studies the relationship and dynamics between the courts and various civil dispute resolution methods in China, which is intended to provide a background for the analyses in subsequent chapters

---

106 Jerome Alan Cohen, "China's Legal Reform at the Crossroads," *Far Eastern Economic Review* 169, no. 2 (2006): 26.

on the procedural systems of civil litigation, arbitration, and mediation that intertwine with the courts at various levels.

4.1 Civil litigation

The system of civil litigation is shaped by the relevant institutional and procedural levels. The impact of the court on civil litigation is mainly reflected on the institutional level.

Institutionally, as discussed in this chapter, the role of the courts has been reviewed by five rounds of the top-down five-year court reform plans since 1999, proposing the better court infrastructure to facilitate civil litigation. However, the commitment to reform did not take full effect, as had been anticipated. Except for the introduction of a unified national judicial exam, the other parts of the first two rounds of court reform (1999–2008) which aimed to institutionalize the court finance and court personnel have yet to be implemented. The third round of court reform (2009–2013) saw a trend of politicization of the courts and its civil procedures, in which courts were required to prioritize mediation over litigation, so as to contain sensitive disputes and societal confrontations. The period of politicization was retreated by the fourth round of court reform (2014–2018), during which the societal disputes were less politicized and courts were no longer required to prioritize mediation. However, the fifth round of court reform (2019–2023) appears again to be politically sensitive in which ensuring the Party leadership has become a concrete task for all aspects of the improvement of the court system and a general objective throughout the whole reform agenda. Unsurprisingly, the current conservative institutional reform tone of the Chinese courts will impact on the procedural reform of the civil litigation too.

The profound effect of the top-down approach in the institutional reforms of the courts is due to its dependence on the socio-political climate of the government and the Party leadership. As we see, the overall political climate of the Party, the change of the SPC leadership, and the associated lack of consistency in their ideologies toward the role of the courts and that of the civil litigation within the dispute resolution ecology has inevitably led to an unstable evolution of the court system that may not necessarily serve the disputants.

At the procedural level, substantive changes to the civil procedure, by way of amendments to the Civil Procedure Law in 2007, 2012, and 2017, will be analyzed in Chapter 3.

4.2 Arbitration

The courts are involved in arbitration in several respects, as indicated later in this chapter.

Courts, particularly the SPC, issue important judicial interpretations that serve as sources of regulations for arbitration. As will be discussed in Chapters 4 and 7, over the past two decades, the SPC has issued an impressive body of judicial interpretations to provide a supportive judicial environment toward arbitration. Second, in China, courts grant and enforce interim measures of protection to assist arbitration proceedings. These interim measures include property and evidence preservation orders in China.[107] Courts also exercise the final check over arbitral jurisdiction, that is, to rule on whether the arbitration agreement is existent or valid.[108] Most powerfully, courts scrutinize the outcome of arbitration, that is, arbitral awards, which they are asked to enforce or set aside. The judicial power to enforce or not to enforce an arbitral award has been regarded as the key measurement of whether a jurisdiction could be termed as "pro-arbitration" or "arbitration-friendly."[109] The judicial policy that guides the decision-making on matters of the effective enforcement of arbitral awards is accurate testimony of a jurisdiction's deposition on arbitration.[110] As will be illustrated in Chapter 7, in the past decade, some of the most controversial cases of arbitral enforcement have been liberally construed by both the SPC and Chinese lower-level courts.

The arbitration system will be analyzed in Chapter 4, and the interactions between the court system and the arbitration system (i.e., judicial review over arbitration) will be studied in Chapter 7.

4.3 Mediation

Chinese courts prefer to use mediation as their main form of decision-making in their adjudicative work. Analyses on the Chinese courts' preference for using mediation have been offered in various areas of the literature. There are strong cultural roots, including Confucianism, for this preference, which emphasizes amicable settlement. Irrespective of whether the dispute has been subject to mediation before the court action is brought, mediation efforts to bring about a settlement voluntarily accepted by both parties will be made at various points of the civil proceedings.[111]

---

107 Zhongcai Fa (仲裁法) [Arbitration Law] (promulgated by the Standing Committee of the National People's Congress, August 31, 1994, effective September 1, 1995), art. 68, http://www.npc.gov.cn/wxzl/wxzl/2000-12/05/content_4624.htm.

108 Ibid., art. 20; Supreme People's Court, *Reply on Several Issues of Ascertaining the Validity of the Arbitration Agreement*, October 26, 1998, http://cicc.court.gov.cn/html/1/218/62/84/671.html.

109 Anselmo Reyes and Gu Weixia, "Conclusion: An Asia Pacific Model of Arbitration Reform," in *The Developing World of Arbitration: A Comparative Study of Arbitration Reform in the Asia Pacific*, eds. Anselmo Reyes and Gu Weixia (Oxford: Hart Publishing, 2018), 279–300.

110 Thomas Carbonneau, "Judicial Approbation in Building the Civilization of Arbitration," in *Building the Civilization of Arbitration*, eds. Thomas Carbonneau and Angelica M. Sinopole (London: Wildy, Simmonds & Hill Publishing, 2010), 335–336.

111 Minshi Susong Fa (民事诉讼法) [Civil Procedure Law] (promulgated by the National People's Congress, June 27, 2017, effective July 1, 2017, arts. 9, 93–99, https://www.pkulaw.com/chl/d33df017c784876fbdfb.html.

The first stage at which mediation is conducted by the court (as distinguished from mediation by people's mediation committees, or by arbitrators in the course of arbitration) is before the trial. The court, acting either through one adjudicator or as a collegiate bench, may conduct mediation. The second and more frequently occurring stage is mediation conducted during trial proceedings, and can be requested by parties on a voluntary basis at any time before the court's judgment is rendered. Furthermore, parties in a judicial mediation in China may invite other relevant parties to assist in the mediation process, such as working units that the litigation parties are attached to.[112] A mediation agreement prepared by the court, more frequently referred to as a "judicial settlement agreement," is binding and enforceable once it is delivered to the parties.[113] Over the past two decades, judicial mediation and extra-judicial mediation systems have both developed in full swing.

The mediation system will be analyzed in Chapter 5, and the interactions between the court system and the mediation system (i.e., judicial mediation) will be examined in Chapter 6.

5 Observations

In concluding this chapter, it is encouraging to note that some limitations of the Chinese court system have been addressed in the past two decades. The Second Five-Year Reform Outline (2004–2008) appeared particularly bold in exploring a number of goals for upgrading the Chinese judicial system. However, the professionalism-building trend of the reform of the Chinese courts and judges was dampened by the publication of the Third Five-Year Reform Outline (2009–2013). The Fourth Five-Year Reform Outline (2014–2018) aimed to depoliticize the courts and published some major changes in the management of the judges' profession. Unfortunately, the reform tone of the current Fifth Five-Year Reform Outline (2019–2023) again appears to be conservative and politically sensitive.

Unlike other transitional economies where judicial justice has been developed to facilitate economic development and political reorientation, in China, the task of maintaining social stability has also been assigned to the judiciary. With the rule of law still being a developing concept, the Chinese courts as part of an authoritarian regime cannot make decisions without considering their political and social consequences. Despite China's impressive economic growth for over more than four decades, reform in China is entering into a crucial stage in which conflicts caused by distribution inequality, wealth polarization, labor dissatisfaction, and environmental pollution that have all accompanied deepening urbanization and

112 Ibid., art. 95.
113 Ibid., arts. 97, 99.

marketization is taking the country to many chaotic societal issues. In this context, it is believed that any future reform of the courts needs to take into account the Chinese social reality. Pragmatic compromises will be required to skillfully handle the complexity of economic, political, and societal transitions. In a huge developing country such as China, insufficient resources, developing legal institutions, and enduring legal culture will all impact the performance of the Chinese courts, and the pace and ways of its reform. In the process, the Chinese Party-State faces the pressure of maintaining both the social order and its regime legitimacy, in addition to enhancing the economic growth.

Many experts have argued that China should liberalize its ideology, moving toward a universal-value-based rule of law (although this has been much challenged as a "Western model" in some mainstream Chinese publications),[114] because a weak judiciary and its resulting limited institutionalization of the dispute resolution will only undermine the ruling regime's legitimacy.[115] But in China, once disputes are classified as sensitive, such as class actions, then even pure commercial lawsuits might catch the attention of the Party. After more than four decades of the economic reform, Zhang observed that the Party's influence determines and will still determine, either directly or indirectly, the results of these cases.[116] With limited judicial independence, the courts may only carry out its responsibility for delivering judicial justice within the authoritarian environment, in which justice may be measured more by other criteria such as social popularity and political correctness than by professional standards. This is most evident in the reform tone of the current fifth round of court reform.

It is fair to say that China is still struggling to find the optimal judicial framework, with the Party leadership in a dilemma with respect to the role of the courts in the Chinese society and governance during transitions. Although it has been strenuously argued that the courts and individual judges should be significantly empowered to play a more active role in adjudication, to fundamentally reform Chinese courts would be a very difficult and complex task that requires an entire rule of law system to be put into practice. The path to rule of law, including the future reform of the Chinese courts, is nevertheless increasingly pushed forward by the more progressive elements in the Chinese society.

114   See, for example, Feng Yuzhang, "Zenyang renshi suowei pushi jiazhi" 怎样认识所谓普世价值, *People's Daily* 人民日报, September 10, 2008, http://www.npc.gov.cn/zgrdw/npc/xinwen/rdlt/sd/2008-09/10/content_1449151.htm; Zhou Xincheng 周新城, "Yixie ren guchui de 'pushi jiachi' shizhi shang jiushi xifang de jiazhi" 一些人鼓吹的"普世价值"实质上就是西方的价值, *Guangming Daily* 光明日报, September 16, 2008, http://epaper.gmw.cn/gmrb/html/2008-09/16/nw.D110000gmrb_20080916_5-09.htm?div=-1.

115   Randall Peerenboom, "Between Global Norms and Domestic Realities: Judicial Reforms in China," in *Law and Development and the Global Discourses of Legal Transfers*, eds. John Gillespie and Penelope Nicholson (Cambridge: Cambridge University Press, 2012), 181–201.

116   Zhang, "Civil Justice Reform with Political Agendas," 253–271.

Bibliography

Balme, Stéphanie. "Local Courts in Western China: The Quest for Independence and Dignity." In *Judicial Independence in China: Lessons for Global Rule of Law Promotion*, edited by Randall Peerenboom, 154–179. New York: Cambridge University Press, 2010.

Carbonneau, Thomas. "Judicial Approbation in Building the Civilization of Arbitration." In *Building the Civilization of Arbitration*, edited by Thomas Carbonneau and Angelica M. Sinopole, 333–365. London: Wildy, Simmonds & Hill Publishing, 2010.

Central Committee of the Communist Party of China. *Zhonggong Zhongyang guanyu goujian shehuizhuyi hexieshehui ruogan zhongda wenti de jueding* 中共中央关于构建社会主义和谐社会若干重大问题的决定, October 11, 2006. http://www.gov.cn/gongbao/content/2006/content_453176.htm.

Chen, Albert H.Y. *An Introduction to the Legal System of the People's Republic of China*, 4th ed. Hong Kong: LexisNexis, 2011.

Chen, Ruihua 陈瑞华. "Faguan yuan'e zhi gaige de lilun fansi" 法官员额制改革的理论反思. *The Jurist* 法学家 no. 3 (2018): 1–14.

Cohen, Jerome Alan. "Body Blows for the Judiciary." *South China Morning Post*, October 18, 2008. http://www.scmp.com/article/656696/body-blow-judiciary.

Cohen, Jerome Alan. "China's Legal Reform at the Crossroads." *Far Eastern Economic Review* 169, no. 2 (2006): 23–27.

Cohen, Jerome Alan. "The PRC Legal System at Sixty." *East Asia Forum*, October 1, 2009. https://www.eastasiaforum.org/2009/10/01/the-prc-legal-system-at-sixty/.

"Dazao guoji jinyong jiufen jiejue youxuan di – Shanghai jinyong fayuan chengli yizhounian jishi" 打造国际金融纠纷解决优选地–上海金融法院成立一周年纪实. *Renmin fayuan bao* 人民法院报, August 20, 2019. http://www.court.gov.cn/zixun-xiangqing-177832.html.

"Explanatory Notes for the 'Decision of the Central Committee of the Communist Party of China on Some Major Issues Concerning Comprehensively Deepening the Reform'." *China.org.cn*, January 16, 2014. http://www.china.org.cn/china/third_plenary_session/2014-01/16/content_31210122.htm.

Faguan Fa (法官法) [Judges' Law] (promulgated by the Standing Committee of the National People's Congress, February 28, 1995, effective July 1, 1995). http://www.lawinfochina.com/display.aspx?lib=law&id=121&CGid=.

"Faguan yuangezhi gaige zai quanguo luoshi 9 wan faguan bei dangzai menwai" 法官员额制改革在全国落实 9万法官被挡在门外. *Zhongguo xinwen wang* 中国新闻网. http://www.chinanews.com/gn/2017/07-05/8269363.shtml.

Fan, Maureen. "China's Party Leadership Declares New Priority: 'Harmonious Society'." *Washington Post*, October 12, 2006.

Feng, Yuzhang 冯虞章. "Zenyang renshi suowei pushi jiazhi" 怎样认识所谓普世价值. *People's Daily* 人民日报, September 10, 2008. http://www.npc.gov.cn/zgrdw/npc/xinwen/rdlt/sd/2008-09/10/content_1449151.htm.

Finder, Susan. "China's Translucent Judicial Transparency." In *Transparency Challenges Facing China*, edited by Fu Hualing, Michael Palmer and Zhang Xianchu, 141–175. London: Wildy, Simmonds & Hill Publishing, 2019.

Fu, Hualing and Michael Palmer. *Mediation in Contemporary China: Continuity and Change*. London: Wildy, Simmonds & Hill Publishing, 2017.

Fu, Hualing and Richard Cullen. "From Mediatory to Adjudicatory Justice: The Limits of Civil Justice Reform in China." In *Chinese Justice: Civil Dispute Revolution in China*, edited by Margaret Y.K. Woo and Mary E. Gallagher, 25–57. Cambridge: Cambridge University Press, 2011.

Fu, Hualing and Richard Cullen. "The Development of Public Interest Litigation in China." In *Public Interest Litigation in Asia*, edited by Yap Po Jen and Lau Holning, 1–29. New York: Routledge, 2010.

Gallagher, Mary E. and Wang Yuhua. "Users and Non-Users: Legal Experience and Its Effect on Legal Consciousness." In *Chinese Justice: Civil Dispute Resolution in Contemporary China*, edited by Mary E. Gallagher and Margaret Y.K. Woo, 204–233. Cambridge: Cambridge University Press, 2011.

Gechlik, Mei Ying. "Judicial Reform in China: Lessons from Shanghai." *Columbia Journal of Asian Law* 19, no. 1 (2005–2006): 122–132.

Halegua, Aaron. "Reforming the People's Mediation System in Urban China." *Hong Kong Law Journal* 35, no. 1 (2005): 747–750.

He, Xin. "A Tale of Two Chinese Cities: Economic Development and Contract Enforcement." *Journal of Law and Society* 39, no. 3 (2012): 384–409.

"Home." Beijing Intellectual Property Court, accessed July 29, 2020. http://bjzcfy. chinacourt.gov.cn/index.shtml.

"Home." China Judicial Process Information Online, accessed July 29, 2020. https:// splcgk.court.gov.cn/gzfwww/.

"Home." *Zhongguo caipan wenshu wang* 中国裁判文书网, accessed July 29, 2020. http://wenshu.court.gov.cn/.

"Home." *Zhongguo tingshen gongkai wang* 中国庭审公开网, accessed July 29, 2020. http://tingshen.court.gov.cn/.

"Home." *Zhongguo zhixing xinxi gongkai wang* 中国执行信息公开网, accessed July 29, 2020. http://zxgk.court.gov.cn/.

Huang, Ying. Discussion with the author.

Li, Yuwen. "Court Reformation in China: Problems, Progress and Prospects." In *Implementation of Law in the People's Republic of China*, edited by Chen Jianfu, Li Yuwen and Jan Michiel Otto. The Hague: Kluwer Law International, 2002.

Liebman, Benjamin. "China's Courts: Restricted Reform." *China Quarterly* 191, no. 1 (2007): 620–638.

Michelson, Ethan and Benjamin L. Read. "Public Attitudes toward Official Justice in Beijing and Rural China." In *Chinese Justice: Civil Dispute Resolution in Contemporary China*, edited by Mary E. Gallagher and Margaret Y. K. Woo, 169–203. Cambridge: Cambridge University Press, 2011.

Minshi Susong Fa (民事诉讼法) [Civil Procedure Law] (promulgated by the National People's Congress, June 27, 2017, effective July 1, 2017). https://www.pkulaw.com/ chl/d33df017c784876fbdfb.html.

Minzner, Carl. "China's Turn Against Law." *American Journal of Comparative Law* 59, no. 4 (2011): 935–984.

"Organisation." The Supreme People's Court of the People's Republic of China, accessed July 29, 2020. http://english.court.gov.cn/organization.html.

Palmer, Michael and Simon Roberts. *Dispute Processes: ADR and the Primary Forms of Decision-Making*. Cambridge: Cambridge University Press, 2020.

Peerenboom, Randall. "Between Global Norms and Domestic Realities: Judicial Reforms in China." In *Law and Development and the Global Discourses of Legal Transfers*, edited by John Gillespie and Penelope Nicholson, 181–201. Cambridge: Cambridge University Press, 2012.

Peerenboom, Randall. *China's Long March Toward Rule of Law*. Cambridge: Cambridge University Press, 2002.

Peerenboom, Randall. "More Law, Less Courts: Legalized Governance, Judicialization, and Dejudicialization in China." In *Administrative Law and Governance in Asia: Comparative Perspectives*, edited by Tom Ginsburg and Chen Albert H.Y., 175–202. London: Routledge, 2009.

Potter, Pitman B. "Legal Reform in China: Institutions, Culture, and Selective Adaptation." *Law & Social Inquiry* 29, no. 2 (2004): 465–495.

Qin, Xudong. "Judicial Reform: A New Round." *Caijing Magazine*, January 24, 2009.

Renmin Fayuan Zuzhi Fa (人民法院组织法) [Organic Law of People's Courts] (promulgated by the Standing Committee of the National People's Congress, July 5, 1979, effective January 1, 1980). http://www.npc.gov.cn/zgrdw/englishnpc/Law/2007-12/13/content_1384078.htm.

Renmin Fayuan Zuzhi Fa (人民法院组织法) [Organic Law of People's Courts] (promulgated by the Standing Committee of the National People's Congress, October 26, 2018, effective January 1, 2019). http://www.lawinfochina.com/display.aspx?id=29192&lib=law.

Reyes, Anselmo and Gu Weixia. "Conclusion: An Asia Pacific Model of Arbitration Reform." In *The Developing World of Arbitration: A Comparative Study of Arbitration Reform in the Asia Pacific*, edited by Anselmo Reyes and Gu Weixia, 279–300. Oxford: Hart Publishing, 2018.

Shanghaishi Renmin Zhengfu 上海市人民政府. *Shanghai sifa tizhi gaige* 上海司法体制改革, May 19, 2017. http://www.shanghai.gov.cn/nw2/nw2314/nw24651/nw42131/nw42135/u21aw1230816.html.

"Shige shuzi, goule 2018 Renmin Fayuan gaimao" 十个数字, 勾勒 2018 年人民法院概貌. *Tengxun Wang* 腾讯网. https://new.qq.com/omn/20190312/20190312A0C5TU.html.

Supreme People's Court. *Outline of the Five-Year Reform of the People's Court (1999–2003)*, October 20, 1999. http://www.iolaw.org.cn/web/special/2015/new.aspx?id=44911.

Supreme People's Court. *Outline of the Second Five-Year Reform of the People's Court (2004–2008)*, October 26, 2005. https://www.cecc.gov/resources/legal-provisions/second-five-year-reform-program-for-the-peoples-courts-2004-2008-cecc#body-chinese.

Supreme People's Court. *Outline of the Third Five-Year Reform of the People's Courts (2009–2013)*, March 17, 2009. http://www.lawinfochina.com/display.aspx?lib=law&id=7380&CGid=.

Supreme People's Court. *Reply on Several Issues of Ascertaining the Validity of the Arbitration Agreement*. October 26, 1998. http://cicc.court.gov.cn/html/1/218/62/84/671.html.

Supreme People's Court. *Zuigao renmin fayuan fabu "siwu gaige gangyao"* 最高人民法院发布"四五改革纲要", July 10, 2014. http://www.court.gov.cn/zixun-xiangqing-8168.html.

The Central Committee of the Communist Party of China. *Decision of the CPC Central Committee on Major Issues Pertaining to Comprehensively Promoting the Rule of Law*, October 23, 2014.

The Supreme People's Court of the People's Republic of China, *The Supreme People's Court of the People's Republic of China*, accessed July 29, 2020. http://www.court.gov.cn/style/system/files/spc_en_cn.pdf.

Thomas, Kristie. "Dynamism in China's Civil Procedure Law: Civil Justice with Chinese Characteristics." In *The Dynamism of Civil Procedure—Global Trends and Developments*, edited by Colin B. Picker and Guy I. Seidman, 119–139. New York: Springer, 2016.

Wang, Shengjun 王胜俊. *Zuigao renmin fayuan gongzuo baogao* 最高人民法院工作报告, March 11, 2010. http://www.gov.cn/test/2012-11/13/content_2264068. htm.

Wang, Shengjun. *Working Report of the Supreme People's Court (2009)*, March 17, 2009.

Wang, Shirong 汪世荣. "Faguan yuan'e zhidu luodi dui sifa neibu guanli jizhi jianshe yiyi zhongda" 法官员额制度落地对司法内部管理机制建设意义重大. *Renmin fayuan bao* 人民法院报, July 8, 2017. https://www.chinacourt.org/article/detail/2017/07/id/2916592.shtml.

Wei, Lisi. "Inside China: Judicial and Legal Reform in the People's Republic." *International Judicial Monitor*. Washington: International Judicial Academy, 2015.

"Zengshe Jing Guang 'hulianwang fayuan' huanjie wangluo jiufen susong nan" 增设京广"互联网法院"缓解网络纠纷诉讼难. *Xinlang sifa* 新浪司法, September 4, 2018. http://news.sina.com.cn/sf/news/fzrd/2018-09-04/doc-ihiixyeu3072377.shtml.

Zhang, Qi 张骐. *Zhongguo sifa xianli yu anli zhidao zhidu yanjiu* 中国司法先例与案例指导制度研究. Beijing: Peking University Press, 2016.

Zhang, Taisu. "The Pragmatic Court: Reinterpreting the Supreme People's Court of China." *Columbia Journal of Asian Law* 25, no. 1 (2012): 1–61.

Zhang, Xianchu. "Civil Justice Reform with Political Agendas." In *The Development of the Chinese Legal System: Change and Challenges*, edited by Yu Guanghua, 253–271. Oxford: Routledge, 2011.

Zhang, Zhiquan 张智全. "Jiceng faguan liushi de duochong lixing sikao" 基层法官流失的多重理性思考. *Zhongguo Fayuan Wang* 中国法院网, May 19, 2014. https://www.chinacourt.org/article/detail/2014/05/id/1297649.shtml.

Zhongcai Fa (仲裁法) [Arbitration Law] (promulgated by the Standing Committee of the National People's Congress, August 31, 1994, effective September 1, 1995). http://www.npc.gov.cn/wxzl/wxzl/2000-12/05/content_4624.htm.

Zhonghua Renmin Gongheguo Xian Fa (中华人民共和国宪法) [Constitution of the People's Republic of China] (promulgated by the National People's Congress, March 11, 2018, effective March 11, 2018). http://en.pkulaw.cn/display. aspx?cgid=311950&lib=law.

Zhou, Qiang 周强. *Zuigao renmin fayuan gongzuo baogao* 最高人民法院工作报告, March 10, 2014. http://www.court.gov.cn/zixun-xiangqing-82562.html.

Zhou, Qiang 周强. *Zuigao renmin fayuan gongzuo baogao* 最高人民法院工作报告, March 12, 2017. http://www.court.gov.cn/zixun-xiangqing-82602.html.

Zhou, Qiang 周强. *Zuigao renmin fayuan gongzuo baogao* 最高人民法院工作报告, March 9, 2018. http://www.court.gov.cn/zixun-xiangqing-87832.html.

Zhou, Qiang 周强. *Zuigao renmin fayuan gongzuo baogao* 最高人民法院工作报告, March 12, 2019. http://www.court.gov.cn/zixun-xiangqing-146802.html.

Zhou, Xincheng 周新城. "Yixie ren guchui de 'pushi jiachi' shizhi shang jiushi xifang de jiazhi" 一些人鼓吹的"普世价值"实质上就是西方的价值. *Guangming Daily* 光明日报, September 16, 2008. http://epaper.gmw.cn/gmrb/html/2008-09/16/nw.D110000gmrb_20080916_5-09.htm?div=-1.

Zu, Xianhai 祖先海. "Jiceng faguan gongzuoliang taida" 基层法官工作量太大. *Renmin Fayuan Bao* 人民法院报, March 12, 2016. http://rmfyb.chinacourt.org/paper/html/2016-03/12/content_109341.htm?div=-1.

"Zuigao renmin fayuan guanyu renmin fayuan jinyibu Shenhua duoyuanhua jiufen jiejue jizhi gaige de yijian" 最高人民法院关于人民法院进一步深化多元化纠纷解决机制改革的意见. *Renmin fayuan bao* 人民法院报, January 8, 2017. https://www.chinacourt.org/article/detail/2017/01/id/2509588.shtml.

"Zuigaofa fabu Renmin Fayuan Wu Wu gaige gangyao" 最高法发布人民法院五五改革纲要. *Xinhua Wang* 新华网, February 27, 2019. http://www.xinhuanet.com/legal/2019-02/27/c_1124169476.htm.

Part II

The laws of and developments in China's major dispute resolution systems

3 Civil litigation

Evolution toward a more litigious society

1 Introduction

1.1 Preliminaries

Civil procedure commonly refers to the body of laws governing the practice of civil litigation in the court system. Civil litigation is the cornerstone of the civil procedural system of a jurisdiction.[1]

This chapter examines the civil litigation system in China. Civil litigation in China is mainly governed by China's Civil Procedure Law, complemented by some ancillary rules and interpretations issued by the Supreme People's Court ("SPC"). To date, all reforms introduced to the regime of civil litigation can be divided into two levels—the court level (institutional level) and the Civil Procedure Law level (procedural level). As the reforms concerning the court level have been examined in the previous chapter, this chapter now focuses on the reforms at the procedural level, in particular, the introduction of public interest litigation and its potential impact on access to justice in China. This chapter further examines the wider political, economic, and societal contextual factors that have led to the civil procedural reform, and analyses the patterns of the reform over the past decade. This chapter concludes that the Chinese path to civil litigation reform is an evolution toward a more litigious society and predicts that the future of the civil litigation regime requires further efforts in both procedural fine-tuning of the public interest litigation rules, and systemic reform to overhaul the court's role and competence in the Chinese societal governance.

1.2 Empirical evidence

Empirical evidence on the entire civil litigation landscape in contemporary China is lacking. The statistics as to the overall caseload and actual disputed

---

1 Guy I. Seidman, "Comparative Civil Procedure," in *The Dynamism of Civil Procedure—Global Trends and Development*, eds. Colin B. Picker and Guy I. Seidman (New York: Springer, 2016), 5.

Table 3.1 First-instance civil litigation concluded by
Chinese courts (2009–2018)

Year	Total number of cases	Year-on-year increase
2009	5,797,160	7.7%
2010	6,112,695	5.4%
2011	6,558,621	7.3%
2012	7,206,331	9.9%
2013	7,510,584	4.2%
2014	8,010,342	6.7%
2015	9,575,152	19.5%
2016	10,763,889	12.4%
2017	11,651,363	8.2%
2018	12,434,826	6.7%

amounts of civil litigation in Chinese courts are generally not available—in particular, they are not available in the China Law Yearbook (or other relevant statistical yearbooks) nor traceable from the annual SPC work reports.

Table 3.1 compiles the total number of first-instance civil litigation concluded by all Chinese courts at various levels in the most recent decade (2009–2018) and an update of its year-on-year caseload increase, as these data are available at the China Law Yearbook (covering the period from 2009 to 2017) and China Statistical Yearbook (covering the year of 2018). Chart 3.1 visualizes the annual caseload of first-instance civil litigation and its trend. At the time when the manuscript is completed, the 2019 data have not been published yet.

The civil litigation caseload increased significantly in the most recent decade. In particular, there was an increase of 19.5% and 12.4% in the two continuous years of 2015 and 2016, respectively. Taking more recent years as an example, in 2017 alone, 11,651,363 first-instance civil litigation cases were concluded in 2017 by different levels of all Chinese courts, and the figure

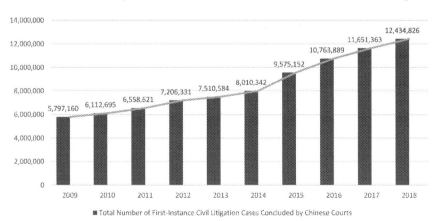

Chart 3.1 First-instance civil litigation concluded by Chinese courts (2009–2018)

rose to 12,434,826 cases in 2018 (a 6.7% increase). However, the caseload data only included those civil litigation cases which had been concluded. As the cases concluded only represented those where civil litigation had led to an end (such as cases concluded by a judgment, a mediation settlement agreement, or withdrawal of suit), empirically, the actual use of civil litigation in China is presumably wider; the overall civil litigation caseload in China could only be higher.

In addition, according to the Yearbooks, civil lawsuits in China are meant to include both civil and commercial cases. However, the Yearbooks did not provide differentiated statistics as to the specific caseload of civil cases vis-à-vis commercial cases so as to distinguish civil contracts from commercial contracts. Moreover, statistics were not provided with respect to the total disputed amount by civil litigation either. It would thus be undesirable to conduct a comparative study between the commercial litigation world and the commercial arbitration world (which is based on commercial contracts in business settings and is considered in Chapter 4), in order to assess empirically which dispute resolution mechanism is more popular in resolving commercial disputes in China.[2, 3]

2 Regulatory framework

2.1 The 1991 civil procedure law

In 1991, China's first Civil Procedure Law was promulgated (the "1991 CPL"),[4] after a decade of practice of the 1982 Provisional Civil Procedure Law,[5] whereby the principles of procedural transparency and formalization were introduced to the Chinese civil procedure system for the first time. Zhang and Peerenboom summarized a chain of reasons for the promulgation of the 1991 CPL and the introduction of formal court procedures to China. First, there was the adoption of the open-door policy by the Party, leading to a shift in policy from revolution to economic modernization. Second, there had been a significant drop in political cases such as those involving counter-revolutionary acts, which used to dominate the workload of the courts. Third, there had been a quantitative and qualitative change

---

2 China Law Society, *The Law Yearbook of China* (2010–2018) (showing the statistics from 2009 to 2017); National Bureau of Statistics of China, *China Statistical Yearbook 2019*, accessed July 8, 2020, http://www.stats.gov.cn/tjsj/ndsj/2019/indexeh.htm (showing the statistics of 2018).

3 Ibid.

4 Minshi Susong Fa (民事诉讼法) [Civil Procedure Law] (promulgated by the National People's Congress, April 9, 1991, effective April 9, 1991), http://www.lawinfochina.com/display.aspx?lib=law&id=19&CGid=.

5 Minshi Susong Fa (Shixing) (民事诉讼法(试行)) [Provisional Civil Procedure Law] (promulgated by the National People's Congress Standing Committee, March 8, 1982), http://www.npc.gov.cn/wxzl/wxzl/2000-12/06/content_4411.htm.

in civil disputes. New types of commercial disputes among strangers arose from the economic developments, such that conflicts were not limited to matrimonial and neighborhood matters, small interpersonal debts and tortious liability among acquaintances. Fourth, civil courts were left with greater autonomy to formulate and implement various court rules in handling these new cases. At that time, the SPC was also given the authority from the National People's Congress ("NPC") to interpret national laws on its own when dealing with civil disputes in real practice.[6] Fundamental changes were therefore initiated by the SPC—these included the need for public trials in civil cases, the demand of formal court rules and procedures, and the recognition of substantive and procedural rights of parties.

The implementation of these procedural safeguards were further crystalized in two subsequent SPC judicial interpretations: the SPC Provisions on Issues Relating to the Reform of the Mode of Adjudication of Civil and Economic Cases in 1998 (the "1998 SPC Provisions"), and the SPC Provisions on Evidence in Civil Litigation in 2001 (the "2001 SPC Provisions").[7] As the 1991 CPL only contained 12 articles on matters of evidence, it failed to provide sufficient legal guidance to parties. In this respect, the 1998 SPC Provisions included more detailed rules on evidence, such as those on the examination and review of evidence in civil procedures.[8] The rules of evidence finally culminated in the 2001 SPC Provisions, which was more often referred to as the "SPC Evidence Provisions." It contained 83 articles covering extensively the issues on various aspects on evidence, including the production of evidence by the parties, the investigation and collection of evidence by the courts,[9] the time period for production of evidence, the exchange of evidence, as well as the examination and verification of evidence.[10] The SPC Evidence Provisions also abolished to a great extent the power of the judges to collect evidence on their own accord, in that courts can only interfere where parties were unable to collect their evidence, and applied for collection of evidence by the judge.[11]

6 Zhang Xianchu, "Civil Justice Reform with Political Agendas," in *The Development of the Chinese Legal System: Change and Challenges*, ed. Guanghua Yu (Oxford: Routledge, 2011), 253; Randall P. Peerenboom, *China Modernizes: Threat to the West or Model for the Rest?* (Oxford: Oxford University Press, 2007), 216.

7 Hu Xiabing and Feng Renqiang, eds., *Research on Judicial Justice and Judicial Reform* 司法公正与司法改革研究综述 (Beijing: Tsinghua University Press, 2001), 265–268.

8 Li Yuwen, "The Civil Trial Process," in *The Judicial System and Reform in Post-Mao China: Stumbling Towards Justice*, ed. Li Yuwen (Oxford: Routledge, 2016), 138.

9 See Supreme People's Court, *Guanyu minshi jingji shenpan fangshi gaige wenti de ruogan guiding* 关于民事经济审判方式改革问题的若干规定, June 19, 1998, arts. 1–4, http://www.people.com.cn/zixun/flfgk/item/dwjjf/falv/9/9-1-1-11.html.

10 See Supreme People's Court, *Guanyu minshi susong zhengju de ruogan guiding* 关于民事诉讼证据的若干规定, December 6, 2001, arts. 32–46, https://www.pkulaw.com/chl/1224979098644812995.html?Customer=tyc.

11 Fu Yulin and Cao Zhixun, "The Position of Judges in Civil Litigation in Transitional China—Judicial Mediation and Case Management," in *Towards a Chinese Civil Code: Comparative and Historical Perspectives*, eds. Chen Lei and C. H. van Rhee (Leiden: Brill, 2012), 506.

The 1991 CPL also provided rules on other aspects. For example, it expanded the parties' scope of recourse toward challenging legal judgments, in light of the increasing judicial errors and issues of corruption. Rules of prosecutorial supervision over civil adjudication were also introduced. However, the parties were not given the full range of procedural rights. Save for decisions on certain interlocutory measures where parties were given the right to object, such as the preservation of assets, parties generally had no right to interfere with the conduct of trial procedures by judges.[12] Nonetheless, the 1991 CPL was introduced as a timely legal response to the macro context when China began to develop itself into a market, where there was an increase in the volume of civil and commercial disputes from 779,999 at first instance in 1982 to around 2.5 million by the time the 1991 CPL was promulgated.[13]

2.2 The 2007 civil procedure law

In 2007, the CPL underwent a partial revision (the "2007 CPL," or the "first amendment") focusing on areas of trial supervision and enforcement, as a result of a perception of rises in judicial errors and complaints against the courts. This turn of events was perhaps prompted by parties not being able to fully grasp their new roles in the courtroom following the procedural formalization with the addition of rules of evidence after the civil procedure developments in 1991, 1998, and 2001. Moreover, although parties were required to bear the burden of proof in civil trials, the trial judges still retained broad procedural powers.[14] As a result, mechanisms of challenging legal judgments by retrials (*zaishen* 再审) were introduced in the 2007 CPL, with provisions on the grounds for retrial and time limits for such applications added. Specifically, greater procedural protections were conferred upon parties on the grounds for retrial—examples would include situations where parties were not given proper notice for attending trials, where they lacked proper legal representation, or where they were prevented from presenting their case.[15]

The 2007 CPL also reinforced parties' rights on enforcement of court judgments. These include extending the time limit for applications of mandatory enforcement (*qiangzhi zhixing* 强制执行) from six months to two years, and

---

12　Fu Yulin, "Zou xiang xiandaihua de minshi susong chengshi" 走向现代化的民事诉讼程式, (presentation, Hong Kong, October 26, 2015). See also Civil Procedure Law 1991, art. 64.

13　"Home," National Bureau of Statistics of China, accessed July 8, 2020, http://www.stats. gov.cn/english/.

14　Donald C. Clarke, "Power and Politics in the Chinese Court System: The Enforcement of Civil Judgments," *Columbia Journal of Asian Law* 10, no. 1 (1996): 27.

15　Minshi Susong Fa (民事诉讼法) [Civil Procedure Law] (promulgated by the National People's Congress, October 28, 2007, effective April 1, 2008), arts. 179(1)–(12), http:// en.pkulaw.cn/display.aspx?cgid=1811a46f52ef6533bdfb&lib=law.

strengthening enforcement mechanisms to boost the compliance rate by judgment debtors.[16] The new Article 203 in the 2007 CPL even specifically provided for plaintiffs to apply for a change of court where there was a delay of enforcement of judgment. Such provision was deemed to contemplate for the then prevalent local protectionism in China which caused delays in enforcement.[17] However, the judiciary generally adopted a retreating stance in the context of the then political background of "social harmonization." Courts frequently refused to carry out strict measures to enforce civil judgments as they were then viewed as means to advance political needs.[18] Most of the reforms made by the SPC in response to the evolving Chinese society in the past sixteen years on evidence and procedure formalization through the 1998 and 2001 judicial interpretations were not incorporated into the 2007 CPL, even though some were arguably relevant to the two main areas of reform agenda under the 2007 CPL, that is: the procedures of retrial, and enforcement.[19]

3 Reform

3.1 The 2012 civil procedure law

In August 2012, the CPL went through a substantial revision (the "2012 CPL," or the "second amendment"). Some have argued that the 2012 CPL contains the most encompassing amendments and reforms since the 1991 CPL, which improves the rights of parties, clarifies the rules of evidence, and most importantly, introduces public interest litigation to address the problem of mass societal claims from the bottom.[20]

The first major reform concerns the use of summary procedures. The summary procedure was first introduced in the 1991 CPL. It is offered at the basic courts and their tribunals when the plaintiff's case is straightforward and the disputed amount is trivial. The civil procedure will be completed within three months upon filing (as compared to six months required for ordinary civil procedure cases at the first instance).[21] In the past, there

---

16 Liao Yong-an and Deng Hejun, "Comments on the Decision to Amend the Civil Procedural Law," *Xiandai Faxue* 现代法学, no. 1 (2009): 150–160.

17 Ibid.

18 Fu Yulin 傅郁林, "Social Harmony at the Cost of Trust Crisis: Goals of Civil Justice in China" 以信任危机为代价的社会和谐: 中国民事司法的目标, *Peking University Law Journal*, no. 2 (2014): 373–390.

19 Liu Jialiang, "It is Necessary to Overhaul the Civil Procedure Law," *Jiancha Ribao* 检察日报, March 18, 2008, 4.

20 Kristie Thomas, "Dynamism in China's Civil Procedure Law: Civil Justice with Chinese Characteristics," in *The Dynamism of Civil Procedure—Global Trends and Developments*, eds. Colin B. Picker and Guy I. Seidman (New York: Springer, 2016), 129; Ariel Ye and Yu Song, "Justice, Efficiency and the New Civil Procedure Law," *China Law and Practice* 20, no. 12 (2012).

21 Civil Procedure Law 1991, arts. 142–146.

were debates on how to assess the "triviality" of disputed amount. The 2012 CPL now alleviates this problem by introducing a "small claims" procedure into the summary procedure under the new Article 162 with a quantitative limitation, such that civil claims involving an amount below 30% of the average annual salary of urban employees of the relevant provincial area in the preceding year would be applied; and rulings through the "small claims" procedure would be final.[22] The exact amount as determined by the 30% benchmark varies from place to place: for example, it would be around 15,000 RMB in Shanghai.[23] The 2012 CPL also grants parties the right to opt for summary procedure if there is mutual consent between the parties.[24] Such right to use the summary procedure by the parties will be subject to the court's assessment and the ordinary procedure can be resorted to if the summary procedure is deemed inappropriate.[25] This is a significant improvement from the provisions in the 2007 CPL where only courts were allowed to apply the summary procedure.

Another major reform concerns the presentation of evidence in trials. New rules in the 2012 CPL have specifically aimed to address the complaints on "surprise evidence" submitted after trials have commenced, due to a lack of clear provisions on the timeline of discovery and exchange of evidence between parties. Under the new Article 65, courts are expressly given the discretion to determine the time period for parties to produce evidence according to circumstances of the case, such as the claims of the parties and the progress of the proceedings. Where there is late submission of evidence, parties may apply to the court for an extension of the timeline, with the power of the court to request the defaulting party to explain on such late submission. If the defaulting party fails to give a satisfactory explanation or refuses to give any explanation, the court may reject such evidence, or accept such evidence by imposing a fine or issuing a warning.[26] In addition, the new Article 66 provides a fresh layer of formality to the evidence process by establishing that the court must provide stamped and dated receipt to the submission of evidence by parties.[27] The 2012 CPL has therefore further reinforced and expanded the evidence rules since the 2001 SPC Evidence Provisions.

There are also substantial revisions brought to the case filing system, by dispensing with the need of pre-filing substantive assessment. Under the new Article 123 of the 2012 CPL, once the basic formality requirements are

---

22 Civil Procedure Law 2012, art. 162.
23 "Shanghai chutai xiao'e susong shenpan gongzuo shishi xize 上海出台小额诉讼审判工作实施细则," *The Supreme People's Court of the People's Republic of China*, December 28, 2012, http://www.court.gov.cn/zixun-xiangqing-11892.html.
24 Civil Procedure Law 2012, art. 157.
25 Ibid., art. 163.
26 Ibid., art. 65.
27 Ibid., art. 66.

satisfied, cases will be registered forthwith. Courts are now required to issue a written receipt within seven days, failing which the plaintiff may lodge an appeal. Such requirements are further consolidated in the "SPC Provisions on Several Questions Regarding Case Registration and Filing" issued on April 15, 2015. All these provisions now aim to impose stricter supervision over the case filing process to prevent courts from arbitrarily refusing to hear certain sensitive cases.[28] On the other hand, to counter the diminished power of courts in the case filing process, the new Article 13 imposes an obligation on parties to conduct litigation in good faith. This is perhaps motivated by the increase in frivolous or malicious lawsuits and the abuse of legal process by litigants, such as falsifying evidence and intentionally delaying proceedings.[29] Where parties engage in collusion or attempt to evade obligations through malicious litigation, the court is now authorized to sanction with fines or detain any party involved in such collusion.[30]

Mediation procedures are also of great importance. Under the new Article 122, parties are required to attempt voluntary mediation if appropriate before filing their civil litigation, unless the parties refuse to do so. Some have argued that because of this provision, courts now have the legal basis to facilitate pre-filing mediation when necessary.[31] A highlight in the mediation procedure as introduced by the 2012 CPL is the judicial confirmation of extra-judicial mediation efforts (i.e., mediation settlement agreements facilitated by people's mediation committees) under the new Articles 194 and 195. The request for such judicial confirmation has to be jointly filed by mediation parties within 30 days from the effective date of the mediation settlement agreement.[32] The reform therefore encourages extra-judicial mediation efforts by way of elevating mediation settlement agreements to the status of judicial judgments, and to thereby enjoy enhanced enforceability.

Among the major reforms introduced in the 2012 CPL, perhaps the greatest emphasis has been on the expansion of parties' procedural rights through the addition of a new cause of civil action, the "public interest litigation" (*gongyi susong* 公益诉讼).

In recent years, Chinese courts have discouraged group litigations and cases with a broader social impact, mainly because of a fear that the cases might have the potential in leading to social unrest. Fears of instability have led courts to withdraw from accepting group litigations. Courts have been

---

28 Fu Yulin, "Zhongguo dalu sifa gaige de mubiao he weidu—chengshi, jizhi, tizhi" 中国大 陆司法改革的目标和维度—程式、机制、体制, (lecture, Hong Kong, October 26, 2015).
29 Jones Day, *Adding More Strings to the Bow: The 2012 Amendments to China's Civil Procedure Law*, accessed July 8, 2020, https://www.jonesday.com/en/insights/2013/01/ adding-more-strings-to-the-bow-the-2012-amendments-to-chinas-civil-procedure-law.
30 Civil Procedure Law 2012, arts. 112–113.
31 Ye and Song, "Justice, Efficiency, and the New Civil Procedure Law."
32 Civil Procedure Law 2012, arts. 194–195.

urged to divide up group litigations into individual lawsuits. In 2006, the All-China Lawyers Association even issued a "guiding opinion" instructing law firms to assign only "politically qualified" lawyers to cases involving ten or more litigants.[33]

The "public interest" under the new Article 55 of the 2012 CPL encompasses two specific areas, namely consumer protection and environmental protection cases. It provides for a generalized recourse in respect to these two areas such that "relevant bodies and organizations prescribed by law may bring lawsuit to the courts against such acts as environmental pollution, harm of consumers' legitimate interests and rights and other acts that undermines the public interest."[34] This procedural revision is particularly meaningful because it recognizes the social significance of some mass torts (e.g., consumer torts and environmental torts), and offers *locus standi* for social organizations to sue tortfeasors on behalf of the victims (the so-called "third-party standing").[35] According to Fu, one of the most prominent scholars on civil procedure based in Beijing, the public interest litigation system constitutes the core theme in the 2012 CPL reform.[36] Due to its critical importance in addressing social unrest arising out of the increasing amount of mass disputes in China, this procedural reform will be looked into more carefully in subsequent sections of this chapter.

Apart from the aforementioned major reforms, the 2012 CPL has also made amendments to other provisions to enhance parties' procedural rights. For example, Article 34 expands the scope of jurisdiction of courts by including not only the domicile of the parties and the place where the subject matter is located, but also "any other place actually connected to the dispute."[37] Transparency over court judgments is also much strengthened. Judges are now required to give public judgments whether the case has been heard publicly or privately.[38] Under the newly added Article 156, the public may also access legally effective judgments and rulings, except those involving state secrets, business secrets, and personal privacy.[39]

All these newly added provisions in the 2012 CPL are in an effort to introduce a multi-tracked litigation system according to the specific needs of various cases, thereby to streamline cases and to counter the exponential rise

33 Margaret Woo, "The Dynamism of China's Civil Litigation System," in *The Dynamism of Civil Procedure—Global Trends and Developments*, eds. Colin Picker and Guy I. Seidman (New York: Springer, 2016), 147.
34 See Civil Procedure Law 2012, art. 55.
35 "Third-party standing" means to stand as the plaintiff even though it may not have been directly injured by defendant's conduct.
36 Fu, "Zhongguo dalu sifa gaige de mubiao he weidu 中國大陸司法改革的目標和維度."
37 Civil Procedure Law 2012, art. 34.
38 Ibid., art. 148.
39 Ibid., art. 156.

in caseload in people's courts.[40] In the eyes of some Western scholars, the 2012 CPL reform shows an unprecedented commitment to efficiency, transparency, and access to justice in the formal legal system in China, and links to the persistent debate surrounding the developing rule of law in China.[41]

3.2 The 2017 civil procedure law

In June 2017, the CPL was revised for the third time (the "2017 CPL" or the "third amendment"). The third amendment was small in scale and it added only one paragraph to Article 55 of the 2012 CPL, that is, the new Article 55(2), which allows Chinese procuratorates to bring public interest lawsuits in addition to the social organizations. As such, the differences between the 2017 CPL and 2012 CPL are minimal.

According to the newly added Article 55(2), the people's procuratorates, which in general serve as the prosecutors in Chinese criminal cases, may file civil lawsuits against acts that compromise public rights and interests in cases related to environmental and natural resources protection, as well as food and drug safety. The added paragraph states that the procuratorates can only initiate civil public interest litigation when it discovers such acts in the course of fulfilling its duties, and when the social organizations are not actively initiating proceedings. If the social organizations have initiated public interest litigation, the procuratorates may support the filing of the lawsuit.[42]

The power to file public interest lawsuits is a new extension of the authority of the procuratorates. This amendment is seen to target recent incidents related to food and drug safety that had visible impact within the civic society. The amendment increases the State's capacity to engage in civil public interest litigations. It is also believed that the entry of the State units into this field of litigation may be helpful in enhancing the enforcement of environmental laws and consumer laws in China by their significant financial resources.[43]

As the current civil procedure system is mainly shaped by the second amendment, that is, the 2012 CPL, the subsequent discussion will focus on the 2012 CPL, with reference to the new development of the 2017 CPL where necessary.

---

40 Wang Huazhong and Wang Jingqiong, "Courts Hit by Rising Number of Lawsuits," *China Daily*, July 14, 2010, http://www.chinadaily.com/cn/china/2010-07/14/content_10102630. htm. The number of cases rose by at least 25% between 2005 and 2009 but the total number of judges remained almost the same.

41 Thomas, "Dynamism in China's Civil Procedure Law," 132.

42 Minshi Susong Fa (民事诉讼法) [Civil Procedure Law] (promulgated by the National People's Congress Standing Committee, June 27, 2017, effective July 1, 2017), art. 55(2), http://en.pkulaw.cn/display.aspx?id=6d9ce94e57cee7afbdfb&lib=law.

43 "China Focus: China Amends Law to Allow Public Interest Litigation by Prosecutors," *Xinhua News* (June 27, 2017), http://www.xinhuanet.com//english/2017-06/27/c_136399032.htm

3.3 A closer look at public interest litigation

The addition of the new Article 55 (on public interest litigation) under the 2012 CPL has been a welcomed leap from the existing Articles 52 to 54 (on joint and representative litigation) following an increase in group litigation in recent years against China's rapid economic reforms and social development.[44] While these provisions all provided for various causes of action to a large number of litigants, Article 55 can be distinguished from Articles 52 to 54 in two ways: (1) the nature of the targeted class of plaintiffs with standing, and (2) the nature of the litigation.

In respect of the targeted class of plaintiffs, Articles 52–54 are targeted at causes of action initiated by identified or specific (*teding* 特定) litigants in large numbers (*duoshuren* 多数人). Under Article 52 which concerns joint litigation (*gongtong susong* 共同诉讼), where there are more than two plaintiffs in a case with common questions of law or facts, the courts are given the right to join these parties and combine the actions after obtaining the parties' consent.[45] In a similar vein, under Articles 53 and 54 which address representative litigation (*daibiaoren susong* 代表人诉讼), where the number of litigants of one side of the case is specific (*teding* 特定) and exceeding ten, that side is considered "large" (*zhongduo* 众多) in litigation size[46] and is given the right to select a certain representative to follow throughout the process of litigation.[47] The subsequent judgment will then bind all parties that were represented. According to Pan, Dean of Peking University Law School and one of the most authoritative scholars on Chinese civil litigation, the newly added Article 55, however, targets at "unspecific" (*buteding* 不特定) and "mass" (*duoshuren* 多数人) litigants. Moreover, the "unspecific" nature of the targeted class of plaintiffs under Article 55 requires that the nature of the litigation initiated thereunder must be concerned with "public interest" (*gongyi* 公益), as opposed to grouped individual civil litigations initiated under Articles 52 and 54 which are of "private interest" (*siyi* 私益).[48]

Before Article 55 was added, the joint and representative litigation systems had a few serious shortages. First, Chinese courts often preferred fewer than ten plaintiffs or defendants in any legal proceedings. Second,

---

44 Sun Lijuan and Xie Jun, "Access to Collective Litigations in China: A Tough Work," *Journal of Politics and Law* (*Zhengzhi yu Falv*) 政治与法律 3, no. 1 (2010): 45. The Mar. 9, 2005 Annual report by the president of the Supreme Court stated that the number of the collective suits has reached 538,941, increased by 9.5% comparing with 2004.

45 Civil Procedure Law 2012, art. 52.

46 The Supreme People's Court defined "large" to be ten or more persons, and that two to five representatives may be chosen.)

47 The difference between Articles 53 and 54 is whether the number of litigants has been fixed at the time of litigation, with Article 53 being "fixed" and Article 54 as "yet to be fixed" (*shangwei queding* 尚未确定).

48 Pan Jianfeng, "The Role of Comparative Law in Teaching and Research," (lecture, Hong Kong, January 19, 2018).

only two to five legal representatives may be appointed in a representative litigation in China.[49] Such practice was explained by the inherently political nature of such litigation in China which might threaten social order and by the attempt to reduce the costs of litigation, rather than to enhance procedural safeguards to the parties. Judges often fear that large numbers of litigants would decrease judicial efficiency and might potentially lead to social unrest. Many courts are hence urged to divide cases into individual lawsuits instead.[50] As such, by not explicitly requiring the identity of the litigants to be specific (i.e., "unspecific") and by not restricting the size of the class (i.e., the general "mass") in public interest litigation, Article 55 has now provided for an additional channel of recourse for cases with large number of plaintiffs to which courts might have been reluctant to accept before. Moreover, Article 55 provides standing for "relevant bodies and organizations prescribed by the law" (*youguan zuzhi* 有关组织) to sue on behalf of the unspecific litigants.[51] The relevant bodies refer to non-governmental social organizations in the fields of consumer and environmental protection, with the specifics to be further defined by relevant laws, that is, the Consumer Protection Law and Environmental Protection Law.[52]

For example, on consumer public interest litigation, Article 35 of the most recent version of China's Consumer Protection Law (amended in 2013) (the "2013 Consumer Law"), provided that courts *must* accept and hear mass consumer cases in a timely manner where they meet the terms of the 2012 CPL.[53] Likewise, on environment public interest litigation, Article 58 of the most recent version of China's Environmental Protection Law (amended in 2014) (the "2014 EPL") was amended following the addition of Article 55 in the 2012 CPL, by expanding the scope of social organizations (*shehui zuzhi* 社会组织) which are eligible to sue to those environmental protection bodies established at the city level or above.[54] This shows much improvement from the earlier draft which only allowed the All-China Environmental Federation, the national-level environment protection social organization, to sue. As such, the amendment will certainly

---

49 Ibid.
50 Woo, "The Dynamism of China's Civil Litigation System," 146.
51 Civil Procedure Law 2012, art. 55.
52 Pan, "The Role of Comparative Law in Teaching and Research."
53 Xiaofeizhe quanyi baohu Fa (消费者权益保护法) [Consumer Protection Law] (promulgated by the National People's Congress Standing Committee, October 25, 2013, effective January 1, 2014), http://www.npc.gov.cn/wxzl/gongbao/2014-01/02/content_1823351.htm.
54 Huanjing baohu Fa (环境保护法) [Environmental Protection Law] (promulgated by the National People's Congress Standing Committee, April 24, 2014, effective January 1, 2015), art. 58, http://en.pkulaw.cn/display.aspx?cgid=4544&lib=law. Two conditions have to be satisfied: (1) the organization has to be registered at the civil affairs departments of people's governments at or above the city level with sub-districts in accordance with the law; and (2) it has to specialize in environmental protection public interest activities for five or more consecutive years, and have no records in violating the law.

enhance access to justice in the field, as many such social organizations are registered at the city level.[55]

The recent SPC Opinion on Environmental Public Interest Civil Litigation in 2015 (the "2015 SPC EPICL Opinion") further provided for extended powers to public-power holders such as procuratorates and departments responsible for environmental protection to assist in the initiation of environmental public interest litigation, or the so-called "pertinent public interest litigation."[56] Equivalent powers for procuratorates in respect of consumer public interest litigation, however, was neither found under the 2013 Consumer Law, nor the SPC Opinion of the Consumer Public Interest Litigation in 2016 (the "2016 CPIL Opinion").[57] Both Article 47 of the 2013 Consumer Law and Article 1 of the subsequent 2016 CPIL Opinion prescribed the "relevant consumer bodies" that can bring consumer public interest litigation are only those consumer protection associations which should be set up at the national level and the provincial level, with the exclusion of those set at the city level, which starkly contrasted with Article 58 of the 2014 EPL.[58] While some Chinese legal scholars and public interest advocates expressed strong encouragement toward more consumer public interest litigation without ill-resourced consumers taking individual actions,[59] others thought that with only some 30 of such consumer associations available, they would be unable to handle the workload and hence, many potential claims will not be brought to court.[60]

Technically, the new Article 55 of the 2012 CPL represented an improvement for the courts and parties in general. Prior to the addition of Article 55, when adjudicating cases under Articles 52–54, courts had to assume the onerous tasks of supervising the appointment of class representatives, and overseeing the distribution of damages to a large number of individuals,

---

55 According to the U.S. based National Resource Defence Council's Beijing office, this will apply to about 300 NGOs in China. See Woo, "The Dynamism of China's Civil Litigation System," 151.

56 Supreme People's Court, *Interpretation of the Supreme People's Court on Several Issues concerning the Application of Law in the Conduct of Environmental Civil Public Interest Litigations* 最高院关于审理环境民事公益诉讼案件适用法律若干问题的解释, January 6, 2015, art. 11, http://pkulaw.cn/(S(pvgjlx45wuwnwm5555df4e55))/fulltext_form.aspx?Db=chl&Gid=f81c55e05ed7c7f6bdfb.

57 Supreme People's Court, *Guanyu Shenli xiaofei minshi gongyi susong anjian shiyong falü ruogan wenti de jieshi*最高院关于审理消费民事公益诉讼案件适用法律若干问题的解释, April 25, 2016, art.1, http://www.court.gov.cn/zixun-xiangqing-20082.html.

58 Consumer Protection Law 2013, art. 47.

59 "Amendments to Consumer Protection Law Allows for Public Interest Lawsuits With Limitations," *Congressional-Executive Commission on China*, January 14, 2014, http://www.cecc.gov/publications/commission-analysis/amendments-to-consumer-protection-law-allows-for-public-interest#_ednref3.

60 See Xiao Jianguo and Huang Zhongshun肖建国 黄忠顺, "Xiaofei gongyi susong zhong de dangshiren shige wenti yanjiu" 消费公益诉讼中的当事人适格问题研究, *Shandong jingcha xueyuan xuebao* 山东警察学院学报no. 6 (2013): 7–10.

even though they had limited resources and were sometimes pressured by political pressures.[61] Under the new Article 55, since specific social organizations are designated with the standing to sue on behalf of multiple individuals, the tasks will have become less onerous since the entity vested with the right of standing will have served as the intermediary in facilitating the litigation process.

With respect to parties, prior to the addition of Article 55, they were often dissuaded from bringing class actions (under Articles 53 and 54) since they would incur extra costs in appointing lawyers, as well as travel expenses and costs associated with the preparation of evidence.[62] The new Article 55 will therefore improve parties' access to justice in two ways. First, it switches the burden to sue to social organizations which will then be responsible for the collection of evidence and associated legal costs. These social organizations are in a better position to represent clients' interests since they are better resourced.[63] Second, it delegates the right to social organizations to sue despite their lack of direct interest or direct standing. The amendments in 2012 CPL, which introduced public interest litigation and extended its scope to social bodies without a direct interest in the case, offer an outlet for the public to express their discontent, and help to maintain social stability.[64]

In practice, however, the question of whether these social organizations are in active pursuit of public interest claims is thornier than expected. Realistically, many of these social organizations are still troubled by the lack of funding. Political concerns are also apparent in relation to consumer claims, with the China Consumers' Association (the "CCA") being the main social organization named under Article 47 of the 2013 Consumer Law, which monopolizes the handling of consumer issues to the exclusion of other consumer protection social organizations.[65] The political connection of the CCA with the Chinese government casts doubts on its status as an independent social organization in that the CCA might be reluctant to deal with more sensitive consumer disputes which are considered as potentially disruptive to social order or challenging the governance of the state. But, without the linkage with the government, its funding might be problematic. To limit the eligibility to sue to those consumer protection organizations at the provincial level or above is also significantly inadequate to

---

61 Benjamin Liebman, "Class Action Litigation in China," *Harvard Law Review*, 111 (1998): 1533.
62 See "Bereaved Parents Compensated by Sanlu," *China Daily*, January 17, 2009, http://www. chinadaily.com.cn/cndy/2009-01/17/content_7405679.htm. (e.g., Shen Xianlai, a lawyer representing a couple from Gansu whose 5-month-old son died from milk poisoning, stated that "the couple was unlikely to get more than 200,000 RMB by taking their case to court in Gansu.")
63 Thomas, "Dynamism in China's Civil Procedure Law," 137.
64 Ibid.
65 Civil Procedure Law 2012; See also Jonathan Benney, *Defending Rights in Contemporary China* (New York: Routledge, 2012), 64.

address China's massive scale of consumer grievances. In this respect, there is a lack of nationwide empirical data collected either by the Yearbooks or the judiciary as to how many consumer public interest litigation cases have been brought since the 2012 CPL and 2013 Consumer Law amendments. According to a recent academic survey, there were altogether only nine public interest litigation cases in the area of consumer protection up till the end of 2017.[66] These data showed the difficulty in actively pursuing public interest claims in the consumer protection area.

Environmental public interest litigations have similar concerns, including those on the independence of the environmental protection social organizations. When compared with consumer public interest litigation, the resources to initiate environment public interest litigation is arguably more robust as environmental protection social organizations at the city level or above are allowed to sue, which might also explain why there have been more environmental public interest litigation cases in China in recent years than consumer public interest litigation cases. In this respect, the SPC started to issue China's Environmental Adjudication White Book (the "White Book") on an annual basis in the past few years. According to the White Book, a total of 58 environment public interest litigation lawsuits were lodged by social organizations nationwide in 2017; the caseload increased to 65 in 2018,[67] and further increased to 179 in 2019.[68] These data empirically indicate the importance in lowering the bar of the social organizations entitled to sue, and the enhancement of access to justice in civil public interest litigation. As discussed earlier in this chapter, the eligibility of city-level social organizations to sue in environmental public interest litigation cases (vis-à-vis provincial-level social organizations in consumer public interest litigation cases) have significantly increased the number of environmental public interest litigation cases.

The standing to bring public interest litigation has been most recently extended to the public procuratorates in the 2017 CPL. Article 55(2) of the 2017 CPL now allows Chinese procuratorates to be the plaintiff in civil public interest litigation cases, in addition to the social organizations. The standing to sue of the procuratorates has two outstanding features that distinguish it from that of the social organizations. First, as aforementioned, the procuratorates can only initiate civil public interest litigation when they discover

66 Chen Lei, "The Role of Comparative Law in Teaching and Research," (conference, Hong Kong, January 19, 2018).
67 Jiang Bixin 江必新, *Zhongguo huanjing ziyuan shenpan 2017–2018* 中国环境资源审判 2017–2018, March 2, 2019, https://www.cenews.com.cn/subject/2019/2019lh/a/201903/t20190302_894317.html.
68 "<Zhongguo huanjing ziyuan shenpan (2019)> ji niandu dianxing anli <Zhongguo huanjing sifa fazhan baogao (2019)> xinwen fabu hui"《中国环境资源审判(2019)》暨年度典型案例《中国环境司法发展报告(2019)》新闻发布会, May 8, 2020, https://www.chinacourt.org/chat/fulltext/listId/52428/template/courtfbh20200508.shtml.

such acts in the course of fulfilling their duties, and when the social organizations are not actively pursuing the proceedings. If the social organizations have initiated public interest litigation, the procuratorates may only be in a supportive role.[69] Second, while environmental public interest litigation cases initiated by the procuratorates are concerned with the general ecological environment and the protection of natural resources, the consumer public interest litigation cases initiated by the procuratorates are restricted to food and drug safety ones.[70] It has been criticized that the unjustified restriction in the 2017 CPL will dismiss other aspects of consumer interests and the procuratorates could have been allowed to bring a broader scope of consumer public interest litigation cases.[71] However, it is generally believed by Chinese scholars and practitioners that, as the statutory supervisory organ of the state, the procuratorates possess a more advantageous position in terms of social status and economic resources. While the involvement of the procuratorates in civil public interest litigations would significantly enhance the enforcement of environmental laws and consumer laws in China, such power should be restricted to very serious cases.[72]

Finally, as a special feature of public interest litigation, in terms of enforcement, courts are given the discretion to consult different social organizations on the various enforcement methods against the defendant. If the defendant fails to comply with its legal obligations, the specific court which makes the judgment has the discretion to directly transfer the matter of enforcement to its enforcement division. This is to be distinguished from the enforcement procedure in ordinary civil litigation cases, where the plaintiff instead will have to apply for compulsory enforcement from the court's enforcement division upon default of the defendant. Such augmentation of the enforcement system is perhaps due to the involvement of public interest which the state deems proper to require an additional layer of supervision.

4 Development analyses

4.1 Penetrating factors of reform

Holistically, the reforms in the 2012 CPL in relation to public interest litigation, refinement of summary procedures, recognition of extra-judicial mediation agreements and improvements in the rules of evidence, have been seen as responses to the change in social and economic conditions in modern China. The main driving force is China's internal domestic socio-economic and socio-political context.

---

69 Civil Procedure Law 2017, art. 55(2).
70 Ibid.
71 Wu Jun 吴俊, "Zhongguo minshi gongyi susong niandu guancha baogao (2017)" 中国民事公益诉讼年度观察报告 (2017), *Dangdai faxue* 当代法学, no. 5 (2018): 141.
72 "China Focus: China Amends Law to Allow Public Interest Litigation by Prosecutors."

China has been undergoing rapid economic development since the 2000s.[73] This generated an increase in both the number and complexity of civil disputes. For example, recent statistics published by the 2012 SPC Working Report suggested that from 2008 to 2012, the number of civil cases concluded at first instance increased by around 40% as compared to that from 2003 to 2007.[74] This perhaps led to the emphasis in the promotion of "judicial efficiency" by the SPC's first two rounds of court reform.[75] The explosion in the use of summary procedures follows as a natural result, and become one of the themes in the 2012 CPL reform. For example, in 2008, judges were evaluated by the proportion of cases to which summary procedure was adopted, in order to cater to the increase in the caseload and to utilize limited judicial resources.[76]

There was also a rise in the complexity of civil disputes. As a statistical backdrop to the 2012 CPL reform, in 2010 alone, Chinese local courts at various levels concluded about 11 million cases of various types. During the year, the courts handled 20,258 cases on foreign-related issues and maritime matters, 3.239 million cases on domestic contracts and commercial relationships, 1.428 million cases on family matters, 578,919 cases on the financial market, 14,694 cases on merger, acquisition and bankruptcy, 48,051 cases on intellectual property infringement, and 12,018 cases on environmental pollution compensation.[77] To successfully drive the economic reform from a centralized planned economy to a market-driven economy, there is consequently more economic disputes brought by new economic entities such as private businesses and foreign-invested enterprises. Coupled with the revamp of state-owned enterprises and the reduction of government interference in these entities, many disputes have now turned to courts via litigation or to arbitral tribunals via commercial arbitration, instead of being resolved by administrative authorities.[78]

---

73 See "The World Bank and Development Research Center of the State Council, the People's Republic of China," *China 2030: Building a Modern, Harmonious, and Creative Society* (Washington: World Bank, 2013), *2030:* XV, 8, http://www.worldbank.org/content/dam/Worldbank/document/China-2030-complete.pdf.

74 Supreme People's Court, "Report on the Work of the Supreme People's Court," May 8, 2014, http://en.chinacourt.org/public/detail.php?id=4867.

75 "Renmin fayuan <'yiwu' gaige gangyao> yu <'erwu' gaige gangyao>"人民法院《"一五"改革纲要》与《"二五"改革纲要》, *Legal Daily China*, April 30, 2009, http://www.legaldaily.com.cn/zbzk/2009-04/30/content_1091822.htm.

76 Thomas, "Dynamism in China's Civil Procedure Law," 136; Some, however, have argued for other reasons for the increased use of summary procedures, one of which is to safeguard SPC's own self-interest to promote its finances rather than reducing the workload of courts. See Zhang Taisu, "The Pragmatic Court: Reinterpreting the Supreme People's Court of China," *Columbia Journal of Asian Law* 25, no. 1 (2012): 34.

77 See "Highlights of work report of China's Supreme People's Court," *China Daily*, March 11, 2011, http://www.chinadaily.com.cn/china/2011npc/2011-03/11/content_12157831.htm.

78 Li Yuwen, *The Judicial System and Reform in Post-Mao China* (New York: Routledge, 2014), 133–164.

Another by-product of the rapid economic development of China is a higher awareness on various domestic problems among Chinese people within the country who are concerned with various rights. This in turn has caused the evolution toward a more litigious society and the frequent occurrence of group actions, which has led eventually to the development of public interest litigation.

There are also environmental problems, with numerous reports on water and air pollution, invariably affecting the human health and living conditions.[79] The increased domestic and international concerns on the matter has also led to an increased awareness on environmental rights in China among the public, a more active civil society community, as well as greater political attention to the issue.[80] Administrative measures were also implemented to respond to the serious environmental problems in China, such as the establishment of an "environmental police force." In addition, there has been an expansion of insurance coverage for environmental claims. Victims are therefore less likely to be left out of pockets due to the insolvency of defendants after succeeding in environmental cases.[81] As such, the development of environmental public interest litigation does not come in a vacuum; rather, there are sufficient contextual factors that drive the legislative development. Prior to the addition of Article 55 to the 2012 CPL, several Chinese environment protection organizations had already initiated a few environmental public interest litigation cases.[82] Some Chinese courts at the provincial- and city-levels had also formulated informal regulations in exploring the standing of some non-governmental organizations (NGOs) to bring environmental public interest litigation cases.[83]

---

79 John C. Nagle, "How Much Should China Pollute?," *Vermont Journal of Environmental Law* 12, (2011): 591–632. Nagle stated that China is the world's greatest polluter. See also Rachel E. Stern, "The Political Logic of China's New Environmental Courts," *The China Journal* 72 (2014): 58.

80 The political endorsement by Chinese leaders in fact started in 2000s where President Hu Jintao introduced the term "ecological civilization." For the first time, meeting pollution targets was included in evaluating local governmental officials' political performance. See Shannon Tiezzi, "China's Fifth Plenum: What You Need to Know," *China Dialogue*, October 29, 2015, http://thediplomat.com/2015/10/chinas-fifth-plenum-what-you-need-to-know/; see also "Woguo huanjing shijian nianjun dizeng 29%" 我国环境事件年均递增 29%, *Caijing* 财经, October 27, 2012, http://tinyurl.com/dycoh82.

81 Anna Lora-Wainwright, Zhang Yiyun, Wu Yunmei, and Benjamin Van Rooij, "Learning to Live with Pollution: How Environmental Protestors Find their Interests in a Chinese Village," *The China Journal* 68, no. 1 (2012): 106–124; see also State Environmental Protection Agency and the Insurance Regulatory Commission, *Opinion on Development of Environmental Pollution Liability Insurance* 关于环境污染责任保险工作的指导意见, December 4, 2007, http://www.gov.cn/zwgk/2008-02/25/content_899905.htm.

82 Wang Xiaogang, "Review of Public Interest Litigation in Fundamental Environmental Law" 透视环境基本法中的公益诉讼, *Environmental Protection* 环境保护, no. 9 (2010): 32–34.

83 Ibid. For example, on November 5, 2008, Kunming authorities issued a document granting relevant social organizations legal standing. In 2009, Yunnan Provincial High Court issued a meeting summary stating that social organizations with the aim of protecting the environment could launch environmental public interest litigations as plaintiff.

Some NGOs, such as the All-China Environmental Federation, filed both civil and administrative lawsuits with respect to environmental pollution, in addition to continuously promoting environmental protection through the Internet and social media.[84]

In a similar vein, consumer awareness on defective consumer products has also intensified following the transformation of the Chinese society from being investment-led to consumption-led, as a result of China's rapid economic development. Since the 1990s, there has been a change in consumer culture from "buyers beware" to a more litigious culture where consumers make complaints when they wish to.[85] This in turn led to an increase in the number of collective actions, as well as confrontations between consumers and producers in courts. For example, before the revision to the 2012 CPL, there had been a series of class actions on defective products, ranging from fake watches to substandard fertilizer.[86] In addition to the rise in consumer awareness, there has also been an increase in media attention on individual consumer cases, although in the early days, most of the media coverage was generated by official media, such as the Xinhua Newsnet, or quasi-governmental media, such as the China Consumer Newspaper, which was in some ways affiliated and controlled by the Chinese government.[87] Moreover, the content reported by the media has shifted to increasingly prioritize sensational stories about and concerns of Chinese consumers, as opposed to issues which were sanctioned by the central government. Examples include the reporting of some extreme consumer rights cases, such as those promoted by Wang Hai, one of the earliest activists on double compensation in consumer cases.[88]

The most influential case during this period of time is the case of Sanlu tainted milk powder which happened in September 2008 (the "Sanlu Incident"). In the Sanlu Incident, 300,000 babies suffered urinary-related

---

84 Yang Guobin, "Environmental NGOs and Institutional Dynamics in China," *The China Quarterly* 181, no. 1 (2005): 46–66.

85 "China Overhauls Consumer Protection Laws," *Hong Kong Lawyer*, October 2013, http://www.hk-lawyer.org/content/china-overhauls-consumer-protection-laws; see also Deborah Davis, "Urban Consumer Culture," *China Quarterly* 183 (2005): 692–702 (arguing that Chinese culture now prioritizes consumer goods and process of consumptions).

86 Fu Hualing and Richard Cullen, "The Development of Public Interest Litigation in China," in *Public Interest Litigation in Asia*, eds. Yap Po Jen and Lau Holning (New York: Routledge, 2010), 1–29; Liebman, "Class Action Litigation in China."

87 See Ho Suk-ching, "Executive Insights: Growing Consumer Power in China: Some Lessons for Managers," *Journal of International Marketing* 9, no. 1 (2000): 64–83. (e.g., in 1999, the China Consumer Newspaper filed a lawsuit on behalf of a university student in Shanghai who was strip-searched in a Watson chain store branch in Shanghai to claim for mental suffering she suffered.)

88 Davis, "Urban Consumer Culture."

diseases with a total of six fatalities from drinking milk from milk powder contaminated by melamine produced by the Sanlu Corporation. This caused public outrage after the revelation of the lack of regulation over food safety and the government's deliberate concealment of the scandal.[89] In addition to media coverage both domestically and internationally, victims of the plight took initiative to use the social media for the first time. For example, Beijing resident Zhao Lianhai decided to set up a website called "Home for Kidney-Stone Babies" after he discovered that his infant son had a two-millimeter kidney stone in his right kidney. Through the website, information was reported and exchanged in relation to poisoned dairy products and a mass of other victims alike was drawn in to join the lawsuits together.[90]

In the meantime, lawyers also became active in filing collective suits on behalf of the victims. A group of lawyers named "Sanlu Melamine Victims' Legal Support Team" filed a tort action in the Shijiazhuang Intermediate People's Court on behalf of 63 victims demanding for compensation for bodily harm and emotional distress arising out of the Sanlu Incident. Others offered free legal advice and attempted to file actions under Articles 54 and 55 of the then 2007 CPL on representative litigation,[91] with the aim to reduce costs for clients, and to potentially force a settlement with Sanlu.[92] In the end, many lawsuits against Sanlu was dismissed by courts for apparent political reasons because of the Party's vested interests in Sanlu as a key state-owned enterprise (the "SOE") and a national dairy product provider champion.[93] A national policy was also put in place to let Sanlu undergo liquidation and address compensation claims for victims,[94] after which many of the victims lost their standing to sue since Sanlu was no longer a legal

---

89 Andrew Jacobs, "Chinese Release Increased Numbers in Tainted Milk Scandal," *The New York Times*, December 2, 2008, http://www.nytimes.com/2008/12/03/world/asia/03milk. html?_r=1.

90 Benney, *Defending Rights in Contemporary China*, 89.

91 Qin Yudong, "Sanlu pochan shanhou nanti shouhaizhe quanyi shuilai baozhang" 三鹿破产善后难题受害者权益谁来保障, *Caijing* 财经, December 25, 2008, http://www.caijing. com.cn/2008-12-25/110042541.html.

92 The distinction between Article 54 and Article 55 is on the number of litigations being known at the time of the litigation (Art 54) or being unknown Art 55. (e.g., led by the Beijing-based lawyer Xu Zhiyong, 15 lawyers decided to bundle up cases of up to 100 families into a single lawsuit against Sanlu seeking for medical expenses, payments for trauma and compensation for the babies who died. In doing so, the lawyers aimed to reduce costs for their clients and to "set a benchmark for compensation.")

93 "Sanlu Faces Class-Action Lawsuit," *Newshub New Zealand*, November 13, 2008, http:// www.newshub.co.nz/world/sanlu-facing-classaction-lawsuit-2008111406#axzz44e-zlYycR. (The collapse of Sanlu would also create enormous economic impact on the market, in that many provinces relied heavily on Sanlu for employment and taxes.)

94 L.M. Katz, "Class Action with Chinese Characteristics: The Role of Procedural Due Process in the Sanlu Milk Scandal," *Tsinghua China Law Review* 2, no. 2 (2010): 421–466.

entity and not an eligible defendant in civil litigation according to Article 108 of the then 2007 CPL.[95]

Unfortunately, at the other side of the story, the All-China Lawyers Association (the "ACLA"), a semi-governmental self-regulatory organization for all Chinese lawyers, issued a guideline in 2006 which discouraged group litigations and contained onerous rules to be represented by lawyers, as well as a "guiding opinion" for law firms to only instruct "politically qualified" lawyers to handle group litigation.[96] In the 2008 Sanlu Incident, lawyers were faced with harassments on not to take up class actions due to their inherent political nature which threatens social stability, and that if they do proceed with such sensitive cases, they may be perceived as inciting political unrests.[97]

Although a political remedy was pursued in the end, the Sanlu Incident, as a landmark case, sparked claims in the areas of consumer protection and product liability of the consumer rights against powerful SOEs. Government authorities, including government-controlled media, have to stifle media coverage on politically-affiliated cases. The case also marked the beginning to use legal means such as collective actions by both lawyers and victims to voice out their grievances, as well as to develop consumer protection activism through non-governmental media and rights activist lawyers, going beyond government-affiliated consumer organizations.

At this juncture, the role of mediation in courts was also questioned. Prior to the Sanlu Incident, Chinese political-legal authorities had promoted the Party-led "grand mediation" in handling complex disputes which could lead to social unrests.[98] In 2007, the SPC even singled out several types of cases where closed-door mediation should be used, including those that involved a large number of litigants and concerned with sensitive social issues, such as product liability torts and land seizures.[99] However, after the outbreaks of

---

95 Ibid., 440. (As part of the national policy of the Central Government, Shijiazhuang Intermediate Court accepted a creditor's bankruptcy petition on December 23, 2008, where Sanlu were to undergo liquidation with its legal personality being discontinued following its liquidation. This would mean that for Sanlu's victims, they would have to establish themselves as legitimate creditors within a restricted time frame after the court's acceptance of the bankruptcy petition, in order to get legal priority over Sanlu's bankruptcy assets. However, most victims were not able to establish creditors rights as most civil actions were rejected by courts prior to the bankruptcy petition, and by the end of the bankruptcy process, victims had lost their standing to sue as Sanlu was no longer a legal person according to the 2007 CPL.)

96 "Guiding Opinion of the All China Lawyers Association Regarding Lawyers Handling Cases of a Mass Nature (CECC Full Translation)," March 20, 2006, http://www.cecc.gov/resources/legal-provisions/guiding-opinion-of-the-all-china-lawyers-association-regarding-lawyers.

97 Edward Wong, "Courts Compound Pain of China's Tainted Milk," *New York Times*, October 16, 2008, http://www.nytimes.com/2008/10/17/world/asia/17milk.html?_r=0.

98 See discussions in Chapter 5.

99 Carl Minzner, "China's Turn against Law," *American Journal of Comparative Law* 59, no. 1 (2011): 942.

some landmark consumer cases, mediation in Chinese courts was no longer seen by the Chinese government as the panacea to pacify social anger. On the contrary, mediation exacerbated the situation, which was contrary to the Party's policy to maintain social harmony. In relation to consumers, some argued that under the 2012 CPL, litigation was often preferred over mediation by consumers because the formal links between consumers and vendors had become increasingly distant and unregulated by the government.[100] Subsequent cases also frequently involved strangers, migrants, or corporate entities disconnected from traditional village or state-owned entities. As such, these disputes were less amenable to resolution by mediation, which relied on existing social ties in leading parties toward narrowing down differences and compromising in disputes.

Courts at this time had a historically low public satisfaction, especially following the Sanlu Incident, as the Bankruptcy Law leading to the termination of the Sanlu Corporation conflicted with the laws on consumer standing under the 2007 CPL.[101] Hence, the new addition of Article 55 in the 2012 CPL was seen as a move by the political leadership to salvage and to maintain the legitimacy of courts, by requiring them to take up civil public interest cases and respond to social grievances.

4.2 Patterns of reform

While civil procedure reforms in other jurisdictions are largely fueled by aims to improve due process in their civil justice system,[102] one noteworthy feature of reforms in civil procedure in China is that they were largely motivated by top-down responses from Chinese authorities to bottom-up societal grievances. A typical trajectory would involve legislative reform by introducing new causes of actions in the CPL with subsequent fine-tuning in implementation by procedural rules, following certain bottom-up triggering events. The trajectory of the reforms in civil litigation (on procedural laws and rules) are thus in contrast with the trajectory of the reforms in the Chinese courts. Reforms of the courts in China are often made in a comparatively more systematic manner through publication of policy documents at the top-down level (i.e., the SPC's issuance of the court reform plans in a five-year-cycle), subject to some versatility in implementation on local practices and the various local economic developments at the bottom-up level.

In addition, on the pattern and trajectory of reforms in civil procedure in China, it is observed that the bottom-up triggering events must have

100 Huang Philip C.C., ed., *Chinese Civil Justice, Past and Present* (Maryland: Rowman & Littlefield, 2010), 125–144.
101 Katz, "Class Action with Chinese Characteristics," 431.
102 Examples included 1998 Woolf Reforms in the United Kingdom and the subsequent 2009 Civil Justice Reform in Hong Kong which mirrored the 1998 Woolf Reforms. See discussions in Chapter 9.

reached a sufficiently serious level or even devastating in nature. Examples would include the series of events following the Sanlu Incident and the Sichuan Earthquake Incident.[103] Legal resolutions were then pursued to address grievances after the general public had been more conscious about the law, including its uses and benefits. Many movements were initiated by individual victims, specifically in the consumer protection area, as they were built on the better awareness among the citizens on consumer rights. In the example of the Sanlu Incident, as a result of intense media coverage and public discontent over the food safety among victimized babies, the Chinese government at the top level responded by correspondingly opening up a new cause of action in the 2012 CPL, in order to allow civil public interest litigations to be initiated on the basis of consumer rights. The same phenomenon and observations are applied in the situation of environmental protection, where there has been extensive media attention and public outrage over environmental pollution in China following the Sichuan Earthquake Incident.

5 The future

There remain deficiencies in the civil litigation landscape which should be addressed by the Chinese central government, in particular, those related to public interest litigation. This section therefore proposes a package of areas that need to be further fine-tuned, clarified, amended, and overhauled, both at the technical procedural level and systematic institutional level.

5.1 Public interest litigation—technical reforms

Technically, the author proposes that the public interest litigation procedure should cover other types of civil and commercial mass claims, apart from those related to consumer rights and environmental protection in China. One emerging area would be labor disputes, particularly with respect to concerns on equality, where many female Chinese workers challenge on the matter of employment discrimination. Although most of these cases resulted in labor mediation with payment compensation, it demonstrated the potential rise in the number of collective actions in the field and the need to develop an alternative channel such as public interest litigation to resolve such disputes.[104] Other examples include securities litigation, where there were a line of landmark collective cases initiated in 2000s, with minority shareholders launching civil compensation claims against the companies

103 Liu Chenglin, "Profits above the law: China's melamine tainted milk incident," *Mississippi Law Journal* 79, no. 2 (2009): 371–418.
104 Woo, "The Dynamism of China's Civil Litigation System," 151.

or majority shareholders, on grounds of insider trading, false statements and misrepresentations, in violation of the Securities Law.[105] Last but not least, medical malpractice incidents have been on the rise in recent years, and some are sufficiently serious to generate wide attention. As such, some scholars have called for public interest litigation to be applied in medical malpractice cases to protect patients' rights.[106]

One might question the legislative intent behind the new Article 55 of the 2012 CPL as to why the list of public interest litigation cases was exhaustively restricted to only those related to consumer rights and environmental protection. This is especially in view of the rise in other aforementioned collective actions. Perhaps the existing restrictive list was intended as a strategy to "start small," to test the floodgates of mass claims which might potentially threaten social stability, and to gauge the public reaction in relation to bottom-up consumer product liability and environmental incidents. In terms of mass claims in tort in China, it is believed that the further development of the civil public interest litigations cannot be viewed in isolation, but needs to be read in conjunction with other recent enactments such as the Tort Liability Law (the "TLL") promulgated in December 2009 and came into effect in July 2010.[107]

The TLL consolidated existing laws concerning tort liability ranging from product liability, environment liability, to medical malpractices.[108] For example, for environmental torts, Article 66 of the TLL specifically provides for the burden of proof to be borne by the defendant on the issues of causation, liability, and mitigation.[109] The promulgation of the TLL therefore dealt with the substantive aspect on various types of torts and clarified the causes of action to be initiated by potential victims, leaving the procedural aspect of these actions to be determined by the rules of civil procedure. The 2012 CPL is therefore a golden opportunity to fill in the gaps in relation to the procedural aspects of these causes of action in relation to various types of torts as clarified by the 2009 TLL. For example, Article 55 of the 2012 CPL clarifies the standing of plaintiffs in collective product liability

---

105 Gu Weixia, "Securities Arbitration in China: A Better Alternative to Retail Shareholder Protection," *Northwestern Journal of International Law and Business* 33, no. 2 (2013): 283–323.

106 See generally, Ding Chunyan, *Medical Negligence Law in Transitional China* (Cambridge: Intersentia Publishing, 2012).

107 Tort Law of the People's Republic of China (promulgated by the National People's Congress Standing Committee, December 26, 2009, effective December 26, 2009), http://www.wipo.int/edocs/lexdocs/laws/en/cn/cn136en.pdf.

108 Ibid., arts 41–47 for product liability; arts. 65–68 for environmental liability; arts. 54–64 for medical malpractice.

109 Ibid., art. 66; see also Supreme People's Court, *Zuigao Renmin Fayuan Guanyu Shenli Huanjing Qinquan Zeren Jiufen Anjian Shiyong Falü Ruogan Wenti de Jieshi* 最高人民法院关于审理环境侵权责任纠纷案件适用法律若干问题的解释, June 1, 2015, http://www.court.gov.cn/fabu-xiangqing-14615.html, where the burden of proof and presumption of liability in environmental tort cases were clarified by the Supreme People's Court.

and environmental liability actions. However, what remains to be seen is whether the legislature would subsequently expand the list of actions under Article 55 to include other types of torts, so as to complement the various substantive types of torts introduced by the TLL and the Securities Law.

The expansion of the current list would certainly be a welcomed move, since the reform of the civil procedural law would undoubtedly encourage reforms of the corresponding civil substantive law. There are already precedents to this, for example, those in the 2013 Consumer Law and the 2014 EPL discussed earlier in this chapter. Mass civil compensation claims on securities and medical malpractices would also benefit from procedural enhancements if Article 55 of the 2012 CPL could be applied. Currently, there are no class action regimes available in labor litigation (where employees could sue discriminative employers), securities litigation (where minority shareholders could sue majority shareholders or the company acting in bad faith), and in medical tort actions (where victimized patients could sue wrongful medical practitioners). The existing group litigation rules (joint action and representative action) proved to be expensive and inoperative in the context of China's massive numbers of migrant laborers, retail shareholders in the commercialized society, and large numbers of medical patients accompanying the aging society. Moreover, civil remedies for torts concerning securities are also inadequate.[110] Therefore, the development of a better procedural system through the improvement of the civil procedure law would hopefully push for reforms in the substantive aspects of civil substantive law: labor regulations, securities regulations and medical law.

5.2 Public interest litigation—systematic reforms

The landscape of civil litigation requires not only the revamp of the civil procedural laws, but also effective reforms of the Chinese courts institutionally. These depend on many crucial concepts, such as the independence of the courts and the judges, as well as the competence of the judicial profession. There have been many positive debates and discussions from various scholars on systematic improvements which are essential to the reform of the Chinese civil procedures. Among the advocates, in 2014, Fu at the Peking University Law School (as this chapter has referred to in numerous occasions), suggested two parallel threads of reforms: (1) judicial structural reform which focuses on de-localization of budgetary control of Chinese courts and (2) revision of the accountability of Chines judges which focuses on enhancement of their specialized competence.[111] As many of these issues have been addressed in the fourth and fifth rounds of the SPC Five-Year Court Reform Outline, which are considered in Chapter 2, the following

110 Gu, "Securities Arbitration in China," 296.
111 Fu, "Social Harmony at the Cost of Trust Crisis," 373–390.

discussion will only outline the necessary reforms which have not been considered in Chapter 2.

First, Fu emphasized that as civil litigation reform has generally responded to changing economic and social circumstances, and with China being a vast country with many geographic divisions, the practical implementation of the formal rules has often been compromised by local practices and limited resources. For example, in economically developed cities such as Beijing and Shanghai where commercial disputes accounted for the majority of cases, judges tend to follow systemic formal rules with stronger emphasis on due process elements, such as the adoption of the adversarial model with corresponding obligations on the parties in terms of burden of proof, etc. However, in economically less developed regions, most courts responded to disputes mostly in a mediatory and inquisitorial fashion.[112] The issue of judicial disparity resulting from the economic disparity among different regions of China reflects that the budgetary system between local courts and local governments should be de-coupled. Fu suggested by gradually realizing centralized financing of various courts in China, the divergences caused by limited resources at the local level could be mitigated.[113]

Second, Fu called for professionalization of Chinese judges in specialist fields to accompany the emergence of specialist courts and tribunals. Fu used the examples of intellectual property law and environmental law.[114] A report in 2010 showed that there were more than 11 environmental tribunals established at the city-level intermediate courts in Southwestern and Eastern China, dealing particularly with environmental torts.[115] The number rose to 61 by early 2012,[116] and there was a significant increase to reach 391 environmental tribunals within China at the end of 2018, with 23 provincial-level high courts having established specific tribunals to handle disputes with respect to protection of environmental and natural resources.[117]

112 Li, *The Judicial System and Reform in Post-Mao China*, 136.
113 Fu, "Social Harmony at the Cost of Trust Crisis," 373–390.
114 Fu Yulin, "Sifa zeren de zhongxin zaiyu quanze jieding he quanze yizhi" 司法责任的重心在于权责界定和权责一致, (lecture, Hong Kong, October 26, 2015).
115 Alex L. Wang and Gao Jie, "Environmental Courts and the Development of Environmental Public Interest Litigation in China," *Journal of Court Innovation* 3 (2010): 38–39.
116 Zhang Sha 张莎, "Renda daibiao jianyi dali tuixing huanbaofating qianghua jianguan" 人大代表建议大力推行环保法庭强化监管, *Sina Green*, March 13, 2012, http://green.sina.com.cn/news/roll/2012-03-13/100424106526.shtml. (NPC Deputy Zhang specifically stated in the report that the National People's Congress is actively advocating the development of environmental courts, in view of the rampant pollution by large corporations who would rather pay fines over clearing up the polluted areas. Such concern has manifested in a multitude of pollution cases in 2011 which included the Jiangxi water pollution, blood lead poison cases along the Eastern coastal areas, Yunnan Qujing factory chromium leakage, and the Wuhan water pollution cases.)
117 *Zhongguo huanjing ziyuan shenpan 2017–2018.*

In terms of the newly introduced environmental public interest litigation, Stern examined whether these specialist environmental tribunals could effectively address environmental problems. In her published paper in 2011, Stern showed that Chinese courts showed greater sympathy to victims in environmental torts, as evidenced by the increase in number of reported cases that qualified as environmental public interest litigation, although some environmental tribunals still assumed a passive role for the sake of the local governments.[118] In her subsequent published empirical study in 2014, Stern looked into the case records in the environmental tribunals in the cities of Guiyang (in Guizhou Province), Wuxi (in Jiangsu Province), and Kunming (in Yunnan Province).[119] All three tribunals showed tentative willingness to broaden the range of plaintiffs with the legal standing to sue. For civil cases, however, the effectiveness of the tribunals suffered from a lack of public interest litigation, the court's lack of experience with trying these cases, and considerable obstacles for NGOs to file the cases. Based on such observations, Stern then suggested that these courts were only established to fulfil the political needs of the government to address environmental problems and social unrests. It has been suggested that until judges are fully trained in the specialized fields (including expertise in environmental science in addition to legal skills on tort claims), specialized tribunals will not be able to fulfil their true functions.[120]

Subtly, public interest litigation as introduced in the CPL will also test the Chinese courts' role to maintain social stability. At the center of civil litigation is always the delicate balance of power between litigants and the court. Earlier, we discussed the impact of sensational cases such as the Sanlu Incident in the development of the 2012 CPL. However, if we slightly modify the timeline such that those cases occurred after the 2012 CPL, will the outcome of those cases be the same? And, will Article 55 of the 2012 CPL be able to deliver its full effect?

Let us postulate two scenarios using the Sanlu Incident as an illustration. In the first scenario, upon occurrence of the Sanlu Incident, in the beginning, there were neither any social movements from activists and victims, nor was there any media attention. In this scenario, things were largely peaceful at first, and the product liability stemmed from a private company. Eventually, after the defective milk products were exposed by the media, the public would demand a cause of action against the private company. In such circumstances, it is suggested that Article 55 would likely be of great assistance to victims in establishing a cause of action in court.

In the second scenario, the initial situation would be the same: there were no social movement from activists and victims, nor was there any media attention.

118 Rachel E. Stern, "From Dispute to Decision: Suing Polluters in China," *The China Quarterly* 206, (2011): 294–312.
119 Stern, "The Political Logic of China's New Environmental Courts," 53–74.
120 Zhang Sha, "Renda daibiao jianyi dali tuixing huanbaofating qianghua jianguan."

However, unlike the first scenario, the product liability stemmed from a public company, for example, an SOE where political interests of the State were involved. Eventually, after the defective milk products were discovered, media activities on reporting would be overwhelmingly stifled by State actors, in order to prevent the public from being notified of the illegal activities of the SOE. In such circumstances, it is suggested that Article 55 might have little or even no use in assisting victims or social organizations to establish a cause of action on public interest litigation. The outcome under the second scenario is explained by the stability-maintenance function of courts in the Chinese society.

The Party-State holds the instrumentalist view that the court was a means to achieve various policy aims, such as economic development and social stability. Civil justice then functions to maintain social stability as part of the State-building process, at the expense of other lofty goals such as fairness and due process.[121] Such a direction is still evident in many official documents such as the 2014 Party Central Committee Decision concerning Some Major Questions in Comprehensively Promoting Governance of the Country According to Law (the "2014 Party Decision").[122] Some have argued that by dedicating an entire session to the topic of law in the 2014 Party Decision, the Party attempted to reassert its role in the legal system to address the weak public trust of the legal system.[123] This announcement was consistent with Article 2 of the 2012 CPL, which stressed that the goals of the civil procedure are to resolve disputes, under the overarching notion of "maintaining social stability."[124]

As the courts are being tasked with the political obligation to maintain social harmony, policy considerations played a big role in the decision-making process of the judges, sometimes at the cost of preserving due process. Such considerations, however, are largely undisclosed in the reasoning of the judgments unless parties have specifically presented or defended those issues.[125] Cases related to social policies are often rejected at the docketing stage, and even if they survived that stage, most judges decline to take on multi-party cases because of the complexity and potential political interference due to the expected wider impact to the society. For these reasons, these cases tend to be mediated, withdrawn by the plaintiffs, or handled by the state through other administrative means.[126] For example, Chinese courts in the Sanlu Incident had become a multi-purpose governance tool

---

121   Jerome Alan Cohen, "Body Blows for the Judiciary," *South China Morning Post*, October 18, 2008, http://www.scmp.com/article/656696/body-blow-judiciary.

122   "Decision of the CCP Central Committee on Major Issues Pertaining to Comprehensively Promoting the Rule of Law," *China Law Translate*, October 28, 2014, http://chinalaw-translate.com/fourth-plenum-decision/?lang=en.

123   Woo, "The Dynamism of China's Civil Litigation System," 153.

124   Civil Procedure Law 2012, art. 2.

125   Fu, "Social Harmony at the Cost of Trust Crisis," 173.

126   Ibid., 177.

rather than the protector of rights in due process, by assuming an active role over the commencement and conclusion of Sanlu Corporation's bankruptcy, which ultimately led to the demise of any litigation in tort.[127] Even though the new Article 55 of the 2012 CPL would seem to have improved the situation, some scholars still argue that this is a mere political move to reduce public discontent due to the rise in public awareness toward a more litigious society and with activist movements in those areas of mass claims in torts. As such, despite the issue of standing to sue has been solved, the Chinese courts are still very cautions on the development of capacity-building in the civil society that may potentially threaten the courts' politically instrumental roles.[128] As such, the new multi-tracked litigation system under the 2012 CPL reform where public interest litigation was introduced has been commented by Woo, leading scholar on China's civil justice in the West, as another political product, where (1) pure commercial cases without socio-economic and socio-political impact can be adjudicated; (2) politically insignificant disputes can be mediated; and (3) mass claims are to be carefully controlled and shaped by the Party State through the tasks to maintain social stability (*weiwen* 维稳) designated to the courts.[129]

6 Conclusion

The civil litigation system in China is constantly evolving, with much development introduced in the past decade. However, unlike contemporary civil procedural reforms in other jurisdictions such as Hong Kong and the United Kingdom that have been driven by procedural efficiency concerns,[130] China's reforms are largely triggered by social grievances at the bottom, which are then responded to by legislative amendments at the top for social stability maintenance as part of its state-building process.

The Chinese path to the civil procedure reform is thus an evolution toward a more litigious Chinese society where civil activism in certain areas of law such as consumer rights and environmental protection could be increasingly accommodated. China has been steered to revise its civil litigation regime as the political entities started to lose popular legitimacy in pacifying the general public. If the movements to reform civil procedure laws were technically motivated by procedural concerns, then the introduction of the public interest litigation system in the 2012 CPL would have also addressed other forms of malfeasance by public bodies and other areas of mass claims with a public interest element.[131]

---

127 Ibid., 179.
128 Thomas, "Dynamism in China's Civil Procedure Law," 138; Woo, "The Dynamism of China's Civil Litigation System," 151.
129 Woo, "The Dynamism of China's Civil Litigation System," 149.
130 See discussions in Chapter 9.
131 Thomas, "Dynamism in China's Civil Procedure Law," 138.

Fortunately, there are also signs of de-politicization of the civil litigation system in progress. Although Article 55 of the 2012 CPL is an enactment motivated by bottom-up movements, in the recent 2014 EPL, environmental protection bodies established at the city level or above are given the standing to sue, and there has been an increase in non-governmental affiliated NGOs established at the city level or above since then. Citizens are also given greater participation opportunities in certain social issues through participating in such public interest cases, which is a move that has certain impact on access to justice. Hence, public interest litigation introduced by Article 55, in connection with the subsequently amended 2013 Consumer Protection Law and 2014 EPL, have pushed the conventional boundary of access to justice of mass tort claims in China.

There are also signs of changes in mindset among both academics and political leaders. An increasing number of Chinese civil procedure scholars argue that the functions of civil litigation system should include the protection of lawful rights of the parties, and emphasize the importance of establishing a legal order as opposed to a social order, in addition to mere dispute resolution. Many have urged courts to exercise their adjudicatory power to declare legal norms and uphold justice. State leaders have started to recognize the defects in the legal system such as judicial structure and resources, as well as the need to enhance judicial competence.

Finally, regardless of the underlying political motivations on the amendments of the existing Chinese civil procedure laws and rules, it is still an important step by China to move toward better due process and access to justice. The legislative amendments also demonstrate China's responsiveness to domestic voices, thereby constantly re-molding the landscape of civil causes of actions. Indeed, the civil procedural laws are merely a facet of civil justice, and inroads must be made and complemented by parallel technical reforms of the procedure and systematic reforms of the courts and judges. As Fu suggested, the reform of parties' procedural rights in mass civil litigation drives systematic reforms such as the revision in the courts' structure and functions, as well as increased professionalism and accountability of the judges.[132] The recent development of the Chinese civil litigation landscape, in particular the evolution of public interest litigation, is one of the ongoing steps to propel China's civil justice reform.

Bibliography

"Amendments to Consumer Protection Law Allows for Public Interest Lawsuits with Limitations." *Congressional-Executive Commission on China*, January 14 2014. http://www.cecc.gov/publications/commission-analysis/amendments-to-consumer-protection-law-allows-for-public-interest#_ednref3.

---

132 Fu 傅郁林, "Social Harmony at the Cost of Trust Crisis: Goals of Civil Justice in China", 以信任危机为代价的社会和谐: 中国民事司法的目标, 170.

Benney, Jonathan. *Defending Rights in Contemporary China*. New York: Routledge, 2012.

"Bereaved Parents Compensated by Sanlu." *China Daily*, January 17, 2009. http://www.chinadaily.com.cn/cndy/2009-01/17/content_7405679.htm.

Chen, Lei. "The Role of Comparative Law in Teaching and Research." Conference, Hong Kong, January 19, 2018.

"China Focus: China Amends Law to Allow Public Interest Litigation by Prosecutors." *Xinhua News*, June 27, 2017. http://www.xinhuanet.com//english/2017-06/27/c_136399032.htm.

China Law Society. *The Law Yearbook of China* (2010–2018). Accessed July 8, 2020. http://www.stats.gov.cn/tjsj/ndsj/2019/indexeh.htm.

"China Overhauls Consumer Protection Laws." *Hong Kong Lawyer*, October 2013. http://www.hk-lawyer.org/content/china-overhauls-consumer-protection-laws.

Clarke, Donald C. "Power and Politics in the Chinese Court System: The Enforcement of Civil Judgments." *Columbia Journal of Asian Law* 10, no. 1 (1996): 1–91.

Cohen, Jerome Alan. "Body Blows for the Judiciary." *South China Morning Post*, October 18, 2008. http://www.scmp.com/article/656696/body-blow-judiciary.

Davis, Deborah. "Urban Consumer Culture." *China Quarterly* 183, (2005): 692–702.

"Decision of the CCP Central Committee on Major Issues Pertaining to Comprehensively Promoting the Rule of Law." *China Law Translate*, October 28, 2014. http://chinalawtranslate.com/fourth-plenum-decision/?lang=en.

Ding, Chunyan. *Medical Negligence Law in Transitional China*. Cambridge: Intersentia Publishing, 2012.

Fu, Hualing and Richard Cullen. "The Development of Public Interest Litigation in China." In *Public Interest Litigation in Asia*, edited by Yap Po Jen and Lau Holning, 1–29. New York: Routledge, 2010.

Fu, Yulin. "Sifa zeren de zhongxin zai yu quanze jieding he quanze yizhi" 司法责任的重心在于权责界定和权责一致. Lecture, Hong Kong, October 26, 2015.

Fu, Yulin 傅郁林. "Social Harmony at the Cost of Trust Crisis: Goals of Civil Justice in China" 以信任危机为代价的社会和谐：中国民事司法的目标. *Peking University Law Journal* 中外法学, no. 2 (2014): 373–390.

Fu, Yulin. "Zhongguo dalu sifa gaige de mubiao he weidu" 中国大陆司法改革的目标和维度. Lecture, Hong Kong, October 26, 2015.

Fu, Yulin. "Zou xiang xiandaihua de minshi susong chengshi" 走向现代化的民事诉讼程式. Presentation, Hong Kong, October 26, 2015.

Fu, Yulin and Cao Zhixun, "The Position of Judges in Civil Litigation in Transitional China—Judicial Mediation and Case Management." In *Towards a Chinese Civil Code: Comparative and Historical Perspectives*, edited by Chen Lei and C. H. van Rhee, 495–520. Leiden: Brill, 2012.

"Guiding Opinion of the All China Lawyers Association Regarding Lawyers Handling Cases of a Mass Nature (CECC Full Translation)." March 20, 2006. http://www.cecc.gov/resources/legal-provisions/guiding-opinion-of-the-all-china-lawyers-association-regarding-lawyers.

Gu, Weixia. "Securities Arbitration in China: A Better Alternative to Retail Shareholder Protection." *Northwestern Journal of International Law and Business* 33, no. 2 (2013): 283–323.

"Highlights of work report of China's Supreme People's Court." *China Daily*, March 11, 2011. http://www.chinadaily.com.cn/china/2011npc/2011-03/11/content_12157831.htm.

"Home." National Bureau of Statistics of China. Accessed July 8, 2020. http://www. stats.gov.cn/english/.

Ho, Suk-ching. "Executive Insights: Growing Consumer Power in China: Some Lessons for Managers." *Journal of International Marketing* 9, no. 1 (2000): 64–83.

Hu, Xiabing and Feng Renqiang, eds. *Research on Judicial Justice and Judicial Reform* 司法公正与司法改革研究综述. Beijing: Tsinghua University Press, 2001.

Huang, Philip C.C., ed. *Chinese Civil Justice, Past and Present*. Maryland: Rowman & Littlefield, 2010.

Huanjing baohu Fa (环境保护法) [Environmental Protection Law] (promulgated by the National People's Congress Standing Committee, April 24, 2014, effective January 1, 2015). http://en.pkulaw.cn/display.aspx?cgid=4544&lib=law.

Jacobs, Andrew. "Chinese Release Increased Numbers in Tainted Milk Scandal." *The New York Times*, December 2, 2008. http://www.nytimes.com/2008/12/03/world/asia/03milk.html?_r=1.

Jiang, Bixin 江必新. *Zhongguo huanjing ziyuan shenpan 2017–2018* 中国环境资源审判 2017–2018, March 2, 2019. https://www.cenews.com.cn/subject/2019/2019lh/a/201903/t20190302_894317.html.

Jones Day. *Adding More Strings to the Bow: The 2012 Amendments to China's Civil Procedure Law*. Accessed July 8, 2020. https://www.jonesday.com/en/insights/2013/01/adding-more-strings-to-the-bow-the-2012-amendments-to-chinas-civil-procedure-law.

Katz, L.M. "Class Action With Chinese Characteristics: The Role of Procedural Due Process in the Sanlu Milk Scandal." *Tsinghua China Law Review* 2, no. 2 (2010): 421–466.

Li, Yuwen. "The Civil Trial Process." in *The Judicial System and Reform in Post-Mao China: Stumbling Towards Justice*, edited by Li Yuwen, 133–164. Oxford: Routledge, 2016.

Li, Yuwen. *The Judicial System and Reform in Post-Mao China*. New York: Routledge, 2014.

Liao, Yong-an and Deng Hejun. "Comments on the Decision to Amend the Civil Procedural Law." *Xiandai Faxue* 现代法学, 1 (2009): 150–160.

Liebman, Benjamin. "Class Action Litigation in China." *Harvard Law Review* 111 (1998): 1523–1541.

Liu, Chenglin. "Profits above the law: China's melamine tainted milk incident." *Mississippi Law Journal* 79, no. 2 (2009): 371–418.

Liu, Jialiang. "It is Necessary to Overhaul the Civil Procedure Law." *Jiancha Ribao* 检察日报, March 18, 2008.

Lora-Wainwright, Anna, Zhang Yiyun, Wu Yunmei, and Benjamin Van Rooij. "Learning to Live with Pollution: How Environmental Protestors Find their Interests in a Chinese Village." *The China Journal* 68 (2012): 106–124.

Minshi Susong Fa (Shixing) (民事诉讼法(试行)) [Provisional Civil Procedure Law] (promulgated by the National People's Congress Standing Committee, March 8, 1982). http://www.npc.gov.cn/wxzl/wxzl/2000-12/06/content_4411.htm.

Minshi Susong Fa (民事诉讼法) [Civil Procedure Law] (promulgated by the National People's Congress, April 9, 1991, effective April 9, 1991). http://www.lawinfochina.com/display.aspx?lib=law&id=19&CGid=.

Minshi Susong Fa (民事诉讼法) [Civil Procedure Law] (promulgated by the National People's Congress, October 28, 2007, effective April 1, 2008). http://en.pkulaw.cn/display.aspx?cgid=1811a46f52ef6533bdfb&lib=law.

Minshi Susong Fa (民事诉讼法) [Civil Procedure Law] (promulgated by the National People's Congress Standing Committee, June 27, 2017, effective July 1, 2017). http://en.pkulaw.cn/display.aspx?id=6d9ce94e57cee7afbdfb&lib=law.

Minzner, Carl. "China's Turn against Law." *American Journal of Comparative Law* 59 (2011): 935–984.

Nagle, John C. "How Much Should China Pollute?" *Vermont Journal of Environmental Law* 12, no. 1 (2011): 591–632.

Pan, Jianfeng. "The Role of Comparative Law in Teaching and Research." Lecture, Hong Kong, January 19, 2018.

Peerenboom, Randall. *China Modernizes: Threat to the West Or Model for the Rest?* Oxford: Oxford University Press, 2007.

Qin, Yudong. "Sanlu pochan shanhou nanti shouhaizhe quanyi shuilai baozhang" 三鹿破产善后难题受害者权益谁来保障. *Caijing Beijing*, December 25, 2008. http://www.caijing.com.cn/2008-12-25/110042541.html.

"Renmin fayuan <'yiwu' gaige gangyao> yu <'erwu' gaige gangyao>"人民法院《"一五"改革纲要》与《"二五"改革纲要》. *Legal Daily China*, April 30, 2009. http://www.legaldaily.com.cn/zbzk/2009-04/30/content_1091822.htm.

"Sanlu Faces Class-Action Lawsuit." *Newshub New Zealand*, November 13, 2008. http://www.newshub.co.nz/world/sanlu-facing-classaction-lawsuit-2008111406#axzz44ezlYycR.

Seidman, Guy I. "Comparative Civil Procedure." In *The Dynamism of Civil Procedure—Global Trends and Development*, edited by Colin B. Picker and Guy I. Seidman, 3–17. New York: Springer, 2016.

"Shanghai chutai xiao'e susong shenpan gongzuo shishi xize" 上海出台小额诉讼审判工作实施细则. *The Supreme People's Court of the People's Republic of China*, December 28, 2012. http://www.civilprocedurelaw.cn/html/fldt_1171_2978.html.

State Environmental Protection Agency and the Insurance Regulatory Commission. *Opinion on Development of Environmental Pollution Liability Insurance* 关于环境污染责任保险工作的指导意见, December 4, 2007. http://www.gov.cn/zwgk/2008-02/25/content_899905.htm.

Stern, Rachel E. "From Dispute to Decision: Suing Polluters in China." *The China Quarterly* 206, no. 1 (2011): 294–312.

Stern, Rachel E. "The Political Logic of China's New Environmental Courts." *The China Journal* 72 (2014): 53–74. http://ssrn.com/abstract=2466534.

Sun, Lijuan and Xie Jun. "Access to Collective Litigations in China: A Tough Work." *Journal of Politics and Law* 3, no. 1 (2010): 45–55.

Supreme People's Court. *Guanyu minshi susong zhengju de ruogan guiding* 关于民事诉讼证据的若干规定, December 6, 2001. https://www.pkulaw.com/chl/1224979098644812995.html?Customer=tyc.

Supreme People's Court. *Guanyu minshi jingji shenpan fangshi gaige wenti de ruogan guiding* 关于民事经济审判方式改革问题的若干规定, June 19, 1998.

Supreme People's Court. *Guanyu Shenli xiaofei minshi gongyi susong anjian shiyong falv ruogan wenti de jieshi* 最高院关于审理消费民事公益诉讼案件适用法律若干问题的解释, April 25, 2016. http://www.court.gov.cn/zixun-xiangqing-20082.html.

Supreme People's Court. *Interpretation of the Supreme People's Court on Several Issues concerning the Application of Law in the Conduct of Environmental Civil Public Interest Litigations*, January 6, 2015. http://pkulaw.cn/(S(pvgj1x45wuwnwm5555df4e55))/fulltext_form.aspx?Db=chl&Gid=f81c55e05ed7c7f6bdfb.

Supreme People's Court. *Report on the Work of the Supreme People's Court.* May 8, 2014. http://en.chinacourt.org/public/detail.php?id=4867.

Supreme People's Court. *Zuigao Renmin Fayuan Guanyu Shenli Huanjing Qinquan Zeren Jiufen Anjian Shiyong Falü Ruogan Wenti de Jieshi* 最高人民法院关于审理环境侵权责任纠纷案件适用法律若干问题的解释, June 1, 2015. http://www.court.gov.cn/fabu-xiangqing-14615.html.

The World Bank and Development Research Center of the State Council, the People's Republic of China. *China 2030: Building a Modern, Harmonious, and Creative Society.* Washington: World Bank, 2013. http://www.worldbank.org/content/dam/Worldbank/document/China-2030-complete.pdf.

Thomas, Kristie. "Dynamism in China's Civil Procedure Law: Civil Justice with Chinese Characteristics." In *The Dynamism of Civil Procedure—Global Trends and Developments*, edited by Colin B. Picker and Guy I. Seidman, 119–139. New York: Springer, 2016.

Tiezzi, Shannon. "China's Fifth Plenum: What You Need to Know." *China Dialogue*, October 29, 2015. http://thediplomat.com/2015/10/chinas-fifth-plenum-what-you-need-to-know/.

Tort Law of the People's Republic of China (promulgated by the National People's Congress Standing Committee, December 26, 2009, effective December 26, 2009). http://www.wipo.int/edocs/lexdocs/laws/en/cn/cn136en.pdf.

Wang, Alex L. and Gao Jie. "Environmental Courts and the Development of Environmental Public Interest Litigation in China." *Journal of Court Innovation* 3 (2010): 38–39.

Wang, Huazhong and Jingqiong Wang. "Courts Hit by Rising Number of Lawsuits." *China Daily*, July 14, 2010. http://www.chinadaily.com/cn/china/2010-07/14/content_10102630.htm.

Wang, Xiaogang. "Review of Public Interest Litigation in Fundamental Environmental Law" 透视环境基本法中的公益诉讼. *Environmental Protection* 环境保护 no. 9 (2010): 32–34.

"Woguo huanjing shijian nianjun dizeng 29%" 我国环境事件年均递增29%. *Caijing* 财经, October 27, 2012. http://tinyurl.com/dycoh82.

Wong, Edward. "Courts Compound Pain of China's Tainted Milk." *New York Times*, October 16, 2008. http://www.nytimes.com/2008/10/17/world/asia/17milk.html?_r=0.

Woo, Margaret. "The Dynamism of China's Civil Litigation System." In *The Dynamism of Civil Procedure—Global Trends and Developments*, edited by Colin B. Picker and Guy I. Seidman, 141–153. New York: Springer, 2016.

Wu, Jun 吴俊. "Zhongguo minshi gongyi susong niandu guancha baogao (2017)" 中国民事公益诉讼年度观察报告(2017). *Dangdai faxue* 当代法学 no. 5 (2018): 136–146.

Xiao, Jianguo and Huang Zhongshun 肖建国　黄忠顺. "Xiaofei gongyi susong zhong de dangshiren shige wenti yanjiu" 消费公益诉讼中的当事人适格问题研究. *Shandong jingcha xueyuan xuebao* 山东警察学院学报 no. 6 (2013): 7–10.

Xiaofeizhe quanyi baohu Fa (消费者权益保护法) [Consumer Protection Law] (promulgated by the National People's Congress Standing Committee, October 25, 2013, effective January 1. 1994), http://www.npc.gov.cn/wxzl/gongbao/2014-01/02/content_1823351.htm.

Yang, Guobin "Environmental NGOs and Institutional Dynamics in China." *The China Quarterly* 181, no. 1 (2005): 46–66.

Ye, Ariel and Yu Song. "Justice, Efficiency and the New Civil Procedure Law." *China Law and Practice* 20, no. 12 (2012).

Zhang, Sha 张莎. "Renda daibiao jianyi dali tuixing huanbaofating qianghua jian-guan" 人大代表建议大力推行环保法庭强化监管. *Sina Green*, March 13, 2012. http://green.sina.com.cn/news/roll/2012-03-13/100424106526.shtml.

Zhang, Taisu. "The Pragmatic Court: Reinterpreting the Supreme People's Court of China." *Columbia Journal of Asian Law* 25, no. 1 (2012): 1–61.

Zhang, Xianchu. "Civil Justice Reform with Political Agendas." In *The Development of the Chinese Legal System: Change and Challenges*, edited by Yu Guanghua, 253–271. Oxford: Routledge, 2011.

"<Zhongguo huanjing ziyuan shenpan (2019)> ji niandu dianxing anli <Zhongguo huanjing sifa fazhan baogao (2019)> xinwen fabu hui"《中国环境资源审判(2019)》暨年度典型案例《中国环境司法发展报告(2019)》新闻发布会, May 8, 2020. https://www.chinacourt.org/chat/fulltext/listId/52428/template/courtfbh20200508.shtml.

4 Arbitration

A synthesis of unique socio-economic dynamics

1 Introduction

1.1 Preliminaries

Arbitration is a binding, non-judicial and consensual[1] means of settling commercial disputes based on an agreement to arbitrate by the parties involved in a transaction. Arbitration has been described as an important part of modern commerce and one of the soft power indicators in the literature.[2] Every significant trading state in the world now hosts at least one important international arbitration center or institution. Both developed and developing economies are increasingly reliant on, and supportive of arbitration in resolving commercial disputes.[3] States have established laws and institutions regulating arbitration to create an arbitration-friendly commercial environment and attract foreign direct investment ("FDI"), which in turn is expected to promote economic growth. Such an environment typically involves the following elements. First, a liberal modern arbitration law that regulates the arbitration activities as ante-control (first element). Second, an impartial judiciary that supervises arbitral awards made in its jurisdiction and decides when to recognize and enforce awards from another state as post-control (second element). Third, an arbitration-friendly environment

---

1 Some literature summarized arbitration's "non-judicial" nature as "quasi-judicial" because the outcome of arbitration is binding on the disputing parties submitting to arbitration; and the "consensual" nature as "private" nature of arbitration. See leading scholar, the late Professor Hans Smit of Columbia University: Hans Smit, "Contractual Modifications of the Arbitral Process," in *Building the Civilization of Arbitration*, eds. Thomas Carbonneau and Angelica Sinopole (London: Wildy, Simmonds & Hill Publishing, 2010), 1–16.
2 Walter Mattli and Thomas Dietz, "Mapping and Assessing the Rise of International Commercial Arbitration in the Globalization Era: An Introduction," in *International Arbitration and Global Governance*, eds. Walter Mattli and Thomas Dietz (Oxford: Oxford University Press, 2014), 1–2.
3 Alec Stone Sweet and Florian Grisel, *The Evolution of International Arbitration: Judicialization, Governance, Legitimacy* (Oxford: Oxford University Press, 2017), 45–46.

would also see the proliferation of arbitration institutions, with market competition promoting a healthy development to attract case (third element).[4]

China's modernization and marketization has led to increased foreign trade and investment and as a natural corollary, commercial disputes. Arbitration as the preferred means of commercial dispute resolution between the Chinese and foreign parties, has been increasingly seen as an important indicator of China's trade and investment environment. Efforts by China to improve its pro-arbitration environment have not been futile.

This chapter first examines the arbitration system in China. China's Arbitration Law ("AL"), promulgated in 1994 (effective in 1995) forms the cornerstone of the Chinese arbitration regulatory framework. A remarkable feature of China's arbitration system is its control on administered arbitration within its territory (more often referred to as "institutional arbitration monopoly"). In the past decade, the AL was only very slightly amended in 2017 and did not address the development concerns. Most of the arbitration reforms introduced so far are prompted by two threads: (1) the regulatory level which is largely led by the SPC's judicial interpretations, and (2) the institutional level which is largely shaped by the Chinese arbitration market. This chapter further examines the wider economic contextual factors that have driven the development of arbitration and analyses the patterns of the reform. This chapter finally concludes that the Chinese path to arbitration reform is a unique synthesis of socio-economic dynamics and predicts that market competition will remain a major driving force for Chinese arbitration development in the future.

1.2 Empirical evidence

Empirical evidence as to how commercial arbitration had developed and is practiced in China is lacking. Such evidence is not offered, for example, in the China Law Yearbook. While leading Chinese arbitration commissions such as the China International Economic and Trade Arbitration Commission ("CIETAC") and Beijing Arbitration Commission ("BAC") have been compiling arbitration data for their own institutional purposes for many years, arbitration data on a national basis in China have not become available until very recently. BAC started to look into the national arbitration data on an annual basis since 2013, and published such materials as *Commercial Dispute Resolution in China: An Annual Review and Overview*. Since 2015, CIETAC, in collaboration with the China Academy of Arbitration Law, has been reviewing the nationwide arbitration statistics in the preceding year, and published their review as *Annual Report on International Commercial Arbitration in China*.

---

4 Anselmo Reyes and Gu Weixia, "Conclusion: An Asia Pacific Model of Arbitration Reform," in *The Developing World of Arbitration: A Comparative Study of Arbitration Reform in the Asia Pacific*, eds. Anselmo Reyes and Gu Weixia (Oxford: Hart Publishing, 2018), 279–280.

Table 4.1 Arbitration statistics (2012–2018)

Year	Total number of Chinese arbitration institutions	Total number of cases	Disputed amount in total (RMB, billion yuan)
2012	219	96,378	131.5
2013	225	104,257	164.6
2014	235	113,660	265.6
2015	244	136,924	411.2
2016	251	208,545	469.5
2017	253	239,360	533.8
2018	255	544,536	695

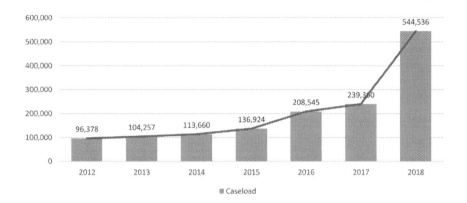

Chart 4.1 Caseload of Chinese arbitration (2012–2018)

Table 4.1 provides an aggregated overview of the Chinese arbitration land-scape, such as the total number of Chinese arbitration institutions, total number of cases and disputed amount, in the most recent years, on the basis of the statistics collected from the BAC and CIETAC's annual reviews and reports.[5,6]

Chart 4.1 then shows the growing popularity of arbitration in China in resolving commercial disputes, reflected by its rapidly developing caseload by years. Chart 4.2 conveys a sense of the vibrant role played by arbitration

---

5 At the time when the book manuscript is submitted, the 2019 data have not become available.

6 For Chinese nationwide arbitration statistics from 2012 to 2013, see Song Lianbin, Peng Liming, Stuart Dutson and Jean-Marc Deschandol, "Annual Review on Commercial Arbitration," in *Commercial Dispute Resolution in China: An Annual Review and Preview*, ed. Beijing Arbitration Commission Institute of Advanced Legal Studies, 1, http://www. bjac.org.cn/attached/file/20160217/2013.pdf. For Chinese nationwide arbitration statistics from 2014 to 2018, see China International Economic and Trade Arbitration Commission and China Academy of Arbitration Law, eds., *Zhong guo guo ji shang shi zhong cai nian du bao gao (2014–2019)* 中国国际商事仲裁年度报告 (2014–2019).

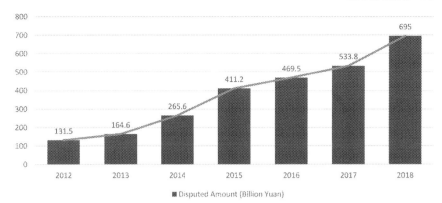

Chart 4.2 Disputed amount of Chinese arbitration (2012–2018)

Table 4.2 CIETAC arbitration statistics (2009–2018)

Year	Total number of cases	Disputed amount (RMB, billion yuan)
2009	1,482	17.313
2010	1,352	13.749
2011	1,435	15.6789
2012	1,060	15.47275
2013	1,256	24.4
2014	1,610	37.8
2015	1,968	42.54
2016	2,181	58.66
2017	2,298	71.888
2018	2,962	101.59

as a legal service sector in the commercial setting of China, shown by the significant increase of the disputed amount in arbitration over the years, which is also indicative of China's economic growth. The trend lines of both caseloads (Chart 4.1) and disputed amount (Chart 4.2) are upward sloping. Take more recent years as an example, in 2017 alone, 239,360 cases were handled by 253 Chinese arbitration institutions with the total disputed amount of 533.8 billion yuan,[7] and the figures rose in 2018 to 544,536 cases (a 127% increase in arbitration caseload) and 695 billion yuan (a 30% increase in disputed amount) as processed by 255 Chinese arbitration institutions.[8]

Table 4.2 and Chart 4.3 then compile the arbitration statistical trend of China's leading arbitration institution and largest by caseload, CIETAC, in the past decade. In 2017, CIETAC included a sizeable portion of China's

7 Ibid.
8 Ibid.

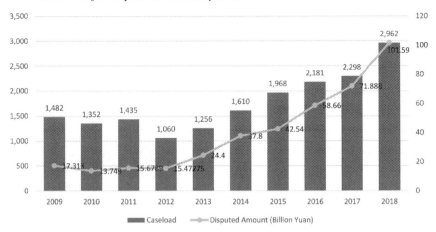

Chart 4.3 CIETAC caseload and disputed amount (2009–2018)

commercial arbitration cases—handled 2,298 cases or about 1% of the total arbitration caseload in China in 2017. Although CIETAC's caseload rose to 2,962 in number in 2018, the total arbitration caseload in China grew even more quickly, and the percentage of share by CIETAC in the total arbitration caseload in China dropped to 0.5%.[9]

2 Regulatory framework

2.1 The arbitration law and other sources of regulation

2.1.1 Arbitration law

China's Arbitration Law (the "AL") was adopted in August 1994 and came into effect in September 1995.[10] The AL was promulgated in light of the increasing popularity of commercial arbitration as a method of dispute resolution flowing from China's legal and economic reforms since the 1980s.[11] Applicable to all arbitrations conducted on the basis of voluntary agreements to arbitrate, the AL covers procedural and substantive rules throughout the arbitral process, from the establishment of arbitral tribunals to the enforcement of arbitral awards.[12] While the United Nations Commission on International Trade Law

---

9 See Yu Jianlong 于健龙, *CIETAC Annual Work Report and Work Plan (2009–2018)*, January 27, 2010, http://cn.cietac.org/.

10 Zhongcai Fa (仲裁法) [Arbitration Law] (promulgated by the Standing Committee of the National People's Congress, August 31, 1994, effective September 1, 1995), http://www.npc.gov.cn/wxzl/wxzl/2000-12/05/content_4624.htm.

11 Katherine Lynch, "The New Arbitration Law," *Hong Kong Law Journal* 16 (1996): 104.

12 See, generally, the Chinese Arbitration Law (1994).

("UNCITRAL") Model Law on International Commercial Arbitration (the "Model Law") formed a guiding reference for the modernization of China's arbitration regime, it was never adopted in China.[13]

2.1.2 State council regulations

State Council (i.e., the Central Government) Notices supplement the AL, providing regulation on matters not covered under the legislation. In particular, such notices guide the establishment of city-based local arbitration commissions, which only occurred and flourished after the promulgation of the AL. For instance, the "1996 Notice"[14] diluted the "dual-track" division of arbitration commissions in China on the basis of jurisdiction bifurcation by permitting local arbitration commissions to arbitrate foreign-related disputes previously monopolized by CIETAC.[15] These provisions allowed, to some extent, the rapid expansion of certain local arbitration commissions, such as BAC, which will be examined further.

2.1.3 Judicial interpretations

In its dual position as both the highest judiciary and a *de facto* rule-making institution in China, the Supreme People's Court ("SPC") has sporadically supplemented the AL by issuing judicial interpretations (*sifa jieshi* 司法解释)[16] supervising the handling of specific arbitration cases in lower level Chinese courts. These judicial interpretations commonly take the form of 'replies' (*pifu* 批复) or 'notices' (*tongzhi* 通知). The SPC's interpretations on arbitration practice were consolidated in 2006 in the SPC Interpretation on Certain Issues Concerning the Application of the Arbitration Law (the "2006 SPC Interpretation").[17] The 2006 SPC Interpretation is highly

---

13 Wang Shengchang, "The Globalization of Economy and China's International Arbitration," (paper delivered, Globalization and Arbitration, Beijing, jointly sponsored by the ICC and CIETAC, October 15, 2002).

14 General Office of the State Council, *Notice Concerning Several Issues to be Clarified for the Purpose of Implementing the PRC Arbitration Law*, June 1996, http://cicc.court.gov.cn/html/1/219/199/200/653.html.

15 Gu Weixia, "Arbitration in China," in *International Commercial Arbitration in Asia*, 3rd ed., eds. Shahla Ali and Tom Ginsburg (New York: Juris Publishing, 2013), 82.

16 Renmin Fayuan Zuzhi Fa (人民法院组织法) [Organic Law of People's Courts] (promulgated by the Standing Committee of the National People's Congress, July 5, 1979, effective January 1, 1980, amended 2006), art. 33, http://www.npc.gov.cn/zgrdw/englishnpc/Law/2007-12/13/content_1384078.htm. However, the scope of SPC's interpretative power is not clearly defined as between *interpreting law* and *making law* although there may be the literal distinction that legislation is the act of making a law, while interpretation is the act of process of ascertaining the meaning of existing laws.

17 Supreme People's Court, *Interpretation on Certain Issues Concerning the Application of the Arbitration Law*, August 23, 2006, http://www.asianlii.org/cn/legis/cen/laws/iotspccsmoaotalotprocl305/.

regarded, not only symbolizing substantive developments in the Chinese arbitral landscape, but also serving as a harbinger of further legislative amendments to the AL.

2.1.4 Arbitration commissions rules

One distinctive feature of the AL is its unique stipulation that all arbitrations in China, regardless of being domestic- or foreign-related in nature, must be administered by Chinese arbitration commissions and conducted in accordance with the rules of the chosen Chinese arbitration commission.[18] This distinction is more often referred to as "institutional arbitration monopoly" in China.[19] As a matter of the institutional arbitration system in China, while rules of the arbitration commissions governing arbitral procedures do not carry the force of law, they are *de facto* viewed as part of the regulatory framework of Chinese arbitration.

Since 1956, CIETAC has amended its rules on eight occasions—most recently in January 2015[20]—to reflect the international trend of enhancing flexibility in arbitration procedure. Further, CIETAC's use of specialized arbitration rules, for instance, the "Arbitration Rules for Financial Disputes," have increased her competitiveness by providing a set of arbitral rules tailored to financial disputes.[21] The China Maritime Arbitration Commission ("CMAC") similarly periodically revises its rules, with its most recent rules taking effect from January 2015. Alongside CIETAC and CMAC, over 200 city-based local arbitration commissions formulate and apply their own sets of arbitration rules. Among them, BAC, drawing experience from CIETAC and international arbitral institutions, has been increasingly recognized as a rising star of arbitration rule-making in China. BAC's 2015 and 2019 arbitration rules, for instance, featured arbitral procedures enhancing arbitrator professionalism and party autonomy.[22]

2.1.5 International agreements

International agreements ratified by China also form part of the regulatory framework of Chinese arbitration. Applicable provisions of such conventions take precedence over their domestic counterparts, except any

---

18 Arbitration Law arts. 16, 18.
19 Gu Weixia, *Arbitration in China: The Regulation of Arbitration Agreements and Practical Issues* (London: Sweet & Maxwell, 2012), 19–24.
20 The eight occasions took place in 1988, 1994, 1995, 1998, 2000, 2005, 2012, and 2014, respectively. The CIETAC rules were most recently revised on November 4, 2014, effective as from January 1, 2015.
21 The CIETAC Financial Arbitration Rules was first adopted in 2003, and were most recently amended in 2014, effective as from January 1, 2015.
22 *Beijing Arbitration Commission Arbitration Rules*, accessed November 15, 2016, http://arbitrator.bjac.org.cn/en/Arbitration/index.html.

reservations made during its accession.[23] For instance, the primary source of regulation with respect to the enforcement of foreign arbitral awards is the Convention on the Recognition and Enforcement of Foreign Arbitral Awards (the "New York Convention"), adopted by the United Nations in 1958 and acceded to by China in December 1986.

2.2 Dual-track mechanism

The Chinese arbitration regulatory framework adopts a dual-track distinction. Although the AL covers both domestic and foreign arbitration and applies equally to both regimes, there are provisional gaps differentiating the two tracks, effectively giving foreign arbitration a more favorable treatment. Chapter VII (Articles 65–73) of the AL specifically regulates the foreign-related track and prescribes a series of privileges exclusively reserved to foreign-related arbitrations, including greater freedom enjoyed by foreign-related arbitration commissions when deciding upon their own organizational structure,[24] more flexible and user-friendly rules governing the application for interim measures of protection, etc. [25] Moreover, Chapter VII of the AL also provides less stringent qualification requirements for foreigners applying to serve as arbitrators in China.

While there is no legislative definition of the term "foreign-related," Article 1 of the "Several Opinions on the Implementation of the Law on the Applicable Laws in Foreign-related Civil Relations" promulgated in 2012 provides that a foreign element exists where: (1) one party or both parties to the contract are foreign entities, foreign legal persons or stateless persons; (2) the subject matter of the contract is located in a foreign country; or (3) the act which gives rise to, modifies or extinguishes the rights and obligations under the contract occurs in a foreign country.[26] Besides the three criteria above, cases involving parties from Hong Kong, Macau, and Taiwan

---

23 Minfa Tongze (民法通则) [General Principles of Civil Law] (promulgated by the National People's Congress, April 12, 1986, effective January 1, 1987), art. 142, http://www.npc.gov. cn/wxzl/wxzl/2000-12/06/content_4470.htm.

24 Pursuant to Arbitration Law art. 66, there is no exact limit for the number of members on a foreign-related arbitration commission. In contrast, Arbitration Law art. 12 limits the number of members on a local arbitration commission to be 16.

25 The relevant rules for domestic arbitrations are stipulated in Arbitration Law art. 46, while that for foreign-related arbitrations are in Arbitration Law art. 68.

26 Supreme People's Court, *Interpretations of the Supreme People's Court on Several Issues Concerning Application of the Law of the People's Republic of China on Choice of Law for Foreign-Related Civil Relationships (1)*, December 28, 2012, https://www.chinacourt.org/ law/detail/2012/12/id/146055.shtml. Similar stipulations were issued by the SPC judicial interpretation relating to the China Civil Procedure Law. See Supreme People's Court, *Zuigao renmin fayuan guanyu shiyong "Zhonghua renmin gongheguo minshi susong fa" ruogan wenti de yijian* 最高人民法院关于适用《中华人民共和国民事诉讼法》若干问题的意见, July 14, 1992, art. 304.

are broadly referred to as foreign-related. This situation remains unchanged with regard to Hong Kong and Macau even after the post-handover period.

While the AL governs both domestic- and foreign-related arbitrations, the latter is given a more favorable treatment under the statute. Chapter VII of the AL prescribes privileges exclusively reserved for foreign-related arbitrations, such as greater autonomy permitted to foreign-related arbitration commissions in determining their organizational structure[27] and more relaxed qualification requirements for foreign arbitrators wishing to serve in China. The greatest disparity between the tracks lies in their respective enforcement of arbitral awards. While the grounds to exercise judicial supervision for setting aside or denial of enforcement of foreign and foreign-related awards in China are limited to procedural grounds,[28] supervision for domestic awards are more rigid and even include substantive matters, such as the effects of the evidence on which the award was based.[29]

With respect to the dual tracks, since 1995, the SPC also operates a "pre-reporting system"[30] in its procedure of review, which aims to limit local protectionist influences over the enforcement of foreign or foreign-related arbitral awards.[31] Under the system, lower level courts may not refuse recognition or enforcement without the SPC's confirmation.[32] The scheme has, however, been criticized for overlooking domestic arbitration and even aggravating the dual-track inequality.[33] To pick up the inequality concern and to present an overall pro-enforcement image, as will be elaborated in Chapter 7, the SPC now extends the application of the "pre-reporting system" to domestic awards.[34]

27 See note 25.
28 Arbitration Law arts. 70, 71, making reference to Minshi Susong Fa (民事诉讼法) [Civil Procedure Law] (promulgated by the National People's Congress, April 9, 1991, effective April 9, 1991), art. 260(1), http://www.lawinfochina.com/display.aspx?lib=law&id=19&CGid=. This is consistent with the New York Convention art. V(2) and international practice.
29 Arbitration Law art. 58.
30 Supreme People's Court, *Zuigao renmin fayuan guanyu renmin fayuan chuli yu shewai zhongcai ji waiguo zhongcai shixiang youguan wenti de tongzhi* 最高人民法院关于人民法院处理与涉外仲裁及外国仲裁事项有关问题的通知, August 28, 1995, http://www.people.com.cn/zixun/flfgk/item/dwjjf/falv/9/9-2-1-05.html. Supreme People's Court, *Zuigao renmin fayuan guanyu chengren he zhixing waiguo zhongcai caijue shoufei ji shencha qixian wenti de guiding* 最高人民法院关于承认和执行外国仲裁裁决收费及审查期限问题的规定, November 14, 1998, http://cicc.court.gov.cn/html/1/218/62/84/660.html. Supreme People's Court, *Zuigao renmin fayuan guanyu renmin fayuan chexiao shewai zhongcai caijue youguan shixiang de tongzhi* 最高人民法院关于人民法院撤销涉外仲裁裁决有关事项的通知, April 23, 1998, http://cicc.court.gov.cn/html/1/218/62/84/663.html.
31 China International Economic and Trade Arbitration Commission, ed., *Symposium Essays on Economic and Trade Arbitration between the Taiwan Straits* (Beijing: China Law Press, 2001), 39.
32 Ibid.
33 Gu, "Arbitration in China," 118.
34 Supreme People's Court, *Relevant Provisions of the Supreme People's Court on Issues concerning Applications for Verification of Arbitration Cases under Judicial Review*, December 26, 2017, https://www.chinacourt.org/law/detail/2017/12/id/149641.shtml.

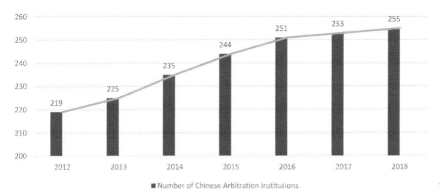

Chart 4.4 Number of Chinese arbitration commissions (2012–2018)

Finally, two types of arbitration commissions, domestic- and foreign-related, cater to the domestic- and foreign-related arbitration tracks, respectively. Foreign-related arbitration cases were monopolized by CIETAC and CMAC until the dual-track jurisdiction was merged under the 1996 State Council Notice. Realistically, with few exceptions such as the BAC and Shenzhen Court of International Arbitration ("SCIA"), it remains difficult for Chinese local arbitration commissions to compete with CIETAC, which has accumulated experience and expertise in handling sophisticated international commercial arbitration matters.

2.3 Institutional framework—Chinese arbitration commissions

The promulgation of the AL has led to the rapid proliferation of locally based arbitration commissions across China in the mid-1990s.[35] The BAC and the Shanghai Arbitration Commission ("SAC") were established in 1995. Then, 1996 and 1997 saw the establishment of the Hangzhou Arbitration Commission ("HAC") and the Wuhan Arbitration Commission ("WAC"), respectively.[36] In tandem with China's urbanization, rising trends in the establishment of city-based local arbitration commissions continue.

As shown previously in Table 4.1, in 2012 there were a total of 219 arbitration commissions in China; increasing to 225 in 2013 and 235 in 2014. The list keeps on expanding, from 235 in 2014, increasing to 244 in 2015; 251 in 2016; 253 in 2017; and further increasing to 255 in 2018. Chart 4.4 tracks the growing bar of the Chinese arbitration commissions in the most recent years (2012–2018), as the 2019 data have not yet become available.

---

35 Arbitration Law art. 10(1) stipulates that arbitration commissions may be established in any Chinese city that may be divided into administrative districts.
36 See the official websites of Beijing, Shanghai, Hangzhou, and Wuhan Arbitration Commissions.

Despite the quickly expanding list of institutions, a dearth in caseload negatively impacts institutional independence and competitiveness, especially for those institutions established to meet administrative, rather than market needs.[37] In particular, commissions reliant on local governments and treasuries for caseload and other financial support are susceptible to administrative interference. [38] Further, arbitral commissions that reap sufficient profits from service charges undergo administrative scrutiny, even if they are not financially reliant on local governments.

While the AL provides that arbitration should be conducted independently, free from external interference,[39] the legislative deficiency of specific implementation rules has given rise to ancillary rules which effectively frustrate the goal of institutional "independence." A 1995 State Council Notice provides that the establishment and operation of local arbitration commissions ought to be supervised by the local government's legislative affairs office, conferring disproportionate influence on matters of the staffing and development of the commissions.[40] Two BAC surveys, conducted in 2006 and 2007, showed, respectively, that 73.9% and 69.3% of the personnel composition of the surveyed local arbitration commissions (2006: 98; 2007: 73) were associated with an administrative organ or the local government.[41] Such a situation contravenes the AL's stipulation that the legal and economic trade professions should make up no less than two-thirds of the members of an arbitration commission. The independence of individual institutions thus turns on the local administrative attitude toward arbitration.

Arbitrators must satisfy several requirements to qualify as arbitrators. First, the legislative requirements set out by Article 13 of the AL stipulate professional conditions for becoming an arbitrator in China, so that apart from being a morally unimpeachable person he/she must have sufficient years of "expertise" in some special areas such as law, trade and economics. Article 13 of the AL states that "expertise" refers to "established years" of at least eight years of working experience in the relevant field.[42] To align the qualification standard required of a legal professional to become an arbitrator with that required to become a lawyer, in 2017, the AL was slightly amended to require staff members with working experience in the arbitration commissions for eight years or above to pass the

---

37 Gu, *Arbitration in China: Regulation and Practical Issues*, 107.
38 Ibid., 106–107.
39 Arbitration Law, arts. 8 and 14.
40 General Office of the State Council, *Guowuyuan bangongting guanyu jin yibu zuohao chongxin zujian zhongcai jigou gongzuo de tongzhi* 国务院办公厅关于进一步做好重新组建仲裁机构工作的通知, May 26, 1995, http://www.gov.cn/zhengce/content/2010-11/12/content_6997.htm.
41 Chen Fuyong 陈福勇, "Wo guo zhong cai ji gou xian zhuang shi zheng yan jiu" 我国仲裁机构现状实证研究, *Legal Studies* 2 (2009): 81–97.
42 Arbitration Law arts. 13(1), (2), (3).

National Unified Law Exam before they could get qualified as arbitrators in China.[43] The National Unified Law Exam is a substitute of the National Judicial Exam since 2018 for all legal professionals intending to practice law, such as lawyers, judges, prosecutors, arbitrators, government counsels and public notary.[44]

Comparative research shows that China sets relatively stringent standards for the professional qualification of arbitrators. [45] As with the dual-track tradition wherein favorable treatment is accorded to the foreign-related track, for appointment of foreign arbitrators (including permanent residents of Hong Kong, Macau, and Taiwan),[46] it is neither subject to the Article 13 restrictions on "expertise" and "established years" nor to any specific qualification requirements.[47] At the institutional level, each individual arbitral commission builds on the basis of the professional standards set by the AL, developing its own qualifications in appointing arbitrators. For example, CIETAC requires its arbitrators to have a good grasp of a foreign language and can adopt it as a working language.[48] No uniform standards exist for the enlisting of arbitrators among the hundreds of arbitration commissions across China.

The Chinese arbitration system operates a "panel arbitrator system," whereby only arbitrators named on a panel list maintained by the arbitration commission administering the case may be appointed by parties.[49] This feature has been criticized for impinging on party autonomy; further, the "panel arbitration system" raises questions as to the impartiality of Chinese arbitration, when viewed against the potential protectionist concerns of personal relations and networks (*guanxi* 关系) pervading the operation of the close-panel arbitral tribunal.[50] When arbitrators are drawn from internal staff of the administering commission, or governmental officials from the same community,[51] standards of impartiality may be compromised by efforts

---

43   Arbitration Law art. 13(1), amended in September 2017.

44   Ministry of Justice, *Implementation Measures for the National Uniform Legal Profession Qualification Examination*, April 28, 2018, http://www.gov.cn/gongbao/content/2018/content_5341398.htm.

45   For example, to be an arbitrator in Taiwan, the candidate shall practise as a lawyer, judge, or accountant for more than five years.

46   The Hong Kong-, Macau- and Taiwan-based arbitrators are considered as foreign arbitrators, and the cases involving elements from these three jurisdictions are considered as foreign-related cases.

47   Arbitration Law, art. 67.

48   China International Economic and Trade Arbitration Commission, *Zhongguo guoji jingji maoyi jingji zhongcai weyuanhui zhongcaiyuan pinren guiding* 中国国际经济贸易仲裁委员会仲裁员聘任规定, accessed July 4, 2020, http://www.cietac.org/index.php?m=Page&a=index&id=57, art. 2(4).

49   Though the panel system is not expressly provided for in the Arbitration Law, it may be inferred form Articles 11 and 13. See Gu, *Arbitration in China*, 124–125.

50   Gu, *Arbitration in China*, 131–133, 136–141.

51   Ibid., 142–148.

to yield an "amicable" majority opinion.[52] The "panel arbitration system" thus exacerbates issues of external influence and impartiality.

The validity of awards rendered by foreign arbitration institutions seated in China remains unsettled.[53] Arbitration commissions in China are statutorily subject to various organizational and constitutional requirements, as well as supervision by the China Arbitration Association. These remain conditions unlikely to be met by foreign institutions.[54] The legal status of such institutions has been judicially considered; in particular, whether awards resulting from arbitrations following the Rules of the International Chamber of Commerce ("ICC") Court of Arbitration are enforceable.[55] Arbitration agreements designating ICC arbitrations have been declared invalid by Chinese courts, notably in *Züblin International GmbH v Wuxi Woco-Tongyong Rubber Engineering Co Ltd*.[56]

Finally, ad hoc arbitration plays no legal role in the Chinese arbitration system, and arbitral awards rendered through ad hoc arbitration are unenforceable until the practice was recently gradually liberalized in some arbitrations that concerned with China's new Free Trade Zone ("FTZ") initiative.[57] The denial to ad hoc arbitration in the Chinese arbitration system stems from the AL's stipulation that "arbitration agreements must designate an arbitration institution to be valid."[58] Accordingly, the SPC has struck down agreements providing for ad hoc arbitration, for example, in *People's Insurance Company of China, Guangzhou v Guanghope Power et al*.[59]

As such, the Chinese arbitration system relies very much on the control from the top such as the institutional arbitration monopoly by the Chinese

---

52 Ibid. See also Gu, "Arbitration in China," 107.

53 "Conducting arbitration" in this context means to choose China as the seat of arbitration, regardless of whether the hearings take place in China.

54 Arbitration Law art. 15. Arbitration Law Chapter VII further provides that foreign-related arbitration commissions must be established by the China Chamber of International Commerce.

55 See discussions on the topic in Robert Briner, "Arbitration in China Seen from the Viewpoint of the International Court of Arbitration of the International Chamber of Commerce" (Roundtable on Arbitration and Conciliation Concerning China, ICCA Congress Series No. 12, Beijing, May 12–14, 2004), compiled in *New Horizons in International Commercial Arbitration and Beyond: ICCA Congress Series No. 12*, ed. Albert Jan van den Berg, (The Hague: Kluwer Law International, 2005).

56 *Züblin International GmbH v Wuxi Woco-Tongyong Rubber Engineering Co Ltd*, Xi Min San Zhong Zi No. 1 (Wuxi Intermediate People's Court, July 19, 2006), cited in Nadia Darwazeh and Friven Yeoh, "Recognition and Enforcement of Awards under the New York Convention: China and Hong Kong Perspectives," *Journal of International Arbitration* 25, no. 6 (2008): 841–42.

57 See discussions in Section 3.1 of Chapter 7.

58 Arbitration Law arts. 16 and 18.

59 Zhongguo renmin baoxian gongsi Guangdongsheng fengongzi yu Guangdong guanghe dianli youxian gongsi deng baoxian hetong jiufen an (中国人民保险公司广东省分公司与广东广合电力有限公司等保险合同纠纷案) [*People's Insurance Company of China, Guangzhou v Guanghope Power et al*] (Shanghai Intermediate People's Court, December 31, 2014).

arbitration commissions, denying access to both ad hoc arbitration and foreign institutional arbitration seated in China. Nonetheless, the traditional view that arbitration agreements must contain "designated arbitration institutions" to become valid in China has been revisited. Recent judicial cases have also relaxed the view that "designated arbitration institutions" encompass only Chinese arbitration commissions. The judicial support of and supervision over arbitration under the latest pro-arbitration move will be discussed and examined in Chapter 7.[60]

3 Reform

3.1 Legislative reform

In terms of legislative reform, the Model Law has never been adopted in China, although the 1985 version of the Model Law served as a guiding reference during the drafting stage of the AL in 1994. The 1994 AL is much outdated and has stalled the development of the Chinese arbitration system. While appeals to reform the AL on the basis of the Model Law have been strong, comprehensive amendments to the same have not taken place so far.[61] In 2017, the AL was only slightly amended with respect to the qualification conditions to admit a person as an arbitrator in China. As aforementioned, the AL now requires the passing of the National Unified Law Exam in addition to eight years' working experience for staff members in the arbitration commissions to qualify as arbitrators in China.[62]

3.2 SPC's judicial interpretations on arbitration

Although the legislative amendment progress is not encouraging, the SPC has however actively filled the regulatory gap on arbitration in many aspects by issuing numerous judicial interpretations in the field which are treated as quasi-laws in Chinese jurisprudence.

The judicial interpretations on arbitration take various forms, ranging from the issuance of sporadic "replies" (*pifu* 批复) and "notices" (*tongzhi* 通知) for individual arbitration cases, to the more systematic "provisions" (*guiding* 规定) and "interpretations" (*jieshi* 解释) for generalized application to all arbitration cases. Those systematic judicial interpretations mainly shape the regulatory advancement on Chinese arbitration when legislative development is lacking. Among them, the most notable one is the SPC's issuance of the 2006

---

60 See discussions in Section 3 of Chapter 7.
61 The SPC Judicial Interpretation on Arbitration was promulgated in 2006, embarking on a nation-wide appeal for the legislative reform of the Arbitration Law in China (see Section 3.2 below). Unfortunately, thus far, there have just been updates in the 2013 Civil Procedure Law in respect of the judicial review over arbitral awards as discussed earlier.
62 Arbitration Law art. 13(1), amended in September 2017.

Interpretation Concerning the Implementation of the Arbitration Law (the "2006 SPC Interpretation"). This is the most comprehensive attempt by the SPC in codifying its opinions on the grey areas of practice of Chinese arbitration unaddressed in the AL since the AL was promulgated in 1994.[63] Under the 2006 SPC Interpretation, for example, drafting pathologies involving "ambiguous and multiple arbitration commissions" are no longer fatal to the validity of arbitration agreements, but are now remediable and enforceable.[64]

Prior to the publication of the 2006 SPC Interpretation, more liberal interpretative techniques had actually been proposed in its Draft Provisions in 2004 (the "2004 SPC Draft Provisions").[65] Among the 2004 SPC Draft Provisions, its most "liberal" Article 27 provided that ad hoc arbitration agreements may be valid and enforceable if both parties to the agreement are nationals of member states of the 1958 New York Convention, and neither country prohibits the practice of ad hoc arbitration.[66] However, some of the 2004 SPC Draft Provisions were not endorsed in the official version of the 2006 SPC Interpretation, and the development of ad hoc arbitration development was abandoned at the crossroads of the SPC-led arbitration reform, until the issue was recently reconsidered by the SPC in context of China's Free Trade Zone initiative as a new national economic policy.[67]

Likewise, the status of foreign institutional arbitration seated in China was similarly not addressed in the 2006 SPC Interpretation, but has been liberally re-interpreted by Chinese courts in the past five years,[68] which will be addressed in Chapter 7.

It is also noteworthy that the SPC has speeded up its regulatory pace on judicial review over arbitration in the past several years, publishing a series of systematic judicial interpretations in the field, particularly with respect to the pre-reporting mechanism. In the provisions published in November 2017, the SPC decided to extend the "pre-reporting system" to judicial reviews over the domestic arbitration regime,[69] which abolished the preferential treatment for over two decades toward the foreign-related arbitration regime.[70] The regulatory developments on judicial review over arbitration will be further examined in Chapter 7.

---

63 For a detailed overview of the 2006 SPC Interpretation, see Gu, *Arbitration in China*, 74–83.

64 Supreme People's Court, *Interpretation on Certain Issues Concerning the Application of the Arbitration Law*, arts. 1–9.

65 Supreme People's Court, *Interpretations to Several Issues on the Application of the China Arbitration Law (Draft Provisions for Opinion Solicitation)*, July 22, 2004.

66 Ibid., art. 27.

67 See discussions in Section 3.1 of Chapter 7.

68 See discussions in Section 4.1 of Chapter 7.

69 See discussions in Section 3.2 of Chapter 7.

70 Supreme People's Court, *Provision on Cases Relating to the Pre-Reporting System of Arbitration*, November 20, 2017, https://www.chinacourt.org/law/detail/2017/12/id/149641.shtml, arts. 1–3.

3.3 Institutional reform—the Chinese arbitration market

In addition to the regulatory reform initiated by the SPC, the Chinese institutional arbitration landscape[71] and its reform are more complicated and the Chinese arbitration market has also been formed.

The landscape of the Chinese arbitration market is mainly formed by the following three forces. First, the AL's promulgation led to the rapid proliferation of city-based local arbitration commissions across China to compete for caseload, where a Chinese arbitration market start to be formed. To date, there are more than 250 such kind of local arbitration commissions. Second, despite the jurisdictional merging under the 1996 State Council Notice, CIETAC, as the most established arbitration institution in China, has continued to dominate the foreign-related arbitration market, until it was recently challenged by the dramatic CIETAC "split incident" in 2013. Third, local arbitration commissions are increasingly proactive in recent years. They regularly and continually update their arbitration rules and present innovative marketing initiatives, which contributed substantially to the Chinese arbitration market. The second and third forces make the Chinese arbitration market more complicated and diversified. Fourth, China's recent Belt and Road Initiative ("BRI") has brought about new pressures and opportunities for China's leading arbitration institutions, as they started to explore investment arbitration businesses.

3.3.1 CIETAC's split incident

The key actors in the CIETAC's Split Incident were the CIETAC South-China sub-commission located in Shenzhen, and the Shanghai sub-commission located in Shanghai. The two sub-commissions were established in 1983 and 1988, following respective requests by the Shenzhen and Shanghai municipal governments, through the assistance of CIETAC's organizer, the China Council for Promotion of International Trade ("CCPIT") attached to the State Council.[72] The two sub-commissions were historically managed under their respective local governments and their establishment as "CIETAC

71　The term "landscape" is inspired by Marc Galanter, "Reading the Landscape of Disputes: What We Know and Don't Know (and Think We Know) about Our Allegedly Contentious and Litigious Society," *UCLA Law Review* 31 (1983): 12.

72　CIETAC South China sub-commission was set up in 1984 and CIETAC Shanghai sub-commission was set up in 1990. CIETAC South China sub-commission bore the name of CIETAC Shenzhen office at its establishment. It was upgraded to CIETAC Shenzhen sub-commission in 1989 and had its name changed to the current one in 2004. For their history of establishment, see Gao Fei 高菲, "Maozhongwei Shanghai, Huanan liang fen hou yu maozhongwei zhi zheng de falv wenti yanjiu (3): maozhongwei Shanghai, Huanan liang fenhui weifa duli de yuanyin yu jiejue" 贸仲委上海、华南两分后与贸仲委之争的法律问题研究（三）:贸仲委上海、华南两分会违法独立的原因与解决,*Present Day Law Science*11, no. 2 (2013): 3–9.

sub-commissions" were largely professional labels.[73] Nonetheless, CIETAC attempted to strengthen its influence by appointing secretary-generals and deputy secretary-generals to the sub-commissions, as well as compulsory application of her rules from 2002 to 2012.[74] In addition, CIETAC and the two sub-commissions were natural competitors in the arbitration market for arbitration fees.[75] This rivalry peaked in 2012, when CIETAC revised its arbitration rules excluding jurisdiction of the sub-commissions.

On 3 February 2012, CIETAC promulgated its revised Arbitration Rules (the "2012 Rules"), with effect from 3 May 2012. The taking into effect of the 2012 Rules was followed by announcements from the Shenzhen and Shanghai sub-commissions claiming independence from CIETAC (the "CIETAC Split Incident").[76] The split was likely triggered by CIETAC's 2012 Rules, in particular Article 2, concerning the jurisdictional power division between CIETAC's headquarters in Beijing and its two sub-commissions.[77]

Article 2 of the 2012 Rules stipulates that "CIETAC sub-commissions or arbitration centers are branches of CIETAC. They accept arbitration applications and administer arbitration cases with CIETAC's authorization."[78] Cases submitted to CIETAC's empire yield three common types of jurisdiction clauses: (1) Parties elect to submit the dispute to CIETAC in Beijing ("Headquarters Clause"); (2) Parties elect to submit the dispute to a specified CIETAC sub-commission ("Sub-commission Clause"); and (3) Parties elect to submit the dispute to "CIETAC, at the place of a specified sub-commission, or where the agreement on the sub-commission is ambiguous" ("Mixed Clause").[79]

Under the 2005 and 2000 CIETAC Rules, where a Headquarters Clause or a Mixed Clause was used, parties could submit their cases to either the CIETAC headquarters in Beijing or the Shenzhen/Shanghai sub-commissions, with the jurisdiction determined upon the claimant's first choice.[80] However, under the 2012 Rules, Headquarters Clause and Mixed Clause cases would both be taken by the CIETAC headquarters in Beijing; the sub-commissions could only handle cases with a clearly written Sub-commission Clause.[81]

73 Ibid., 6–7.
74 Ibid.
75 Ibid.
76 See, for example, Chen Meng, "Is CIETAC Breaking Apart? An Analysis of the Split in the CIETAC System," *Contemporary Asia Arbitration Journal* 6, no. 1 (2013): 107–132.
77 Article 2 is titled 'The Structure and Duties'.
78 China International Economic and Trade Arbitration Commission, *Arbitration Rules*, February 3, 2012, art. 2 para. 3.
79 Ibid., art. 2 para. 6.
80 China International Economic and Trade Arbitration Commission, *Arbitration Rules*, January 11, 2005, art. 2 para. 8; China International Economic and Trade Arbitration Commission, *Arbitration Rules*, February 3, 2012, art. 2 para. 6.
81 China International Economic and Trade Arbitration Commission, *Arbitration Rules*, February 3, 2012, art. 2 para. 6.

Years of competition, catalyzed by changes to the jurisdictional power division and its impacts on the sub-commissions' income from case filing fees—coupled with CIETAC's declaration of effective control over the sub-commissions—led to the announcement of independence by the sub-commissions.[82] CIETAC subsequently announced on August 1, 2012 its termination of authorization to the Shanghai and South-China sub-commissions for accepting and administering any CIETAC-related cases, including cases with Sub-commission Clauses.[83] The two sub-commissions responded by renaming themselves as, respectively, the Shenzhen Court of International Arbitration/South China International Economic and Trade Arbitration Commission ("SCIA/SCIETAC") in October 2012 and the Shanghai International Arbitration Center/Shanghai International Economic and Trade Arbitration Commission ("SHIAC/SIETAC") in April 2013.[84] In May 2013, SCIA and SHIAC each announced a set of new arbitration rules, stating that they would no longer accept cases with the Headquarters Clause, but would as usual accept cases with the Sub-commission Clause.[85]

An immediate issue afterwards was whether previous agreements with Sub-Commission Clauses, which had been accepted by the two sub-commissions prior to the CIETAC split, remained valid. Judicial challenges on grounds that the original sub-commissions had no jurisdiction to arbitrate following CIETAC's announcement on 1 August 2012 were largely refused, for the maintenance of stability in the arbitration regime.

The uncertainty lingered until the SPC issued its official stance on 4 September 2013 (the "2013 Notice").[86] The 2013 Notice requested all cases

---

82 See report by China's leading economic news media, Yicai.com, on the "CIETAC split episode": "Shewai zhongcai nao 'fen zhi': zhengyi beihou shenfen chengmi" 涉外仲裁闹·分治·:争议背后身份成谜, *Yicai.com*, May 4, 2012, http://www.yicai.com/news/1691426.html.

83 China International Economic and Trade Arbitration Commission, *Zhongguo guoji jingji maoyi zhongcai weiyuanhui guanyu yueding you Zhongguo Guoji Jingji Maoyi Zhongcai Weiyuanhui Shanghai Fenhui, Zhongguo Guoji Jingji Maoyi Zhongcai Weiyuanhui Huanan Fenhui zhongcai de anjian de guanli gonggao* 中国国际经济贸易仲裁委员会关于约定由中国国际经济贸易仲裁委员会上海分会、中国国际经济贸易仲裁委员会华南分会仲裁的案件的管理公告, August 1, 2012, http://cn.cietac.org/notes/notes094.shtml.

84 SIETAC and SCIETAC also use the new name of as Shanghai International Arbitration Centre (SIAC) and Shenzhen Court of International Arbitration (SCIA), respectively. See reports by *Yicai.com* on the aftermath of the "CIETAC split episode": "Huanan Guozhong, Shanghai Maozhong: Duli zhongcai jigou bucunzai shouquan zhishuo" 华南国仲、上海贸仲: 独立仲裁机构不存在授权之说 [CIETAC Huanan, CIETAC Shanghai: There is No Theory of Authorization on Independent Arbitration Organizations], *Yicai.com*, January 31, 2013, http://www.yicai.com/news/2463616.html; "Shanghai Maozhong gengming: Xiayue qiyong xinguize xinmingce" 上海贸仲更名: 下月启用新规则新名册, *Yicai.com*, April 12, 2013, http://www.yicai.com/news/2621445.html.

85 Ibid.

86 Supreme People's Court, *Notice on Certain Issues Relating to Correct Handling of Judicial Review of Arbitration Matters*, September 4, 2013, http://cicc.court.gov.cn/html/1/218/62/84/666.html.

arising out of the jurisdictional dispute to be reported to the SPC and stated that such cases could only be decided after a reply from the SPC was obtained. At least two cases followed the SPC's 2013 Notice. The first concerned the effect of an award following an arbitration agreement selecting "CIETAC Shanghai Sub-commission." On 31 December 2014, the Shanghai No. 2 Intermediate People's Court upheld the effectiveness of the arbitration: since the Shanghai Sub-commission had its name changed to SIETAC, the case would be deemed to have been accepted by SIETAC.[87] Similarly, on 13 January 2015, the Beijing No. 2 Intermediate People's Court confirmed the jurisdiction of SCIETAC.[88] Both judgments were confirmed by the SPC. The 2013 SPC Notice, however, fell short of articulating the principles by which the appropriate forum for arbitration would be determined pursuant to an affected clause.

On 15 July 2015, the SPC issued a further judicial interpretation on the matter in the form of a joint reply to the Shanghai Higher People's Court, the Jiangsu Higher People's Court and the Guangdong Higher People's Court (the "2015 Reply").[89] The 2015 Reply offers guidance as to which institution should exercise jurisdiction and under what circumstances. This reply, effective on 17 July 2015, splits the timeline into three periods.

1   Prior to the renaming of the sub-commissions as a result of the split (the "Pre-renaming Period");
2   On the date or after the renaming but prior to the effective date of the 2015 Reply (the "Transition Period"); and
3   After the effective date of the 2015 Reply (the "New Period").

According to the 2015 Reply, SIETAC and SCIETAC would have jurisdiction over arbitration agreements submitted to them made during the Pre-renaming period, as was the case previously.[90] However, CIETAC held jurisdiction over all arbitration agreements entered into during the

---

87   Hu Er Zhong Min Reng (Zhong Ban) Zi No. 5 (沪二中民认 (仲协) 字第5号民事裁定书) (Shanghai Intermediate People's Court, December 31, 2014), http://www.shiac.org/upload/day_150104/201501040219323425.pdf.

88   Jinda rongzi danbao youxian zeren gongzi yu Zhongguo taiping baoxian (Xianggang) youxian gongsi deng shenqing queren zhongcai xieyi xiaoli yishen minshi caiding shu (金达融资担保有限责任公司与中国太平保险 (香港) 有限公司等申请确认仲裁协议效力一审民事裁定书) (Beijing Intermediate People's Court, May 18, 2015). The Beijing Court recognised that CIETAC South-China Sub-commission was established in 1984 in accordance with law and had its name changed to SCIETAC; and that the parties in the case had made a clear designation of the arbitration institution. Therefore, the arbitration application shall be made to SCIETAC in accordance with law.

89   Supreme People's Court, *Zuigaoyuan jiu maozhongwei Huanan fenhui, Shanghai fenhui tiaokuan anjian de guanxia ji caijue de sifa jiandu shensha wenti zuochu pifu* 最高院就贸仲委华南分会、上海分会条款案件的管辖及裁决的司法监督审查问题作出批复, July 17, 2015, http://cn.cietac.org/NewsFiles/NewsDetail.asp?NewsID=1532.

90   Ibid., art. 1 para. 1.

Transitional and New Periods.[91] By so prescribing, the SPC aimed to mitigate the side effects of the CIETAC split and to maintain stability and clarity in the arbitration market.[92] Thus, the SPC guidelines confirm the jurisdiction of SIETAC and SCIETAC, and the jurisdictional battle following the CIETAC split has finally been resolved.

The CIETAC split indicates that the unrivalled position and the historical near-monopoly of the foreign-related arbitration market held by CIETAC in the Chinese arbitration system is susceptible to challenge. The declarations of independence by SCIETAC and SIETAC have been bolstered by their respective promulgations of new arbitration rules seeking to match with international standards. In addition, the utilization of unique geographic advantages by SCIETAC and SIETAC—located in the Shanghai and Guangdong Free Trade Zones, respectively—have created still fiercer competition for CIETAC. SCIETAC in particular has fully capitalized on its geographic proximity to Hong Kong and Macau; of the 34 foreign arbitration awards enforced by Hong Kong courts in 2014, five were awards rendered by SCIETAC, being the largest portion of foreign awards delivered by one individual institution outside Hong Kong.[93] The dynamics of arbitration commissions using their niches to thrive and compete has extended to local arbitration commissions, as discussed later.

3.3.2 *Competition among local arbitration commissions*

The expansion, maturation and increasingly competitive nature of the market for Chinese local arbitration commissions may be attributed to several factors. These include the proliferation of local arbitration commissions following the promulgation of the 1994 AL, the blurring of the dual-track jurisdiction following the 1996 State Council Notice, the desire of local arbitration commissions to attract foreign caseload in the "shadow" of CIETAC, as well as their continuing efforts to improve institutional independence, integrity, and competitiveness.

Regular updates by local arbitration commissions of their arbitration rules serves to enhance their market competitiveness, with features threefold. First, to attract foreign-related caseload, local commissions are incentivized to bring their rules in line with international standards, with greater respect accorded to procedural autonomy and flexibility. For instance, BAC

---

91 Ibid., art. 1 paras. 2–3.
92 See for example, comments by foreign law firms: Norton Rose Fulbright, *China Arbitration: New Judicial Guidance on the CIETAC Split*, August 2015, http://www.nortonrosefulbright.com/knowledge/publications/131227/china-arbitration-new-judicial-guidance-on-the-cietac split.
93 Shenzhen Court of International Arbitration, *Huanan Guozhong ju Xianggang fayuan zhixing neidi zhongcai caijue shuliang zhi shou* 华南国仲居香港法院执行内地仲裁裁决数量之首, January 22, 2015, http://www.sccietac.org/web/news/notice_detail/1517.html.

updated its arbitration rules in April 2015[94] and September 2019,[95] respectively. The most recently updated BAC Arbitration Rules in 2019 specifically includes a Chapter (Chapter VIII) on "Special Provisions for International Commercial Arbitration," introducing rules with regard to interim measures of protection[96] and emergency arbitrators,[97] as well as specifying increased scope and flexibility of procedural measures.[98] The BAC Rules in 2019 further implements a new fee structure and is the first among the Chinese arbitration institutions to clearly separate the arbitrator's fees (remunerations) from the institution's administration fees (case filing and processing fees).[99] Similar efforts have occurred in local arbitral commissions in other economically developed Chinese cities such as Shenzhen.[100] In the past couple of years, the Shenzhen Court of International Arbitration ("SCIA"), since its split from the CIETAC in 2012, has earned the reputation as the most diligent among all Chinese arbitration institutions in updating her rules. SCIA updated its arbitration rules in December 2016[101] and February 2019[102] to enhance the procedural management in its international commercial arbitration. The most recently updated SCIA Rules in 2019, benchmarked against the world institutional arbitration giants such as the ICC Court of Arbitration in Paris, has introduced all major international arbitration procedural reforms such as joinder of parties in arbitration,[103] consolidation of arbitration in multiple contracts,[104] emergency arbitration,[105] etc.

Second, to enhance their competitive edges, local commissions seek to nurture a higher degree of professionalism. Privileged by its location in Beijing, BAC is renowned in its recruitment of talents in law, economics, technology, and trade, such that many of its arbitrators are renowned scholars and leading professionals in the fields both in China

94 Beijing Arbitration Commission, *Beijing Arbitration Commission Rules*, July 9, 2014, http://www.bjac.org.cn/english/page/zc/guize_en.html.
95 Beijing Arbitration Commission, *Beijing Arbitration Commission Rules*, July 4, 2019, http://www.bjac.org.cn/english/page/zc/guize_en2019.html.
96 Ibid., art. 62.
97 Ibid., art. 63.
98 Ibid., art. 35.
99 Ibid., annex 2.
100 Shenzhen Court of International Arbitration ("SCIA") started to amend its arbitration rules in 2016 and 2019 to enhance the procedural management (such as emergency arbitration and consolidation of arbitration) in its international commercial arbitration.
101 Shenzhen Court of International Arbitration, *Shenzhen guoji zhongcaiyuan zhongcai guize (2016 nian 12 yue 1 ri qi shixing)* 深圳国际仲裁院仲裁规则 (2016年12月1日起施行), December 1, 2016, http://www.sccietac.org/index.php/Home/index/rule/id/798.html.
102 Shenzhen Court of International Arbitration, *SCIA Arbitration Rules (effective from February 21, 2019)*, February 21, 2019, http://www.sccietac.org/index.php/Home/index/rule/id/791.html.
103 Ibid., arts. 20–21.
104 Ibid., arts. 17–19.
105 Ibid., art. 26.

and globally.[106] Further, BAC has maintained a tradition of high elimination rate of its arbitrators who have not participated in any cases in the past few years.[107] In 2013, 267 out of the 391 BAC panel arbitrators were involved in handling arbitration cases; just one out of the 57 newly appointed arbitrators in that year failed to handle any cases.[108] BAC is also the only institution in China which imposes strict ethical restrictions on its arbitrators acting as counsel in other cases submitted to BAC.[109] This prohibition seeks to ensure the ethics and integrity of BAC arbitrators to offset the negative influence of personal relations and networks (*guanxi* 关系) existing delicately within the operation of arbitral tribunals in China. Similar efforts have been seen at the SCIA in Shenzhen. The SCIA, located in the Shenzhen Special Economic Zone, and by taking advantage of its strategic role of connecting with Hong Kong, compiled a most common-law-featured roster of its international panel arbitrators, many of whom were drawn from legal professionals who were residents in Hong Kong. In 2019, SCIA's updated roster of panel arbitrators had as high as 41% of its arbitrators drawn from overseas (385 out of 933 panel arbitrators), making SCIA the most internationalized in terms of arbitrators' background among Chinese arbitration institutions.[110]

Third, local arbitration commissions proactively capitalize on their best local features to attract caseload in the competitive arbitration market. In June 2015, the Guangzhou Arbitration Commission ("GAC")—located in the capital city of the Guangdong province—started the process of amending its arbitration rules and published its Internet Arbitration Rules to promote online arbitration as its unique selling point.[111] In Hubei province, the Wuhan Arbitration Commission ("WAC") boasts successful mediation (settlement) rate for arbitration cases as high as 97.13% from

---

106 BAC's current Chairman is Professor Liang Huixing, a most impactful jurist in civil and commercial law in today's China. See *"Jingwai zhongcai jigou jinzhu Zhongguo shichang jiaju jingzheng, zhuanjia yu feixingzhenghua"* 境外仲裁机构进驻中国市场加剧竞争, 专家吁非行政化, *Fazhi ribao* 法制日报, September 29, 2015, http://www.chinanews.com/cj/2015/09-29/7549384.shtml.

107 "Beizhong shizhounian gongzuo zongjie" 北仲十周年工作总结, Beijing Arbitration Commission, accessed July 4, 2020, http://www.bjac.org.cn/page/gybh/sznzj.html.

108 "Beizhong 2013 nian gongzuo zongjie" 北仲2013年工作总结, Beijing Arbitration Commission, accessed July 4, 2020, http://www.bjac.org.cn/page/gybh/2013zj.html.

109 "Beizhong zhongcaiyuan shouze" 北仲仲裁员守则, Beijing Arbitration Commission, accessed July 4, 2020, http://www.bjac.org.cn/page/zc/zcygf.html.

110 Shenzhen Court of International Arbitration, *Instructions for the Panel of Arbitrators*, accessed July 4, 2020, http://www.scia.com.cn/files/fckFile/file/%E6%B7%B1%E5%9C%B3%E5%9B%BD%E9%99%85%E4%BB%B2%E8%A3%81%E9%99%A22019%E4%BB%B2%E8%A3%81%E5%91%98%E5%90%8D%E5%86%8C.pdf.

111 Guangzhou Arbitration Commission, *2015 Guangzhou Internet Arbitration Rules*广州仲裁委员会网络仲裁规则2015, accessed July 4, 2020, http://www.gzac.org/WEB_CN/AboutInfo.aspx?AboutType=4&KeyID=100b1ae3-9f15-4bfc-bf59-a90273778fa5.

2002 to 2012, with an arbitration caseload consistently ranked as the highest among all Chinese arbitration institutions in that decade.[112] Given plentiful local financial activity (and corresponding financial disputes), the Wenzhou Arbitration Commission ("WEAC") in Zhejiang province has focused its efforts on promoting financial arbitration services.[113] The WEAC Financial Arbitration Rules, taking effect in May 2015, feature flexibility in application of financial laws, norms, customs and rules in the financial profession, as well as principles of equity and fairness in the financial market, all as admissible governing regulations in arbitrating financial disputes at WEAC.[114] Thus, ever intensified competition among local commissions in the Chinese arbitration market is pushing the system toward qualitative advancement.

3.3.3 China's Belt and Road Initiative and investment arbitration business

The "One Belt One Road" vision was unveiled by Chinese President Xi Jinping in autumn 2013 during his visits to Kazakhstan and Indonesia.[115] It is the name of a development strategy by the Chinese government to revive the historical land and maritime Silk Roads dating back to the days of Marco Polo. The strategy covers 65 countries in Eurasia, Africa, and the Mediterranean, with the ambition for China to address the infrastructural deficits and untapped development potential across the region.[116]

Officially referred to as the "Belt and Road Initiative" ("BRI") (*yidai yilu* 一带一路) by the Chinese government since 2015, the BRI has now become the core of China's foreign strategy and outbound economic strategy, to expand regional markets and facilitate economic integration across the region.[117] Within this context of a steadily increasing volume of cross-border transactions and joint commercial enterprises, a well-functioning dispute

---

112 See the news report: "Wuhan Zhongcaiwei shouanshu lianxu shinian weiju quanguo diyi" 武汉仲裁委受案数连续十年位居全国第一, *Changjiang Daily* 长江日报, February 7, 2013, http://news.ifeng.com/gundong/detail_2013_02/07/22024260_0.shtml.
113 Wenzhou Arbitration Commission, *2015 Wenzhou Financial Arbitration Rules* 温州仲裁委员会金融仲裁规则 2015, accessed August 19, 2015, http://www.wzac.org/News_Detail.aspx?CateID=18&ID=397.
114 Ibid., art. 12.
115 See the official report by China's Ministry of Commerce: "Yidai yilu changyi de tichu" 一带一路"倡议的提出, The History of Commerce, accessed July 4, 2020, http://history.mofcom.gov.cn/?newchina=%E4%B8%80%E5%B8%A6%E4%B8%80%E8%B7%AF%E5%80%A1%E8%AE%AE%E7%9A%84%E6%8F%90%E5%87%BA.
116 Ibid.
117 "Visions and Actions on Jointly Building Silk Road Economic Belt and 21st-Century Maritime Silk Road," National Development and Reform Commission (NDRC) People's Republic of China, March 28, 2015, http://en.ndrc.gov.cn/newsrelease/201503/t20150330_669367.html.

resolution system is required to support and facilitate the development of the BRI. It further yields the secondary benefit of increasing transactional efficiency and reducing transactional costs for private investors and state parties to infrastructure projects relating to the BRI. The BRI development has already been regarded as a game-changer on the landscape of dispute resolution, triggering a proliferation of arbitration business.[118] The BRI development has further brought about new pressures and opportunities for China's leading arbitration institutions, as they started to explore a new arbitration business, investment arbitration.

China's leading institutions are not high in number and are concentrated in first-tier cities. According to CIETAC's survey, of the 253 Chinese arbitration institutions in 2017, only 60 handled "foreign-related" arbitration cases.[119] This number remained stable from 2016, when 62 institutions handled "foreign-related" cases.[120] According to CIETAC, only CIETAC, BAC, SCIA, GAC and Shanghai International Arbitration Center ("SHIAC," the post-CIETAC-split Shanghai institution) remained leading Chinese arbitration institutions in handling many of the "foreign-related" cases in 2016.[121] These numbers, however, are missing from the 2018 report. The vast majority of Chinese arbitration institutions do not concern themselves with cases involving a foreign party, foreign subject-matter, or the performance of obligations outside China.[122] Therefore, market competition of BRI arbitration business, and of arbitration business more generally, is shaped by only a handful of leading Chinese arbitration institutions.

While commercial arbitration is a comparatively developed area of Chinese arbitration, investment arbitration is a more recent phenomenon in China arising out of the BRI investor-state dispute resolution context. Again, SCIA and CIETAC are leading the development. SCIA revised

---

118 Matthew Erie, "The New Legal Hubs: The Emerging Landscape of International Commercial Dispute Resolution," *Virginia Journal of International Law* 59, no. 3 (2020): 225–298, Pamela Bookman, "The Adjudication Business," *Yale Journal of International Law* 45, no. 2 (2020): 227–283.

119 China International Economic and Trade Arbitration Commission, *Zhongguo guoji shangshi zhongcai niandu baogao 2017* 中国国际商事仲裁年度报告2017, accessed July 4, 2020, http://www.cietac.org/Uploads/201810/5bd6d2e9b333e.pdf.

120 China International Economic and Trade Arbitration Commission, *Zhongguo guoji shangshi zhongcai niandu baogao 2016* 中国国际商事仲裁年度报告2016, accessed July 4, 2020, http://www.cietac.org/Uploads/201710/59df3824b2849.pdf.

121 Ibid.

122 These are the three main circumstances where the court would deem a case to be "foreign-related." The SPC introduced a fourth limb to "foreign-relatedness," where both companies were wholly-foreign-owned enterprises registered in a free trade zone in Shanghai in 2015, in Ximenzi guoji maoyi (Shanghai) youxian gongsi yu Shanghai huangjin zhidi youxian gongsi shenqing chengren he zhixing waiguo zhongcai caijue an (西门子国际贸易(上海)有限公司与上海黄金置地有限公司申请承认和执行外国仲裁裁决案) [*Siemens International Trading (Shanghai) Co Ltd v Shanghai Golden Landmark Co Ltd*] (Shanghai Intermediate People's Court, November 27, 2015).

its rules in 2016 to include investor-state disputes as one of its arbitrable matters, becoming the first Chinese arbitration institution to do so.[123] The 2016 SCIA Rules mandated that all investment arbitrations submitted to SCIA will be governed by the ready-made international benchmark in the field (i.e., the UNCITRAL Rules applied to ad hoc investment treaty arbitration), and will be subject to the SCIA UNCITRAL Guidelines.[124] This development has been confirmed in the 2019 SCIA Rules.[125]

CIETAC, on the other hand, specially devised a set of rules for investor-state disputes in 2017 independent of its commercial arbitration rules.[126] To date, SCIA, CIETAC, and BAC[127] are the only three Chinese arbitration institutions that accept investor-state disputes. Indeed, there is traditionally little interest in arbitrating with China as a host state for investment, or arbitrating with other host states by Chinese investors under the ICSID Convention, which went into force in China in 1993.[128] As of April 2020, only five cases have been filed by Chinese investors against other host states, and only three cases have been filed by foreign investors against China as a host state.[129]

4 Development analyses

4.1 Penetrating factors of reform

In the absence of legislative development, judicial interpretations have plugged the gaps of the AL, clarifying issues uncertain in arbitral practice. Simultaneously, the rising competition among Chinese arbitration commissions represents a push toward professionalism and internationalization of the Chinese arbitration landscape. Both developments are commendable in their tendency to address defects of different aspects in the Chinese arbitration system.

---

123 Shenzhen Court of International Arbitration, *Shenzhen guoji zhongcaiyuan zhongcai guize (2016 nian 12 yue 1 ri qi shixing)* 深圳国际仲裁院仲裁规则 (2016年12月1日起施行), December 1, 2016, http://www.sccietac.org/index.php/Home/index/rule/id/798.html.
124 Ibid., art. 3(5).
125 Shenzhen Court of International Arbitration, *SCIA Arbitration Rules (effective from February 21, 2019)* arts. 2(2), 3(4), (5).
126 See the 2017 CIETAC International Investment Arbitration Rules.
127 Beijing Arbitration Commission and Beijing International Arbitration Center, *Rules for International Investment Arbitration*, accessed November 2, 2019, http://www.bjac.org.cn/page/data_dl/2019%E6%8A%95%E8%B5%84%E4%BB%B2%E8%A3%81%E8%A7%84%E5%88%990905%20%E8%8B%B1%E6%96%87.pdf.
128 Qi Tong, "How Exactly Does China Consent to Investor-State Arbitration: On the First ICSID Case against China," *Contemporary Asia Arbitration Journal* 5 (2012): 265, 268.
129 See the official website of the ICSID database at "Advanced Case Search," International Centre for Settlement of Investment Disputes, accessed March 13, 2019, https://icsid.worldbank.org/en/Pages/cases/AdvancedSearch.aspx.

As mentioned previously, the SPC serves a dual function as the highest court in China, as well as a de facto rule-making power-holder through the issuance of judicial interpretations. In both capacities, the SPC brings certainty to legal issues where existing legislation fails to provide clear or satisfactory solutions, particularly as arbitration is in close connection with the overall quality of China's investment environment. In its interpretative function, the 2006 SPC Interpretation clarified what amounts to an "unclear yet curable designation of arbitration commissions" under Articles 16 and 18 of the AL. The SPC's power to clarify and supplement the legislation is significant to the reform of the arbitration system in China, where laws often lag behind the pace of economic development and practical needs. Accordingly, the SPC has shouldered much of the burden of legal reform of the Chinese arbitration system in the past decade.

Unlike the judiciary, arbitration commissions are "private institutions" (*minjian jigou* 民间机构), or have as their objective to be private institutions (*minjianxing* 民间性). The driving force behind reform initiatives spearheaded by such commissions lies in their intent to enhance institutional competitiveness, independence and self-sufficiency vis-à-vis other commissions. On one hand, competition exists among Chinese city-based local arbitration commissions, particularly with respect to economically better developed cities. On the other hand, city-based arbitration commissions—including the former CIETAC sub-commissions—have grown to rival the traditional giant, CIETAC. Local arbitration commissions have pro-actively amended their arbitration rules on their local advantages, geographically, economically, culturally, or otherwise. Similarly, actions undertaken by SCIA and SHIAC illustrate how previous CIETAC partners strive to compete for a larger share of their legacies in the arbitration market. Institutional initiatives thus improve the arbitration regime in favor of quality and competitiveness, and eventually, to reform the Chinese arbitration system for qualitative development.[130]

4.2 *Patterns of reform*

On the patterns of arbitration reform in China, a distinction between the regulatory reform led by the SPC and institutional reform shaped by the arbitration market is made, which shows different ways in which they influence stakeholders of the arbitration system, the former being top-down while the latter bottom-up.

---

130 The Chinese arbitration regime has been challenged as over-developed in terms of number of arbitration institutions. The establishment of over 240 arbitration commissions spreading Chinese cities has been criticized as catering to administrative needs rather than real market demand. See Section 3.3 above.

SPC's top-down approach has a wide and direct scope of application, with its jurisprudence binding (or highly influential)[131] on arbitration practices on the similar types of issues in the future. In contrast, bottom-up changes such as those pursued by an individual arbitration commission are prima facie limited to that specific institution. An arbitration rule amendment by BAC, for instance, is applicable only to BAC itself, with only limited and indirect impact on external arbitral practices. However, bottom-up initiatives are no less important in the reform of the Chinese arbitration system. As the forerunners of Chinese arbitral practice, spearheading commissions are by nature sensitive to the market needs of both domestic and international arbitration businesses and users, and have the flexibility and capacity to respond to needs more quickly than either the legislature or the judiciary.

The most prevalent attributes in the development path of Chinese arbitration are the fast-developing economy and a comparatively weaker rule of law situation resulting from its historically rooted administrative-governance system.[132]

Chinese arbitration commissions (in particular, city-based local commissions), which have long tolerated administrative controls by local governments, have been anticipating legislative reform to embrace the real "private and market" nature of their institutional foundation and development.[133] However, as there has been no timetable set in the national legislative agenda for revision of the AL, certain frontline arbitration commissions have partaken in institutional strengthening and applied their best efforts in modernizing their rules. While arbitration commission rules do not carry the force of law and do not remedy deficiencies in the legal framework, they promote arbitral practice, facilitate legislative progress and imply development trends under China's institutional arbitration system,

During the interim period and before the revision of the AL, a significant attribute of China's arbitration reform is the mixture of the SPC-led, top-down regulatory developments and arbitration-commission-driven, bottom-up institutional efforts. In particular, due to the rapidly developing

---

131 China follows the civil law jurisdiction where case judgments do not carry force of law (*stare decisis* rule) as in common law jurisdictions. But it has been a general practice in China that SPC judgments are highly influential (or highly persuasive) on subsequent rulings of the same (or similar) types of issues as lower courts would be very reluctant to dis-follow the SPC precedent due to the system of appeal.

132 For example, among the wave of arbitration reform and development in Asia Pacific jurisdictions, Australia owes the major attribute of reform as inhered in the influence of the common law legal tradition and strong rule of law tradition. Australia owes its success of arbitration reform (in particular, the amendment of the International Arbitration Act in 2010) to be in response to the federal system of jurisdiction. See Leon Trakman, "Australia's Contribution to International Commercial Arbitration in Asia," (presentation, The Developing World of Arbitration: A Comparative Study of the Arbitration Reform in China and Asia Pacific, Hong Kong, October 27, 2015).

133 See Section 3.3.2 above.

Chinese national economy, both inbound and outbound strategies (such as the BRI economic strategy) and the corresponding increase in the demand for dispute resolution have made market-driven bottom-up institutional initiatives a persuasive force for arbitration development motivating top-down reforms, either from the judiciary or the legislature. The SPC's judicial efforts at the central level, and the institutional efforts at the local level collectively should elicit a positive response from the state legislature—that is, revision to the AL.

As such, the Chinese path to arbitration development and reform is that it is led from the top, such as the institutional arbitration monopoly in the AL and the SPC's top-down regulatory efforts, reflecting China's controlling ideology on arbitration. Fortunately, the system accommodates and is even reliant on market competition at the bottom level to make Chinese arbitration an attractive option for dispute resolution by domestic and foreign investors. The Chinese trajectory is thus an attempt to synthesize a unique socio-economic dynamic, with both a controlling element and features of free market. Interestingly, despite the Chinese arbitration system being monopolized by Chinese arbitral commissions, it does not prevent these commissions from being market players. From the bottom-up perspective, the Chinese arbitration market has been formed and even flourished. Intensifying competitions amongst leading city-based arbitration commissions, competing among themselves and with CIETAC internally, and even with traditional giants in the region externally, have formed a most exciting force of arbitration development in China in recent years, promoting the quality development of the Chinese arbitration market players, that is, the arbitration commissions. Hence, the free market features have become a more important force driving arbitration reform in China over the past decade and it will remain vigorous in driving the Chinese arbitration development trajectory in the future.

5 The future

5.1 AL revision

As addressed in numerous occasions in this chapter, the AL should be overhauled. Looking into the future, in amending the AL, the Chinese legislature should take advantage of the 2006 amended version of the Model Law,[134] which is widely considered a reflection of international best arbitration practices and

---

134 The United Nations Commission on International Trade Law (UNCITRAL) Model Law on International Commercial Arbitration was adopted in June 1985, and comprehensively amended in July 2006; see United Nations Commission On International Trade Law, *UNCITRAL Model Law on International Commercial Arbitration 1985 with amendments as adopted in 2006*, accessed November 17, 2016, https://www.uncitral.org/pdf/english/texts/arbitration/ml-arb/07-86998_Ebook.pdf.

the adoption of which is deemed a primary gate to access the international commercial market.[135] Moreover, the revisions to the AL must address both external alignment with international arbitration norms, and internal consistency among different sources of arbitral regulations in China. Internally, the Chinese legislature should review, for consistency, the manifold sources of arbitration regulations. Inconsistencies abound among the AL and other arbitral regulations in China. Further, given the merging of the dual track jurisdiction system by the 1996 State Council Notice, the concept of "foreign-related arbitration commission" should be discarded to curb practical confusion. Only the concept of "foreign-related arbitration"[136] would be retained.

Another "essential" ingredient to a successful arbitration reform is a pro-arbitration judiciary, which is critical to ensure the proper direction of legislative reform. Over the past decade, the SPC has issued an impressive body of interpretations, such as the 2006 Interpretation on AL, to bring certainty to legal issues which have either been left out by the AL or where the existing system fails to provide solutions. Moreover, the SPC has been supportive to arbitration in the past decade through concrete judicial practice. In fixing the jurisdictional mess after the 2015 CIETAC split episode, the SPC has exhibited judiciary leniency, exerting efforts to give effect to arbitration agreements as much as possible. Chinese lower-level judiciaries are also taking efforts to emulate SPC's pro-arbitration jurisprudence. As will be examined in Chapter 7, the SPC's efforts on establishing China as a pro-arbitration jurisdiction could only be realized by its lower-level courts' judicial attitude toward arbitration cases.

5.2 Competitiveness and independence of Chinese arbitration commissions

Future reform should also target at achieving institutional independence and competitiveness of Chinese arbitration commissions, which is particularly important to China as an institution-arbitration-dominated jurisdiction. Institutional reform should aim to comprehensively restructure the players of the arbitration market and by so doing, Chinese arbitration commissions will develop and thrive on the basis of market demand, rather than administrative needs.

To achieve independence and self-sufficiency, arbitration commissions must be decoupled from the influence of local governments. The personnel composition within a commission must consist of legal professionals rather

---

135 Australia is one of the first to adopt the 2006 amendments to the Model Law, as a reflection of embracing international best practice. See Doug Jones, *Commercial Arbitration in Australia*, 2nd ed. (Australia: Thomson Reuters, 2012); Richard Garnett and Luke Nottage, *International Arbitration in Australia* (Australia: Federation Press, 2010).

136 In accordance with judicial interpretations of both General Principles of Civil Law and Civil Procedure Law.

than representatives of administrative departments. On financial matters, commissions should rely solely on arbitration fees for their operation and development. Self-sufficiency not only establishes the institutional independence of local arbitration commissions, but edges them toward quality development in the market. Local governments should be prohibited from forcing local enterprises to use local arbitration commissions under a localization sentiment. In this regard, BAC is a shining example of restructuring in terms of integrity and quality, winning rising fame in professionalism within the larger arbitration market beyond China. However, BAC's success has neither been easy; nor will its path be easily reproduced by other arbitration commissions without sufficient market demand. Without market demand, well-intended institutional reform endeavors will fail—this will be a real possibility given that many commissions were established to meet administrative rather than actual needs. The competition within the Chinese arbitration market is an ever-intensifying, yet inevitable trend, wherein only the fittest arbitral service providers may thrive. It is thus proposed that less developed local commissions which have very little caseload to support their operation will be eliminated from the market.

In association with the modernization of Chinese arbitration commissions, the arbitrator profession in China should be established as an integral part of the success of the reform.

First, arbitrators must have high professional ability and moral integrity. Second, China must establish an environment in which arbitrators may work impartially. While the AL has established professional requirements no less stringent than other jurisdictions, accreditation is even more difficult for that it has been controlled by individual arbitration commissions. Changes to the accreditation scheme are needed to incentivize arbitral talents. The China Arbitration Association ("CAA") would be a most appropriate self-regulating authority for the qualification and accreditation of arbitrators, given its mandate to coordinate all arbitration commissions in China.[137] Further experience may be drawn from international arbitrator self-regulatory bodies such as the Chartered Institute of Arbitrators ("CIArb") with respect to examining and training Chinese and foreign nationals to become accredited and remain competent.[138] In this regard, the rising fame of BAC in arbitrator professionalism is particularly built on its success in achieving institutional independence in the first place and BAC's experience is research-wise. With CAA taking the lead in accreditation, and with individual arbitration commissions ensuring institutional

---

137 Arbitration Law, art. 15, para. 2.
138 CIArb is a world recognized self-regulatory institutional leader in providing accreditation and training to arbitrators and mediators. See "The Chartered Institute of Arbitrators," The Chartered Institute of Arbitrators, accessed December 10, 2016, http://www.ciarb.org.

independence and competitiveness, it is expected that arbitrator professionalism will be established in China in the not too distant future.

6 Conclusion

The arbitration arrangements established by China stand out as distinctive among major trading nations in the world—in theory, law, institutions, practice, and moreover, reform patterns and development discourse—as a function of its unique socio-economic context. While China's AL introduced substantial changes to the arbitration landscape in the nation, the road to arbitration modernization has not always been smooth. As a developing rule of law jurisdiction, the administrative-governance arbitration system originally practiced in China is incompatible with international norms emphasizing party autonomy and arbitral independence; indeed, her regulatory system for arbitration remains scattered and in need of development.

Faced with the overall backdrop of China's deepening marketization and further opening up, the current framework of the AL must be revisited. Legislative reform benchmarked against the 2006 Model Law standards should take place in China's arbitral regime soon. Although the consolidated 2006 SPC Interpretation and its numerous judicial interpretative documents to align Chinese arbitration with international norms and practices are much commendable, an apparent lack of official legislative support will leave SPC's judicial initiatives with many restrictions. China may lose its competitiveness in the international arbitration market due to slow progress in macrolegislative development, despite her strong vigor in economic competitiveness.

The formation of a modern and liberal arbitration environment is critical to China's trade and investment interests. Given China's rapidly expanding economic prominence, the number of international disagreements involving Chinese entities is expected to continue to grow, particularly in light of China's ambitious BRI development. In view of the lack of competence of Chinese courts and the reluctance of Chinese litigants to put their fate in the hands of foreign courts, arbitration remains the best choice for Sino-foreign commercial dispute resolution. The Chinese government should take China's development to become a favorable international arbitration forum a serious commitment and make it a continuous endeavor.

Bibliography

"Advanced Case Search." International Center for Settlement of Investment Disputes, accessed March 13, 2019. https://icsid.worldbank.org/en/Pages/cases/AdvancedSearch.aspx.

Beijing Arbitration Commission and Beijing International Arbitration Center. *Rules for International Investment Arbitration*, accessed November 2, 2019. http://www.bjac.org.cn/page/data_dl/2019%E6%8A%95%E8%B5%84%E4%BB%2%E8%A3%81%E8%A7%84%E5%88%990905%20%E8%8B%B1%E6%96%87.pdf.

Beijing Arbitration Commission, *Arbitration Rules*, April 1, 2015. https://www.bjac. org.cn/english/page/data_dl/zcgz_en.pdf.

Beijing Arbitration Commission. *Beijing Arbitration Commission Rules*, July 9, 2014. http://www.bjac.org.cn/english/page/zc/guize_en.html.

Beijing Arbitration Commission. *Beijing Arbitration Commission Rules*, July 4, 2019. http://www.bjac.org.cn/english/page/zc/guize_en2019.html.

"Beizhong 2013 nian gongzuo zongjie" 北仲2013年工作总结. Beijing Arbitration Commission, accessed July 4, 2020. http://www.bjac.org.cn/page/gybh/2013zj.html.

"Beizhong shizhounian gongzuo zongjie" 北仲十周年工作总结. Beijing Arbitration Commission, accessed July 4, 2020. http://www.bjac.org.cn/page/gybh/sznzj.html.

"Beizhong zhongcaiyuan shouze" 北仲仲裁员守则. Beijing Arbitration Commission, accessed July 4, 2020. http://www.bjac.org.cn/page/zc/zcygf.html.

Bookman, Pamela, "The Adjudication Business." *Yale Journal of International Law* 45, no. 2 (2020): 227–283.

Briner, Robert, "Arbitration in China Seen from the Viewpoint of the International Court of Arbitration of the International Chamber of Commerce." Roundtable on Arbitration and Conciliation Concerning China, ICCA Congress Series No. 12, Beijing, May 12–14, 2004. Compiled in New Horizons in International Commercial Arbitration and Beyond: ICCA Congress Series No. 12, edited by Albert Jan van den Berg. The Hague: Kluwer Law International, 2005.

Chen, Fuyong 陈福勇. "Wo guo zhong cai ji gou xian zhuang shi zheng yan jiu" 我国仲裁机构现状实证研究. *Legal Studies* 2, no. 1 (2009): 81–97.

Chen, Meng. "Is CIETAC Breaking Apart? An Analysis of the Split in the CIETAC System." *Contemporary Asia Arbitration Journal* 6, no. 1 (2013): 107–132.

China International Economic and Trade Arbitration Commissio. *Zhongguo guoji jingji maoyi zhongcai weiyuanhui guanyu yueding you Zhongguo Guoji Jingji Maoyi Zhongcai Weiyuanhui Shanghai Fenhui, Zhongguo Guoji Jingji Maoyi Zhongcai Weiyuanhui Huanan Fenhui zhongcai de anjian de guanli gonggao* 中国国际经济贸易仲裁委员会关于约定由中国国际经济贸易仲裁委员会上海分会、中国国际经济贸易仲裁委员会华南分会仲裁的案件的管理公告, August 1, 2012. http://cn.cietac. org/notes/notes094.shtml.

China International Economic and Trade Arbitration Commission, ed. *Symposium Essays on Economic and Trade Arbitration between the Taiwan Straits*. Beijing: China Law Press, 2001.

China International Economic and Trade Arbitration Commission. *Arbitration Rules*, January 11, 2005. http://www.cietac.org/index.php?m=Article&a=show&id=17.

China International Economic and Trade Arbitration Commission. *Arbitration Rules*, February 3, 2012. http://www.cietac.org/index.php?m=Article&a=show&id=18.

China International Economic and Trade Arbitration Commission. *Zhongguo guoji jingji maoyi jingji zhongcai weyuanhui zhongcaiyuan pinren guiding* 中国国际经济贸易仲裁委员会仲裁员聘任规定, accessed July 4, 2020. http://www.cietac.org/index. php?m=Page&a=index&id=57.

China International Economic and Trade Arbitration Commission. *Zhongguo guoji shangshi zhongcai niandu baogao 2017* 中国国际商事仲裁年度报告2017, accessed July 4, 2020. http://www.cietac.org/Uploads/201810/5bd6d2e9b333e.pdf.

China International Economic and Trade Arbitration Commission. *Zhongguo guoji shangshi zhongcai niandu baogao 2016* 中国国际商事仲裁年度报告2016, accessed July 4, 2020. http://www.cietac.org/Uploads/201710/59df3824b2849.pdf.

Darwazeh, Nadia and Friven Yeoh, "Recognition and Enforcement of Awards under the New York Convention: China and Hong Kong Perspectives." *Journal of International Arbitration* 25, no. 6 (2008): 837–856.

Erie, Matthew. "The New Legal Hubs: The Emerging Landscape of International Commercial Dispute Resolution." *Virginia Journal of International Law* 59, no. 3 (2020): 225–298.

Galanter, Marc. "Reading the Landscape of Disputes: What We Know and Don't Know (and Think We Know) about Our Allegedly Contentious and Litigious Society." *UCLA Law Review* 31 (1983): 4–71.

Gao, Fei 高菲. "Maozhongwei Shanghai, Huanan liang fen hou yu maozhongwei zhi zheng de falv wenti yanjiu (3): maozhongwei Shanghai, Huanan liang fenhui weifa duli de yuanin yu jiejue" 贸仲委上海、华南两分后与贸仲委之争的法律问题研究 (三): 贸仲委上海、华南两分会违法独立的原因与解决. *Present Day Law Science* 11, no. 2 (2013): 3–9.

Garnett, Richard and Luke Nottage, *International Arbitration in Australia*. Australia: Federation Press, 2010.

General Office of the State Council. *Guowuyuan bangongting guanyu jin yibu zuohao chongxin zujian zhongcai jigou gongzuo de tongzhi* 国务院办公厅关于进一步做好重新组建仲裁机构工作的通知, May 26, 1995. http://www.gov.cn/zhengce/content/2010-11/12/content_6997.htm.

General Office of the State Council. *Notice Concerning Several Issues to be Clarified for the Purpose of Implementing the PRC Arbitration Law*, June 1996. http://cicc.court.gov.cn/html/1/219/199/200/653.html.

Gu, Weixia, *Arbitration in China: The Regulation of Arbitration Agreements and Practical Issues*. London: Sweet & Maxwell, 2012.

Gu, Weixia. "Arbitration in China." In *International Commercial Arbitration in Asia*, 3rd ed, edited by Shahla Ali and Tom Ginsburg, 77–132. New York: Juris Publishing, 2013).

Guangzhou Arbitration Commission. *2015 Guangzhou Internet Arbitration Rules* 广州仲裁委员会网络仲裁规则 2015, accessed July 4, 2020. http://www.gzac.org/WEB_CN/AboutInfo.aspx?AboutType=4&KeyID=100b1ae3-9f15-4bfc-bf59-a90273778fa5.

Hu Er Zhong Min Reng (Zhong Ban) Zi No. 5 (沪二中民认(仲协)字第5号民事裁定书) (Shanghai Intermediate People's Court, December 31, 2014). http://www.shiac.org/upload/day_150104/201501040219323425.pdf.

"Huanan Guozhong, Shanghai Maozhong: Duli zhongcai jigou bucunzai shouquan zhishuo" 华南国仲、上海贸仲:独立仲裁机构不存在授权之说 [CIETAC Huanan, CIETAC Shanghai: there is no theory of authorization on independent arbitration organizations]. *Yicai.com*, January 31, 2013. http://www.yicai.com/news/2463616.html.

Jinda rongzi danbao youxian zeren gongzi yu Zhongguo taiping baoxian (Xianggang) youxian gongsi deng shenqing queren zhongcai xieyi xiaoli yishen minshi caiding shu (金达融资担保有限责任公司与中国太平保险(香港)有限公司等申请确认仲裁协议效力一审民事裁定书) (Beijing Intermediate People's Court, May 18, 2015).

"*Jingwai zhongcai jigou jinzhu Zhongguo shichang jiaju jingzheng, zhuanjia yu feixingzhenghua*" 境外仲裁机构进驻中国市场加剧竞争,专家吁非行政化. *Fazhi ribao* 法制日报, September 29, 2015. http://www.chinanews.com/cj/2015/09-29/7549384.shtml.

Jones, Doug. *Commercial Arbitration in Australia*, 2nd ed. Australia: Thomson Reuters, 2012.

Lynch, Katherine. "The New Arbitration Law." *Hong Kong Law Journal* 16 (1996): 104–120.

Mattli, Walter and Thomas Dietz. "Mapping and Assessing the Rise of International Commercial Arbitration in the Globalization Era: An Introduction." In *International Arbitration and Global Governance*, edited by Walter Mattli and Thomas Dietz, 1–21. Oxford: Oxford University Press, 2014.

Minfa Tongze (民法通则) [General Principles of Civil Law] (promulgated by the National People's Congress, April 12, 1986, effective January 1, 1987). http://www.npc.gov.cn/wxzl/wxzl/2000-12/06/content_4470.htm.

Ministry of Justice. *Implementation Measures for the National Uniform Legal Profession Qualification Examination*, April 28, 2018. http://www.gov.cn/gongbao/content/2018/content_5341398.htm.

Minshi Susong Fa (民事诉讼法) [Civil Procedure Law] (promulgated by the National People's Congress, April 9, 1991, effective April 9, 1991). http://www.lawinfochina.com/display.aspx?lib=law&id=19&CGid=.

Norton Rose Fulbright. *China Arbitration: new Judicial Guidance on the CIETAC Split*, August 2015. http://www.nortonrosefulbright.com/knowledge/publications/131227/china-arbitration-new-judicial-guidance-on-the-cietac split.

Renmin Fayuan Zuzhi Fa (人民法院组织法) [Organic Law of People's Courts] (promulgated by the Standing Committee of the National People's Congress, July 5, 1979, effective January 1, 1980). http://www.npc.gov.cn/zgrdw/englishnpc/Law/2007-12/13/content_1384078.htm.

Reyes, Anselmo and Gu, Weixia. "Conclusion: An Asia Pacific Model of Arbitration Reform." In *The Developing World of Arbitration: A Comparative Study of Arbitration Reform in the Asia Pacific*, edited by Anselmo Reyes and Gu Weixia, 279–300. Oxford: Hart Publishing, 2018.

"Shanghai Maozhong gengming: Xiayue qiyong xinguize xinmingce" 上海贸仲更名: 下月启用新规则新名册. *Yicai.com*, April 12, 2013. http://www.yicai.com/news/2621445.html.

Shenzhen Court of International Arbitration. *Huanan Guozhong ju Xianggang fayuan zhixing neidi zhongcai caijue shuliang zhi shou* 华南国仲居香港法院执行内地仲裁裁决数量之首', January 22, 2015. http://www.sccietac.org/web/news/notice_detail/1517.html.

Shenzhen Court of International Arbitration. *Instructions for the Panel of Arbitrators*, accessed July 4, 2020. http://www.scia.com.cn/files/fckFile/file/%E6%B7%B1%E5%9C%B3%E5%9B%BD%E9%99%85%E4%BB%B2%E8%A3%81%E9%99%A22019%E4%BB%B2%E8%A3%81%E5%91%98%E5%90%8D%E5%86%8C.pdf.

Shenzhen Court of International Arbitration. *SCIA Arbitration Rules (effective from Feb. 21, 2019)*, February 21, 2019. http://www.sccietac.org/index.php/Home/index/rule/id/791.html.

Shenzhen Court of International Arbitration. *Shenzhen guoji zhongcaiyuan zhongcai guize (2016 nian 12 yue 1 ri qi shixing)* 深圳国际仲裁院仲裁规则(2016年12月1日起施行), December 1, 2016. http://www.sccietac.org/index.php/Home/index/rule/id/798.html.

Shenzhen Court of International Arbitration. *Shenzhen guoji zhongcaiyuan zhongcai guize (2016 nian 12 yue1 ri qi shixing)* 深圳国际仲裁院仲裁规则(2016年12月1日起施行). http://www.sccietac.org/index.php/Home/index/rule/id/798.html.

"Shewai zhongcai nao 'fen zhi': zhengyi beihou shenfen chengmi" 涉外仲裁闹'分治':争议背后身份成谜. *Yicai.com*, May 4, 2012. http://www.yicai.com/news/1691426.html.

Smit, Hans. "Contractual Modifications of the Arbitral Process." In *Building the Civilization of Arbitration*, edited by Thomas Carbonneau and Angelica Sinopole, 1–16. London: Wildy, Simmonds & Hill Publishing, 2010.

Song, Lianbin, Peng Liming, Stuart Dutson and Jean-Marc Deschandol, "Annual Review on Commercial Arbitration." In *Commercial Dispute Resolution in China: An Annual Review and Preview*, edited by Beijing Arbitration Commission Institute of Advanced Legal Studies, 1–28, LexisNexis, 2013.

Supreme People's Court. *Interpretation on Certain Issues Concerning the Application of the Arbitration Law*, August 23, 2006. http://www.asianlii.org/cn/legis/cen/laws/iotspccsmoaotalotproc1305/.

Supreme People's Court. *Interpretations of the Supreme People's Court on Several Issues Concerning Application of the Law of the People's Republic of China on Choice of Law for Foreign-Related Civil Relationships (I)*, December 28, 2012. https://www.chinacourt.org/law/detail/2012/12/id/146055.shtml.

Supreme People's Court. *Interpretations to Several Issues on the Application of the China Arbitration Law (Draft Provisions for Opinion Solicitation)*, July 22, 2004.

Supreme People's Court. *Notice on Certain Issues Relating to Correct Handling of Judicial Review of Arbitration Matters*, September 4, 2013. http://cicc.court.gov.cn/html/1/218/62/84/666.html.

Supreme People's Court. *Opinions of the Supreme People's Court on Some Issues Concerning the Application of the Civil Procedure Law of the People's Republic of China*, July 14, 1992. http://www.lawinfochina.com/display.aspx?id=6690&lib=law.

Supreme People's Court. *Provision on Cases Relating to the Pre-Reporting System of Arbitration*, November 20, 2017. https://www.chinacourt.org/law/detail/2017/12/id/149641.shtml.

Supreme People's Court. *Relevant Provisions of the Supreme People's Court on Issues concerning Applications for Verification of Arbitration Cases under Judicial Review*, December 26, 2017. https://www.chinacourt.org/law/detail/2017/12/id/149641.shtml.

Supreme People's Court. *Zuigao renmin fayuan guanyu chengren he zhixing waiguo zhongcai caijue shoufei ji shencha qixian wenti de guiding* 最高人民法院关于承认和执行外国仲裁裁决收费及审查期限问题的规定, November 14, 1998. http://cicc.court.gov.cn/html/1/218/62/84/660.html.

Supreme People's Court. *Zuigao renmin fayuan guanyu renmin fayuan chuli yu shewai zhongcai ji waiguo zhongcai shixiang youguan wenti de tongzhi* 最高人民法院关于人民法院处理与涉外仲裁及外国仲裁事项有关问题的通知, August 28, 1995. http://www.people.com.cn/zixun/flfgk/item/dwjjf/falv/9/9-2-1-05.html.

Supreme People's Court. *Zuigao renmin fayuan guanyu renmin fayuan chexiao shewai zhongcai caijue youguan shixiang de tongzhi* 最高人民法院关于人民法院撤销涉外仲裁裁决有关事项的通知, April 23, 1998. http://cicc.court.gov.cn/html/1/218/62/84/663.html.

Supreme People's Court. *Zuigaoyuan jiu maozhongwei Huanan fenhui, Shanghai fenhui tiaokuan anjian de guanxia ji caijue de sifa jiandu shensha wenti zuochu pifu* 最高院就贸仲委华南分会、上海分会条款案件的管辖及裁决的司法监督审查问题作出批复, July 17, 2015. http://cn.cietac.org/NewsFiles/NewsDetail.asp?NewsID=1532.

Sweet, Alec Stone and Florian Grisel. *The Evolution of International Arbitration: Judicialization, Governance, Legitimacy*. Oxford: Oxford University Press, 2017.

"The Chartered Institute of Arbitrators." The Chartered Institute of Arbitrators, accessed December 10, 2016. http://www.ciarb.org.

Qi, Tong. "How Exactly Does China Consent to Investor-State Arbitration: On the First ICSID Case against China." *Contemporary Asia Arbitration Journal* 5 (2012): 265–291.

Trakman, Leon. "Australia's Contribution to International Commercial Arbitration in Asia." Presentation, The Developing World of Arbitration: A Comparative Study of the Arbitration Reform in China and Asia Pacific, Hong Kong, October 27, 2015.

United Nations Commission on International Trade Law. *UNCITRAL Model Law on International Commercial Arbitration 1985 with amendments as adopted in 2006*, accessed November 17, 2016. https://www.uncitral.org/pdf/english/texts/arbitration/ml-arb/07-86998_Ebook.pdf.

"Visions and Actions on Jointly Building Silk Road Economic Belt and 21st-Century Maritime Silk Road." National Development and Reform Commission (NDRC) People's Republic of China, March 28, 2015. http://en.ndrc.gov.cn/newsrelease/201503/t20150330_669367.html.

Wang, Shengchang. "The Globalization of Economy and China's International Arbitration." Paper delivered, Globalization and Arbitration, Beijing, jointly sponsored by the ICC and CIETAC, October 15, 2002.

Wenzhou Arbitration Commission. *2015 Wenzhou Financial Arbitration Rules* 温州仲裁委员会金融仲裁规则 2015, accessed August 19, 2015. http://www.wzac.org/News_Detail.aspx?CateID=18&ID=397.

"Wuhan Zhongcaiwei shouanshu lianxu shinian weiju quanguo diyi" 武汉仲裁委受案数连续十年位居全国第一. *Changjiang Daily* 长江日报, February 7. 2013, http://news.ifeng.com/gundong/detail_2013_02/07/22024260_0.shtml.

Ximenzi guoji maoyi (Shanghai) youxian gongsi yu Shanghai huangjin zhidi youxian gongsi shenqing chengren he zhixing waiguo zhongcai caijue an (西门子国际贸易(上海)有限公司与上海黄金置地有限公司申请承认和执行外国仲裁裁决案) [*Siemens International Trading (Shanghai) Co Ltd v Shanghai Golden Landmark Co Ltd*] (Shanghai Intermediate People's Court, November 27, 2015).

"Yidai yilu changyi de tichu" "一带一路"倡议的提出. The History of Commerce, accessed July 4, 2020. http://history.mofcom.gov.cn/?newchina=%E4%B8%80%E5%B8%A6%E4%B8%80%E8%B7%AF%E5%80%A1%E8%AE%AE%E7%9A%84%E6%8F%90%E5%87%BA.

Yu, Jianlong 于健龙. *CIETAC Annual Work Report and Work Plan (2009–2018)*, 2010. http://cn.cietac.org/.

Zhongcai Fa (仲裁法) [Arbitration Law] (promulgated by the Standing Committee of the National People's Congress, August 31, 1994, effective September 1, 1995). http://www.npc.gov.cn/wxzl/wxzl/2000-12/05/content_4624.htm.

Zhongguo renmin baoxian gongsi Guangdongsheng fengongzi yu Guangdong guanghe dianli youxian gongsi deng baoxian hetong jiufen an (中国人民保险公司广东省分公司与广东广合电力有限公司等保险合同纠纷案) [*People's Insurance Company of China, Guangzhou v Guanghope Power et al*] (Shanghai Intermediate People's Court, December 31, 2014).

Züblin International GmbH v Wuxi Woco-Tongyong Rubber Engineering Co Ltd, Xi Min San Zhong Zi No. 1 (Wuxi Intermediate People's Court, July 19, 2006).

5 Mediation

Scattered regime and socio-political orientations

1 Introduction

1.1 Preliminaries

Mediation is a form of third-party intervention conducted with the consent of the interested parties and assisted by a neutral entity, the mediator, who has no determinative power over the outcome of the dispute process. The mediation process emphasizes harmonious relationship building and generally tries to avoid a "win-lose" outcome in the dispute resolution.[1] Chinese culture traditionally favors benevolence and harmony between predefined social relations, as a result of the influence of Confucianism.[2] Cohen had argued more than half a century ago that Chinese mediation had historically been at the core of the Chinese legal tradition,[3] which is still valid today. A first feature of Chinese mediation is that it is rooted in Chinese legal tradition.

Contemporary literature has identified the culture-laden feature of mediation, where mediation has been argued to be the most effective process in assisting parties to work toward a mutually sustainable solution, and has a special value in the context of relationship-keeping cultural settings such as the Chinese society.[4] In the meantime, literature has shown that the Chinese approach to mediation is fairly different to the international understanding of that process. Mediation as practiced in the Western jurisdictions is regarded to be cooperative, voluntary, and party-centered. Mediators are expected to be mainly facilitators and to respect the autonomy and choice of the parties. Even in evaluative mediation in the West, mediators are required

---

1 Carrie Menkel-Meadow, *Mediation and Its Applications for Good Decision Making and Dispute Resolution* (Cambridge: Intersensia, 2016).
2 Chen Albert H.Y., "Confucian Legal Culture and Its Modern Fate," in *The New Legal Order in Hong Kong*, ed. Raymond Wacks (Hong Kong: Hong Kong University Press, 1999), 515, 517–18.
3 Jerome Alan Cohen, "Chinese Mediation on the Eve of Modernisation," *California Law Review* 54, no. 3 (1966): 1201–1226.
4 Jacqueline Nolan-Haley, "Mediation: The Best and Worst of Times," *Cardozo Journal of Conflict Resolution* 16, no. 1 (2014): 731–740.

not to be adjudicatory.[5] However, Chinese mediation is more "adjudicatory, aggressive, and interventionist."[6] A second feature of the mediation in
China thus lies in its persisting and distinctive "evaluative" approach in the
mediatory intervention, which is contrary to the understanding of evaluative mediation in the modern international ADR discourse.[7]

More subtly, the Party's concern with leadership popularity and social
stability in an authoritarian state such as China has furthered its reliance
on mediation. Lubman had earlier argued the political-socialism distinction of the Chinese mediation in Communist China under Mao.[8] The view
was shared by Fu with respect to the Chinese mediation in the post-Mao
era.[9] Confucianism favors less contentious means in dispute resolution
with an emphasis on mediation. While the ends are the same, the state
governance justification to promote mediation is more instrumentalist.
The Hu Jintao–Wen Jiabo administration (the "Hu–Wen administration")
(2002–12) propagandized "harmonious society" (*hexie shehui* 和谐社会)
and prioritized mediation to maintain social order.[10] Under the current
Xi Jingping leadership (2012–13 till now), the Party's concern with political stability has intensified in context of its "China dreams" (*zhongguo
meng* 中国梦) slogan. Fu and Cullen argued that the reliance on mediation reflected a growing lack of faith in the capacity of the law to solve
the growing and intensifying social conflicts that had accompanied the
massive economic development and societal change.[11] Fu further argued,
together with Palmer, that the Party-State has officially promoted mediation as a way of suppressing discontent which is infused with its political control, justified by a responsibility to maintain stability and promote
harmony.[12] Mediation is used to promote better governability of the civil
society and to reduce visible and publicized conflicts that might potentially reduce the legitimacy of the Party-State. As such, a third and more

---

5 Jacqueline Nolan-Haley, *Alternative Dispute Resolution in A Nutshell*, 2nd ed. (Minnesota: West Academic, 2017), 60–63.
6 Fu Hualing and Richard Cullen, "From Mediatory to Adjudicatory Justice: The Limits of Civil Justice Reform in China," in *Chinese Justice: Civil Dispute Resolution in Contemporary China*, eds. Margaret Woo and Mary Gallagher (Cambridge: Cambridge University Press, 2011), 33.
7 See Michael Palmer and Simon Roberts, *Dispute Processes: ADR and The Primary Forms of Decision Making*, 3rd ed. (Cambridge: Cambridge University Press, 2020), Chapter 7.
8 Stanley Lubman, "Mao and Mediation: Politics and Dispute Resolution in Communist China," *California Law Review* 55, no. 5 (1967): 1284–1359.
9 Fu Hualing, "Understanding People's Mediation in Post-Mao China," *Columbia Journal of Asian Law* 5, no. 2 (1992): 211.
10 Hu's thoughts were added to the 2018 amendment to the Chinese Constitution.
11 Fu and Cullen, "From Mediatory to Adjudicatory Justice," 32.
12 Fu Hualing and Michael Palmer, "Introduction," in *Mediation in Contemporary China: Continuity and Change*, eds. Fu Hualing and Michael Palmer (London: Wildy, Simmonds & Hill Publishing, 2017), 2.

important feature of the Chinese mediation (more accurately, the contemporary Chinese mediation) is that it has been consistently under political imperatives, even more so than before.

Mediation is thus designed to meet both the cultural legacy and political needs of dispute resolution in China. In the meantime, unlike civil litigation and commercial arbitration, both of which have unified governance at the national level, mediation is not a unified regime in China. Rather, it is composed of many different types under various programs, regulated or non-regulated. Among the Asian jurisdictions where mediation have been significantly promoted and reformed in the past decade, Hong Kong passed a Mediation Ordinance (effective in 2013),[13] and Japan passed a unified ADR Act (effective in 2007).[14] In contrast, China has neither developed a standalone and unified civil mediation law to govern mediation (as in Hong Kong) nor regulated mediation in a unified statute on ADR (as in Japan), despite her continuing emphasis and reliance on mediation. In China, mediation is a rather scattered regime consisting of various types and initiatives in search of reform at different levels and in different scales, which is the fourth but distinctive feature of the Chinese mediation (or more accurately, as it is practiced today).

In 2017, the leading research book on mediation in China co-edited by Fu and Palmer, *Mediation in Contemporary China: Continuity and Change*, studied those different types and initiatives of mediation developed domestically in China over the past decade, and the Chinese authorities' revived concerns with social stability and harmonious society in all these types of mediation.[15] As this author summarizes from Fu and Palmer's edited book, and through her personal research and practice experience, today, six different types of mediation exist in China. Each has a different context within which mediation is used for handling specific disputes. They are (1) people's mediation (*renmin tiaojie* 人民调解); (2) administrative mediation (*xingzheng tiaojie* 行政调解); (3) judicial mediation (*sifa tiaojie* 司法调解); (4) mediation combined with arbitration or med-arb (*tiaojie yu zhongcai xiangjiehe or tiaozhong* 调解与仲裁相结合或者调仲); (5) international commercial mediation (*guoji shangshi tiaojie* 国际商事调解); and (6) private mediation (*siren tiaojie* 私人调解).

People's mediation (type 1) is carried out by people's mediation committees. This is primarily a form of local community dispute resolution, as regulated nationally by the People's Mediation Law (2010).[16] Administrative

---

13 Mediation Ordinance (Cap. 620) (Hong Kong).
14 Shusukei Kakiuchi, "Regulating Mediation in Japan: Latest Development and Its Background," in *New Developments in Civil and Commercial Mediation*, eds. Carlos Esplugues and Louis Marquis (New York: Springer, 2015), 367–368.
15 Fu Hualing and Michael Palmer, eds., *Mediation in Contemporary China: Continuity and Change* (London: Wildy, Simmonds & Hill Publishing, 2017).
16 See discussions on people's mediation later in this chapter.

mediation (type 2) is conducted by government officials. This is often focused on disputes in specific areas of Chinese government administration in various socio-civil-legal contexts, such as labor relations and consumer protection,[17] with the more prominent example as labor mediation legalized nationally by the Labor Dispute Mediation and Arbitration Law (2008).[18] Judicial mediation (type 3) is carried out by Chinese judges in and around Chinese courts, and is a distinctive feature of the Chinese justice system (the "mediatory justice").[19] Med-arb (type 4) is a hybrid dispute resolution process where mediation is combined with commercial arbitration under the auspices of the Chinese arbitration commissions, and is a popular means of commercial dispute resolution in China.[20] International commercial mediation (type 5) is conducted by some specialized international mediation centers which are set up to mediate China-related international trade and commercial disputes, such as the Mediation Center set up by the China Council for the Promotion of International Trade ("CCPIT").[21] Private mediations (type 6) are carried out without any specific institutional support.[22]

Among the six types of mediation illustrated earlier in this chapter, judicial mediation (type 3) and med-arb (type 4) are mediation incorporated into umpiring systems (i.e., into courts and arbitration commissions) and will be examined in Chapters 6 and 8, respectively.

Specialized international commercial mediation (type 5) such as that carried out by the CCPIT Mediation Center mainly addresses international commercial and trade disputes. Hence, it has not been used on a scale comparable to the Chinese mainstream mediation systems, such as people's mediation and labor mediation (type 1 and type 2); it does not have specialized laws either. In August 2019, China signed the United Nations Convention on International Settlement Agreements Resulting from Mediation (also

---

17 Ling Zhou, *Access to Justice for the Chinese Consumer: Handling Consumer Disputes in Contemporary China* (Oxford: Hart, 2020). In the Introduction, the author identifies consumer mediation as a new type of administrative mediation in China.

18 See discussions on labor mediation later in this chapter.

19 Fu and Cullen, "From Mediatory to Adjudicatory Justice," 39–42. See discussions in Chapter 6. See also discussions in Chapter 3.

20 Gu Weixia, "The Delicate Art of Med-Arb and Its Future Institutionalization in China," *UCLA Pacific Basin Law Journal* 31, no. 2 (2014): 97–99. See also discussions in Chapter 7.

21 Mediation Center set up by the China Council for the Promotion of International Trade ("CCPIT") as early as 1987; and Shanghai Commercial Mediation Center set up by the Shanghai Municipal Government Commission of Commerce since 2011.

22 For example, there is the novel but already very popular bottom-up phenomenon of "reality television mediation" on family disputes, which has a combination of education and entertainment forms. The programs attract high audience ratings. Both the TV station and TV mediators are given nationwide acclamation. See Zhao Yixian, "Divorce Disputes and Popular Legal Culture of the Weak: A Case Study of Chinese Reality TV Mediation," in *Mediation in Contemporary China: Continuity and Change*, eds. Fu Hualing and Michael Palmer (London: Wildy, Simmonds & Hill Publishing, 2017), 319–341.

known as the "Singapore Mediation Convention") to show her commitment to promote international commercial mediation, and to advocate the adoption of the same in transnational disputes arising out of the ambitious Belt and Road Initiative development led by China. Despite the foregoing, China has never promulgated specific domestic laws to govern commercial mediations. The primary mediation-related legislations in China, as will be discussed later, all appear to gear toward resolving domestic civil disputes and facilitate social stability maintenance.

Efforts on private mediation (type 6) are mostly laissez-faire and scattered, which have not had consolidated developments legislatively or institutionally.

The global trend to formalize ADR shares the aim that, by increasing the availability of mediation for disputants, the caseload of courts can be reduced and hence access to justice can be improved.[23] In contrast, the Chinese developments over the past two decades tend to focus on political imperatives of retaining social harmony and containing societal disputes. As with the theme of this book, the extent to which Chinese mediation develops is also largely shaped by the socio-political and socio-economic conditions of China.

As the book focuses on civil dispute resolution in China, this chapter focuses on the laws of and developments in people's mediation (type 1) and labor mediation (type 2), which are the two Chinese mainstream mediation systems for resolving domestic civil disputes (though labor relations are in between the governance by civil law and administrative law and labor mediation is in essence an administrative mediation in China). Judicial mediation and med-arb are to be explored in Chapters 6 and 8.

Over the past one to two decades, in response to the rapid socio-political and socio-economic changes, there have been top-down attempts in China to legalize the people's mediation and labor mediation systems, to make them more formalized and institutionalized, and to give them more legitimacy and legal force. This chapter examines the extent of legalization, professionalization and formalization, as well as the contextual factors that have led to the development and reform patterns. In doing so, it gauges the effectiveness and identifies major technical and systematical weaknesses. This chapter concludes that China's contemporary mediation, though deep-rooted in Chinese culture and tradition, is not a unified regime. More subtly, the two mainstream domestic mediation systems of people's mediation and labor mediation have in fact been manipulated by political orientations. Mediators (whether in people's mediation or labor mediation) have to consider the social and political impact of what they mediate, even more so than before.

---

23 Michael Palmer and Simon Roberts, *Dispute Processes: ADR and the Primary Forms of Decision Making*, 3rd ed. (Cambridge: Cambridge University Press, 2020), Chapter 7.

Table 5.1 People's mediation statistics (2008–2018)

Year	Total number of PMCs	Total number of civil disputes mediated by PMCs
2008	827,412	4,981,370
2009	824,000	5,797,300
2010	818,130	8,418,393
2011	811,000	8,935,341
2012	817,121	9,265,855
2013	820,025	9,439,429
2014	802,957	9,404,544
2015	798,417	9,331,047
2016	784,000	9,019,000
2017	759,000	8,741,000
2018	752,000	9,532,000

1.2 Empirical evidence

1.2.1 People's mediation

Empirical evidence on the use of people's mediation is available in the China Law Yearbook (covering the statistics from 2008 to 2015) and China Statistical Yearbook (covering the statistics from 2016 to 2018). Table 5.1 compiles the annual total number of the people's mediation committees ("PMCs") in China and civil disputes that PMCs mediated in the most recent decade as compiled by the author using the relevant data from the Yearbooks.

Due to its strong cultural roots, the people's mediation system had existed in China for resolving civil disputes prior to the existence of State-level regulatory documents to govern the same.[24] The People's Mediation Law ("PML"), which started to officially legalize China's people's mediation system at the state-level, was promulgated in 2010, in the context of the then "harmonious society" national propaganda and "grand mediation" national campaign[25] under the Hu–Wen administration (2002–2012) where mediation was widely promoted and even prioritized to maintain social stability. Despite the overall societal atmosphere, in order to ascertain the direct impact (if any) of the PML alone on access to justice in the people's mediation system, the chronological figures compiled in the most recent decade is extended to cover the period from two years before the promulgation of the PML (2008 and 2009) to the most recent time when nation-wide data in the field are available (2018) so that a comparative sense might be obtained.

24 Cohen, "Chinese Mediation on the Eve of Modernisation."; Lubman, "Mao and Mediation," 1284–1359.
25 See Section 4.2.2 of this chapter.

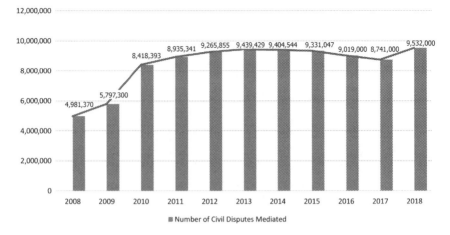

Chart 5.1 Number of civil disputes mediated by PMCs (2008–2018)

As shown in Table 5.1, there were 4,981,370 and 5,797,300 civil disputes mediated by the PMCs throughout China in 2008 and 2009, respectively. The caseload figures significantly increased since the PML was enacted in 2010. Statistics show that in 2011 alone (one year after PML's enactment), PMCs mediated more than 8.935 million cases, approximately twice as many as they did in 2008 (4,981 thousand). The caseload kept on growing and further increased to more than 9.265 million in 2012, maintained the same high level throughout the next few years, and reached the peak of 9.532 million in 2018 (except in 2017 when the caseload number went below 9 million). Chart 5.1 shows a clear upward trend of the civil dispute caseload handled by the people's mediation system since the PML was promulgated. As such, empirically, the PML has led to a significant growth of the adoption or usage of the people's mediation system in China. This empirical finding is important as it reflects the positive link between legalization and formalization of the civil dispute resolution system and the relevant enhancement of access to justice.

On the other hand, the total number of the PMCs is on a downward slope. As shown in Table 5.1, in 2008 and 2009, there were over 820,000 PMCs throughout China. The figures slightly decreased and maintained between 810,000 and 820,000 PMCs from 2010 till 2013. The figures kept on going down, decreasing from 802,000 in 2014; 798,000 in 2015; 784,000 in 2016; and further decreasing to around 750,000 in 2017 in 2018. Hence, empirically, the promulgation of the PML and its associated legalization and institutionalization of the people's mediation system have not brought about the increase of its handling institutions (PMCs). On the contrary, the number of the PMCs is declining rather quickly (see Chart 5.2).

As will be explained later in this chapter, while the PMCs have served as powerful socio-political institutions to mobilize the masses in China to maintain

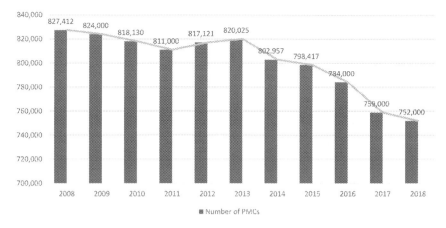

Chart 5.2 Number of PMCs (2008–2018)

social stability, under the present PML, the PMCs are insufficiently funded, and people's mediators do not enjoy occupational security. Their incentive of involvement in the mediation work is largely derived from their sense of social responsibility toward the achievement of a harmonious society.[26] The empirical results stand in stark contrast with those of the arbitration landscape in Chapter 4, where the promulgation of the Arbitration Law has led to significant increases in both the caseload of arbitration and total number of the Chinese arbitration commissions.[27] While mediation and arbitration are both treated as important dispute resolution mechanisms in China to handle civil and commercial disputes, as arbitration focused solely on commercial disputes, there are in fact very different social functions performed by the PMCs vis-à-vis the Chinese arbitration commissions, as well as the different social roles of the people's mediators vis-à-vis the arbitrators.[28, 29, 30]

1.2.2 Labor mediation

Empirical statistics on China's adoption of labor mediation is provided by neither the China Law Yearbook nor China Statistical Yearbook. But some related statistics are found in the China Labor Statistical Yearbook. Similar

26 See Sections 4.1 and 5.1 of this chapter. See also Fu Yulin, "Dispute Resolution and China's Grassroots Legal Services," in *Chinese Justice: Civil Dispute Resolution in Contemporary China*, eds. Margaret Woo and Mary Gallagher (Cambridge: Cambridge University Press, 2011), 335–338.
27 See Table 4.1 and Chart 4.4.
28 China Law Society, *The Law Yearbook of China* (2010–2018) (showing the statistics of 2009–2017); National Bureau of Statistics of China, *China Statistical Yearbook* (2016–2019).
29 Ibid.
30 Ibid.

Table 5.2 Labor dispute statistics (2007–2017)

Year	Total number of labor disputes filed	Total number of labor disputes concluded	Total number of labor disputes concluded by labor mediation and arbitration under LDMAL
2007	350,182	340,030	119,436
2008	693,465	622,719	221,284
2009	684,379	689,714	251,463
2010	600,865	634,041	250,131
2011	589,244	592,823	278,873
2012	641,202	643,292	302,552
2013	665,760	669,062	311,806
2014	715,163	711,044	321,598
2015	813,859	812,461	362,814
2016	828,410	827,717	389,109
2017	785,323	790,448	390,278

to people's mediation, labor mediation practices had existed before the Labor Dispute Mediation and Arbitration Law ("LDMAL") was enacted in 2008.[31] However, in the context of the "harmonious society" atmosphere in the 2000s, the LDMAL was promulgated with the aim to institutionalize the labor mediation and arbitration systems.

Table 5.2 compiles the annual caseload of all labor disputes that were filed in China (the second column), concluded in China (the third column), and those concluded through labor mediation and arbitration under the LDMAL (the fourth column), in the most recent decade where the data are available under the China Labor Statistical Yearbook (2007–2017).

As Table 5.2 shows, within the first year of LDMAL's enactment, the total number of labor disputes filed in China doubled from 350,182 in 2007 to 693,465 in 2008. There was then a decrease to a low of around 589,000 in 2011, before reaching the peak of more than 828,000 in 2016. On the other hand, the total number of concluded labor disputes in China rose significantly since 2008. However, these data (the second and third columns in Table 5.2) had included labor disputes handled through various Chinese labor dispute resolution channels (such as litigation, mediation, arbitration, and other means) and were not exclusively applied to labor mediation cases. In the meantime, while the China Labor Statistical Yearbook did calculate the total number of labor disputes concluded by labor mediation and arbitration under the LDMAL, the data did not divide the caseload among labor mediation, labor arbitration, and labor mediation and arbitration combined. As such, it is hard to discern that empirically, to what extent the LDMAL promulgation has impacted on the total number of labor mediation cases, so as to reflect the enhancement in the workers' access to seek redress for labor

---

31 See Section 2.2 of this chapter.

rights through labor mediation, despite a clear upward trend in the number of overall labor disputes (both filed and concluded) since 2008.[32]

2 Regulatory background

As explained, other than judicial mediation and med-arb, people's mediation and labor mediation are the two Chinese mainstream mediation systems for resolving domestic civil disputes which have developed formal laws in the past two decades. They are different from the regulatory and development patterns of judicial mediation and med-arb too.

2.1 People's mediation

People's mediation is conducted by PMCs on the basis of parties' consent, and with a view to secure voluntary agreements. It develops from its foundations in traditional Chinese legal culture of community mediation. The State Council started to legalize people's mediation as early as 1989 by promulgating the Organic Regulations on People's Mediation, which laid down the community nature of the people's mediation system.[33] The PMCs were established under neighborhood committees for urban areas, and village committees for rural areas, under the supervision of its corresponding Basic People's Court and Basic People's Government.[34] The design of the PMCs allow disputes that arise at the community-level to be resolved without relying on more formal institutions such as the court system, and aims to promote a more stable Chinese society.[35]

However, the popularity of people's mediation declined in the 1990s, in contrast to the increasing adoption of the ADR mechanisms around the world at the same time. Under an increasingly mobilized "stranger society" in China in the 1990s, litigation was more favored and no longer considered shameful or dishonorable.[36] Meanwhile, litigation proved to be insufficient in providing a satisfactory solution to the influx of disputes. People's mediation struggled to respond to the rapidly changing social circumstances of China in the 1990s, and resulted in a relative decline in its usage since the 1990s until the mid-2000s. According to statistics from the China Law Yearbook, 2,824,162 family disputes were mediated through people's mediation in 1991, which was reduced to 1,005,181 in 2007, recording a 64.4%

---

32 Department of Population and Employment Statistics and Ministry of Human Resources and Social Security, *China Labor Statistical Yearbook* (2008–2018).

33 Organic Regulations on People's Mediation (*Remin Tiaojie Weiyuanhui Zuzhi Tiaoli* 人民调解委员会组织条例), promulgated by the State Council, in June 1989.

34 Ibid., art. 2.

35 Ibid., art. 1 cites promoting the "unity of the people" and the "protection of social stability" as motivations for institutionalizing PMCs.

36 Di Xiaohua and Wu Yuning, "*The Developing Trend of the People's Mediation in China*," *Sociological Focus* 42, no. 1 (2009): 228.

reduction. Similarly, people's mediation resolved 859,857 disputes over homestead matters in 1991 and that figure dropped to 350,105 in 2007, a 59.3% decrease,[37] before the statistics gradually rose after the promulgation of the People's Mediation Law (previously referred to as the "PML") in 2010.

With the danger of social discontent and conflicts arose out of overly rapid economic development and growingly complex social structures, the Chinese government adopted a different approach toward people's mediation, with efforts to provide some normative framework to the people's mediation system so as to better regularize it.

In 2002, two rounds of reforms were introduced which aimed to impose greater institutional control over the people's mediation system in China. The first round was the 2002 SPC Judicial Interpretation Regarding Some Provisions on Trying Civil Cases Involving the People's Mediation Agreements (the "2002 Interpretation").[38] The 2002 Interpretation clarified the legal status of mediation settlement agreements reached at the PMCs, by granting them a status equivalent to that of civil contracts which could not be arbitrarily changed or absolved by the parties.[39] It also emphasized the voluntariness of the mediation settlement agreement, such that coercion in the mediation process and harm to the public interest would void its effect.[40] The second round of the reform was marked by the released of the document titled Some Provisions Concerning the Work of People's Mediation issued by the Ministry of Justice in the same year.[41] It sought to make people's mediation more attractive by standardizing the mediation procedure. Specific provisions were made to outline the scope of disputes available under people's mediation such as family and neighborhood disputes[42] and a one-month time limit was set for people's mediation of a case.[43]

Before the promulgation of the PML in 2010, there were concerns over legalization and institutionalization of the people's mediation system. In particular, there are concerns that legalization would lead to a rigidified mediation procedure, which would be contradictory to its underlying rationale.[44] In the initial legislative draft of the PML, the mediation process had been characterized as formalized, limiting the flexibility of the mediation process.

---

37 China Law Society, *The Law Yearbook of China* (1991–2007).

38 Supreme People's Court, *Interpretation Regarding Some Provisions on Trying Civil Cases Involving the People's Mediation Agreements* 最高人民法院关于审理涉及人民调解协议的民事案件的若干规定, http://www.npc.gov.cn/zgrdw/huiyi/lfzt/rmtjfzfjc/2010-06/17/content_1577196.htm.

39 Ibid., art. 1.

40 Ibid., art. 7.

41 Ministry of Justice, *Some Provisions Concerning the Work of People's Mediation*, September 26, 2002, http://www.lawinfochina.com/display.aspx?lib=law&id=2465&CGid=.

42 Ibid., art. 20.

43 Ibid., art. 33.

44 Fan Yu 范愉, "An Evaluation of the People's Mediation Law of China" 《中华人民共和国人民调解法》评析, *The Jurist* 法学家 no. 2 (2011): 1.

The final version of the PML, in an attempt to dilute the impression of people's mediation being too legalistic in nature, supported a more flexible and less standardized process of mediation.[45]

2.2 Labor mediation

Compared to people's mediation, labor mediation was legalized in China even earlier. In 1994, China published its first statute governing labor relations. The 1994 Labor Law already outlined a three-step process for handling labor dispute resolution.[46] The three steps consisted of labor mediation, followed by labor arbitration through labor arbitration committees overseen by local Labor Bureaus, and civil court adjudication in the event of an appeal of an unsatisfactorily arbitrated decision.[47] The process can be explained as follows. First, the parties can apply to the labor dispute mediation committee for labor mediation once a labor dispute arises. Second, if the dispute cannot be settled through mediation and a party asks for arbitration, application can be filed to a labor dispute arbitration commission for arbitration. Third, if any party refuses to enforce the labor arbitral award obtained in the prior step, an application should be made to a relevant people's court to enforce the arbitral award.[48]

The past two decades have seen the rise of labor disputes through both official and unofficial channels. The phenomenal economic growth in China transformed the labor relations from one under the planned economy to a freer, more market-oriented economy. Through replacing the traditional allocation of jobs by the state with a labor contract system to enhance efficiency and flexibility, the economic reform brought about various labor issues, including unemployment, poor working conditions, and generally, reduced labor rights and benefits of the workers.[49] All these socio-economic conditions resulted in a rise in the number and an increase

---

45 For example, the legislative bill originally stated that people's mediation should be based on "law, regulations, rules, and policies, as well as follow social morality, community agreements, and society's good customs without breaking the law, regulations, and rules." This is later modified into conducting mediation "without infringing the law, regulations, and state policies" as presented in the current PML.

46 Laodong Fa (劳动法) [Labour Law] (promulgated by the National People's Congress Standing Committee, May 7, 1994, effective January 1, 1995, http://www.lawinfochina.com/display.aspx?id=705&lib=law.

47 Zhao Yun, "China's New Labor Dispute Resolution Law: A Catalyst for the Establishment of Harmonious Labor Relationship?," *Comparative Labor Law & Policy Journal* 30 (2009): 409, 411–12.

48 Shen Jie, "Labor Litigation in China," in *The Strategies of China's Firms: Resolving Dilemmas*, eds. Yang Hailan, Stephen Morgan and Wang Ying (Cambridge: Chandos Publishing, 2015).

49 Virginia Ho, *Labor Dispute Resolution in China: Implications for Labor Rights and Legal Reform* (California: Institute of East Asian Studies, 2005).

in the complexity of labor disputes, and many involved large-scale protests over non-payment of wages and sub-standard working conditions.[50]

In response to the context of "harmonious society" in the 2000s, the goal of building "harmonious labor relations" became widely espoused by Chinese policymakers as a vital indicator of the country's socio-economic stability. In pursuing this goal, the Chinese government was eager to institutionalize the labor dispute resolution system that corresponded to the state policy of "ruling according to the law" while maintaining social stability. As such, over 400 labor-related legislative documents had been enacted by 2010.[51] This wave reached a climax in 2008, when some most important pieces of labor legislation were enacted, such as the Labor Contract Law, the Labor Dispute Mediation and Arbitration Law, and the Employment Promotion Law.[52] Among all, the Labor Dispute Mediation and Arbitration Law (previously referred to as the "LDMAL"),[53] published in 2008, is the most notable piece enhancing workers' access to seek redress for labor rights violation through official dispute resolution channels.

3 Reform

3.1 People's mediation

In 2010, the PML was promulgated by the National People's Congress Standing Committee and is commonly regarded as one of the most significant legislative achievements in China's mediation development since it represents the official recognition of the need to increase the legitimacy of people's mediation.[54]

---

50 Mary Gallagher, "Changes in the World's Workshop: The Demographic, Social, and Political Factors behind China's Labor Movement," in *Dragon Versus Eagle: The Chinese Economy and U.S.–China Relations*, eds. Huang Wei-Chiao and Zhou Huizhong (Michigan: Upjohn Institute, 2012).

51 Eli Friedman and Lee Ching Kwan, "Remaking the World of Chinese Labour: A 30-Year Retrospective," *British Journal of Industrial Relations* 48, no. 3 (2010): 507–533.

52 Laodong hetong Fa (劳动合同法) [Labor Contract Law] (promulgated by the National People's Congress Standing Committee, June 29, 2007, effective January 1, 2008, amended on December 18, 2012), https://www.6laws.net/6law/law-gb/中華人民共和國勞動合同法.htm; Laodong zhengyi tiaojie zhongcai Fa (劳动争议调解仲裁法) [Labor Dispute Mediation and Arbitration Law] (promulgated by the National People's Congress Standing Committee, December 29, 2007, effective January 5, 2008), http://www.lawinfochina.com/display.aspx?id= 6584&lib=law; Jiuye cujin Fa (就业促进法) [Employment Promotion Law] (promulgated by the National People's Congress Standing Committee, April 24, 2015, effective January 1, 2008), http://www.npc.gov.cn/zgrdw/npc/xinwen/lfgz/flca/2007-03/25/content_362938.htm.

53 Laodong zhengyi tiaojie zhongcai Fa (劳动争议调解仲裁法) [Labor Dispute Mediation and Arbitration Law] (promulgated by the National People's Congress Standing Committee, December 29, 2007, effective May 1, 2008), http://www.lawinfochina.com/display.aspx?id=6584&lib=law&EncodingName=big5.

54 Renmin tiaojie Fa (人民调解法) [People's Mediation Law] (promulgated by the National People's Congress Standing Committee, August 28, 2010, effective January 1, 2011), http://www.lawinfochina.com/display.aspx?id=8266&lib=law.

The PML codifies the principles and rules governing people's mediation. At the outset, the PML sets the goal of the people's mediation system as a dispute resolution "to timely resolve disputes among the people and maintain social harmony and stability."[55] The expression, "disputes among the people," limits on the range of disputes that could be subject to people's mediation. Literature shows that typical types of disputes that people's mediation handles include non-stranger disputes such as those concerning the family and the neighborhood, labor disputes, and disputes of compensation for minor harm.[56] The expression, "maintain social harmony and stability," indicates the political orientation and societal function of people's mediation in China.

The PML lays down a strong institutional and legal basis for the establishment of PMCs in order to mediate civil disputes, and provides guide as to the organization and establishment of the PMCs in China. The PMCs are mainly established in association with residence, such as those in villagers' committees and city neighborhood committees.[57] Trade unions in the enterprises and industry-based specialized sectors, such as those associated with businesses and consumers associations, were not supportive of the idea of establishing PMCs within the enterprises and these sectors. However, the PML bypassed this resistance by prescribing that "work units, enterprises and other organizations may also have the discretion to organize the PMCs to mediate civil disputes based on need."[58] In this way, people's mediation system remains fragmented in different sectors.

As to the mediation process, the PML requires voluntariness as a guiding principle throughout the process.[59] People's mediators may adopt flexible methods and techniques to mediate and promote an agreement according to circumstances.[60] The PML has a pro bono dimension in that people's mediators are not allowed to charge fees for the services they provide.[61] The justice bureaus in the corresponding local level provide vocational training for the people's mediators on a regular basis.[62] Meanwhile, local people's courts offer professional guidance to the PMCs.[63]

Regarding the mediation outcome, mediation settlement agreements are legally binding on the disputants and the PML expressly provides for

55 Ibid., art. 1.
56 Wu Yuning, "People's Mediation Enters the 21st Century," in *Mediation in Contemporary China: Continuity and Change*, eds. Fu Hualing and Michael Palmer (London: Wildy, Simmonds & Hill Publishing, 2017), 34–58.
57 People's Mediation Law, art. 4.
58 Ibid. See also Ministry of Justice, *Report on the Development of People's Mediation System*, October 18, 2012.
59 People's Mediation Law, art. 22.
60 Ibid., arts. 21–22.
61 Ibid., art. 4.
62 Ibid., art. 14.
63 Ibid., art. 10.

the enforcement mechanism.[64] A written or oral agreement can be made by the PMC once there is an agreement between the disputants[65] and the PMC will oversee the fulfillment of the obligations as agreed.[66] This fills the gap in the 2002 Interpretation in which disputants to a mediation settlement agreement could still attempt to back out and avoid enforcement of the civil contract.[67] The 2010 PML further provides for a new procedure whereby disputants can jointly apply to the people's court for judicial confirmation within thirty days from the day the mediation settlement agreement takes effect.[68] The court shall conduct a review of the mediation settlement agreement promptly and confirm the validity according to law. After the court confirmation, if one party fails to perform the agreement, the other party can apply to the court for mandatory enforcement.[69]

The subsequent issuance of the SPC People's Mediation Provision in 2011 further standardizes the procedure for judicial confirmation and enforceability of the PMC mediation settlement agreements.[70] The 2012 CPL confirms the approach achieved through the 2010 PML and 2011 SPC Mediation Provision and brings consistency to the PML reform.[71] As Table 5.1 shows, in 2011 alone (one year after the PML promulgation), PMCs handled approximately twice as many cases as they did in 2008. The year 2011 also evidenced the steady increase of people's mediation to level off.[72]

The revival of the people's mediation is not simply a rehash of the traditional process of mediation. Rather, it has taken some new directions such as an increased institutionalization of the PMCs, a heavier intervention of the government, and an enhanced collaboration between different social and governmental agencies. As will be studied in the subsequent section on reform analyses, these reforms highlight the political and societal orientation of people's mediation in maintaining social stability.

---

64 Ibid., art. 31.
65 Ibid., art. 28.
66 Ibid., art. 31.
67 Zhang Xianchu, "Rethinking the Mediation Campaign," in *Mediation in Contemporary China: Continuity and Change*, eds. Fu Hualing and Michael Palmer (London: Wildy, Simmonds & Hill Publishing, 2017), 59–86.
68 People's Mediation Law., art. 32–33.
69 Ibid.
70 Ibid., art. 33; Supreme People's Court, *Guanyu renmin tiaojie xieyi sifa queren chengxu de ruogan guiding* 关于人民调解协议司法确认程序的若干规定, December 13, 2011, art. 13, http://www.court.gov.cn/shenpan-xiangqing-3473.html.
71 *Minshi Susong Fa* (民事诉讼法) [Civil Procedure Law] (promulgated by the National People's Congress, August 31, 2012, effective October 3, 2012), arts. 194–195, http://www.lawinfochina.com/display.aspx?lib=law&id=19&CGid=; See also discussion in Section 3.1, Chapter 3.
72 See Table 5.1.

3.2 Labor mediation

Aiming to further refine the existing procedures to allow workers to seek redress for labor right violations through official channels, the LDMAL was promulgated by the NPC in 2008 and expanded the scope of disputes that could be submitted to labor mediation and arbitration.[73] Moreover, the LDMAL contained several important reforms.

First and foremost, the emphasis in the official dispute resolution system for labor disputes is on "mediation." Pursuant to the LDMAL, any party is entitled to mediation or arbitration if the parties fail to reach a settlement agreement.[74] Hence, the legislative emphasis is on mediation over the more formal procedures of arbitration and litigation—mediation can be the sole method used in handling a labor dispute, or the primary step in a dispute that in due course might lead to arbitration or litigation.

As to the mediation process and mediation outcome, the LDMAL stresses the voluntariness of the mediation process and crystalizes the effect of the labor mediation settlement agreement.[75] Any agreement reached as a result of the labor mediation must be documented in writing and signed or sealed by the employer, the employee and the mediator, which shall be legally binding upon both the employer and the employee. In some special circumstances, the employee may apply to the people's court directly for an order of payment if the employer fails to perform the mediation settlement agreement within the time limit prescribed in the agreement.[76]

With respect to the procedure leading to a more formal labor dispute resolution, the LDMAL recognizes the previous three-step framework designed by the 1994 Labor Law, namely mediation, arbitration, then litigation. However, the LDMAL also stresses on the consultation before proceeding with the three-step process. Workers are encouraged to engage in consultation with the employer, either directly or by requesting the trade union to jointly engage in the consultation with the employer, in order to reach a settlement agreement.[77] Such an arrangement helps to

---

73 Labor Dispute Mediation and Arbitration Law, art. 2. The eligible labor disputes include: (1) disputes on affirmation of the labor relations; (2) disputes on formation, performance, alternation and termination of the labor contract; (3) disputes concerned with lay-off; (4) disputes regarding working duration, leave arrangement, social insurance, working benefit, training, etc.; (5) disputes on labor remuneration, medical expenses for job-related injury, economic compensation, etc.; and (6) other labor disputes.

74 Ibid., art. 5.

75 Ronald C. Brown, "Resolving Labor Disputes by Mediation, Arbitration, and Litigation," in *Understanding Labor and Employment Law in China*, ed. Ronald C. Brown (Cambridge: Cambridge University Press, 2010), 168, 171.

76 Labor Dispute Mediation and Arbitration Law, art. 16. The special circumstances include payment of labor remuneration, medical expenses for job-related injury, statutory severance payment and punitive compensation.

77 Ibid., art. 4.

offer the workers various options and opportunities to protect their own interests. During the stage of labor arbitration, the policy emphasis is again on mediation. The labor dispute arbitration committee is required to attempt mediation to settle the dispute before a formal adjudication and can issue a mediation settlement agreement if the mediator's efforts prove to be successful.[78]

Most noticeably, a broader range of "labor dispute mediation committees" (the "LDMC") are provided for under the LDMAL. There are three official categories of LDMCs: (1) LDMCs established at the enterprise level; (2) LDMCs set up at the PMCs at the grassroot level as authorized by the relevant laws; and (3) any other bodies for mediating labor disputes established at the township level or in the neighborhood community.[79] According to Zhao, these three categories are all special types of PMCs. While the first category functions with the official trade union system to resolve disputes within the enterprises in-house, and the All-China Federation of Trade Unions (the "ACFTU") has inherently perceived itself as a mediator,[80] the second and third categories belong to the PMCs functioning outside the enterprises without any involvement of the ACFTU, such as those operated by the community or NGOs.[81] This broader scope of LDMCs reflects the continued emphasis of mediation. Such a broad scope opens up various channels by making use of social resources in establishing LDMCs and provides alternatives for workers in private enterprises where there are no internal mediation commissions.[82] The promotion of mediation in labor dispute resolution reflects a broader trend toward mediated settlements in the Chinese legal system in the past decade.[83]

Lastly, new provisions on labor arbitration under the LDMAL extends the period for workers to lodge labor arbitration complaints to one year through the labor arbitration process.[84] Labor arbitration institutions are established by the corresponding level labor administration departments[85] and financially sponsored by the state treasury. Labor arbitration services are thus required

---

78 Ibid., art. 42.
79 Ibid., art. 10.
80 Gonghui Fa (工会法) [Trade Union Law] (promulgated by the National People's Congress, August 27, 2009, effective August 27, 2009), art. 28, http://www.lawinfochina.com/display.aspx?id=22786&lib=law.
81 Zhao, "China's New Labor Dispute Resolution Law," 411–412.
82 Zou Mimi, Pan Xuanming and Han Sirui, "Regulating Collective Labour Disputes in China: A Tale of Two Actors," in *Mediation in Contemporary China: Continuity and Change*, eds. Fu Hualing and Michael Palmer (London: Wildy, Simmonds & Hill Publishing, 2017), 392–410.
83 Randy Peerenboom and He Xin, "Dispute Resolution in China: Patterns, Causes and Prognosis," *University of Pennsylvania East Asia Law Review* 4, no. 1 (2009): 36–37.
84 Labor Dispute Mediation and Arbitration Law, art. 27.
85 Ibid., arts 17–18.

to be free of charge.[86] These provisions show the administrative nature of and the government's intervention in labor dispute resolution in China.

As Table 5.2 shows, within the first year of the enactment of LDMAL, the total number of labor disputes in China doubled from 350,182 in 2007 to 693,465 in 2008.[87] Most labor disputes clustered in regions with high economic growth, such as Guangdong Province, Shanghai Municipality, and Jiangsu Province.[88]

The revival of labor mediation is also a response to the surge in arbitration and litigation cases involving individual and collective labor disputes.[89] A recent empirical study of a nationwide campaign by the government aiming to promote labor mediation revealed that mediation was used in over 60% of the labor disputes studied.[90] The initial motivation of this campaign was to ease the pressure of the overloading civil courts and to deal better with the surging amount of labor disputes. But the study further suggested that the reinforcement of labor mediation was also a result of local bureaucratic interests in maintaining social stability,[91] as will be studied in the subsequent section which analyzes the reforms.

4 Reform analyses

4.1 Penetrating factors of reform

While China is experiencing profound social and economic changes, mediation has become the first line of defense to maintain social stability and promote harmony. The government is conscious of the perils of social inequality and tightens both formal and informal social control. Since the mid-2000s, the Chinese government has called for the building of "harmonious society," and since the early 2010s, the pursuit of the "Chinese dreams," to inspire its governance populace. One of the government imperatives to promote both is to uphold the traditional Chinese cultural ideal of mediation.

The 2010 PML came into being at a time when China has seen and continues to see a surge of social contradictions and conflicts, manifested by numerous popular grievances, collective complaints and demonstrations. These incidents have posed serious threats to social stability and state control. In response to the social disorder, the Party propagandizes the "harmonious society" campaign. One of the strategies used in the campaign is the

---

86 Ibid., art. 53.
87 See Table 5.2.
88 National Bureau of Statistics, *Labor Statistics Yearbook 2009* (Beijing: China Statistics Press, 2009), 9.1, 9.3.
89 Zou, Pan and Han, "Regulating Collective Labour Disputes in China."
90 Zhuang Wenjia and Cheng Feng, "Mediate First: The Revival of Mediation in Labor Dispute Resolution in China," *The China Quarterly* 222, no. 1 (2015): 380–422.
91 Ibid.

promotion of people's mediation, to alleviate social conflicts before they escalate to mass incidents.[92] In this respect, the positive influence of mediation in maintaining social stability has been noted. One official report provided that people's mediation successfully kept over 50,000 civil disputes from escalating into criminal cases, and stopped nearly 100,000 group fights.[93]

On the front of labor mediation, China's rapidly changing economy and massive urbanization wave have generated growing issues of inequality, insecurity, and instability in employment relations. China's market reform took place against the backdrop of an underdeveloped legal and social welfare system combined with corruption and abuse of power, which intensified disputes between different interest groups and sometimes widespread conflicts.[94] One of the unfolding problems has been the failure of the Chinese local governments to regulate fairly and expeditiously the labor relations, as well as their unwillingness to extend legal protection to workers, especially migrant works who have contributed significantly to China's urbanization development.[95]

It was reported that the number of "mass incidents" (*quntixing shijian* 群体性事件) drastically increased from 8,700 in 1993 to 87,000 in 2005, and further doubled to 180,000 in 2010, even though only around one-tenth of those incidents were successfully settled without use of threat or violence.[96] Among the reported mass incidents, labor disputes and land seizures were recognized as the largest causes.[97] A report released by the China Academy of Social Security estimated that there were 270 mass labor incidents in 2012 alone, involving more than 30 participants per incident.[98] Another study by the China Academy of Social Science found that, in the first three quarters of 2013, 30.65% of the mass incidents in China were labor-related, which constituted the largest proportion of mass incidents.[99]

---

92 "Mediation Law Could Ease Tension," *People's Daily*, June 23, 2010.

93 Wang Jue 王珏, "A Brief Argument on the Foundation for the Legislation on the People's Mediation" 简论人民调解立法的实践基础, *Justice of China* 中国司法 5, no. 1 (2005): 48.

94 Zhang, "Rethinking the Mediation Campaign."

95 Fu and Palmer, "Introduction," 31.

96 The term "mass incidents" was coined in 2005 by Zhou Yongkang, then Minister of Public Security, as "any kind of planned or impromptu gathering that forms because of 'internal contradictions,' including mass public speeches, physical conflicts, airing of grievances or other forms of group behavior that may disrupt social stability." This broad definition varies across provinces and incorporates sit-ins, strikes, marches, and rallies, participation in cults or organized crime, and gambling, among other things. See Will Freeman, "The Accuracy of China's 'Mass Incidents,'" *Financial Times*, March 2, 2010, https://www.ft.com/content/9ee6fa64-25b5-11df-9bd3-00144feab49a.

97 Li Lin and Tian He, *The Annual Report on China's Rule of Law No. 12 (2014)* (Beijing: Social Sciences Academic Press, 2014), 12.

98 "Shehui lanpi shu: meinian gezhong quntixing shijian duoda shuwan qi" 社会蓝皮书: 每年各种群体性事件多达数万起, *Renmin Wang* 人民网, December 18, 2012, http://society.people.com.cn/n/2012/1218/c1008-19933666.html.

99 Li and Tian, *The Annual Report on China's Rule of Law No. 12 (2014)*, 270.

With increasing tension generated within the society, workers began to seek a more formal labor dispute process to resolve their tensions. Pressures from increasingly organized collective labor actions have prompted regulatory responses from the state in the form of new laws and institutions.[100] The 2008 LDMAL regulating labor mediation emerged in the context, with an aim to contribute to the "harmonious labor relations."

This ideology of harmony, however, is not without criticism. Hundreds of thousands of the PMCs and the LDMCs served as powerful institutions to mobilize the masses and to prevent social conflicts. With their heavy focus on social stability, the people's mediation system and labor mediation system are instrumentalist in nature, to prevent expression of disagreements rather than to actually deal with the conflict. The growth of labor dispute mediation shows an even stronger concern now than in the past with dispute suppression. It delivers mediation as an important way of avoiding the labor petitioning, mass labor incidents, and possible labor litigation, which are expressions of the social dislocation spawned by China's rapid economic growth and labor movement.

Besides the internal domestic political factors which are triggered by societal concerns, according to the studies by Minzner, China's mediation reform has also been influenced by movements in other jurisdictions such as the United States and India.[101] These jurisdictions invariably shifted their focus back to mediation in the recent decades, also with an aim to explore alternatives to resolve societal grievances and enhance the access to civil justice. However, unlike China's shift which was motivated by top-down authoritarian political reaction to societal unrests and protection of central officials from citizens' petitions, the movement in these other jurisdictions was motivated by non-political legal actors and entities with a certain degree of independence.[102] As such, scholars have argued that mediation reform in China has a unique but strong political undertone that distinguishes it from contemporary civil mediation reform in the rest of the world.[103]

4.2 Patterns of development

4.2.1 Top-down and bottom-up

At the central level, the Chinese government adopts a top-down approach to legally reform mediation so as to make mediation politically operate as an instrumentalist channel to contain societal conflicts; and technically, to enable mediation toward possibly becoming a possible alternative to

---

100 Zou, Pan and Han, "Regulating Collective Labour Disputes in China."
101 Carl Minzner, "China's Turn Against Law," *American Journal of Comparative Law* 59, no. 4 (2011): 937
102 Ibid.
103 Wu, "People's Mediation in the 21st Century," 33–34.

litigation in the court. The top-down approach is reflected in the regulatory responses from the state in the form of promulgating new laws and setting up new institutions, such as those stipulated in the 2010 PML and the 2008 LDMAL, to legalize and institutionalize people's mediation and labor mediation systems.

With this top-down approach, people's mediation and labor mediation have entered a new era of consolidation and expansion. At the same time, there have been concerted efforts of mediation and problem-solving by multiple governments and social organizations.[104] The civil nature of mediation process is thus socialized and socially controlled to a significant degree.

In addition, there are significant patterns of bottom-up local initiatives noted in the mediation development trajectory.

For people's mediation, there is a diversification of the people's mediation organizations in addition to the PMCs prescribed by the 2010 PML, as well as the practice of mediation. For example, several new varieties on mediation were introduced in Shanghai, such as the people's mediation agreements review system, leading people's mediator system, and people's mediation studios.[105] Among these initiatives, the integration of the people's mediation studios into the broad mediation system, with the collaborative network of the local government and residential committees, was perhaps the most unconventional.[106] Xiong conducted field study on one of these mediation studios—the "Yang's Studio" in Shanghai. The studio was a non-profit civil organization and was part of the street level mediation committee. The studio handled more serious disputes for the government, including minor criminal cases referred to by the local police, while the residential committees handled less serious disputes. The government purchased mediation services from the studio, and the studio was responsible for drafting all the mediation settlement agreements using standard and professional languages.[107]

For labor mediation, the introduction of grassroot people's mediation organization and mediation bodies at the township level or in the neighborhood community seem to provide scope for NGOs to mediate labor disputes.[108] As such, attempts of collaboration between NGOs and the local government to provide labor mediation service are observed. One example is the setting up of "Little Bird PMC" mediation office in Donghuamen sub-district of Beijing by an NGO named Little Bird and the Beijing Bureau of Justice in 2004. Before the establishment of the Little Bird PMC, it is estimated that the NGO had only been able to recover around 4 million RMB of

---

104 Ibid., 49.
105 Ibid.
106 Ibid.
107 Xiong Yihan, "Socialization and Reorganization of People's Mediation: A Case Study of Yang Boshou's Workroom in Shanghai," *Chinese Journal of Sociology* 26, no. 6 (2006): 100–121.
108 Zou, Pan and Han, "Regulating Collective Labour Disputes in China."

workers' salaries.[109] However, Little Bird managed to recover over 15 million RMB in its first year as a PMC.[110] This new status as a PMC grants Little Bird more power in the mediation negotiation process since it now appears as a government organ, and more pressure is put on employers to settle the dispute by allowing NGOs to take an active role in labor mediation.[111]

4.2.2 Grand mediation

Among all the recent initiatives on mediation, grand mediation (*datiaojie* 大调解) is probably the most controversial. International literature has cautioned against the use of mediation in public disputes.[112] The grand mediation is one such that it has blurred the boundary of traditional parameters of mediation.

Grand mediation aims to have the grassroot government officials identify potential large-scale disputes before they escalate into mass incidents, and then through working with the disputants and related institutions, help to resolve the conflicts and defuse the tension.[113] It is a hybrid process involving multiple parties designed to resolve complex disputes at the basic level, and engages all levels of mediation, including administrative mediation, people's mediation, and judicial mediation.[114] These types of mediation are not used competitively against each other and the disputants could opt for more than one type of mediation in the same dispute.[115] Initiated in Nantong, Jiangsu Province in 2003, and subsequently introduced to other Chinese cities in various forms, grand mediation represents a comprehensive method of mediation by mobilizing authorities and resources from different social and governmental agencies for problem-solving.[116] Typical types of disputes handled by grand mediation include collective disputes involving land expropriation, labor disputes, environment disputes, and conflicts involving socio-economic rights and entitlements such as pensions and medical claims. Legal and extra-legal actors are encouraged, and often required, to bypass legal rules and procedures in the interests of political expediency and achieving proper social impact in "resolving" disputes.[117]

---

109 Aaron Halegua, "Getting Paid: Processing the Labor Disputes of China's Migrant Workers," *Berkeley Journal of International Law* 26 (2008): 254, 300.

110 Ibid.

111 Zou, Pan and Han, "Regulating Collective Labour Disputes in China."

112 Sarah S. Matari, "Mediation to Resolve the Bedouin-Israeli Government Dispute for the Negev Desert," *Fordham International Law Journal*, 34, no. 4 (2010): 1089–1130.

113 Keith Hand, "Resolving Constitutional Disputes in Contemporary China," *University of Pennsylvania East Asia Law Review* 7 (2012): 51.

114 Cao Liqun, Ivan Y. Sun and Bill Hebenton, *The Routledge Handbook of Chinese Criminology* (Oxford: Routledge, 2013), 121.

115 Zhao, *Mediation in Contemporary China*.

116 Hu Jieren, "Grand Mediation in China: Mechanism and Application," *Asian Survey* 51, no. 6 (2011): 1065.

117 Ibid.

Scholars are critical of the policy. Hand characterizes grand mediation as a party-political tool and part of the social management system to contain complex disputes at the basic level, in the pretense of "building a harmonious society" and promoting social stability.[118] In a similar vein, Wu and Hu argue that grand mediation is in a natural tension with mediation. While people's mediation emphasizes principles such as voluntariness and flexibility, grand mediation has a close connection with the state power and government conduct, and does not offer the benefit of disputant autonomy.[119] In promoting grand mediation, not only the boundary of traditional parameters of mediation is blurred, but the distinction between legal and socio-political processes is also intentionally blurred.

5 The future

This section analyzes challenges for prospective development of the people's mediation and labor mediation systems. While technical challenges such as lack of professionalism might be gradually remediable, systematical challenges are embedded within the rule of law governance of China's dispute resolution mechanism.

5.1 People's mediation

Historically, people's mediation operated within communities and ostensibly encouraged social cohesion in the face of disharmony. But with the global growth of the ADR movement, people's mediation is now closely associated with the Chinese civil justice system. However, the mediator profession in China remains disjointed and makes only limited attempts to engage in progress. Fu and Palmer argue there are cultural barriers for its professionalization and specialization.[120]

Technically, in Chinese legal traditions, mediation is regarded as an art rather than a science. A mediator is successful because of his or her personality, passion and life experience. The skills are passed through subtle cultivation rather than structured teaching and learning. This cultural understanding of the "true nature" of mediation weighs heavily against the attempt to make community mediation as formal area of knowledge and skills that might for example be a subject taught in law schools.[121]

---

118 Hand, *Resolving Constitutional Disputes in Contemporary China.*
119 Hu, *Grand Mediation in China: Mechanism and Application*; Wu Yuning, "People's Mediation in China," in Cao Liqun, Ivan Y. Sun and Bill Hebenton, *The Routledge Handbook of Chinese Criminology* (Oxford: Routledge, 2013), 116.
120 Fu and Palmer, "Introduction."
121 Ibid.

According to the 2010 PML, the composition of the PMCs includes three to nine members elected for a three-year term[122] and the mediators are adult citizens of China who are impartial and dedicated to the people's mediation work, with a certain level of education, and understanding of law and policy.[123] The PML, however, does not clearly provide for the educational, occupational, and ethical qualifications required of the people's mediators. Literature shows people's mediators are mainly from the following three sources: (1) volunteers from local judicial bureaus and organizations such as unions and associations, (2) those elected by local villages or employees in an institution, and (3) part-time government officials from local judicial administrative stations. Only a small portion of the people's mediators are chosen through competitive applications.[124] This is to be contrasted with Japan, where mediation is also heavily relied on in the civil dispute resolution system. Japan's Civil Mediation Law provides that the members in a mediation committee are mainly elected from the following three types: (1) those with lawyer qualification and legal expertise, (2) professionals who could make use of their knowledge to propose proper solutions, and (3) elder people (between the age of 40 and 70) with considerable social experience.[125]

Systematically, as mentioned earlier in this chapter, mediation in China has a persisting and distinctive "evaluative" feature, in both moral and socio-political aspects, in the mediatory intervention. In China, such evaluation is not solely an assessment of the disputing parties' respective legal positions and the likely outcome (similar to the evaluative-styled mediation in the international modern mediation discourse).[126] Instead, the Chinese mediation process is often infused with concerns about the parties' social relationships and the political impact of the dispute resolution outcome.[127] This distinctive "socio-politically evaluative mediation" is a reflection of China's socialist morality and the Party ideals. Mediation continues to be used in a manner that takes into account the policy goals of the Party, even more so than before. As the Chinese leadership prioritizes its felt-need to maintain political stability, it has become correspondingly difficult to move away from the preference for the distinctive Chinese "socio-politically evaluative mediation," and the government becomes particularly proactive to intervene in troubling situations.

122 People's Mediation Law, art. 9.
123 Ibid., art. 14.
124 Wu, "People's Mediation in China."
125 Katja Funken, "Comparative Dispute Management: Court-Connected Mediation in Japan and Germany," *German Law Journal* 3, no. 2 (2002).
126 Michael Palmer and Simon Roberts, *Dispute Processes: ADR and The Primary Forms of Decision Making*, 3rd ed. (Cambridge: Cambridge University Press, 2020), Chapter 7.
127 Ibid.

Moreover, under the present PML, the PMCs are insufficiently funded, and people's mediators do not enjoy any occupational security.[128] Their incentive of involvement in mediation work is purely derived from their sense of social responsibility toward the harmonious society achievement. Some Western scholars have uncritically compared Chinese mediation with the American model, but Chinese mediation ought to be viewed less simplistically.[129] Extra-judicial mediation in China is likely to focus on group interest and social harmony, instead of following the protection of individual rights despite the growing acceptance of law-based rights. It is thus difficult for the people's mediation system to effectively institutionalize professionally in actual practice.

5.2 Labor mediation

Inadequate professionalism is a shared problem in labor mediation in China. The lack of professional training and resources pose serious challenges to the labor mediation system.

Technically, successful labor mediation relies on the labor-intensive efforts of experienced mediators who can persuade parties imbalanced in power (i.e., employers and employees) to reach an agreement. Hensler has long argued the difficulties of weaker parties to enter into labor agreements due to power imbalances.[130] In China, successful mediators in labor dispute mediation are not only required to possess delicate personal skills, but they also need to mobilize social pressure that has a bearing on the parties as well.[131] The objectives are to bring a labor dispute to an effective end. Given the perceived nature of mediation, labor mediation that is too formalized and structured within a firm legal framework is seen as undermining the effectiveness of mediation.

Systematically, as mentioned earlier in this chapter, collective labor disputes, which constitute one of the largest portions of "mass incidents," is an increasing concern to the Chinese dispute resolution system. The increased promotion of collective bargaining by the government in China has taken place within the context of an increase of strikes and rapid social and policy changes. Chan and Hui argued that, driven by growing labor protests, the collective negotiation process in China is undergoing a transition, from "collective consultation as a formality," through a stage of "collective bargaining by riot," and toward "Party-State-led collective bargaining." This transition, however, is unlikely to reach the stage of "worker-led collective

---

128 Fu, "Dispute Resolution and China's Grassroots Legal Services," 335–338.
129 Stanley Lubman, "Bird in a Cage: Chinese Law Reform after Twenty Years," *Northwestern Journal of International Law & Business* 20 (2000): 383, 388.
130 Deborah R. Hensler and Linda J. Demaine, "Volunteering to Arbitrate through Pre-Dispute Arbitration Clauses," *Law and Contemporary Problems* 67 (2004): 55–74.
131 Fu and Palmer, "Introduction," 8.

bargaining" in the near future.[132] The Chinese government not only faces the need to ease the pressure of the courts, but also the need to reform mediation into an effective institutional avenue for workers to ease grievances in order to maintain social stability.[133]

One relatively more feasible suggestion is, however, to enable NGOs to play a more active role in the labor mediation system.[134] Grassroot NGOs are mostly formed by an underprivileged group of workers, and their staffs are also closely connected with the workers through regular gatherings and visits.[135] Allowing a stronger supporting role of these NGOs in the regulatory framework for labor mediation, together with the trade union such as the ACFTU, would give workers some institutional space for negotiation and act as an effective and formal channel for workers to ease their grievances.

However, despite the increasing institutionalization and formalization of the labor mediation in China, it has been argued that the revival of mediation as the primary method to resolve labor disputes in China is a significant departure from the commitment to the rule of law. The approach by both the central and local governments in dealing with labor disputes has been the same—to use mediatory intervention to control disputes so that harmony and social stability is maintained.[136] In a similar vein, the state has also tried to carefully shape the ways in which labor litigation is conducted, again with political goals in mind.[137]

6 Conclusion

Half a century ago, two leading Chinese law specialists in the West, Cohen, and Lubman in the United States, debated on whether mediation in China was primarily traditional (Cohen)[138] or socialist (Lubman) in nature.[139] Revisiting this earlier debate, it is clear that both are correct in their own way. It is also the case that contemporary Chinese mediation has developed other distinctive facets over the ensuing years.

Faced with deepening economic and societal reform, as the Chinese leadership prioritizes its felt-need to maintain social stability and leadership populace, it has become correspondingly difficult to move away from the

---

132 Chan Chris King-Chi and Hui Elaine Sio-Ieng, "The Development of Collective Bargaining in China: From 'Collective Bargaining by Riot' to 'Party-State-Led Wage Bargaining,'" *The China Quarterly* 217 (2014): 221–242.

133 Ibid.

134 Zou, Pan and Han, "Regulating Collective Labour Disputes in China."

135 Ibid.

136 Zhuang and Chen, "Mediate First," 222.

137 Aaron Halegua, "Access to Justice for China's Workers," *NYU Labor and Employment Law News* 13 (2017).

138 Cohen, "Chinese Mediation on the Eve of Modernisation."

139 Lubman, "Mao and Mediation."

preference for the distinctive Chinese "socio-politically evaluative mediation." Despite the increasing institutionalization and professionalization of the people's mediation and labor mediation systems in China, though limited in extent, hundreds of thousands of the people's mediation committees and labor mediation committees have served as powerful institutions to mobilize the masses and to prevent social conflicts. Mediators are found to be particularly proactive in intervention in trouble situations to maintain the harmonious society, and they have to care about the social and political impact of what they mediate, even more so than before. Confucian harmony has become socialist stability.

With its strong focus on "harmonious society" building, the people's mediation system and labor mediation system are instrumentalist in nature, to prevent expression of disagreements rather than to really deal with the conflict. Mediation is used to promote better governability of the civil society and to reduce visible and publicized conflicts that might potentially reduce the legitimacy of the Party-State. This official promotion of mediation is justified by a political responsibility to maintain stability and promote harmony, particularly in times of crisis.[140] Hence, the Chinese approach to the promotion and governance (legalization and formalization) of mediation, unlike contemporary mediation developments in other jurisdictions in both the East and the West, has been carrying a strong political undertone.[141]

The Chinese path in developing mediation, though led from the top, is a checkered one, and the author has explained the socio-political contextual factors and systematic challenges that have led to the restrictions in its reform. Contrary to the Cohen–Lubman debate on the tradition–socialism dichotomy of the Chinese mediation earlier, this chapter concludes that contemporary mediation in China, though rooted in the Chinese tradition, is a scattered regime (in many different types, forms and initiatives), and has developed under strong socio-political orientation.

Bibliography

Brown, Ronald C. "Resolving Labor Disputes by Mediation, Arbitration, and Litigation." In *Understanding Labor and Employment Law in China*, edited by Ronald C. Brown. Cambridge: Cambridge University Press, 2010.

Cao, Liqun, Ivan Y. Sun and Bill Hebenton, *The Routledge Handbook of Chinese Criminology*. Oxford: Routledge, 2013.

Chan, Chris King-Chi. and Hui Elaine Sio-Ieng. "The Development of Collective Bargaining in China: From 'Collective Bargaining by Riot' to 'Party-State-Led Wage Bargaining'." *The China Quarterly* 217 (2014): 221–242.

---

140 Fu and Palmer, "Introduction."
141 Zhuang and Chen, "Mediate First."

Chen, Albert H.Y. "Confucian Legal Culture and Its Modern Fate." In *The New Legal Order in Hong Kong*, edited by Raymond Wacks, 505–534. Hong Kong: Hong Kong University Press, 1999.

China Law Society. *The Law Yearbook of China* (1991–2018).

Cohen, Jerome Alan. "Chinese Mediation on the Eve of Modernisation." *California Law Review* 54, no. 3 (1966): 1201–1226.

Department of Population and Employment Statistics and Ministry of Human Resources and Social Security. *China Labor Statistical Yearbook* (2008–2018).

Di, Xiaohua and Wu Yuning. "The Developing Trend of the People's Mediation in China." *Sociological Focus* 42 (2009): 228–245.

Fan, Yu 范愉. "An Evaluation of the People's Mediation Law of China" 《中华人民共和国人民调解法》评析. *The Jurist* 法学家 no. 2 (2011): 1–12.

Freeman, Will. "The Accuracy of China's 'Mass Incidents.'" *Financial Times*, March 2, 2010. https://www.ft.com/content/9ee6fa64-25b5-11df-9bd3-00144feab49a.

Friedman, Eli and Lee Ching Kwan. "Remaking the World of Chinese Labour: A 30-Year Retrospective." *British Journal of Industrial Relations* 48, no. 3 (2010): 507–533.

Fu, Hualing and Michael Palmer. "Introduction." In *Mediation in Contemporary China: Continuity and Change*, edited by Fu Hualing and Michael Palmer, 1–33. London: Wildy, Simmonds & Hill Publishing, 2017.

Fu, Hualing, "Understanding People's Mediation in Post-Mao China." *Columbia Journal of Asian Law* 5, no. 2 (1992): 211–246.

Fu, Hualing and Richard Cullen. "From Mediatory to Adjudicatory Justice: The Limits of Civil Justice Reform in China." In *Chinese Justice: Civil Dispute Resolution in Contemporary China*, edited by Margaret Woo and Mary Gallagher, 25–97. Cambridge: Cambridge University Press, 2011.

Fu, Yulin. "Dispute Resolution and China's Grassroots Legal Services." In *Chinese Justice: Civil Dispute Resolution in Contemporary China*, edited by Margaret Woo and Mary Gallagher, 314–339. Cambridge: Cambridge University Press, 2011.

Funken, Katja. "Comparative Dispute Management: Court-Connected Mediation in Japan and Germany." *German Law Journal* 3, no. 2 (2002), E1.

Gallagher, Mary. "Changes in the World's Workshop: The Demographic, Social, and Political Factors behind China's Labor Movement." In *Dragon Versus Eagle: The Chinese Economy and U.S.–China Relations*, edited by Huang Wei-Chiao and Zhou Huizhong, 119–132. Michigan: Upjohn Institute, 2012.

Gonghui Fa (工会法) [Trade Union Law] (promulgated by the National People's Congress, August 27, 2009, effective August 27, 2009). http://www.lawinfochina.com/display.aspx?id=22786&lib=law.

Gu, Weixia. "The Delicate Art of Med-Arb and Its Future Institutionalization in China." *UCLA Pacific Basin Law Journal* 31, no. 2 (2014): 97–126.

Halegua, Aaron. "Access to Justice for China's Workers." *NYU Labor and Employment Law News* 13 (2017).

Halegua, Aaron. "Getting Paid: Processing the Labor Disputes of China's Migrant Workers." *Berkeley Journal of International Law* 26 (2008): 254–322.

Hand, Keith. "Resolving Constitutional Disputes in Contemporary China." *University of Pennsylvania East Asia Law Review* 7 (2012): 51–159.

Hensler, Deborah R. and Linda J. Demaine. "Volunteering to Arbitrate Through Pre-Dispute Arbitration Clauses." *Law and Contemporary Problems* 67 (2004): 55–74.

Ho, Virginia. *Labor Dispute Resolution in China: Implications for Labor Rights and Legal Reform.* California: Institute of East Asian Studies, 2005.

Hu, Jieren. "Grand Mediation in China: Mechanism and Application." *Asian Survey* 51, no. 6 (2011): 1065–1089.

Jiuye cujin Fa (就业促进法) [Employment Promotion Law] (promulgated by the National People's Congress Standing Committee, April 24, 2015, effective January 1, 2008). http://www.npc.gov.cn/zgrdw/npc/xinwen/lfgz/flca/2007-03/25/content_362938.htm.

Kakiuchi, Shusukei. "Regulating Mediation in Japan: Latest Development and Its Background." In *New Developments in Civil and Commercial Mediation*, edited by Carlos Esplugues and Louis Marquis, 367–392. New York: Springer, 2015.

Laodong Fa (劳动法) [Labour Law] (promulgated by the National People's Congress Standing Committee, May 7, 1994, effective January 1, 1995). http://www.lawinfochina.com/display.aspx?id=705&lib=law.

Laodong hetong Fa (劳动合同法) [Labor Contract Law] (promulgated by the National People's Congress Standing Committee, December 18, 2012, effective July 1, 2013). https://www.6laws.net/6law/law-gb/中華人民共和國勞動合同法.htm.

Laodong zhengyi tiaojie zhongcai Fa (劳动争议调解仲裁法) [Labor Dispute Mediation and Arbitration Law] (promulgated by the National People's Congress Standing Committee, December 29, 2007, effective January 1, 2008). http://www.lawinfochina.com/display.aspx?id=6584&lib=law;

Lin, Li and He Tian. *The Annual Report on China's Rule of Law No. 12 (2014).* Beijing: Social Sciences Academic Press, 2014.

Lubman, Stanley. "Bird in a Cage: Chinese Law Reform after Twenty Years." *Northwestern Journal of International Law & Business* 20, no. 1 (2000): 383–424.

Lubman, Stanley. "Mao and Mediation: Politics and Dispute Resolution in Communist China." *California Law Review* 55, no. 5 (1967): 1284–1359.

Matari, Sarah. "Mediation to Resolve the Bedouin-Israeli Government Dispute for the Negev Desert." *Fordham International Law Journal* 34, no. 4 (2010): 1089–1130.

Mediation Ordinance (Cap. 620) (Hong Kong).

Menkel-Meadow, Carrie. *Mediation and Its Applications for Good Decision Making and Dispute Resolution.* Cambridge: Intersensia, 2016.

Ministry of Justice. *Report on the Development of People's Mediation System*, October 18, 2012.

Ministry of Justice. *Some Provisions Concerning the Work of People's Mediation*, September 26, 2002. http://www.lawinfochina.com/display.aspx?lib=law&id=2465&CGid=.

Minshi Susong Fa (民事诉讼法) [Civil Procedure Law] (promulgated by the National People's Congress, August 31, 2012, effective October 3, 2012). http://www.lawinfochina.com/display.aspx?lib=law&id=19&CGid=

Minzner, Carl. "China's Turn Against Law." *American Journal of Comparative Law* 59, no. 4 (2011): 935–984.

National Bureau of Statistics. *Labor Statistics Yearbook 2009.* Beijing: China Statistics Press, 2009.

National Bureau of Statistics of China. *China Statistical Yearbook* (2016–2019).

Nolan-Haley, Jacqueline. "Mediation: The Best and Worst of Times." *Cardozo Journal of Conflict Resolution* 16 (2014): 731–740.

Nolan-Haley, Jacqueline. *Alternative Dispute Resolution in a Nutshell*, 2nd ed. Minnesota: West Academic, 2017.

Palmer, Michael and Simon Roberts. *Dispute Processes: ADR and the Primary Forms of Decision Making*, 3rd ed. Cambridge: Cambridge University Press, 2020.

Peerenboom, Randy and He Xin, "Dispute Resolution in China: Patterns, Causes and Prognosis." *University of Pennsylvania East Asia Law Review* 4, no. 1 (2009): 1–61.

Renmin tiaojie Fa (人民调解法) [People's Mediation Law] (promulgated by the National People's Congress Standing Committee, August 28, 2010, effective January 1, 2011). http://www.lawinfochina.com/display.aspx?id=8266&lib=law.

"Shehui lanpi shu: meinian gezhong quntixing shijian duoda shuwan qi" 社会蓝皮书: 每年各种群体性事件多达数万起. *Renmin Wang* 人民网, December 18, 2012. http://society.people.com.cn/n/2012/1218/c1008-19933666.html

Shen, Jie, "Labor Litigation in China." In *The Strategies of China's Firms: Resolving Dilemmas*, edited by Yang Hailan, Stephen Morgan and Wang Ying, 41–52. Cambridge: Chandos Publishing, 2015.

Supreme People's Court. *Interpretation Regarding Some Provisions on Trying Civil Cases Involving the People's Mediation Agreements* 最高人民法院关于审理涉及人民调解协议的民事案件的若干规定. http://www.npc.gov.cn/zgrdw/huiyi/lfzt/rmtjfzfjc/2010-06/17/content_1577196.htm.

Supreme People's Court. *Guanyu renmin tiaojie xieyi sifa queren chengxu de ruogan guiding* 关于人民调解协议司法确认程序的若干规定, December 13, 2011. http://www.court.gov.cn/shenpan-xiangqing-3473.html.

Wang, Jue 王珏. "A Brief Argument on the Foundation for the Legislation on the People's Mediation" 简论人民调解立法的实践基础. *Justice of China* 中国司法 5 (2005): 48–51.

Wu, Yuning. "People's Mediation Enters the 21st Century." In *Mediation in Contemporary China: Continuity and Change*, edited by Fu Hualing and Michael Palmer, 34–58. London: Wildy, Simmonds & Hill Publishing, 2017.

Wu, Yuning. "People's Mediation in China." In Cao Liqun, Ivan Y. Sun and Bill Hebenton, *The Routledge Handbook of Chinese Criminology*, 116–129. Oxford: Routledge, 2013.

Xiong, Yihan. "Socialization and Reorganization of People's Mediation: A Case Study of Yang Boshou's Workroom in Shanghai." *Chinese Journal of Sociology* 26, no. 6 (2006): 100–121.

Zhang, Xianchu. "Rethinking the Mediation Campaign." In *Mediation in Contemporary China: Continuity and Change*, edited by Fu Hualing and Michael Palmer, 59–86. London: Wildy, Simmonds & Hill Publishing, 2017.

Zhao, Yixian. "Divorce Disputes and Popular Legal Culture of the Weak: A Case Study of Chinese Reality TV Mediation." In *Mediation in Contemporary China: Continuity and Change*, edited by Fu Hualing and Michael Palmer, 319–341. London: Wildy, Simmonds & Hill Publishing, 2017.

Zhao, Yun. "China's New Labor Dispute Resolution Law: A Catalyst for the Establishment of Harmonious Labor Relationship?." *Comparative Labor Law & Policy Journal* 30 (2009): 409–430.

Zhou, Ling. *Access to Justice for the Chinese Consumer: Handling Consumer Disputes in Contemporary China.* Oxford: Hart, 2020.

Zhuang, Wenjia and Feng Cheng. "Mediate First: The Revival of Mediation in Labor Dispute Resolution in China." *The China Quarterly* 222 (2015): 380–422.

Zou, Mimi, Pan Xuanming and Han Sirui. "Regulating Collective Labour Disputes in China: A Tale of Two Actors." In *Mediation in Contemporary China: Continuity and Change*, edited by Fu Hualing and Michael Palmer, 392–410. London: Wildy, Simmonds & Hill Publishing, 2017.

Part III

Interaction between litigation, arbitration, mediation and China's hybrid dispute resolution systems and developments

6 Judicial mediation

The juggling path between adjudicatory and mediatory justice

1 Introduction

1.1 Preliminaries

Literature has identified two different areas in which civil litigation could cross paths with mediation. The first area is mediation processes carried out within civil proceedings and conducted by the judges or court-authorized mediator professionals, that is, the "judicial mediation" system.[1] The second area concerns the courts' confirmation of settlement agreements in order to recognize mediation efforts outside the court and litigation system,[2] such as the judicial confirmation of people's mediation agreements, under the People's Mediation Law and Civil Procedure Law in China. As the second aspect has been separately addressed in other chapters. This chapter focuses on the first aspect, the judicial mediation system.

Chinese courts prefer to rely on mediation for decision-making in their adjudicative work. Zhao, the author of the leading text on mediation in China, has argued for the centrality of judicial mediation as a dispute resolution process in the Chinese litigation culture.[3] Fu and Cullen also argued that judicial mediation carried out by Chinese courts is a distinctive feature of the Chinese civil justice system, and called it "mediatory justice."[4] In addition, there are utilitarian motives of using judicial mediation as the Chinese courts increasingly embrace the more general values of the ADR movement elsewhere in the world. More subtly, the utilitarian

---

1 Jacqueline Nolan-Haley, "Mediation: The Best and Worst of Times," *Cardozo Journal of Conflict Resolution* 16, no. 1 (2014): 731–740.
2 Ibid.
3 Zhao Yun, *Mediation Practice and Skills*, (Beijing: Tsinghua University Press, 2015).
4 Fu Hualing and Richard Cullen, "From Mediatory to Adjudicatory Justice: The Limits of Civil Justice Reform in China," in *Chinese Justice: Civil Dispute Revolution in China*, eds. Margaret Woo and Mary Gallagher (Cambridge: Cambridge University Press, 2011), 25–57.

motives have infused with the Chinese leadership's political emphasis on judicial mediation as a social stability imperative. The development of the judicial mediation reflects the juggling path between adjudicatory and mediatory justice in China, as well as the tension between professional and popular justice.[5]

As the author summarizes from reading the existing literature and through her personal research experience, so far, four different stages may be identified in the development of judicial mediation in China.

The first stage (before 1991) showed that mediation was the major method of dispute resolution for various disputes in the Chinese courts. It was not until the enactment of the 1991 Civil Procedure Law were cases not required to be mediated first before adjudication by the Chinese courts when the former had failed.[6]

The second stage (1991 to mid-late 2000s) still preferred mediation, but with civil litigation strengthened under the Chinese court reform of formal justice and dispute resolution from 1998 to 2008.[7] Voluntary mediation was also stressed in the second stage such that the Chinese judges respected parties' feelings regarding whether mediation should take place.[8]

The third stage (late 2000s to early 2010s) was featured as the stage of prioritizing mediation under the Chinese "mediation campaign."[9] Mediation was largely politicized to achieve social stability maintenance and mediation was adopted throughout the Chinese courts. Parties entered into judicial mediation often due to pressure from the judges. The judges were in turn under pressure of performance targets to settle cases through mediation and were assessed by mediation rates both professionally and politically.[10] In the meantime, judicial mediation was deemed as a significant means of "popular justice" under specific judicial policies and there were different judicial mediation working models developed by the Chinese judges.[11]

The fourth stage (early-mid-2010s to present) adopts a more nuanced approach toward the use of judicial mediation.[12] The Chinese courts have realized the problems of a resulting ineffectiveness of mediation when there

---

5 Gu Weixia, "Responsive Justice in China During Transitional Times: Revisiting the Juggling Path Between Adjudicatory and Mediatory Justice," *Washington University Global Studies Law Review* 14, (2015): 50–58.
6 Zhang Xianchu, "Rethinking the Mediation Campaign," in *Mediation in Contemporary China: Continuity and Change*, eds. Fu Hualing and Michael Palmer (London: Wildy, Simmonds & Hill Publishing, 2017), 59–86.
7 See Sections 2.2 and 3.2 of this chapter.
8 Fu and Cullen, "From Adjudicatory to Mediatory Justice."
9 Zhang, "Rethinking the Mediation Campaign."
10 Carl Minzner, "China's Turn Against Law," *American Journal of Comparative Law* 59, no. 4 (2011): 935–984.
11 See Section 4.2 of this chapter.
12 Gu, "Responsive Justice in China During Transitional Times," 50–58.

has been overreliance on it as a dispute resolution process, which has then led to the marginalized place for courts and formal dispute resolution in the Chinese society as well as the loss of rule of law. Research work, including some carried out by the Chinese courts themselves, has shown that the impact of enhanced emphasis on judicial mediation has not necessarily increased political stability and social harmony.[13]

This chapter will first empirically analyze to what extent judicial mediation is adopted in civil litigation in China so as to test whether it is a popular hybrid system for resolving civil and commercial disputes. It then highlights the regulatory landscape governing judicial mediation from time to time and points out the importance of judicial policy in the field, in particular the politicization moves of the judicial mediation in the late 2000s and early 2010s. In response to the politicization and concerns of overuse, there have been recent top-down attempts after 2013 to put more precautions on judicial mediation, to make the system more nuanced, and to give them more legitimacy. This chapter further examines the development trajectory and unveils challenges for prospective reforms. In looking forward, it discusses the proper role of mediatory justice in China's civil justice reform and rule of law development.

1.2 Empirical evidence

Table 6.1 and Chart 6.1 compile the total number of first-instance civil litigation concluded by all Chinese courts[14] and those concluded through judicial mediation in the most recent decade (2009–2018), as these data are available from the China Law Yearbook and China Statistical Yearbook published annually.[15] At the time when the book manuscript is completed, the 2019 data have not been published yet. According to the Yearbooks, civil litigation meant to include both civil and commercial cases. These most recent data may present empirically whether judicial mediation is a popular hybrid dispute resolution in resolving civil and commercial disputes in China, and how.

In general, the percentage of judicial mediation to conclude first-instance civil cases in China has been consistently higher than 25%, except in 2017 when it drops slightly to below 25% (see Table 6.1 and Chart 6.1). These data empirically demonstrate that Chinese courts commonly adopt judicial mediation to resolve various civil disputes and the popularity of judicial mediation in the Chinese civil litigation system. On closer inspection, even in 2017 when the judicial mediation rate was the lowest

---

13 Zhang, "Rethinking the Mediation Campaign."
14 The data are also available in Table 3.1.
15 China Law Society, *The Law Yearbook of China* (2010–2019). Relevant data are published in "Chapter 11: Statistics of the Yearbook."

Table 6.1 Judicial mediation in China's first-instance civil litigation (2009–2018)

Year	Total number of first-instance civil litigation concluded by all Chinese courts	Total number of first-instance civil litigation concluded by judicial mediation	Percentage of judicial mediation in all concluded civil litigation
2009	5,797,160	2,099,024	36.21%
2010	6,112,695	2,371,683	38.80%
2011	6,558,621	2,665,178	40.64%
2012	7,206,331	3,004,979	41.70%
2013	7,510,584	2,847,990	37.92%
2014	8,010,342	2,672,956	33.37%
2015	9,575,152	2,754,843	28.77%
2016	10,763,889	2,787,475	25.90%
2017	11,651,363	2,885,318	24.76%
2018	12,434,826	3,133,015	25.20%

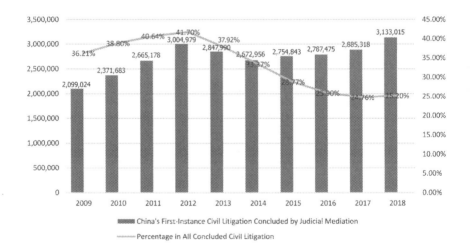

Chart 6.1 Judicial mediation in China's first-instance civil litigation (2009–2018)

in the past decade, among the 11,651,363 first-instance civil cases that all Chinese courts resolved, 5,172,571 were concluded through judgments (44.4% of the total civil caseload), and 2,885,318 were concluded through judicial mediation ending in mediation settlement agreements or mediation statements (24.76% of the total civil caseload). The remaining cases were closed as they were dismissed, withdrawn, or terminated for other reasons.[16] As the cases concluded through judicial mediation only represented those where judicial mediation attempts were successful, the actual

16 China Law Society, *The Law Yearbook of China* (2010–2018), Chapter 11.

adoption of judicial mediation in China's civil litigation could only be higher. This finding is important, as it empirically shows judicial mediation as a popular hybrid civil dispute resolution mechanism in China and reflects the importance in studying and improving the system.

Judicial mediation figures reached the peak in 2011 (40.64%) and 2012 (41.70%). By 2012, two out of every five first-instance civil cases handled by the Chinese courts were disposed by means of judicial mediation.[17] The figures, however, decreased steadily after 2013, and became stabilized after 2016.[18] With judicial mediation having an important but not so overwhelming role to play for the handling of civil cases by Chinese courts since the mid-2010s, the figures throughout the period of 2016 (25.9%), 2017 (24.76%), and 2018 (25.2%) continuously do a 15% decline since the peak point in 2011–2012 (above 40%).[19] The underlying reasons will be discussed in this chapter.

Tables 6.2 and 6.3 then empirically analyze the civil cases concluded by judicial mediation in different case categories. In the period from 2009 to 2016, based on the Yearbooks, China's first-instance civil cases concluded through judicial mediation were divided into three main subject areas: (1) disputes of family, marriage and inheritance (collectively referred to as "family disputes"), (2) contract disputes, and (3) ownership and tortious disputes. As highlighted in Table 6.2, with the exception of 2016, family disputes consistently occupy more than 40% of the civil lawsuits concluded by judicial mediation throughout the period. These data empirically prove the importance of judicial mediation in handling relationship-maintaining-oriented civil disputes such as family disputes, and indirectly mirror its function of building social harmony.[20]

Since 2017, China Law Yearbook has sub-divided civil disputes into more specific case types. As shown in Table 6.3, in 2018, 38.17% of the family lawsuits were concluded through judicial mediation. The rates of judicial mediation to conclude civil lawsuits in the categories of torts, labor, personality, contracts, and property in 2018 were 36.33%, 30.31%, 24.92%, 21.51%, and 16.81% respectively. This distribution was largely along the statistical trend in 2017 where the rates of judicial mediation to conclude civil lawsuits ranked in a decreasing degree in the categories of family (36.97%), torts (35.15%), labor (28.10%), personality (23.71%), contracts (20.69%), and property (18.12%). Likewise, judicial mediation rates were as high as 27.21% in 2017 and 19.97% in 2018 in concluding "maritime and commercial issues combined," which demonstrated the frequent use of judicial mediation in resolving pure commercial disputes in the Chinese courts. Specific to the

17 China Law Society, *The Law Yearbook of China* (2010–2012)
18 China Law Society, *The Law Yearbook of China* (2010–2018) (showing the statistics of 2009–2017); National Bureau of Statistics of China, *China Statistical Yearbook 2019*, accessed July 8, 2020, http://www.stats.gov.cn/tjsj/ndsj/2019/indexeh.htm (showing the statistics of 2018).
19 Ibid.
20 China Law Society, *The Law Yearbook of China* (2010–2017).

Table 6.2 Judicial mediation in Chinese first-instance civil litigation by categories (2009–2016)

Year	Subject area	Total number of first-instance cases	Total number of cases concluded by judicial mediation	Percentage
2009	Family Disputes	1,380,762	659,065	**47.73%**
	Contract Disputes	3,154,347	1,010,991	32.05%
	Ownership and Tort Disputes	1,262,051	428,968	33.99%
2010	Family Disputes	1,428,340	698,900	**48.93%**
	Contract Disputes	3,239,740	1,108,861	34.23%
	Ownership and Tort Disputes	1,444,615	563,922	39.04%
2011	Family Disputes	1,609,801	768,238	**47.72%**
	Contract Disputes	3,286,997	1,199,000	36.48%
	Ownership and Tort Disputes	1,661,823	697,940	42.00%
2012	Family Disputes	1,647,464	803,919	**48.80%**
	Contract Disputes	3,720,160	1,426,117	38.33%
	Ownership and Tort Disputes	1,838,707	774,943	42.15%
2013	Family Disputes	1,611,903	770,437	**47.80%**
	Contract Disputes	3,957,002	1,385,334	35.01%
	Ownership and Tort Disputes	1,941,679	692,219	35.65%
2014	Family Disputes	1,618,904	724,776	**44.77%**
	Contract Disputes	4,375,771	1,295,072	29.60%
	Ownership and Tort Disputes	2,015,667	653,108	32.40%
2015	Family Disputes	1,733,299	706,628	**40.77%**
	Contract Disputes	5,616,624	1,420,597	25.30%
	Ownership and Tort Disputes	2,225,229	627,618	28.20%
2016	Family Disputes	1,752,052	674,866	**38.52%**
	Contract Disputes	6,686,934	1,524,761	22.80%
	Ownership and Tort Disputes	2,324,903	587,848	25.28%

mediation rate of each different civil dispute type, family, tortious and labor disputes have always come out as the first, second and third highest ranked case category where the rates of judicial mediation to conclude these civil lawsuits have been higher.[21]

The data analyses empirically show the heavier reliance on judicial mediation in pure civil disputes than in commercial disputes, as the former is more closely related to harmonious society building. Meanwhile, the data collected by the Yearbooks only represent those where civil lawsuits were concluded by judicial mediation, that is, where judicial mediation attempts were successful. They did not include those cases where judicial mediation attempts were futile, that is, where judicial mediation was adopted in the civil litigation process but for various reasons did not lead to a mediation

21 China Law Society, *The Law Yearbook of China* (2018); National Bureau of Statistics of China, *China Statistical Yearbook 2019*.

Table 6.3 Judicial mediation cases in Chinese first-instance civil litigation by categories (2017–2018)

Year	Subject matter	Total number of first-instance cases	Total number of cases concluded by judicial mediation	Percentage
2017	Personality Disputes	186,654	44,254	23.71%
	Family Disputes	1,830,023	676,606	**36.97%**
	Property Rights Disputes	329,842	59,771	18.12%
	Contract Disputes	7,179,398	1,485,132	20.69%
	Intellectual Property Rights and Competition Disputes	192,938	14,872	7.71%
	Labor Disputes	470,669	132,245	**28.10%**
	Maritime and Commercial Disputes	16,610	4,520	27.21%
	Civil Disputes Relating to Companies, Securities, Insurance, Bills, etc.	219,713	50,361	22.92%
	Tort Liability Dispute	1,186,649	417,087	**35.15%**
	Others	38,867	470	1.21%
2018	Personality Disputes	178,847	44,569	24.92%
	Family Disputes	1,814,441	692,657	**38.17%**
	Property Rights Disputes	329,220	55,342	16.81%
	Contract Disputes	7,952,001	1,710,597	21.51%
	Intellectual Property Rights and Competition Disputes	273,945	27,677	10.10%
	Labor Disputes	450,589	136,577	**30.31%**
	Maritime and Commercial Disputes	16,181	3,232	19.97%
	Civil Disputes Relating to Companies, Securities, Insurance, Bills, etc.	252,647	57,476	22.75%
	Tort Liability Dispute	1,112,755	404,301	**36.33%**
	Others	54,200	587	1.08%

settlement result. In conclusion, while the empirical evidence of overall adoption data is lacking, the actual adoption rate of judicial mediation in Chinese civil lawsuits could only be higher than the data presented in the above tables and charts, which reassure the popularity of judicial mediation in China's civil litigation.

2 Regulatory framework

2.1 The civil procedure law

The legislation which is most relevant with the governance of judicial mediation in China is the Civil Procedure Law ("CPL"). It was not until the enactment of the 1991 CPL were cases not required to be mediated first before adjudication by the Chinese courts when the former had failed.[22] In the past decade or so, the CPL has been revised three times – in 2007, 2012, and 2017 respectively.[23] In the 2007 amendment to the CPL, a whole chapter, Chapter 8 (Articles 85–91), was devoted to the adoption of judicial mediation. The 2007 CPL emphasized the principles of voluntariness and lawfulness for judicial mediation to take place.[24] Mediation agreements resulting from judicial mediation processes, more frequently referred to as "judicial settlement agreements," had the same effect as the court judgments and thus binding and enforceable once they were delivered to the parties,[25] although the parties had the residual right to apply for retrial if the agreement was not entered into voluntarily or was contrary to law.[26]

The judge or collegiate panel handling the case was empowered to carry out judicial mediation but also to continue with the adjudication process should mediation fail.[27] Critiques by leading Chinese scholars such as Fan, at Renmin University Law School, had pointed out the problem of role conflict of the judge-turned-mediator and vice versa for the same civil case.[28] There were various suggestions on how to improve the situation, one being that the judge should channel the case to another unit for mediation. To relieve the procedural concerns, the 2007 CPL stated that the courts could appoint a relevant entity or individual to carry out mediation.[29]

Earlier on, the SPC issued in 2004 a judicial interpretation concerning civil mediation work in the people's courts (the "2004 SPC Interpretation on Mediation").[30] It offered more concrete guidance on judicial mediation in civil lawsuits such as the scope of civil cases where mediation could be applied, to ensure correct adoption of judicial mediation and economize on judicial resources. Pursuant to this Interpretation, mediation may be utilized at any stage of the civil litigation processes, except in cases where special procedures are employed, such as those for bankruptcy and hastening

22 Zhang Xianchu, "Rethinking the Mediation Campaign."
23 See discussions in Chapter 3.
24 Minshi Susong Fa (民事诉讼法) [Civil Procedure Law] (promulgated by the National People's Congress, October 28, 2007, effective April 1, 2008), arts. 85, 88, http://en.pkulaw.cn/display.aspx?cgid=1811a46f52ef6533bdfb&lib=law.
25 Ibid., art. 89.
26 Ibid., art. 91.
27 Zhao Yun, "Mediation in Contemporary China: Thinking About Reform," in *Mediation in Contemporary China: Continuity and Change*, eds. Fu Hualing and Michael Palmer (London: Wildy, Simmonds & Hill Publishing, 2017), 87–111.
28 Fan Yu 范愉, *Research on ADR Mechanisms* 非诉讼纠纷解决机制研究 (Beijing: Renmin University of China Press, 2000), 583–600.
29 Civil Procedure Law 2007, art. 87.
30 Supreme People's Court, *Provisions of the Supreme People's Court about Several Issues Concerning the Civil Mediation Work of the People's Court*, September 16, 2004, http://pkulaw.cn/fulltext_form.aspx?Db=chl&Gid=51834caf365c39a9bdfb.

debt repayment, publication of notice for assertion of claims, confirmation of marriage and identity, etc.[31]

The CPL was further revised in 2012 and 2017, details of which will be addressed subsequently in Section 3.1 of this chapter.

2.2 Judicial policies in the 2000s

More specifically, the SPC established a series of judicial policies which had a significant impact on judicial mediation. As mentioned in Chapter 2, since 1999, the SPC has initiated five rounds of court reform in the form of consecutive Five-Year Reform Outlines of the People's Courts. For the first (1999–2003) and second (2004–2008) rounds of the court reform, despite their bold objectives to cultivate judicial professionalism, judicial reform projects underwent criticism for being under the influence of Western legal concepts, and that the Chinese courts had been led astray from their populist roots.[32] The economic boom in the 1990s and 2000s has led to massive socio-economic issues, and the courts and formal adjudication cannot resolve all such tensions and conflicts within Chinese society. With a sudden surge in the number of petitions to the central authorities in Beijing in the early 2000s due to litigants' dissatisfaction with court decisions, the earlier judicial reforms became a scapegoat. It was determined that the courts had failed to make positive contributions to maintaining social stability by containing disputes.[33] As the number of civil cases began steadily rising, the Party believed that the more formal adjudicatory justice in responding to civil disputes in the 1990s and 2000s failed to deliver the necessary levels of political stability and social harmony. Alongside the castigation of judicial formalism, the reality of Chinese courts and judges being overloaded, as well as the limitations of judicial resources, judicial mediation gradually regained popularity since the mid-2000s.

Additionally, to implement the "harmonious society" State policy post-2006, the Chinese courts have placed an increasing emphasis on mediation.[34]

---

31 Ibid., art. 2.
32 See discussions in Section 2 of Chapter 2.
33 The problems were aggravated by bureaucratic case handling, excessive court fees, corruption, and even enhanced expectations when people did not get substantive justice. Donald Clarke, Peter Murrell and Susan Whiting, "The Role of Law in China's Economic Development," in *China's Great Economic Transformation*, eds. Thomas Rawski and Loren Brandt (Cambridge: Cambridge University Press, 2008): 375–428. See also Randall Peerenboom and He Xin, "Dispute Resolution in China: Patterns, Causes, and Prognosis," *University of Pennsylvania East Asia Law Review* 1, no. 4 (2009): 1–61.
34 See generally Central Committee of the Communist Party of China, *Zhonggong Zhongyang guanyu goujian shehuizhuyi hexieshehui ruogan zhongda wenti de jueding* 中共中央关于构建社会主义和谐社会若干重大问题的决定, October 11, 2006, http://www.gov. cn/gongbao/content/2006/content_453176.htm; Maureen Fan, "China's Party Leadership Declares New Priority: 'Harmonious Society'," *Washington Post*, October 12, 2006.

Corresponding to the subtler societal change and public manifestation of discontent, judges were provided with training to deal with social unrest cases through judicial mediation. To emphasize the importance of mediation and mediatory justice, in 2007, the SPC published Several Opinions on Further Increasing the Positive Role of Mediation in Litigation in Constructing Socialism and a Harmonious Society (the "2007 Opinion").[35] Article 5 of the 2007 Opinion provided a list of cases where judicial mediation should be pursued. These cases involved: (1) community interests that require the assistance of governments, (2) class action lawsuits, (3) complex facts or emotional confrontations between the parties, (4) insufficient evidence or evidence which do not clearly support the matter, (5) sensitive socio-economic issues, or (6) requests for retrial.[36] The Opinion further mandated that Chinese judges should undergo mediation training on an annual basis and that mediation should be included in the judicial performance assessment.[37] Thus, the SPC has given a clear message that judicial mediation has become a target and has direct career consequences upon Chinese judges.[38] This judicial policy clearly transmitted the signal that there are incentives for Chinese judges to shift their role and appraise mediation actively.

Accordingly, in contrast to the declining trend of judicial mediation in the early 2000s, in SPC's annual work report in 2008, 59% of the civil cases were settled by judicial mediation, as compared to the 26.7% resolved between 2004 and 2008.[39] Judicial mediation was vigorously promoted for being conducive to social stability and harmony and reached the peak in the early 2010s,[40] as will be explained later in this chapter.

2.3 Judicial prioritization in the late 2000s and early 2010s

More checkered developments on judicial mediation were pushed for by different judicial policies. In March 2009, in response to the rise of social conflicts that came as a by-product of rapid economic growth, the SPC published its Third-Five-Year Reform Outline (2009–2013).[41] The Third

35 Supreme People's Court, *Several Opinions of the Supreme People's Court on Further Displaying the Positive Roles of Mediation in Litigation in the Building of a Socialist Harmonious Society*, March 7, 2007, http://www.lawinfochina.com/display.aspx?id=5930&lib=law.
36 Ibid., art. 5.
37 Ibid., arts. 20, 24.
38 See Section 3.2 of this chapter on "target responsibility system."
39 Vicki Waye and Xiong Ping, "The Relationship between Mediation and Judicial Proceedings in China," *Asian Journal of Comparative Law* 6, no. 1 (2011): 1–34.
40 Stanley Lubman, "Chinese Law after Sixty Years," East Asia Forum, October 2, 2009, http://www.eastasiaforum.org/2009/10/02/chinese-law-after-sixty-years/.
41 Supreme People's Court, *Renmin Fayuan Di'sange Wunian Gaige Gangyao 2009–2013*人民法院第三个五年改革纲要 2009–2013, February 24, 2010, http://www.court.gov.cn/shenpan-xiangqing-323.html.

Five-Year Reform Outline placed more emphasis on the "mass line" and popular justice. It prioritized the use of judicial mediation and mandated that judicial reform must be politically correct.[42] The consequent reversal from adjudicatory to mediatory justice in China was comparable to the development of "responsive law" as per the arguments of Nonet and Selznick in *Law and Society in Transition*, where the authors argued that contemporary law was in the process of evolving to a higher legal stage of "responsive law" involving a "renewal of instrumentalism … for more objective public ends."[43] While some authors opined that this court reform agenda would help facilitate social harmony, Minzner, a Chinese law expert at the Fordham Law School in the United States, attacked the judicial policy an artificial panacea for social stability and "China's turn against law," through the illustration of a practice known as the "target responsibility system" which manipulated judges' behavior.[44]

The "target responsibility system" referred to by Minzner was used to evaluate, reprimand, and reward judges, by linking careers and salaries with their success in attaining performance goals—which were usually numerical—including higher use of mediation.[45] As Chinese courts prioritized mediation since the late 2000s, they elevated the required mediation target rates for civil litigation. In some cases, targets could reach unbelievably high figures. For instance, Legal Daily (*Fazhi Ribao* 法制日报), China's mainstream legal newspaper, revealed that the successful mediation rate at the Henan Provincial High Court of its first instance civil disputes was as high as 60% to 80%.[46] The implementation of this target system, which guaranteed that higher mediation rates corresponded with higher incomes, resulted in substantial increases in the number of cases resolved by mediation in civil lawsuits, and even mediation competition among many Chinese courts.[47] Meanwhile, there were problematic judicial behavior as Chinese judges' careers were put at stake, which thus pressured them into forcing parties to settle. He and Yang, leading law and society

42 Wang Jiangyu, "China: Legal Reform in an Emerging Socialist Market Economy," *in Law and Legal Institutions in Asia: Traditions, Adaptations and Innovations*, eds. Ann Black and Gary F. Bell (Cambridge: Cambridge University Press, 2011), 56.

43 Brian Z. Tamanaha, "The Tension between Legal Instrumentalism and the Rule of Law," 33 *Syracuse Journal of International Law and Commerce* 33, no. 1 (2005): 131–149, quoting Philippe Nonet and Philip Selznick, *Law and Society in Transition: Toward Responsive Law* (New Jersey: Transaction Publishers, 2000).

44 For a discussion of "target responsibility" see Supreme People's Court, *Renmin Fayuan Di'sange Wunian Gaige Gangyao 2009–2013*人民法院第三个五年改革纲要 2009–2013, 1(3).

45 Minzner, "China's Turn Against Law," 956, 963.

46 Wang Hongwei, "Yichangjiufen, tiaojie haishi panjue" 一场纠纷, 调解, 还是判决, *Legal Daily*, October 21, 2009 (detailing the requirement of the Henan Province High People's Court that between 60 and 80 percent of first instance civil disputes be successfully mediated).

47 Minzner, "China's Turn Against Law," 958.

scholars on Chinese justice, studied that in order to achieve the goal of dissolving street protests organized by unpaid workers, courts had redirected their efforts away from adjudicating cases to appease workers. Rather, they took illogical measures to reach private, backroom settlements by paying workers' wages using court budgets.[48] As Minzner commented on the practice, the shortsighted concessions (in the "pretense" of social harmony) aggravated social problems, as disputants could orchestrate protests without resorting to legal channels at all.[49]

As the examples discussed earlier in this chapter demonstrate, heightened instrumentalism of law, where legal rules are tools to achieve desired policy objectives, requires judges to focus on attaining both legal justice and goal-oriented substantive policy justice. While modern judges engage in two types of analysis in accordance with law and policy goals respectively, Chinese judges have grown to be partial to the instrumentalist view and policy objective of the law, which—in Tamanaha's commentary on the tension between instrumentalism and rule of law—requires judges to manipulate legal rules to reach the desired result when the legally right outcome differs from the policy-oriented outcome.[50]

In the face of this seemingly monolithic drift to judicial mediation, while there are some advantages such as those general values of the alternative dispute resolution movement elsewhere in the world, there are problems in the resulting ineffectiveness of the overuse of mediation as a dispute resolution process, the loss of rule of law standards, and the marginalized place for courts in the Chinese society. The "redress" described earlier in this chapter shows that the judicial prioritization policy of mediation does not contribute to social stability, as it fails to solve the underlying problems of public discontentment. Given that circumstances in various cases are unlikely to be identical, the same set of priority of judicial mediation must be reshaped to bring about specific results. Legal instrumentalism in China, made manifest in the priority of mediation in judicial reform, could only lead to inconsistency and unpredictability in rule application.[51]

The Chinese judicial system is aware that the irrational expansion of the judicial mediation may produce potential injustice and unfairness. Research work, including some carried out by the courts themselves, has shown the impact of enhanced emphasis on mediation has not necessarily enhanced political stability and social harmony.[52] Meanwhile, a high judicial mediation rate has not necessarily led to high enforcement rate of mediation

---

48 Yang Su and He Xin, *Street as Courtroom: State Accommodation of Labor Protest in South China, Law and Society Review* 44, no. 1 (2010): 157–170.

49 Minzner, "China's Turn Against Law," 962.

50 Tamanaha, "The Tension between Legal Instrumentalism and the Rule of Law," 150.

51 Ibid.

52 Zhang, "Rethinking the Mediation Campaign."

settlement agreements. On the contrary, most judicial settlement agreements were not honored voluntarily by parties such that parties had to apply for compulsory enforcement at the enforcement divisions of Chinese courts.[53] As such, unfavorable result of the prioritization of judicial mediation has eventually aggravated the enforcement pressure and hence, exacerbated dispute resolution and social harmonization.

3 Reform

3.1 Legislative reform

The CPL was comprehensively revised in 2012.[54] On judicial mediation, the 2012 CPL largely continued the approach taken in Chapter 8 of the 2007 CPL. Chapter 8 of the 2012 CPL (Articles 93–99) incorporated the counterpart provisions of the 2007 CPL in verbatim.

In addition, under the 2012 CPL, parties were newly required to attempt mediation if appropriate when filing their civil litigation, unless the parties refuse to do so.[55] Some argued that because of this provision, courts now had the legal basis to facilitate pre-filing mediation when necessary. It thus reiterated the legislative tone to emphasize mediation and mediatory justice throughout.[56] Another highlight introduced by the 2012 CPL concerned the judicial confirmation of mediation settlement agreements concluded by the people's mediation committees.[57] The reform therefore encouraged extra-judicial mediation efforts such as those of the people's mediation system by way of elevating them to the status of judicial judgments to enjoy enforceability.

The CPL was most recently revised in 2017. As with its prior versions, the 2017 CPL devoted one whole chapter, Chapter 8 (Articles 93–99), to the adoption of judicial mediation,[58] which stressed the important role of mediation in Chinese civil litigation system continuously over the passage of time. Despite the foregoing, Woo, one of the leading American scholars on Chinese civil justice system, argued that, judicial mediation is one viable, rather than dominant, option for the disputing parties in China; it is for the

---

53 Ibid.
54 See discussions in Chapter 3.
55 Minshi Susong Fa (民事诉讼法) [Civil Procedure Law] (promulgated by the National People's Congress, August 31, 2012, effective October 3, 2012), arts. 122, http://www.lawinfochina.com/display.aspx?lib=law&id=19&CGid=.
56 Ye Ariel and Yu Song, "Justice, Efficiency, and the New Civil Procedure Law," *China Law & Practice*, November 1, 2012.
57 Civil Procedure Law 2012, arts. 194, 195.
58 Minshi Susong Fa (民事诉讼法) [Civil Procedure Law] (promulgated by the National People's Congress Standing Committee, June 27, 2017, effective July 1, 2017), arts. 93–99, http://en.pkulaw.cn/display.aspx?id=6d9ce94e57cee7afbdfb&lib=law.

parties to decide voluntarily on whether to resort to mediation in the civil litigation proceedings.[59] As to the role conflict of the same judge or panel that serves as both the judge(s) and mediator(s) for the same case, the CPL 2017 has not moved further than the stances taken in its prior versions. The judge hearing the case could (rather than "should") appoint relevant entity or individual, instead of the judge in the case, to carry out mediation; and the relevant entity or individual appointed should assist in the judicial mediation process.[60] On encouraging pre-filling voluntary mediation between disputing parties[61] and confirming mediation efforts resulting from people's mediation,[62] the 2017 CPL confirmed the approaches taken in the 2012 CPL.

3.2 More nuanced judicial approach after 2013

The assumption of power by Xi Jinping in late 2012 started to shift the focus from the highly politicized reform back to a rejuvenation of the rule of law. The white paper issued by the State Council that same year utilized a more objective language in contrary to previous leaderships, that China should set a new reform direction focusing on the "use of judicial authority."[63] On the judiciary's front, given a new round of the rule of law reform, albeit one to which commitment appears less than full,[64] and in light of the growing complexity and value diversity of the Chinese society, any moves would require a more nuanced judicial approach toward the role of mediation in the civil justice system.

To echo Xi's "rule of law" move, Zhou Qiang, the first Chief Justice trained in law in the post-cultural-revolution era, was appointed to be the President of the SPC in 2013. In Fu and Palmer's observation, Zhou's appointment is a clear indication of re-embracing judicial formalism such that mediation would no longer receive the same priority it once did.[65]

Not surprisingly, with SPC's launch of the Fourth Five-Year Reform Outline (2014–2018), the Chinese courts adopted a more prudential attitude toward the adoption of judicial mediation in civil litigation. The Fourth

---

59 Margaret Woo, "Bonded Legality: China's Developmental State and Civil Dispute Resolution," *Maryland Journal of International Law* 27, (2012): 235, 240–41.

60 Civil Procedure Law 2017, arts. 94, 95.

61 Ibid., art. 122.

62 Ibid., arts. 194, 195.

63 Fu Hualing and Michael Palmer, "Introduction," in *Mediation in Contemporary China: Continuity and Change*, eds. Fu Hualing and Michael Palmer (London: Wildy, Simmonds & Hill Publishing, 2017), 4.

64 In the summer of 2013, there was a clumsy attempt to restrict the pro-constitutionalist academic and popular discourse that had begun to take hold in the wake of Xi's December 2012 speech. The Chinese leadership indicated that it intends to maintain the one-Party rule, and that this is the political reality within which any legal reform will have to operate.

65 Fu and Palmer, "Introduction," 4.

Five-Year Reform Outline responded to some of the international calls for rule of law, and took a more nuanced approach between adjudicatory justice and mediatory justice.[66] It re-assured the establishment of a Chinese lawsuit system centered on adjudication and proposed the improvement of the rules of proof in civil proceedings.[67] It further proposed that a more balanced policy in the handling of civil cases (both inside and outside the courts) should be pursued, in the spirit of creating a more scientific diversified dispute resolution mechanism so that disputants are offered a genuine choice of processes.[68] In tandem with the Fourth Five-Year Reform Outline, in 2016, the SPC published the Opinions on Further Revolution of the ADR System (the "2016 ADR Opinion").[69]

The 2016 ADR Opinion required the Chinese courts to approach judicial mediation institutionally. It adopted a more rational approach in the promotion of mediation and proposed the separation of mediation and litigation such that a full-time mediator system could be explored in China. Pursuant to the 2016 ADR Opinion, the Chinese judicial system now requires the lower level courts to respect the parties' desires in adopting judicial mediation, and removes the mediation target rate from the performance assessments of both judges and courts.[70] The courts are expected to develop *modus operandi* in dispute resolution with which to regain judicial credibility and effectiveness. The possibility to appoint Chinese judges with both mediation skills and abundant mediation experience to conduct the judicial mediation proceedings is explored.[71] One of the leading scholars on Chinese mediation and civil dispute resolution, Wu at the Nanjing University Law School, noted that while some Chinese courts actively executed this SPC policy on judicial mediation, they were not all successful; others encountered challenges at different extents in implementation.[72] Wu concluded that the employment of the same judge as the mediator is still the predominant practice in Chinese judicial mediation currently, despite the international trend of separating mediation and litigation proceedings and their relevant personnel under rising concerns

---

66 Supreme People's Court, *Zuigao renmin fayuan fabu "siwu gaige gangyao"* 最高人民法院发布 "四五改革纲要," July 10, 2014, http://www.court.gov.cn/zixun-xiangqing-8168.html.

67 Ibid.

68 Ibid.

69 "Zuigao renmin fayuan guanyu renmin fayuan jinyibu Shenhua duoyuanhua jiufen jiejue jizhi gaige de yijian" 最高人民法院关于人民法院进一步深化多元化纠纷解决机制改革的意见, *Renmin fayuan bao* 人民法院报, January 8, 2017, https://www.chinacourt.org/article/detail/2017/01/id/2509588.shtml.

70 Ibid.

71 Ibid.

72 Wu Yingzi 吴英姿, "Priority of Mediation" 调解优先: 改革范式与法律解读 以O市法院改革为样本, *Peking University Law Journal* 中外法学 no. 3 (2013): 536–555; Wu Yingzi 吴英姿, "Justice Identity: Crisis and Reestablishment" 论司法认同: 危机与重建, *China Legal Science* 中国法学, no. 3 (2016): 186–206.

on the fairness and justice in dispute resolution.[73] The apparent relegal-ization policies have seemingly had some relaxation in the emphasis on mediation generally and a gradual moving away from the prioritization of judicial mediation specifically, which was regarded as the normalization of judicial mediation in China to re-embrace judicial formalism.[74]

The analyses above echo the reduced emphasis in judicial mediation empirically shown in Section 1.2 of this chapter, reflecting a continuous decline in the rate of mediated outcomes in civil lawsuits since 2012. The judicial mediation rate dropped from the peak of more than 40% in 2011–2012 to becoming stabilized at around 25% after 2016.[75] The levelling off may indeed be a sign of the use of a more nuanced judicial approach, with medi-ation still having an important role but not overwhelmingly prioritized role to play in China's civil justice system.

Likewise, the most recent Fifth Five-Year Reform Outline (2019–2023) stressed more nuanced and balanced judicial policies in the handling of civil and commercial cases, calling for the establishment of a sound and diversified dispute resolution mechanism connecting among mediation, arbitration and litigation.[76] The collaboration between judicial mediation, arbitration, and civil litigation systems has been emphasized to promote a "diversified" (*duoyuanhua* 多元化) channel for dispute settlements.[77] This revision of a more balanced approach in dispute resolution indicated a new trend of normalization of the judicial mediation, which includes the creation of more specialized tracks of dispute resolution, such as those catered to international disputes. This is especially so with respect to the Belt and Road Initiative (the "BRI") national diplomatic and economic strategy that the Chinese government has been enthu-siastically promoted since 2015.[78]

4 Development analyses

The following section examines the recent development trajectory of judi-cial mediation in China, combining analyses of both the penetrating factors that have led to its checkered development and the development patterns such as top-down and bottom-up.

---

73 Ibid.
74 Fu and Palmer, "Introduction," 4.
75 See statistics in Section 1.2 of this chapter.
76 "'Wuwu gaige gangyao' ji Zhongguo fayuan sifa gaige baipishu xinwen fabu hui" "五五改革纲要"暨中国法院司法改革白皮书新闻发布会, *Zuigao renmin fayuan wang* 最高人民法院网, February 27, 2019, http://www.court.gov.cn/zixun-xiangqing-144172.html.
77 Ibid.
78 National Development and Reform Commission, *Visions and Actions on Jointly Building Silk Road Economic Belt and 21st-Century Maritime Silk Road*, March 28, 2015, https://reconasia-production.s3.amazonaws.com/media/filer_public/e0/22/e0228017-7463-46fc-9094-0465a6f1ca23/vision_and_actions_on_jointly_building_silk_road_economic_belt_and_21st-century_maritime_silk_road.pdf.

4.1 Judicial mediation in social transitions from top-down

In academic literature, the objectives of thin approaches to rule of law are to "ensure stability," to "secure the government in accordance with law by limiting its arbitrariness," to "enhance predictability," to "provide fair dispute resolution mechanisms," and "to reinforce the legitimacy of the government."[79] Despite their shared acceptance of the aforementioned broad goals, states may apportion different weight to these objectives, which in turn results in remarkable variations in legal discourses. In periods of rapid economic or social transformation, as have been occurring in China in the past decade or so, the modernization project is soon challenged by the escalation of social conflicts in the transitional period.

It has been reported that "public order disturbances" grew significantly in recent years.[80] The Rule of Law Development Report published by the Chinese Academy of Social Science in 2010 revealed that the financial crisis, high unemployment, and a polarized society have led to a grave situation of political instability with an increasing number of social unrest cases.[81] This influx of cases and disputes poses a serious challenge to the courts' efficiency in judging, adversely impacting access to justice. The failure to address these disputes has pushed the excluded or dissatisfied to seek redress through other channels, such as the letters and visits system.[82] Zhu, former dean of the Peking University Law School and Chinese leading law and society scholar, argued that all of these have endangered political and social stability, which has been the top priority of the Chinese Party-State.[83] On the other hand, despite the bold advocacy and impressive progress made in the past several decades, Ng and He, authors of the leading empirical work on Chinese courts, vigorously argue that Chinese court system is still more a political regime than a separate professional institution.[84] As the judiciary has been increasingly subject to political control, the challenges facing the judiciary and judicial reform in China include not only the intense conflicts associated with full-scale social and

---

79 Randall Peerenboom, "Varieties of Rule of Law: An Introduction and Provisional Conclusion," *SSRN*, September 23, 2003, https://papers.ssrn.com/sol3/papers.cfm?abstract_id=445821.

80 Christian Göbel and Lynette H. Ong, "Social Unrest in China," *Europe China Research and Advice Network (ECRAN) Paper*, (2012), 8, http://www.chathamhouse.org/sites/files/chathamhouse/public/Research/Asia/1012ecran_gobelong.pdf.

81 See Li Lin and Tian He, *Annual Report On China's Rule Of Law No. 8* (2010), February 1, 2010, https://www.pishu.com.cn/skwx_ps/bookdetail?SiteID=14&ID=1093493.

82 By 2011, many Chinese courts had set up a department to take in complaint letters, petitions, or visits concerning judicial grievances.

83 Zhu Suli, "Political Parties in China's Judiciary," *Duke Journal of Comparative & International Law* 17 (2007): 538–41.

84 Ng Kwai Hang and He Xin, *Embedded Courts: Judicial Decision-Making in China* (Cambridge: Cambridge University Press, 2017), Chapters 1 and 4.

economic transitions, but also the unpredictable struggle of political ideology to deal with the pressing reality.[85]

In this context, according to Zhang's observation, leaving aside other
factors such as biased rulings, judicial corruption, and unbalanced
enforcement, the entire judicial system is institutionally inaccessible and
ineffective, creating an "institutional alienation."[86] The judiciary has been
caught in between judicial justice, realized through an independent judiciary exercising impartial adjudication of disputes, and practical popularity
as a means to provide the political regime with much needed legitimate
support.[87] As a result, under the direction of political policy, some judicial
mechanisms, or "judicial policy," must be deployed to settle disputes that
may not be suitable for their application in a rule-of-law context at all. The
popularity of mediation, apart from drawing on Chinese historical and
cultural roots of harmony, is perceived more as a means to divert disputes
from the overtaxed judiciary, to massage social conflicts, and to ensure
that the judicial system operates in accordance with political policy.[88] The
rise of, and even priority of, judicial mediation is one such judicial policy
and exemplifies the "institutional alienation" of the Chinese judiciary in
transitional times.

Mediation has been widely used in all kinds of civil proceedings to support
the political policy of maintaining social stability.[89] It has been concluded
that after the transition from a planned economy to market economy that
took over several decades, the judicial reform on mediation has taken a full
cycle—from "mediation first" in the 1980s, to mediation on the basis of law
and parties' consent in the 1990s, to deployment of mediation and judgment
in accordance with the nature of disputes in the early 2000s, to the return
in the prioritization of mediation since 2009, and finally, to a more nuanced
approach after 2013.[90] Compared with the prevalence of mediation in the
1980s, the judicial policy toward judicial mediation since the late 2000s, as a
distinctive Chinese response by the justice system to economic and societal
transition, is largely a political arrangement to achieve stability.

As pushed top-down by the SPC's Third Five-Year Reform Outline from
2009 to 2013, a process of de-legalization was set in train and litigation
thus became marginalized in the late 2000s and early 2010s. A politicized

85 Ibid.
86 ZhangXianchu, "Civil Justice Reform with Political Agendas," in *The Development of the
   Chinese Legal System*, ed. Yu Guanghua (New York: Routledge, 2011), 259.
87 Ibid.
88 Waye and Xiong, "The Relationship between Mediation and Judicial Proceedings in
   China," 33.
89 The application of judicial mediation before the social transition towards a market economy was primarily limited to small-scale cases, such as family, neighborhood, and labor
   disputes. See Zhang Xianchu, "Civil Justice Reform with Political Agendas," 259.
90 Zhang, 'Rethinking the Mediation Campaign.'

priority of judicial mediation had been pushed in which the primary test of an outcome was its political impact. The practice has been revisited by the SPC in its fourth and fifth rounds of court reform in the context of China's relegalization judicial policy after 2013. Judicial mediation has thus been adopted in a more prudent and balanced manner. The SPC now stresses the parties' true willingness in adopting judicial mediation and removes the mediation target rate from the performance assessments of both the Chinese judges and courts. The most recent precautions on judicial mediation and the re-embracement of judicial formalism reflects the Chinese top judiciary's response to the international calls for rule of law. As such, the top-down development pattern has been obvious.

4.2 Judicial mediation in social transitions from bottom-up

Scholars have argued that effective access to justice is fundamental to the promotion of the rule of law and that this can be accomplished by both formal and informal measures.[91] A combination of formal and informal access to justice can be found in most societies, as the high costs of litigation imply that there are insufficient judicial resources to deal with the community's demand for redress.[92] Such societal problems have been particularly severe during China's rapid urbanization, which is not comparable to an established economy in ordinary times.[93] Scarce resources aside, tough socio-economic cases tend to raise novel issues for which courts often lack clear legislative or judicial guidance. Benchmarked against developed countries' standards, with regard to the general correlation between wealth and institutional development, Peerenboom, one of the most prolific Chinese law experts in the West, argued that governance institutions in China nonetheless remain relatively weak.[94]

Fu and Peerenboom argued that in the case of China, given the courts' inability to provide an effective remedy in the socio-economic cases, access to the courts should be limited.[95] Moreover, the dejudicialization of

---

91 Edgardo Buscaglia and Paul B. Stephen, "An Empirical Assessment of the Impact of Formal Versus Informal Dispute Resolution on Poverty: A Governance-Based Approach," *International Review of Law and Economics* 25, no. 1 (2005): 89.

92 Christopher Hodges, Stefan Vogenauer and Magdalena Tulibacka, "Costs and Funding of Civil Litigation: A Comparative Study," *SSRN*, November 27, 2009, http://papers.ssrn.com/sol3/papers.cfm?abstract_id=1511714.

93 Randall Peerenboom, "Judicial Independence in China: Common Myths and Unfounded Assumptions," *SSRN*, October 12, 2008, http://papers.ssrn.com/sol3/papers.cfm?abstract_id=1283179.

94 Ibid., 22.

95 Fu Yulin and Randall Peerenboom, "A New Analytical Framework for Understanding and Promoting Judicial Independence in China," in *Judicial Independence in China: Lessons for Global Rule of Law Promotion*, ed. Randall Peerenboom (Cambridge: Cambridge University Press, 2010), 115.

socio-economic cases has become evident as the government has directed such disputes away from court adjudication toward alternative mechanisms such as mediation, in view of the courts' lack of resources and competence to provide effective relief in such cases.[96] Subsequently, with the restrictions imposed on both access to the courts and the courts' roles, non-judicial mechanisms such as mediation have been strengthened to address citizens' concerns in such cases. Correspondingly, there has been a re-emergence and revitalization of judicial mediation among Chinese courts, and a gradual acceptance of judicial mediation among Chinese judges themselves bottom-up in response to the sharp increase in socially-oriented cases since 2006.[97] Overall, Ng and He argued that there has been a gradual transformation in the perspective of Chinese judges and a remodeling of their role from mere passive involvement to an active appraisal of mediation with flexible implementation.[98]

The judges' initial passivity was prompted by their pursuit of professionalism. As in the first two rounds of court reform (1998–2008), substantive and procedural laws proliferated and the professionalization of judges and efficacy of litigation improved.[99] Mediation, which was previously associated with the Confucian cultural influence and Maoist attempts to impose socialist ideology,[100] came to be viewed as inconsistent with China's aspirations for the development of the rule of law.[101] Moreover, given the pressures for efficiency, mediation was further challenged by Chinese judges as being time-consuming.[102] Judicial mediation in China was also challenged by scholars in the West who viewed adjudication and mediation as two entirely separate dispute resolution processes, the blending of which without proper safeguards was deemed to destroy the sanctity of justice and impartiality.[103] While Western-styled court-annexed mediation promotes mediation as a problem-solving process supportive of the parties' self-determination, judicial mediation in China takes a more evaluative role that is likely to involve the directing of parties.[104] There are also concerns about the conflicting roles

---

96 Ibid., 112.
97 Waye and Xiong, "The Relationship between Mediation and Judicial Proceedings in China," 24.
98 Ng and He, *Embedded Courts*, Chapter 2.
99 Fu and Cullen, "From Mediatory to Adjudicatory Justice: The Limits of Civil Justice Reform in China," 42.
100 Stanley Lubman, *Bird in a Cage: Legal Reform in China after Mao* (Stanford: Stanford University Press, 2002), Chapter 3.
101 Peerenboom and He, "Dispute Resolution in China: Patterns, Causes and Prognosis," 10–11.
102 Ibid.
103 Waye and Xiong, "The Relationship between Mediation and Judicial Proceedings in China," 21–22.
104 See generally He Xin and Ng Kwai Hang, "Internal Contradictions of Judicial Mediation," *Law and Social Inquiry* 39, no. 2 (2014): 285.

of mediators and judges and associated breaches of confidentiality because the mediator-turned-judge is allowed to participate in private caucuses with parties and may inadvertently use information that he or she would not have access to in litigation.[105]

Since the SPC engaged in a deliberate policy of revival of mediation in the third round of court reform (2009–2013), judges began to gradually accept and even actively appraised mediation for a variety of reasons.[106] Insofar as difficult disputes over access to resources and participation in decision making about developments resulting from China's economic transformation are concerned, judicial mediation is more attractive than litigation because it obviates the need for articulation of a clear legal position and is more likely to avoid any enforcement difficulties that may follow.[107] In association with the escalation of socio-economic and socio-political conflicts, fewer adjudicatory approaches in litigation could make Chinese judges respond more effectively to the needs of litigants, allowing them to take into account political and social considerations in decision-making and thus contribute to social stability.[108]

Using Tamanaha's theory of legal instrumentalism and rule of law, as the practice of law reinforces the approach of utilizing law instrumentally, Chinese judges inevitably are affected and thus view law in instrumental terms.[109] With the popularity and priority of mediation, Chinese judges changed from expert (*zhuanjia faguan* 专家法官) and elite judges (*jingying faguan* 精英法官) to more populist (*pingmin faguan* 平民法官) and stability-minded judges (*weiwen faguan* 维稳法官).[110]

After 2013, in the context of a more nuanced judicial policy toward judicial mediation, there has been some newfound evidence of Chinese judges' support for and quick adaptation of mediation under the "new normal" (*xinchangtai* 新常态).[111] Interestingly, the strategy of handling cases by involving mediation has become increasingly innovative and flexible. Chinese judges are altering their initial approach as neutral middlemen (*juzhong tiaojie* 居中调解) who only mediate on the basis of facts and evidence they are directly exposed to, to the current adoption of "mediation all around" (*quanmian tiaojie* 全面调解), where judges make use of all information they can procure from disputants.[112] Though no longer prioritized

---

105 Waye and Xiong, "The Relationship between Mediation and Judicial Proceedings in China," 22.
106 Minzner, "China's Turn Against Law," 936.
107 Waye and Xiong, "The Relationship between Mediation and Judicial Proceedings in China," 24.
108 Ng and He, *Embedded Courts*, Chapters 2 and 6.
109 Ibid., 149.
110 Gu, "Responsive Justice in China during Transitional Times," 77.
111 Ng and He, *Embedded Courts*, Chapters 2 and 6.
112 Interview with Judge Xian Yifan (May 2015).

and more prudently approached, there might be a silver lining to the cloud of the bottom-up preference of judicial mediation by Chinese judges in economic and societal transitions, such as the emergence of a more "conversational-infused" approach, such as "communicative justice" to handling socio-economic cases, especially between power imbalanced parties, to achieve its potential in China.[113]

5 The future

While the judicial policy toward mediation has been more rational, there remain inadequacies in the judicial mediation landscape that should be further addressed, fine-tuned, amended, and overhauled, at both the technical procedural level and systematic institutional level, as the directions for future reform.

5.1 Technical challenges

To begin with, even though Chinese judges have continuously practiced mediation over several decades, most judges conduct judicial mediation processes in a manner similar to litigation.[114] In mediation initiated by judges, parties can easily yield to the judges' authority or are reluctant to reveal information that may be used to be against them in subsequent litigation proceedings. Some Chinese scholars appealed to separate the mediation and litigation processes to avoid one judge from performing both roles in two separate proceedings.[115]

These include a clearer separation of roles into an "adjudicating judge" and a "mediating judge" in a revised procedural system (*tiaoshen shidu fenli* 调审适度分离) that might also usefully include the creation of a specific division within the courts dedicated to judicial mediation, with stricter standards of confidentiality. The CPL attempted to address the role conflict by providing that the judge is required to file a judgment if pre-trial mediation agreement is unsuccessful,[116] in effect allowing the judge to have an idea of the likely adjudicatory decision.[117] Nonetheless, this may have the effect

113 Xian Yifan, "Grassroots Judges of China in the Resurgence from Adjudicatory to Mediatory Justice: Transformation of Roles and Inherent Conflict of Identities," in *Mediation in Contemporary China: Continuity and Change*, eds. Fu Hualing and Michael Palmer (London: Wildy, Simmonds & Hill Publishing, 2017), 167–187.
114 Li Hao 李浩, "Separate the Mediation and Litigation in Civil Judiciaries" 调解归调解, 审判归审判: 民事审判中的调审分离, *Zhongguo Faxue* 中国法学 no. 3 (2013): 5–18.
115 Ibid. See also Zhou Cui, "Relationship between Mediation and Adjudication: Rethink and Restatement," *Comparative Legal Research* no. 1 (2014): 52.
116 See discussions in Section 3.1 of this chapter.
117 Chen Yongzhu, "The Judge as Mediator in China and Its Alternatives: A Problem in Chinese Civil Justice," in *Mediation in Contemporary China: Continuity and Change*, eds. Fu Hualing and Michael Palmer (London: Wildy, Simmonds & Hill Publishing, 2017), 140–166.

of dissuading disputants from disclosing information in the pre-trial mediation since such confidential information may well be taken into account in the trial hearing. Meanwhile, pre-trial mediation retains an uncertain legal status, and gives the judge a wide-ranging discretionary authority in handling cases. There are critiques pointing out that a chance was missed in the 2012 revisions to the CPL to regularize the situation, so that in practice, mediating judges in China are not only faced with the role conflict but also have been left in a legal limbo.[118]

Comparative research shows that in Canada, the issue of role conflict has been well taken. In Quebec in particular, the Code of Civil Procedure (2014) sets out a good model for separation between the judge and mediator in the judicial mediation procedure. The confidential information is also protected under the pre-trial settlement conference. Any details of the mediation are not to be shared with other unless such information is expressly authorized by both parties. Unauthorized disclosure would impose civil responsibility on the part of mediator. Judicial mediators are also obliged to destroy documents used in the mediation at the end of the case. These reform measures help maintain a clear separation of the mediatory and trial stages of the case.[119]

The situation is not without hope. Some Chinese local courts have started to explore innovations. For example, the Nanjing Intermediate Court of the Jiangsu Province responded to the call for separating mediation and litigation procedure, altering the current court practice in which the judge plays a dual role. The Nanjing Court divided judges into separated categories of mediation and litigation based on their characteristics, specialties and preferences. Optimistic result has been observed, with the mediation rate increased by 11.29% and a drop of 8% in undecided cases from 2012 to 2013.[120] It remains to be seen, however, as to how the general application of the separation of mediation and litigation procedure would have an overall impact in compliance with the rule of law and improving judicial efficiency, and how it could overcome potential obstacles such as the regulation of mediation behavior and compliance with current legislation.

Local initiatives are also seen in setting up special mediation units within the court. Since 2009, the Dongguan Second Intermediate Court of the Guangdong Province has set up special mediation centers in the court filing division as a forum for transferal and better management of the cases. Its internal regulations divided civil disputes into three main categories according to their individual circumstances: neighborhood civil disputes;

---

118 Xian, "Grassroots Judges of China in the Resurgence from Adjudicatory to Mediatory Justice."

119 Chen, "The Judge as Mediator in China and Its Alternatives."

120 Yang Wen 杨文, "Si fa diao jie de mo shi tan suo—yi nan jing zhong ji ren min fa yuan diao shen shi du fen li wei li" 司法調解的模式探索—以南京中級人民法院调审适度分离为例, *Jin Ling Law Review* 金陵法律评论 25, no. 2 (2013): 150.

commercial disputes; and complicated mass disputes. Following the allocation, the mediation mechanism for the three categories varied, with the more professional and experienced judges and mediators handling civil disputes of higher sensitivity.[121] Arguably, the special mediation units relieved the burden of the court.

5.2 Systematic challenges

Apart from those technical challenges, China's judicial mediation faces obstacles embedded within the legal system. In a transitional society like China, the legal system is under-developed in resolving the influx of cases to the basic courts. In view of the heavy caseload, the Chinese government has made good effort to enhance the efficiency and legitimacy of its dispute resolution system by streamlining the disputes to relieve pressure of the courts and confirming the enforceability of mediation agreements. One major shortcoming is, however, envisaged in China's dispute resolution system, in terms of the lack of respect for fairness and rule of law. An added complication faced by Chinese judges is the assessment mechanism for their performances, which stresses the importance of mediation settlement rate. Being result-oriented, judges and mediators often attach much importance to the final outcome of dispute settlement, neglecting procedural fairness in the process of decision-making. The sub-standard manner of practice by the judges is likely to damage the level of confidence by citizens with regards to the judicial system and the rule of law in China, prompting unsatisfied citizens to seek alternative non-legal routes to resolve their disputes. This challenge is more evident in judicial mediation, as compared and contrasted with the people's mediation system. The success of performance by people's mediators is to a lesser extent based on government objectives and is more dependent on the mediator's personal connections and experiences, such as their social reputation and previous mediation outcomes.[122]

He, leading scholar of Chinese law and society, through extensive empirical studies, finds that the incorporation of mediation as part of the official judicial process creates a set of internal contradictions.[123] In addition to the inherent role conflict of a judge acting also as a mediator, adjudication and mediation stages are organized by different principles. When the rather rigid format of adjudication is carried over to in-trial mediation, it curtails the flexible, non-legalistic approach that mediation is meant to promote, all of which shows the limit of judicial mediation as one important aspects of informal

---

121 Ibid.
122 Wu Yuning, "People's Mediation Enters the 21st Century," in *Mediation in Contemporary China: Continuity and Change*, eds. Fu Hualing and Michael Palmer (London: Wildy, Simmonds & Hill Publishing, 2017), 34–58.
123 He and Ng, "Internal Contradictions of Judicial Mediation in China."

justice. This also reflects the orthodox Chinese legal culture with regard to mediation and civil procedural law, which takes the consequentialist approach to justice, favoring the substantive result of law over procedural justice.[124]

There are subtler political barriers. The Party's "turn against law" under the Hu–Wen leadership and "reliance on mediation" was a political response to social instability, and moreover, a response to the perceived failure of judicial formalism of the rule-based and court-centric litigation.[125] In response, the Party intervened in dispute resolution directly, but in an informal, ad hoc, and politically expedient manner, such as by judicial mediation. Xi's leadership abandoned the prioritized policy for judicial mediation. Though being more nuanced in the judicial approach, through discerning the most recent SPC judicial interpretations on judicial mediation, the Party has still been keeping a special role for its comfort zone of judicial mediation, which is a culturally appraised, politically reliable, and procedurally acceptable dispute resolution, whether domestically or in the international arena.

6 Conclusion

By placing the task of maintaining social stability in the hands of the judiciary, Chinese courts in the late 2000s and early 2010s deployed various layers of mediation so that decisions were made to balance political and social consequences. China's judicial mediation development, where mediation is prioritized and abused, has been seen as a dejudicialization of the courts and an undermining of the rule of law,[126] and the mediatory justice has been seen as the "stability-driven responsive justice."[127]

While China's politicization in judicial mediation has been challenged as a "turn against law," what is the road ahead for China's mediatory justice, the revitalization of which is thought to blend China's own traditions and historical legacy? Should judicial mediation be precautioned, or completely abandoned? Fu, leading scholar on Chinese law and development, recently proposed three developmental models of mediation (both judicial mediation and extra-judicial mediation) in the dispute resolution governance of the society: (1) the civil justice model, (2) the competition model, and (3) the political model.[128]

124 Margaret Woo and Mary Gallagher, "Introduction," in *Chinese Justice: Civil Dispute Resolution in Contemporary China*, eds. Margaret Woo and Mary Gallagher (New York: Cambridge University Press, 2011), 13.
125 He Xin and Feng Yuqing, "Mismatched Discourses in the Petition Office of Chinese Courts," *Law & Social Inquiry* 41, no. 1 (2016): 212–241.
126 Minzner, "China's Turn Against Law," 944, 960.
127 Gu, "Responsive Justice in China during Transitional Times," *49–85*.
128 Fu Hualing, "Mediation and the Rule of Law: The Chinese Landscape," in *Formalization and Flexibilization in Dispute Resolution*, eds. Joachim Zekoll, Moritz Bälz and Iwo Amelung (Leiden: Brill, 2014), 108–129.

Fu argued that first, in the civil justice model, although mediation is encouraged as an alternative dispute resolution method, the application of law is emphasized as expounded by the courts through their decisions. Mediation, including both judicial and extra-judicial mediation, is subject to judicial control. The judicial control allows the court to have substantial power over the exercise of mediation and its scope.[129] Second, in the competition model, the court-based litigation and mediation operate in parallel, with both dispute resolution methods exerting influence in their respective spheres. Instead of being in the shadow of the law, mediation operates as the primary form of dispute resolution, and there is a clear separation of mediation and adjudication. As its name suggests, this model introduces competition between litigation and mediation.[130] Lastly, the political model sees that mediation dominates the dispute resolution landscape to the extent that it hinders rule-based resolution and judicial professionalism. Law loses its autonomy and is driven by social and economic forces, as well as political imperatives. A defining characteristic of this model is that disputes are regarded as undermining social stability and are strongly suppressed by extensive use of informal and extra-legal measures such as the prioritization of both judicial and extra-judicial mediation.[131] Applying Fu's models, it is evident that the development of China's judicial mediation in the late 2000s and early 2010s falls squarely within the political model. As Fu predicts, the better road ahead is the civil justice model. But this is very demanding in terms of the court's ability to be an independent and efficient oversight institution of mediation (such as the very popular judicial mediation in China), and as Fu has noted, Chinese courts have yet to demonstrate such capability.[132]

Scholars have argued that judicial mediation in itself is not a weakness.[133] China's shift away from civil trials and toward mediation is not entirely unique. Beginning in the West, and now spread to the developing world, parties in many countries face prohibitive litigation costs.[134] National judiciaries are overloaded and are increasingly challenged by insufficient access to justice or lengthy trial delays.[135] Many jurisdictions in the world, including developed (such as the United States) and developing rule-of-law

---

129 Ibid., 110–112. Fu proposed three stages of judicial control over mediation. First, the court is empowered to establish rules regarding mediation and is in the position to invalidate any mediation that contravenes those rules. Second, courts can refer cases to mediation both before or after entering the judicial process. By determining which cases are suitable for mediation, the court exercises judicial oversight. Third, the court determines the enforceability of the mediation outcome by evaluating its voluntariness and legality.

130 Ibid., 112–113.

131 Ibid., 113–114.

132 Ibid., 112.

133 Minzner, "China's Turn Against Law," 974.

134 See generally Hodges, Vogenauer and Tulibacka, "Costs and Funding of Civil Litigation," 70.

135 He and Ng, "Internal Contradictions of Judicial Mediation in China," 35.

jurisdictions (such as India and Argentina), are actively incorporating mediation into court adjudication for enhancement of better access to civil justice.[136]

Does mediation have a proper role to play in the civil justice reform, given China's deepening marketization and intensifying social movements? As the prevailing economic, historical, and sociological contexts determine a country's legal framework, the structure of its legal institutions, and its society's pathways to justice, the balance between formal and informal dispute resolution will inevitably be path dependent.[137] Scholars have argued that the architecture of one civil justice system should not be transposed to another since, in practice, the outcome of such transplantation is that the imported Western rule-of-law reforms mesh poorly with local realities.[138] Such failure results in "backlash" consisting of experiments with traditional or community mediation institutions that respond better to local conditions.[139]

It is acknowledged that China's own traditions and historical legacy will continue to play a significant role in determining the future course of its judicial reform and civil justice reform. Nevertheless, the shift of dispute resolution patterns such as advocacy of mediatory justice, and the pressurizing "target responsibility" system to achieve political objectives should not be applied by Chinese authorities to curb rule of law and judiciary autonomy.[140] In short, judicial mediation and its associated mediatory justice should not be abused and over-used as a means for exercising political will. On the contrary, judicial mediation should be rationally treated as a dispute resolution method for channeling judicial caseload and achieving a socio-economically better outcome.

Carefully drafted policies on judicial mediation are still necessary and will help solve some imminent problems in China. In light of China's socio-economic situation and its prevalent economic and social conflicts, judicial mediation could help produce a socially acceptable result,

---

136 For example, the Civil Justice Reform in Hong Kong. See "Home," Civil Justice Reform, accessed July 11, 2020, http://www.civiljustice.gov.hk/eng/home.html. See also Timothy K. Kuhner, "Court-annexed Mediation Compared: The Cases of Argentina and the United States," *ILSA Journal of International & Comparative Law* 11, no. 1 (2005): 519–553; Hiram Chodosh, Stephen A. Mayo, A.M. Ahmadi and Abhishek M. Singhvi, "Indian Civil Justice System Reform: Limitation and Preservation of the Adversarial Process," *New York University Journal of International Law and Politics* 30, no. 1 (1997/1998): 1–78.

137 Waye and Xiong, "The Relationship between Mediation and Judicial Proceedings in China," 2.

138 Ibid., 3.

139 Ethan Michelson, "Popular Attitudes Towards Dispute Processing in Urban and Rural China," *Foundation for Law, Justice and Society* (2008), https://www.fljs.org/content/popular-attitudes-towards-dispute-processing-urban-and-rural-china.

140 Minzner, "China's Turn Against Law," 978.

reducing protests, and letters and visits. This is also evident in judges' growing acceptance of employing judicial mediation in resolving civil disputes bottom-up.[141]

In a huge developing country such as China, insufficient resources, developing (rather than firmly established) legal institutions, and an enduring legal culture will all impact the manner of performance of Chinese justice and the pace and means of its future reform. During this process, the Chinese Party-State faces the pressure of maintaining both social order and regime legitimacy. The Chinese government needs to re-consider the relevance of its home-grown mediation alternatives of civil justice during transitional times; most importantly, how judicial mediation and its associated mediatory justice should be properly adopted under the rule of law.

Bibliography

Buscaglia, Edgardo and Paul B. Stephen. "An Empirical Assessment of the Impact of Formal Versus Informal Dispute Resolution on Poverty: A Governance-Based Approach." *International Review of Law and Economics* 25, no. 1 (2005): 89–106.

Central Committee of the Communist Party of China. *Zhonggong Zhongyang guanyu goujian shehuizhuyi hexieshehui ruogan zhongda wenti de jueding* 中共中央关于构建社会主义和谐社会若干重大问题的决定, October 11, 2006. http://www.gov.cn/gongbao/content/2006/content_453176.htm.

Chen, Yongzhu. "The Judge as Mediator in China and Its Alternatives: A Problem in Chinese Civil Justice." In *Mediation in Contemporary China: Continuity and Change*, edited by Fu Hualing and Michael Palmer, 140–166. London: Wildy, Simmonds & Hill Publishing, 2017.

China Law Society. *The Law Yearbook of China* (2010–2019).

Chodosh, Hiram, Stephen A. Mayo, A.M. Ahmadi and Abhishek M. Singhvi, "Indian Civil Justice System Reform: Limitation and Preservation of the Adversarial Process." *New York University Journal of International Law and Politics* 30, no. 1 (1997/1998): 1–78.

Clarke, Donald, Peter Murrell and Susan Whiting. "The Role of Law in China's Economic Development." In *China's Great Economic Transformation*, edited by Thomas Rawski and Loren Brandt, 375–428. Cambridge: Cambridge University Press, 2008.

Fan, Maureen. "China's Party Leadership Declares New Priority: 'Harmonious Society'." *Washington Post*, October 12, 2006.

Fan, Yu 范愉. *Research on ADR Mechanisms* 非诉讼纠纷解决机制研究. Beijing: Renmin University of China Press, 2000.

Fu, Hualing. "Mediation and the Rule of Law: The Chinese Landscape." In *Dispute Resolution: Alternatives to Formalization*, edited by Joachim Zekoll, Moritz Bälz and Iwo Amelung, 108–129. Leiden: Brill, 2014.

Fu, Hualing and Michael Palmer. "Introduction." In *Mediation in Contemporary China: Continuity and Change*, edited by Fu Hualing and Michael Palmer, 1–33. London: Wildy, Simmonds & Hill Publishing, 2017.

---

141   See Section 4.2 of this chapter.

Fu, Hualing and Michael Palmer, eds. *Mediation in Contemporary China: Continuity and Change*. London: Wildy, Simmonds & Hill Publishing, 2017.

Fu, Hualing and Richard Cullen. "From Mediatory to Adjudicatory Justice: The Limits of Civil Justice Reform in China." In *Chinese Justice: Civil Dispute Revolution in China*, edited by Margaret Woo and Mary Gallagher, 25–97. Cambridge: Cambridge University Press, 2011.

Fu, Yulin and Randall Peerenboom. "A New Analytical Framework for Understanding and Promoting Judicial Independence in China." In *Judicial Independence in China: Lessons for Global Rule of Law Promotion*, edited by Randall Peerenboom, 95–133. Cambridge: Cambridge University Press, 2010.

Göbel, Christian and Lynette H. Ong. "Social Unrest in China." *Europe China Research and Advice Network (ECRAN) Paper* (2012). http://www.chathamhouse. org/sites/files/ chathamhouse/public/Research/Asia/1012ecran_gobelong.pdf.

Gu, Weixia. "Responsive Justice in China During Transitional Times: Revisiting the Juggling Path Between Adjudicatory and Mediatory Justice." *Washington University Global Studies Law Review* 14, (2015): 49–85.

He, Xin and Ng Kwai Hang, "Internal Contradictions of Judicial Mediation." *Law and Social Inquiry* 39, no. 2 (2014): 285–312.

He, Xin and Yuqing Feng. "Mismatched Discourses in the Petition Office of Chinese Courts." *Law & Social Inquiry* 41, no. 1 (2016): 212–241.

Hodges, Christopher, Stefan Vogenauer and Magdalena Tulibacka. "Costs and Funding of Civil Litigation: A Comparative Study." *SSRN*, November 27, 2009. http://papers.ssrn.com/sol3/papers.cfm?abstract_id=1511714.

"Home." Civil Justice Reform, accessed July 11, 2020. http://www.civiljustice.gov.hk/ eng/home.html.

Kuhner, Timothy K. "Court-annexed Mediation Compared: The Cases of Argentina and the United States." *ILSA Journal of International & Comparative Law* 11, (2005): 519–553.

Li, Hao 李浩. "Separate the Mediation and Litigation in Civil Judiciaries" 调解归 调解，审判归审判：民事审判中的调审分离. *China Legal Science* 中国法学 no. 3 (2013): 5–18.

Li, Lin and Tian He. *Annual Report On China's Rule Of Law No. 8 (2010)*, February 1, 2010. https://www.pishu.com.cn/skwx_ps/bookdetail?SiteID=14&ID=1093493.

Lubman, Stanley. "Chinese Law after Sixty Years." *East Asia Forum*, October 2, 2009. http://www.eastasiaforum.org/2009/10/02/chinese-law-after-sixty-years/.

Michelson, Ethan. "Popular Attitudes Towards Dispute Processing in Urban and Rural China." *Foundation for Law, Justice and Society* (2008), https://www.fljs.org/ content/popular-attitudes-towards-dispute-processing-urban-and-rural-china.

Minshi Susong Fa (民事诉讼法) [Civil Procedure Law] (promulgated by the National People's Congress, October 28, 2007, effective April 1, 2008. http://en.pkulaw.cn/ display.aspx?cgid=1811a46f52ef6533bdfb&lib=law.

Minshi Susong Fa (民事诉讼法) [Civil Procedure Law] (promulgated by the National People's Congress, August 31, 2012, effective October 3, 2012. http://www. lawinfochina.com/display.aspx?lib=law&id=19&CGid=.

Minshi Susong Fa (民事诉讼法) [Civil Procedure Law] (promulgated by the National People's Congress Standing Committee, June 27, 2017, effective July 1, 2017). http:// en.pkulaw.cn/display.aspx?id=6d9ce94e57cee7afbdfb&lib=law.

Minzner, Carl. "China's Turn Against Law." *American Journal of Comparative Law* 59, 4 (2011): 935–984.

National Bureau of Statistics of China. *China Statistical Yearbook 2019*, accessed July 8, 2020. http://www.stats.gov.cn/tjsj/ndsj/2019/indexeh.htm.

National Development and Reform Commission. *Visions and Actions on Jointly Building Silk Road Economic Belt and 21st-Century Maritime Silk Road*, March 28, 2015. https://reconasia-production.s3.amazonaws.com/media/filer_public/e0/22/ e0228017-7463-46fc-9094-0465a6f1ca23/vision_and_actions_on_jointly_building_ silk_road_economic_belt_and_21st-century_maritime_silk_road.pdf.

Ng, Kwai Hang and He Xin, *Embedded Courts: Judicial Decision-Making in China*. Cambridge: Cambridge University Press, 2017.

Nolan-Haley, Jacqueline. "Mediation: The Best and Worst of Times." *Cardozo Journal of Conflict Resolution* 16, (2014): 731–740.

Nonet, Philippe and Philip Selznick. *Law and Society in Transition: Toward Responsive Law*. New Jersey: Transaction Publishers, 2000.

Peerenboom, Randall. "Judicial Independence in China: Common Myths and Unfounded Assumptions." *SSRN*, October 12, 2008. http://papers.ssrn.com/sol3/ papers.cfm?abstract_id=1283179.

Peerenboom, Randall. "Varieties of Rule of Law: An Introduction and Provisional Conclusion." *SSRN*, September 23, 2003. https://papers.ssrn.com/sol3/papers. cfm?abstract_id=445821.

Peerenboom, Randy and He Xin, "Dispute Resolution in China: Patterns, Causes and Prognosis." *University of Pennsylvania East Asia Law Review* 4, no. 1 (2009): 1–61.

Supreme People's Court. *Provisions of the Supreme People's Court about Several Issues Concerning the Civil Mediation Work of the People's Court*, September 16, 2004. http://pkulaw.cn/fulltext_form.aspx?Db=chl&Gid=51834caf365c39a9bdfb.

Supreme People's Court. *Renmin Fayuan Di'sange Wunian Gaige Gangyao 2009–2013* 人民法院第三个五年改革纲要 2009–2013, February 24, 2010. http://www.court. gov.cn/shenpan-xiangqing-323.html.

Supreme People's Court. *Several Opinions of the Supreme People's Court on Further Displaying the Positive Roles of Litigation Mediation in the Building of a Socialist Harmonious Society*, March 7, 2007. http://www.lawinfochina.com/display. aspx?id=5930&lib=law.

Supreme People's Court. *Zuigao renmin fayuan fabu "siwu gaige gangyao"* 最高人民 法院发布 "四五改革纲要," July 10, 2014. http://www.court.gov.cn/zixun-xiangqing- 8168.html.

Tamanaha, Brian Z. "The Tension between Legal Instrumentalism and the Rule of Law." *Syracuse Journal of International Law and Commerce* 33, no. 1 (2005): 131–149

Wang, Hongwei. "Yichangjiufen, tiaojie haishi panjue" 一场纠纷, 调解, 还是判决. *Legal Daily*, October 21, 2009.

Wang, Jiangyu. "China: Legal Reform in an Emerging Socialist Market Economy." In *Law and Legal Institutions in Asia: Traditions, Adaptations and Innovations*, edited by Ann Black and Gary F. Bell, 24–61. Cambridge: Cambridge University Press, 2011.

Waye, Vicki and Ping Xiong. "The Relationship between Mediation and Judicial Proceedings in China." *Asian Journal of Comparative Law* 6, no. 1 (2011): 1–34.

Woo, Margaret and Mary Gallagher. "Introduction." In *Chinese Justice: Civil Dispute Resolution in Contemporary China*, edited by Margaret Woo and Mary Gallagher, 1–24. New York: Cambridge University Press, 2011.

Woo, Margaret. "Bonded Legality: China's Developmental State and Civil Dispute Resolution." *Maryland Journal of International Law* 27, no. 1 (2012): 235–262.

"'Wuwu gaige gangyao' ji Zhongguo fayuan sifa gaige baipishu xinwen fabu hui" 五五改革纲要"暨中国法院司法改革白皮书新闻发布会. Zuigao renmin fayuan wang最高人民法院网, February 27, 2019. http://www.court.gov.cn/zixun-xiangqing-144172.html.

Wu, Yingzi 吴英姿. "Justice Identity: Crisis and Reestablishment" 论司法认同：危机与重建. *China Legal Science* 中国法学, no. 3 (2016): 186–206.

Wu, Yingzi 吴英姿. "Priority of Mediation" 调解优先：改革范式与法律解读 以O市法院改革为样本. *Peking University Law Journal* 中外法学, no. 3 (2013): 536–555.

Wu, Yuning. "People's Mediation Enters the 21st Century." In *Mediation in Contemporary China: Continuity and Change*, edited by Fu Hualing and Michael Palmer, 34–58. London: Wildy, Simmonds & Hill Publishing, 2017.

Xian, Yifan. "Grassroots Judges of China in the Resurgence from Adjudicatory to Mediatory Justice: Transformation of Roles and Inherent Conflict of Identities." In *Mediation in Contemporary China: Continuity and Change*, edited by Fu Hualing and Michael Palmer, 167–187. London: Wildy, Simmonds & Hill Publishing, 2017.

Xian, Yifan. Interview. May 2015.

Yang, Su and He Xin. "Street as Courtroom: State Accommodation of Labor Protest in South China." *Law and Society Review* 44, no. 1 (2010): 157–170.

Yang, Wen. "Si fa diao jie de mo shi tan suo—yi nan jing zhong ji ren min fa yuan diao shen shi du fen li wei li" 司法调解的模式探索—以南京中级人民法院调审适度分离为例. *Jin Ling Law Review* 金陵法律评论 25, no. 2 (2013): 145–154.

Ye, Ariel and Yu Song. "Justice, Efficiency, and the New Civil Procedure Law." *China Law & Practice*, November 1, 2012.

Zhang, Xianchu. "Civil Justice Reform with Political Agendas." In *The Development of the Chinese Legal System: Change and Challenges*, edited by Yu Guanghua, 253–271. Oxford: Routledge, 2011.

Zhang, Xianchu. "Rethinking the Mediation Campaign." In *Mediation in Contemporary China: Continuity and Change*, edited by Fu Hualing and Michael Palmer, 59–86. London: Wildy, Simmonds & Hill Publishing, 2017.

Zhao, Yun. "Mediation in Contemporary China: Thinking About Reform." In *Mediation in Contemporary China: Continuity and Change*, edited by Fu Hualing and Michael Palmer, 87–111. London: Wildy, Simmonds & Hill Publishing, 2017.

Zhao, Yun. *Mediation Practice and Skills*. Beijing: Tsinghua University Press, 2015.

Zhou, Cui. "Relationship between Mediation and Adjudication: Rethink and Restatement" 调解与审判的关系：反思与重述. *Comparative Legal Research* 比较法研究, no. 1 (2014): 46–64.

Zhu, Suli. "Political Parties in China's Judiciary." *Duke Journal of Comparative & International Law* 17, no. 1 (2007): 533–560.

"Zuigao renmin fayuan guanyu renmin fayuan jinyibu Shenhua duoyuanhua jiufen jiejue jizhi gaige de yijian" 最高人民法院关于人民法院进一步深化多元化纠纷解决机制改革的意见. *Renmin fayuan bao* 人民法院报, January 8, 2017. https://www.chinacourt.org/article/detail/2017/01/id/2509588.shtml.

7 Judicial enforcement of arbitration

Extending a pro-arbitration judicial embrace

1 Introduction

1.1 Preliminaries

Worldwide, the topic of mixing the processes of litigation and arbitration often centers on the court's interaction with arbitration.[1] Such interaction is manifested in situations where the courts grant and enforce interim measures of protection to assist arbitral proceedings. More importantly, the courts supervise the effectiveness of the arbitration agreements and arbitral awards. Between the two, the latter is more critical and has been regarded as the key measurement of whether a jurisdiction could be termed as "pro-arbitration" or "arbitration-friendly."[2] It is usually measured on its infrastructure to enable arbitral awards to be effectively enforced in accordance with best practices under the New York Convention. The judicial policy that guides the decision-making on matters concerning the effective enforcement of arbitral awards is accurate testimony of a jurisdiction's deposition on arbitration.[3]

This chapter focuses on arbitral award enforcement in China and related matters. Following these prefatory comments, it first presents the empirical status quo of the enforcement landscape. The chapter then looks into the regulatory background, and particularly highlights SPC's decade or so regulatory efforts. The most recent SPC rules exhibit China's ambition to create a pro-arbitration judicial environment in China. This chapter further studies important court decisions in the last decade on some of the most controversial

---

1 George A. Bermann, "The Role of National Courts at The Threshold of Arbitration," *American Review of International Arbitration* 28, no. 3 (2018): 291–308.
2 Thomas Carbonneau, "Judicial Approbation in Building the Civilization of Arbitration," in *Building the Civilization of Arbitration*, eds. Thomas Carbonneau and Angelica M. Sinopole (London: Wildy, Simmonds & Hill Publishing, 2010), 353–357. See also Anselmo Reyes and Gu Weixia, *The Developing World of Arbitration: A Comparative Study of Arbitration Reform in the Asia Pacific* (Oxford: Hart Publishing, 2018), 297–298.
3 Thomas Carbonneau, "Judicial Approbation in Building the Civilization of Arbitration," *Penn State Law Review* 113, no. 4 (2009): 1346.

cases of arbitral enforcement by both central and local courts. Commendably, the Chinese judiciary as a whole is now generally paying more deference to arbitration and has exhibited more judicial support toward arbitral enforcement. The reform analysis shows that arbitration is vital to China's economic and investment interests, especially in the context of the national economic development strategies such as the Free Trade Zone, the Belt and Road Initiative, and the Great Bay Area.

1.2 Empirical evidence

Only when the enforcement of an arbitral award is challenged will the enforcement become a publicly available statistic. As discussed in Chapter 4, since 1995, China has started to operate a unique "pre-reporting system" to curb local protectionist influences[4] over the challenge of enforcement of foreign or foreign-related arbitral awards (i.e., non-domestic arbitral awards). Under the system, if lower-level Chinese courts intend to refuse enforcement of the non-domestic awards (i.e., those "negative" enforcement cases), they need to seek approval from the SPC in Beijing.

Shen and Shang studied all the publicly available non-enforcement cases in China under the pre-reporting system from 1995 to 2015.[5] Their empirical work covered a two-decade period since the system was implemented. They identified 98 cases through collecting all the SPC letters of reply to the lower-level courts in the period, with an average of 49 cases to be reported per decade as they observed. Among the 98 cases, they further found that most of the applications to set aside or not to enforce an award were initiated by foreign parties, showing foreign investors' heavier reliance on this pre-reporting system.[6]

To unveil the empirical side of the most recent decade,[7] this chapter conducted an exhaustive statistical study of all the annual and cumulative number of the "negative" enforcement cases under the pre-reporting system by following Shen and Shang's methodology. By going through key Chinese legal research databases in the field,[8] the statistics are compiled on basis of all the publicly available SPC letters of reply on "negative" enforcement cases with respect to non-domestic arbitral awards under the pre-reporting system in the past decade (2009–2018).

---

4 See discussions in Sections 2.1.2 and 3.2 of Chapter 4 on the pre-reporting system.
5 Shen Wei and Shang Shu, "Tackling Local Protectionism in Enforcing Foreign Arbitral Awards in China: An Empirical Study of the Supreme People's Court's Review Decisions, 1995–2015," *The China Quarterly* 241, no. 1 (2019): 1–25.
6 Ibid., 6.
7 At the time when the book manuscript is submitted, the 2019 data have not yet become available.
8 Chinalawinfo.com, accessed July 16, 2020, http://www.chinalawinfo.com/. Chinalawinfo.com, established by the Peking University Law School, collects all SPC letters of reply under the pre-reporting system.

This is, however, not the entire empirical picture of the enforcement of arbitral awards in China. First, if arbitral awards are voluntarily enforced by disputing parties (whether domestic or non-domestic) and do not meet any challenges at the enforcement stage, due to the confidential nature of arbitration, the "positive" enforcement data will not become publicly available as they do not go through the Chinese court system. Second, non-domestic arbitral awards (foreign or foreign-related) whose enforcement are challenged before the Chinese lower-level courts but have finally been enforced at the same court will also be calculated as "positive" enforcement cases. These cases do not need to be reported to the SPC in Beijing and therefore do not have national data officially compiled. Thus, those "positive" enforcement cases which occupies the biggest proportion of the arbitral enforcement landscape in China do not have nationwide public data. Hence, what has become publicly available with respect to arbitral award enforcement on a national basis are only those "negative" enforcement cases which have gone through the pre-reporting system. Third, challenges to the enforcement of domestic arbitral awards did not need to go through the pre-reporting system and statistics on the non-enforcement of domestic arbitral awards were not made publicly available until 2018 when the pre-reporting system extended its application.[9] As such, the nationwide data compiled below only represent those publicly available "negative" enforcement data pertinent to the pre-reporting system. They are concerned with the non-domestic case sample that were denied enforcement at Chinese lower-level courts before 2018, and the counterpart domestic case sample in 2018 alone when the pre-reporting system started to be applied to domestic cases.[10]

From 2009 to 2018, an exhaustive search has found a total of 55 SPC replies of letters in relation to enforcement cases under the pre-reporting system by the Chinese lower-level courts (see Table 7.1). Compared to Shen and Shang's observation of 49 cases of pre-reporting on average per decade, there is a slight increase (55) in the most recent decade. These most recent data empirically reflect a continuation of reliance on the pre-reporting system by non-domestic investors. Among the 55 cases, 20 cases were confirmed not to be enforced by the SPC (including those set aside by the SPC) in its replies to the Chinese lower-level courts. There were another 29 cases where the SPC rectified the position of the lower-level courts and the awards were finally enforced by the SPC. Finally, six remaining cases were categorized as "other types," which either concerned partial enforcement or had lingering pre-emptive arbitral issues such as a lack of jurisdiction.[11]

9 Since 2018, to present an overall pro-enforcement image, the pre-reporting scheme has now been extended even to domestic awards. See Section 3.2 of this chapter.
10 See Section 3.2 of this chapter.
11 Chinalawinfo.com.

Table 7.1 Enforcement under the pre-reporting system—cumulative (2009–2018)

Total number of pre-reporting cases to the SPC	Total number of cases confirmed to be non-enforced by the SPC	Total number of cases enforced by the SPC	Total number of other cases
55	20	29	6

Table 7.2 Enforcement under the pre-reporting system—annual (2009–2018)

Year	Total number of pre-reporting cases	Total number of cases enforced by the SPC	Enforcement rate
2009	8	5	62.50%
2010	8	5	62.50%
2011	3	1	33.33%
2012	1	0	0.00%
2013	12	5	41.67%
2014	0	0	0.00%
2015	**17**	**10**	**58.82%**
2016	6	3	50.00%
2017	0	0	0.00%
2018	0	0	0.00%
Total	**55**	**29**	**52.73%**
			(on average, for the past decade)

Table 7.2 then tracks the annual breakdown of the pre-reporting cases and their associated enforcement rate, where Chart 7.1 visualizes the data by column effect. From 2009 to 2018, the pre-reporting system had recorded 29 enforced cases in total, an average of 52.73% overall enforcement rate (highlighted in Table 7.2). That means more than half of the cases reported were actually wrongfully adjudicated by the Chinese lower-

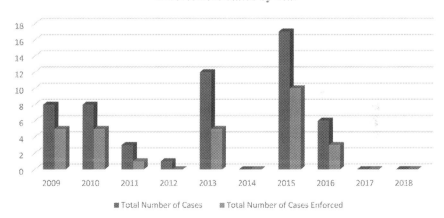

Chart 7.1 Enforcement under the pre-reporting system—annual (2009–2018)

level courts and finally rectified by the SPC. These data are important as they empirically prove the popularity and importance of the pre-reporting system.

Moreover, the pre-reporting cases increased significantly in 2013 and 2015, having more than 10 reported cases in the two respective years, as the foreign-investment-tailored national economic strategies such as the Free Trade Zone and the Belt and Road Initiative started to bite.[12] The year 2015 is a crucial year for China's investment environment record because in 2015, China's outward foreign direct investment ("OFDI") ranked second in the world for the first time.[13] As such, the year 2015 recorded the peak in arbitration reporting, with 17 "negative" enforcement decisions rendered by lower-level courts with respect to foreign or foreign-related awards reported to the SPC. The SPC finally rectified and enforced more than half of them (10 cases in total, and 58.82% in overall enforcement rate, highlighted in Table 7.2). These data empirically reflect the economic-sensitive and investment-sensitive roles of arbitral award enforcement. The number of pre-reporting cases significantly went down after 2015.[14] Continuously throughout 2017 and 2018, there were zero pre-reporting case in both years, implying a 100% "positive" enforcement rate by Chinese lower-level courts, as the national diplomatic and economic strategies such as the Belt and Road Initiative started to exert positive pressure on China's overall investment environment, and the China International Commercial Court started to take shape to centralize the judicial enforcement on Belt and Road arbitration.[15] Again, the statistical findings empirically reflect that arbitral enforcement data are one of the key indicators of China's investment environment.[16, 17, 18]

---

12 See Sections 3.1, 4.3, and 5 of this chapter.
13 Ministry of Commerce, National Bureau of Statistics and State Administration of Foreign Exchange, *2016 Statistical Bulletin of China's Outward Foreign Direct Investment* (Beijing: China Statistical Press, 2016), http://cdi.cnki.net/Titles/SingleNJ?NJCode=N2017120333. See also Karl P. Sauvant and Michael Nolan, "China's Outward Foreign Direct Investment and International Investment Law," *Journal of International Economic Law* 36, no. 1 (2015): 1–42.
14 2015 is the year that the Belt and Road Initiative has been officially recognized by the Chinese government as a national development strategy. See National Development and Reform Commission, *Visions and Actions on Jointly Building Silk Road Economic Belt and 21st-Century Maritime Silk Road*, March 28, 2015), http://en.ndrc.gov.cn/newsrelease/201503/t20150330_669367.html.
15 See discussions in Sections 3.3, 4.4, and 5 of this chapter.
16 Chinalawinfo.com.
17 "Year" is based on the issue date of the SPC letters of reply. Up to the time when the manuscript is completed, the most recent SPC letter of reply regarding the enforcement of arbitral awards was issued in September 2016, therefore the statistics of 2017 and 2018 are included.
18 Chinalawinfo.com.

2 Regulatory framework

Chapter 4 has explained the Chinese arbitration system in some detail. China's Arbitration Law ("AL") came into effect in 1995, and has had little amendment ever since. A key feature of the Chinese arbitral award enforcement scheme is that it is not united, but rather dependent on the type (origin) of awards, including: (1) foreign awards, which are made outside China,[19] (2) foreign-related awards, which are rendered by Chinese arbitral institutions in China[20] as involving at least a "foreign-element," and (3) domestic awards, which are rendered by Chinese arbitral institutions in China without any foreign-element involved.[21] In determining whether a case involves a "foreign element," the three-limb test is used.[22] Since the 1996 State Council Notice, there is no longer a jurisdictional bifurcation on the two types of Chinese arbitration commissions, and dual-track jurisdiction has largely been blurred. Hence, awards rendered in China are no longer categorized as domestic or foreign-related based on the arbitration institution that renders them, but rather, the domestic or international nature of the case itself.[23] This tripartite structure is a departure from the bipartite categorization of domestic and foreign awards as defined in the New York Convention and the UNCITRAL Model Law.[24]

Under the AL, there are two separate sets of procedures through which an arbitral award can be challenged to be invalidated—setting aside (*chexiao* 撤销) and non-enforcement (*buyuzhixing* 不予执行). The procedure to set aside can be initiated by any party up to six months after the arbitral award is made, whereas the procedure for non-enforcement can only be initiated by the losing party after the arbitral award is recognized by a Chinese court.[25] According to China's AL and Civil Procedure Law ("CPL"), both procedures have to be determined by a panel of three judges at the intermediate people's court ("IPC") level where the enforceable asset or the award-rendering arbitral institution is located.[26] As to grounds to invalidate an arbitral award, there

---

19 This does not include awards made in Hong Kong, Macau and Taiwan, in which cases enforcement in China would be using the Mutual Arbitration Arrangements. See Gu Weixia, "Arbitration in China," in *International Commercial Arbitration in Asia*, 2nd ed., eds. Thomas Ginsburg and Shahla Ali (New York: Juris Publishing, 2013), 126–129.

20 Chinese arbitral institutions have been setting up overseas branches these years. For example, CIETAC established its CIETAC's Hong Kong Arbitration Center in Hong Kong in 2012, and CIETAC's North America Center in Vancouver in 2018.

21 Gu, "Arbitration in China," 115–124.

22 See discussions in section 2.1.2 of Chapter 4 on the "foreign-related" element.

23 Ibid.

24 Shen and Shang, "Tackling Local Protectionism in Enforcing Foreign Arbitral Awards in China," 5.

25 Zhongcai Fa (仲裁法) [Arbitration Law] (promulgated by the Standing Committee of the National People's Congress, August 31, 1994, effective September 1, 1995), arts. 70–71, http://www.npc.gov.cn/wxzl/wxzl/2000-12/05/content_4624.htm.

26 Ibid.

are significate disparities when it comes to different types (origins) of awards. For foreign and foreign-related arbitral awards, the grounds for the exercise of judicial supervision in setting aside, or the non-enforcement of, such arbitral awards are limited to procedural grounds, in line with Article V(2) of the New York Convention and international practice.[27] In contrast, for domestic awards, the review involves more substantive matters, such as effects of the evidence on which the award is based, and mistakes in application of the law.[28] The broad power held by the courts to "refuse enforcement" of domestic arbitral awards has, however, been narrowed with the current China's CPL, amended in 2012. Under the 2012 CPL, the "incorrect application of the law" was removed as a ground for refusing enforcement of domestic awards, so that one of the substantive aspects of review on the ground of wrongful legal application are now curbed.[29] While substantive grounds relating to the correctness of evidence still remain, the broad ground of "insufficiency in the main evidence" was replaced by two grounds of "fabrication" and "withholding of main evidence," both of which carry higher standards of burden of proof than the previous "insufficiency" ground.[30] These approaches were confirmed in the most recent amendment to the CPL in 2017.[31]

Apart from the inequality in the grounds of review, as previously discussed in the empirical statistical review, the pre-reporting system introduced by the SPC in the procedure of review, was initially designed to cater exclusively to the enforcement of non-domestic arbitral awards. This system requires that any IPC that decides not to enforce an award shall first report the case to the provincial higher people's court ("HPC") in the same province, which then reports to the SPC. Only when the SPC has confirmed can the non-domestic award be denied enforcement in China by the lower-level courts.[32] Accordingly, a "negative" enforcement ruling made by the courts at the lower level, but not a "positive" one, would be subject to "pyramidal scrutiny" by the higher level. The pre-reporting system is operated by way of a "reply letter," which is channeled through a higher-level court to a lower-level one, without any executive or Party interventions.[33]

---

27 Ibid., arts. 70–71.
28 Ibid., art. 58.
29 Minshi Susong Fa (民事诉讼法) [Civil Procedure Law] (promulgated by the National People's Congress, August 31, 2012, effective January 1, 2013), art. 237(2), http://www.lawinfochina.com/display.aspx?id=11161&lib=law.
30 Ibid. The two new grounds under the amended CPL are "the evidence on which an arbitration case is adjudicated is forged" and "the opposing party withholds any evidence from the arbitral institution, which suffices to affect the fairness of the awards."
31 Minshi Susong Fa (民事诉讼法) [Civil Procedure Law] (promulgated by the National People's Congress Standing Committee, June 27, 2017, effective July 1, 2017), art. 274, http://en.pkulaw.cn/display.aspx?id=6d9ce94e57cee7afbdfb&lib=law.
32 Ibid.
33 Shen and Shang, "Tackling Local Protectionism in Enforcing Foreign Arbitral Awards in China," 5.

As aforementioned, while the pre-reporting system aims to prevent local protectionist influences over arbitral enforcement and to improve China's image in terms of international arbitral enforcement,[34] the scheme has been criticized as one of the most controversial judicial policies toward arbitration, as it overlooked the interests of domestic arbitration. As will be discussed later, the controversy was recently addressed by the SPC in late 2017 and the pre-reporting system is now extended to the domestic arbitration regime.

In practice, there are more controversial cases in the enforcement of arbitral awards. One situation would be the enforcement of *ad hoc* awards delivered in China. While *ad hoc* awards delivered outside China (foreign *ad hoc* awards) can be enforced under the New York Convention, *ad hoc* awards delivered in China cannot get enforced as *ad hoc* arbitration plays no legal role in the Chinese arbitration system. This area of law is gradually reformed by the SPC's regulatory move since 2016 in some arbitrations that concerned with China's new FTZ initiative. Another controversial scenario would be the enforcement of awards delivered by foreign arbitration institutions seated in China. There is Chinese literature treating them as non-domestic awards for enforcement purposes.[35] These awards are largely unenforceable, and the seed for reform is recently seen through some leading cases. The following discussions will detail regulatory reforms in the field and important court decisions in these controversial cases.

3 Reform—regulatory moves

As explained in Chapter 4, the AL has largely remained same since its promulgation more than two decades ago. However, the SPC has spearheaded regulatory reforms on the judicial enforcement of arbitration. The SPC, in its interpretative function, has published a series of impressive regulatory documents pertaining to the judicial support toward enforcement of arbitration, which has developed in an exceptionally rapid pace moving exceptionally fast in the past couple of years.

3.1 SPC opinion on free trade zone (2016)

In 2011, the China Free Trade Zone ("FTZ") national economic policy was initiated by the Chinese national government as a trial for China's new round of reform and opening up, which aimed at liberalization on capital account and trade facilitation.[36] In 2013, the Shanghai (Pudong) Pilot Free

---

34 Ibid., 1–25.
35 Gu Weixia, "Piercing the Veil of Arbitration Reform in China: Promises, Pitfalls, Patterns, Prognoses and Prospects," *American Journal of Comparative Law* 65, no. 4 (2017): 833.
36 Yao Daqing, "The China (Shanghai) Pilot Free Trade Zone: Background, Developments and Preliminary Assessment of Initial Impacts," *National Bureau of Economic Research (NBER) Working Paper Series* (2015), https://www.nber.org/papers/w20924.pdf.

Trade Zone was first established, which was subsequently followed by similar FTZ establishments in Tianjin, Shenzhen and Qingdao.[37] In response to the dispute resolution needs arising out of the FTZ, the SPC issued, in late 2016, its Opinions on the Free Trade Zones (the "2016 FTZ Opinion"),[38] giving recognition and effect to the possibility and potential of *ad hoc* arbitration in China.

By providing that "[w]here both enterprises registered in the FTZ have agreed to settle relevant disputes by a specific arbitrator (or arbitrators) in accordance with the specific arbitration rules at a specific place in China (the "three specifics" criteria), the arbitration agreement may be deemed valid,"[39] Article 9(3) of the FTZ Opinion is deemed to have conditionally permitted the practice of *ad hoc* arbitration in China. At the SPC's press conference held in the beginning of 2017, Zhang Yongjian, the then Head of SPC's Civil Division No. 4,[40] commented on the interpretation of Article 9(3) as follows.[41] First, eligible parties who can invoke *ad hoc* arbitration are required to be enterprises registered in the FTZs. In other words, enterprises registered outside the FTZs are excluded. Second, eligible *ad hoc* arbitration shall meet the "three specifics" criteria. Third, by using the term "may" instead of "shall," even though an arbitration takes place between enterprises registered in the FTZs and has satisfied the "three specifics" requirements, the arbitration might not necessarily become valid. The expression "may" gives the supervisory court a discretionary power in deciding whether the arbitration agreement is valid or not.[42] The discretion also displays the court's cautious attitude toward the opening up of the *ad hoc* arbitration market.[43]

Nevertheless, Zhang's comment indicates the supportive judicial attitude toward gradually defrosting the *ad hoc* arbitration practice in China. However, the 2016 FTZ Opinion only governs decision-making by courts on

---

37 Ibid.
38 Supreme People's Court, *Opinions of the Supreme People's Court on Providing Judicial Guarantee for the Building of Pilot Free Trade Zones*, December 30, 2016, http://en.pkulaw.cn/display.aspx?cgid=441e185f12e602a2bdfb&lib=law.
39 Ibid., para. 9.
40 Civil Division No. 4 is exclusively tasked to handle international commercial cases and arbitration cases in Mainland China.
41 Cao Yajing, *"Fahui Shenpan Zhineng Zuoyong: Cujin Zi Mao Shiyan Qu Jiankang Fazhan"* 发挥审判智能作用: 促进自贸区健康发展, *People's Court Daily*, January 10, 2017, http://rmfyb.chinacourt.org/paper/html/2017-01/10/content_120669.htm?div=-1.
42 Zhu Huafang 朱华芳, "Yu Wai Zhongcai yu Linshi Zhongcai Liang Da Tupo × Zui Gao Fayuan She Zi Mao Qu Zhongcai Sifa Shencha Xin Gui Guancha" 域外仲裁与临时仲裁两大突破——最高法院涉自贸区仲裁司法审查新规观察, *Tiantong Susong Quan* 天同诉讼圈, February 23, 2017, https://mp.weixin.qq.com/s?__biz=MjM5NjA3NDc-5MA==&mid=2654696850&idx=1&sn=c864902c091fffc287073604c5fabbb3&chksm=bd2111db8a5698cd06709e175fb79f4a0191a77fbf5470acl48713f9df348399fa6f6571b4c0#rd.
43 Ibid.

the validity of *ad hoc* arbitration and its consequent awards. It does not provide specific details in procedures as to how an *ad hoc* arbitration is to be carried out in China. The problems may arise in respect of the appointment of arbitrator(s), the application for interim measures, the decision on jurisdictional challenges, the organization of oral hearings, as well as the making of arbitral awards. Without new legislation that treats *ad hoc* arbitration as a recognized category and provides specific implementation details governing the arbitral processes, *ad hoc* arbitration cannot be effectively practiced in China.

Despite the absence of formal legislation, one of the local arbitration commissions, the Zhuhai Arbitration Commission in Guangdong Province, recently took initiative by promulgating the rules for prospective *ad hoc* arbitration practice arising out of the Hengqin (Zhuhai–Macao) FTZ in 2017.[44] As the very first set of *ad hoc* arbitration rules in China, it is a bold step attempted by Chinese arbitral institutions.

In light of the special status of the FTZs as both a trade and legal experiment of Chinese out-going economic reform, it is particularly meaningful to first allow the practice of *ad hoc* arbitration in FTZs. The 2016 FTZ Opinion paves ways for the FTZs to conduct such legal experiments, and the successful experience will then shed light on the future reform of the entire arbitration market (and arbitration service) in China.

3.2 SPC provisions on judicial review over arbitration (2017–2018)

The pre-reporting system, established by the SPC in 1990s, had been applied exclusively to foreign and foreign-related arbitration case. Shen and Shang's empirical study concludes that, along with a variety of recent SPC regulatory directives that have been introduced either to correct abuses of local protectionism or to strengthen the SPC's centralized control on arbitration, the pre-reporting system is the most effective.[45] But local protectionism concerns not only foreign and foreign-related arbitral awards, but Chinese domestic awards rendered outside the local cities or local provinces. To create an overall pro-enforcement and pro-arbitration judicial image, the SPC has now made the pre-reporting system available to the domestic arbitration regime.

In November 2017, the SPC amended the prior pre-reporting mechanism through its issuance of the Provisions on Cases Relating to the Pre-Reporting System of Arbitration (the "2017 SPC Provisions on Pre-reporting").[46] Despite

44 See Zhuhai Arbitration Commission, *Hengqin ziyou maoyi qu linshi zhongcai guize* 横琴自由贸易试验区临时仲裁规则, April 15, 2017, http://cn.oversea.cnki.net/law/detail/detail.aspx?filename=la202001020059&dbcode=CLKLP&dbname=CLKLP.

45 Shen and Shang, "Tackling Local Protectionism in Enforcing Foreign Arbitral Awards in China," 21.

46 Supreme People's Court, *Relevant Provisions of the Supreme People's Court on Issues Concerning Applications for Verification of Arbitration Cases under Judicial Review*, December 26, 2017, http://www.lawinfochina.com/display.aspx?id=27182&lib=law.

the high cost of judicial resources involved in the pre-reporting system, the SPC is now willing to expand the jurisdictional scope to cover even domestic arbitral awards.[47] Hence, the pre-reporting system is now equally applied to domestic arbitration cases, that is, arbitration conducted within Mainland China without any foreign element.[48] According to the new rules, when first instance courts have provisionally decided to refuse the enforcement of an award or to vacate an award, it must first report such decision to its superior HPC in the same province. Only when the HPC agrees with the lower court's finding can the lower court render a decision to frustrate the arbitration outcome. Special rules apply when the HPC's decision is to not enforce or to vacate the award made on the ground of public policy. In these circumstances, the HPC must in turn report the case to the SPC. Only when both the SPC and the HPC agree with the lower court's finding can the lower court render its decision to set aside the arbitral award.[49] Therefore, under the new rules of the pre-reporting system, the decision to invalidate an arbitration award, irrespective of its origin and type, may only be made after the SPC's centralized review. This new SPC regulatory scheme has made even domestic arbitral awards more difficult to be set aside by lower courts.

Moreover, there are two sets of new rules on judicial review procedures published by the SPC in December 2017 and January 2018: the Provisions on Several Issues Relating to the Judicial Review over Arbitration (the "2017 SPC Provisions on Arbitration Review")[50] and the Provisions on Several Issues Relating to the Enforcement of Arbitration Awards (the "2018 SPC Provisions on Award Enforcement").[51] Both Provisions aimed to clarify and streamline the procedure on judicial review over arbitration in China such that the case should be handled by the intermediate court level hierarchically and heard by the collegiate bench organizationally.[52] Moreover, the governing law of the arbitration agreement should be severed from that of the main contract,[53] and the timeline for review should generally be limited to two months.[54]

47 Ibid., arts. 1–3.
48 Ibid., art. 2(2).
49 Ibid., art. 3(2).
50 Supreme People's Court, *Provisions of the Supreme People's Court on Several Issues concerning Trying Cases of Arbitration-Related Judicial Review*, December 26, 2017, http://www.lawinfochina.com/display.aspx?id=27178&lib=law.
51 Supreme People's Court, *Provisions of the Supreme People's Court on Several Issues concerning the Handling of Cases regarding Enforcement of Arbitral Awards by the People's Courts*, February 22, 2018, http://www.lawinfochina.com/display.aspx?id=30284&lib=law.
52 Supreme People's Court, *Provisions of the Supreme People's Court on Several Issues concerning Trying Cases of Arbitration-Related Judicial Review*, art. 11
53 Ibid., arts. 13–14.
54 Supreme People's Court, *Provisions of the Supreme People's Court on Several Issues concerning the Handling of Cases regarding Enforcement of Arbitral Awards by the People's Courts*, art. 12.

Because all the three new sets of rules published by the SPC in 2017 and 2018 concern judicial review over arbitration, for ease of reference, as the section title indicates, the author collectively refers to the three as the "SPC Provisions on the Judicial Review of Arbitration." The author believes that the SPC's aggressive regulatory pace on judicial review of arbitration in the most recent years is a response to China's macro backdrop development such as the FTZ and the Belt and Road Initiative. Because legislative reforms, such as promulgating a new law or amending existing laws, require rigid procedure and usually take a long time, the judiciary is in the position to respond to and resolve legal issues arising out of the day-to-day changing circumstances of the stakeholders quicker than the legislature is able to. As a result, the SPC is expected to support arbitration from a macro regulatory approach in a more proactive manner.[55]

3.3 SPC provisions on the China international commercial court (2018)

Arbitration has the potential to offer commercially flexible solutions, and international commercial arbitration is particularly suitable for mitigating conflicts among different legal systems. Considering the traditional distrust and reluctance of investors to resolve business disputes through foreign courts, with which they may not be familiar, international commercial arbitration will, under market forces, form a preferred, indeed optimal, vehicle for commercial dispute resolution under the Belt and Road Initiative ("BRI").[56] In association with such dispute resolution needs out of China's BRI development, in June 2018, the SPC established the Chinese International Commercial Court ("CICC"),[57] with an aim to improve the legal environment for cross-border investment arising out of the BRI transactions.

The CICC consists of two courts: a sea-route-based one in Shenzhen, Guangdong Province, for taking care of disputes arising out of the Maritime Silk Road (*haishang sichouzhilu* 海上丝绸之路), and a land-route-based one in Xi'an, Shaanxi Province, for taking care of disputes

---

55 Gu Weixia 顾维遐, "Arbitration outside China without Foreign-related Elements" 无涉外因素争议的域外仲裁问题, *Peking University Law Journal* 30, no. 3 (2018): 651–670.

56 Hong Kong's former Secretary for Justice Rimsky Yuen envisioned that opportunities for outward expansion of the local legal and arbitration sectors lay in providing services to alleviating the "legal uncertainties" along "One Belt, One Road" countries. See "Secretary for Justice Promotes Hong Kong's Legal and Dispute Resolution Service in Beijing (with Photos)," Department of Justice, August 18, 2015, https://www.info.gov.hk/gia/general/201508/18/P201508180765.htm.

57 "Zhonggong zhongyang bangongting, guowuyuan bangongting yinfa <guanyu jianli 'yidai yilu' guoji shangshi zhengduan jiejue jizhi he jigou de yijian> 中共中央办公厅、国务院办公厅印发《关于建立"一带一路"国际商事争端解决机制和机构的意见》, *Xinhua She* 新华社, June 27, 2018, http://www.gov.cn/zhengce/2018-06/27/content_5301657.htm.

arising out of the Silk Road Economic Belt (*sichouzhilu jingjingdai* 丝绸之
路经济带). Shenzhen is chosen for its reformist role as a test bed for new
legal and economic policies as well as being a core hub of the Guangdong–
Hong Kong–Macau Great Bay Area. Xi'an is chosen for its historical role
as the starting point of the ancient Silk Road and a hub of economies in
China's vast west regions.[58] The two new courts are permanent bodies
within the SPC.[59] Its judges are selected from senior judges who are familiar with international laws and norms and possess working proficiency in
both English and Chinese.[60] As of May 2020, all thirteen judges appointed
to the CICC are mainland Chinese and have a postgraduate degree in law,
where eight judges have either visited or studied at a university outside
mainland China.[61]

In late June 2018, the SPC further published two important judi-
cial interpretations concerning the CICC: the Provisions on Several
Issues Concerning the Establishment of the International Commercial
Court (the "2018 CICC Provisions"),[62] and the Opinions Concerning the
Establishment of the Belt and Road Initiative International Commercial
Dispute Resolution Mechanism and Institutions (the "BRI Mechanism and
Institutions Opinion").[63]

Article 14 of the 2018 CICC Provisions concerns specifically judicial
review over BRI-related and other high-profile arbitration cases in China.
When a party makes an application to the CICC to set aside or seek non-
enforcement of an arbitral award rendered by an international commercial
arbitration institution "designated" by the CICC, the CICC shall accept the
case.[64] To clarify on the designation scheme, in December 2018, the SPC
announced its first batch of the "CICC-designated" or "CICC-accredited"
international arbitration institutions[65] by virtue of the SPC's Notice on the

---

58 "Weishenme zai Shenzhen, Xian she guoji shangshi fating? Zuigaofa huiying" 为什么在深
圳、西安设国际商事法庭? 最高法回应, *Zhongguo Xinwen Wang* 中国新闻网, June 28, 2018,
http://www.chinanews.com/gn/2018/06-28/8549700.shtml.

59 Supreme People's Court, *Provisions of the Supreme People's Court on Several Issues
Concerning the Establishment of the International Commercial Courts*, July 1, 2018,
art. 1, https://cgc.law.stanford.edu/belt-and-road/b-and-r-texts/20180701-provisions-re-intl-
commercial-courts/.

60 Ibid., art. 4.

61 See "Judges," China International Commercial Court, accessed July 14, 2020, http://cicc.
court.gov.cn/html/1/218/19/151/index.html.

62 Supreme People's Court, *Provisions of the Supreme People's Court on Several Issues
Concerning the Establishment of the International Commercial Courts*.

63 "Zhonggong zhongyang bangongting, guowuyuan bangongting yinfa <guanyu jianli
'yidai yilu' guoji shangshi zhengduan jiejue jizhi he jigou de yijian>" 中共中央办公厅、国
务院办公厅印发《关于建立"一带一路"国际商事争端解决机制和机构的意见》.

64 Supreme People's Court, *Provisions of the Supreme People's Court on Several Issues
Concerning the Establishment of the International Commercial Courts*. arts. 11, 14.

65 See discussions in Section 3.3 of Chapter 8.

CICC One-Stop Dispute Resolution Arbitration and Mediation Institutions (the "CICC One-Stop Institution Notice").[66]

The first batch of the five arbitration institutions are all Chinese leading home-grown international arbitral institutions. They are: CIETAC, BAC, SCIA, SHIAC, and China Maritime Arbitration Commission ("CMAC").[67] These five arbitral institutions are considered the most experienced, capable and credible Chinese arbitration institutions in handling cross-border arbitration cases,[68] and are expected to be the forefront practitioners in BRI-related arbitration. Arbitration cases under these five designated institutions can be linked with the CICC for direct judicial support and supervision so that they can apply to the CICC for arbitral jurisdiction determination, and recognition and enforcement of their arbitral awards. Such linkage is designed to significantly enhance the quality of judicial review over arbitration from these five arbitral institutions as cases submitted to them are deemed as among the most important arbitration cases in China, as well as to cut down the time costs involved in pre-reporting.[69] As the two CICCs are established as permanent bodies within the SPC, the new judicial scheme could be understood as SPC providing direct support and supervision over BRI-related arbitration. So far, out of the first batch of the five judgments issued by the CICC, three are concerned with judicial support over arbitration under the CICC-designated Chinese arbitration institutions.[70]

4 Reform—recent judgments to relax controversial arbitration cases in China

In the meantime, the Chinese judiciary (both the SPC and lower-level courts) have published a series of impressive judgments to clarify some of the most controversial issues concerning arbitral enforcement in China.

4.1 Foreign institutional arbitration seated in China

As discussed in Chapter 4, arbitration agreements designating foreign institutional arbitration seated in China were treated as invalid and their

---

66 Supreme People's Court, *Notice of the Supreme People's Court on Inclusion of the First Group of International Commercial Arbitration and Mediation Institutions in the "One-stop" Diversified International Commercial Dispute Resolution Mechanism*, December 5, 2018, art. 2, http://cicc.court.gov.cn/html/1/219/208/210/1144.html.

67 Ibid.

68 The arbitration institutions listed by CICC exclude those of Hong Kong, Macau and Taiwan.

69 Supreme People's Court, *Provisions of the Supreme People's Court on Several Issues Concerning the Establishment of the International Commercial Courts*. art. 4.

70 Qiao Wenxin 乔文心, "Zuigao renmin fayuan diyi guoji shangshi fating gaoxiao shenjie shoupiwujiananjian"最高人民法院第一国际商事法庭高效审结首批五件案件, December 30, 2019, http://cicc.court.gov.cn/html/1/218/149/156/1545.html.

resulting awards unenforceable.[71] Two cases in the past decade have called this assumption into question.

In 2009, the Ningbo Intermediate People's Court (in Zhejiang Province) in *Duferco SA v Ningbo Art & Craft Import & Export Corp ("Duferco")* confirmed and enforced an arbitral award following the Arbitration Rules of the International Chamber of Commerce ("ICC") Court of Arbitration seated in Beijing. This is also the first reported case of a Chinese court allowing the enforcement of an ICC award made in China.[72] In the judgment, the Ningbo Intermediate Court importantly stated that the arbitral award in question should be categorized as a "non-domestic award" under the New York Convention and as such, should be recognized and enforced under the Convention.[73] However, the respondent in this case had failed to raise its jurisdictional objection before the first oral hearing of the arbitral proceeding and hence, was deemed to have waived the right to challenge the validity of the arbitral agreement in a timely manner.[74] Ultimately, the case was concluded on the basis of the respondent's waiver without discussing much about the status of ICC arbitration seated in Mainland China. As a result, doubts remain as to whether the ruling would have been different had the respondent raised the objection in time.

More recently, in 2013, the similar issue arose in *Longlide Packaging Co Ltd v BP Agnati SRL ("Longlide")*.[75] In this case, the arbitration clause in dispute provided that any dispute shall be submitted to arbitration by the ICC Court of Arbitration and that the place of arbitration shall be in Shanghai. The claimant disputed the validity of the agreement on three grounds. First, the ICC Court of Arbitration is not a "designated arbitration institution" in China. Second, allowing the ICC to arbitrate a case seated in China would violate China's public policy. Third, in any event, the award should be considered as a Chinese domestic award such that the New York Convention should not be applicable for its recognition and enforcement.[76] The case went before the Anhui Provincial Higher People's Court, which consulted the SPC

---

71 See discussions in Section 2.2 of Chapter 4.
72 Degao gangtie gongsi yu Ningbo shi gongyipin jinchukou youxian gongsi [*Duferco SA v Ningbo Art & Craft Import & Export Corp*] (Ningbo Intermediate People's Court, April 22, 2009).
73 Such ruling has been described as a "helpful step in the right direction." See Freshfields Bruckhaus Deringer, *First Reported Case of a China ICC Award Being Enforced in China*, October 2009, https://www.lexology.com/library/document.ashx?g=b989a013-d798-4784-b1fe-3767336de095.
74 There is a timing requirement spelled out by the SPC when interpreting Article 13 of the Arbitration Law; that a court shall not accept a party's application to nullify an arbitration agreement where the party failed to raise its objection prior to the first hearing in the arbitration proceeding.
75 Anhui Longlide Baozhuang Yinshua Youxian Gongsi yu BP Agnati SRL [*Longlide Packaging Co Ltd v BP Agnati SRL*] (Anhui Higher People's Court, January 30, 2013).
76 Ibid.

for a reply on the three issues raised by the claimant. In the reply, the SPC merely responded to the first issue and upheld the validity of the arbitration agreement, the implication of which is that the ICC Court of Arbitration, despite being a foreign arbitration institution, was accepted as a valid "designated arbitration institution."[77] The SPC, however, did not go on to address the second and third issues, such that the questions of whether the current jurisprudence now extends to allow foreign arbitration institutions to administer arbitration in China, and whether awards rendered by such institutions in China should be categorized as "non-domestic," remain unclear.

While the two recent cases, *Duferco* and *Longlide*, exhibit judicial leniency toward foreign institutional arbitration seated in China, uncertainty still looms over the highest Chinese judiciary as to the official legality of foreign institutional arbitration seated in China. On a separate note, the application of the New York Convention is limited to recognition and enforcement of arbitral awards from a "foreign" state.[78] Although China made a "reciprocity" reservation in its accession to the New York Convention,[79] this reservation does not affect the nature of the enforceable award in China under the Convention as entirely "foreign."[80] It is therefore confusing and somewhat disappointing that the SPC failed to address or clarify the issue of whether ICC arbitral awards rendered in China should be categorized as "non-domestic awards," and hence failed to address the proper scope and application of the New York Convention in China.

4.2 Public policy

Public policy works as the safety valve to deny recognition and enforcement of foreign arbitral awards under Article V(2) of the New York Convention.[81] The implementation of the public policy ground has become one of the most controversial areas in international arbitration enforcement as well

---

77 Supreme People's Court, *Reply of the Supreme People's Court to the Request for Instructions on Application for Confirming the Validity of an Arbitration Agreement in the Case of Anhui Long Li De Packaging and Printing Co Ltd v BP Agnati SRL*, March 25, 2013, http://en.pkulaw.cn/display.aspx?cgid=233828&lib=law.
78 The New York Convention, art. 1, para. 1, provides that "[t]he member State will apply the Convention only to recognition and enforcement of awards made in the territory of another contracting state."
79 The "reciprocity" reservation that China made during accession.
80 See Supreme People's Court, *Circular of Supreme People's Court on Implementing Convention on the Recognition and Enforcement of Foreign Arbitral Awards Entered by China*, December 31, 1986, http://www.cietac.org/index.php?m=Article&a=show&id=2413&l=en. Article 1 of the Circular provides that "[i]n accordance with the reciprocity reservation statement made by China when entering the Convention, this Convention shall apply to the recognition and enforcement of an arbitral award made in the territory of another contracting State."
81 New York Convention, Article V(2)(b).

as a key measurement of the judicial attitude toward arbitration in a given jurisdiction.[82]

Because of the pre-reporting system, Chinese judiciaries at both the central and local levels had to deal with international awards in a very prudent and cautious manner. Public policy was actually not invoked by the Chinese courts to vacate any single foreign arbitral award, in the time period from 2000 to 2007.[83] In a recently published study, from 2000 to 2012, there were a total of twelve cases with respect to enforcement of foreign arbitral awards in China which involved public policy issues.[84] The case of *Hemofarm DD et al v Jinan Yongning Pharmaceutical* (*"Yongning"*) in 2009 was the only one in which a foreign award was denied recognition and enforcement on the ground of public policy.[85]

Yongning concerned a leasing dispute arising between a Chinese investor (Yongning) and its investing joint venture (the "JV"). The Jinan People's Intermediate Court (the "Jinan Court," in Shandong province) ruled in favor of Yongning and imposed property preservation upon the JV. The JV ceased operation and went bankrupt. The foreign investors commenced ICC arbitration in Paris. The ICC arbitral tribunal criticized the interim measures imposed by the Chinese local court and ruled against Yongning. Subsequently, the foreign investors sought to enforce the ICC award at the Jinan Court where Yongning was domiciled. The Jinan Court, however, held that the arbitration clause in the JV contract could only bind disputes between the contracting parties (the investors), but not the leasing dispute between the investor and the JV (the investee). It further held that a foreign tribunal could not criticize the judicial measures by the Chinese court. The non-enforcement decision by the local court was then reported all the way to the SPC under the pre-reporting system. In 2009, the SPC ruled that as the series of event (the

---

82 UNCITRAL Secretariat, Emmanuel Gaillard and George A. Bermann, eds., *Guide on the Convention on the Recognition and Enforcement of Foreign Arbitral Awards: New York, 1958* (The Hague: Brill Nijhoff, 2017).

83 Speech by Wan E'xiang, Deputy Chief Justice of the SPC, at the international symposium "50th Anniversary of the New York Convention" (June 6, 2008, Beijing). Justice Wan stated that, from 2000 to 2007, a total of twelve foreign arbitral awards were not recognized and denied enforcement by the SPC. Among these twelve awards, four were refused because the statute of limitations for application for enforcement had expired, five were refused because the concerned parties had not reached an arbitral agreement or the arbitration clause had been invalid, one was refused because the concerned party against which the arbitral award was enforced did not have any enforceable assets within China, and the remaining award was refused because the concerned party against which the arbitral award was enforced had not received the notice for appointment of arbitrators and arbitration procedure.

84 He Qisheng, "Public Policy in Enforcement of Foreign Arbitral Awards in the Supreme People's Court of China," *Hong Kong Law Journal* 43, no. 1 (2013): 1037.

85 Supreme People's Court, *Letter of Reply of the Supreme People's Court to a Request for Instructions on the Non-Recognition and Non-Enforcement of an Arbitration Award of the ICC International Court of Arbitration.* June 2, 2008, http://www.lawinfochina.com/display.aspx?lib=law&id=14615&CGid=.

leasing dispute, the property preservation order and JV's associated bank-ruptcy) which gave rise to the ICC arbitration were not covered by the parties' arbitration clause, the ICC tribunal had overstepped its jurisdiction. The SPC opined that the jurisdiction rightfully belonged to the independent jurisdic-tion of the Chinese courts, and confirmed that enforcement of the ICC award would violate China's judicial sovereignty.[86]

The SPC's 2009 decision in *Yongning* holds the distinction of being the only case in the past decade in which a "public policy" argument has succeeded in barring recognition and enforcement of a foreign award in China.[87] In *Yongning*, the ICC award was denied on the newly delineated grounds that its enforcement would violate "judicial sovereignty"—thus confirming "judicial sovereignty" as a component of China's "public policy."[88] However, the decision of *Yongning* in 2009 contrasts with the *Castel Electronics Ptd Ltd* case ("*Castel*") in 2013, under which the "public policy" argument was rejected by the SPC.[89] In *Castel*, a disagreement between an Australian arbitration institution and a Chinese Intermediate People's Court[90] on the validity of an arbitration agreement did not amount to a violation of the "judicial sovereignty" or China's public policy.[91]

Castel could be distinguished from *Yongning* in two aspects. First, in *Yongning*, Yongning did not participate in the ICC arbitral proceed-ings. However, in *Castel*, through voluntary participation, TCL did not raise objections to the arbitral jurisdiction but actively counterclaimed against Castel in the Australian arbitral proceedings. Second, in *Castel*, the Australian arbitral tribunal made the decision on arbitral jurisdiction before the Chinese court ruled on the same matter. Hence, the foreign arbi-tral tribunal neither ignored nor criticized the Chinese court's decision.

Castel has far-reaching impact on the issue of public policy in judicial review over arbitration. This is the first time that China's highest court clearly defines public policy in detail and makes it clear that the Chinese court judg-ment is not equivalent to public policy, and such delineation clearly reflects an arbitration-friendly approach. More recent cases echoed the generally "pro-arbitration" stance taken by the Chinese judiciary. In 2014, the SPC

86 Ibid.
87 Ibid.
88 *Hemofarm DD et al v Jinan Yongning Pharmaceutical Co Ltd*, Reply of the SPC Concerning the Request for Refusal to Recognize and Enforce the Arbitral Award of the International Court of Arbitration of ICC (2009) Min Si Ta Zi No. 11, compiled in Zhao Xiuwen 赵秀文, "Refusing Recognition and Enforcement of Foreign Arbitral Awards on the Ground of Public Policy from the Case of Yongning Corporation 从永宁公司案看公共政策作为我国法院拒绝执行外国仲裁裁决的理由, *The Jurist* 法学家 no. 4 (2009): 101–103.
89 Supreme People's Court, *Reply of the SPC to Application of Castel Electronics Pty Ltd for Recognition and Enforcement of a Foreign Arbitral Award* (2013) Min Si Ta Zi No. 46.
90 Zhongshan Intermediate Court, Guangdong Province.
91 Supreme People's Court, *Reply of the SPC to Application of Castel Electronics Pty Ltd for Recognition and Enforcement of a Foreign Arbitral Award*.

aided in clarification as to the substantive contents of public policy. In *Fujian Zongheng Media Express Technology v Starr Investments Cayman II Inc* ("*Starr Investments*"), the SPC ruled out contravention of mandatory administrative regulations—in the particular case, infringement of foreign currency regulations—as a violation of China's public policy.[92]

4.3 Foreign-related element

The Chinese arbitration system adopts a dual-track distinction where disputes with a "foreign-related" element[93] are treated more liberally. In 2015, a local Chinese court decision in *Siemens v Shanghai Golden Landmark* ("*Golden Landmark*") challenged the conventional wisdom as to what could constitute a "foreign-related" element in China.[94]

Golden Landmark concerned a claim for breach of equipment supply agreement between two foreign investment enterprises ("FIEs") in China, Siemens and Shanghai Golden Landmark. The agreement provided for arbitration under the Singapore International Arbitration Center ("SIAC"). Golden Landmark commenced arbitral proceedings against Siemens and Siemens filed counterclaims. The SIAC tribunal ruled in favor of Siemens. Siemens sought to enforce the SIAC award before the Shanghai No. 1 Intermediate People's Court (the "Shanghai Court"). Golden Landmark challenged enforcement on several grounds. Most notably, as a dispute arising out of a domestic contract between two domestic Chinese companies, it argued that the arbitration contained no "foreign-related elements" and could not select overseas arbitration institutions.[95] Golden Landmark also raised public policy to resist enforcement.

The Shanghai Court opined that the background of the parties and their performance differentiated the current dispute from a purely domestic one. First, both parties were to some extent foreign-related. Both were wholly foreign owned Enterprises ("WFOEs"), and their source of capital, ultimate profits and decision-making processes were all outside China. Second, the equipment was shipped from abroad to the Shanghai FTZ for customs clearance before it was finally delivered to the designated construction site. The performance of the contract, such as the delivery process, resembled that of

---

92 *Starr Investments Cayman II Inc v Fujian Zongheng MediaExpress Technology Inc, Fujian Fenzhong Media Inc, Zheng Cheng* (2014) Rong Zhi Jian Zi No. 51 (Fuzhou Intermediate People's Court, November 5, 2014).

93 See discussions in Section 2.1.2 of Chapter 4.

94 Ximenzi guoji maoyi (Shanghai) youxian gongsi yu Shanghai huangjin zhidi youxian gongsi shenqing chengren he zhixing waiguo zhongcai caijue an (西门子国际贸易(上海)有限公司与上海黄金置地有限公司申请承认和执行外国仲裁裁决案) [*Siemens International Trading (Shanghai) Co Ltd v Shanghai Golden Landmark Co Ltd*] (Shanghai Intermediate People's Court, November 27, 2015).

95 The Chinese company law treats all types of FIEs incorporated in Mainland China as Mainland Chinese companies and there is a lack of "foreign-related element." Purely Chinese domestic disputes are not allowed to apply for overseas arbitration before *Golden Landmark*. See Gu, "Arbitration outside China without Foreign-related Elements."

international sales of goods. The Shanghai Court concluded that the factors outlined above constituted "other circumstances" that may be considered as foreign-related, and that the arbitration clause selecting SIAC arbitration was valid. It also dismissed the public policy challenge.

Golden Landmark is important. For the first time, a local court exercised its discretion liberally in finding foreign elements among unconventional circumstances. However, *Golden Landmark*'s decision contrasts with that of the *Beijing Chaolaixinsheng* case in 2014, under which the "foreign-related" argument out of similar factual scenarios was rejected by the Beijing No. 2 Intermediate People's Court and the SPC (through the pre-reporting system).⁹⁶ The only difference between the two cases lies in the background of the disputing parties, where both parties in *Golden Landmark* were WFOEs in the FTZ. *Golden Landmark* is therefore of particular appeal to foreign parties operating in China through Chinese presence in the FTZs, and who are interested in offshore arbitration.

The jurisprudence in *Golden Landmark* was subsequently confirmed by the SPC in late 2016 in the 2016 FTZ Opinion.⁹⁷ According to Article 9 of the 2016 FTZ Opinion, disputes without conventional foreign elements, such as those arising out of WFOEs registered in FTZs, can also be submitted to overseas arbitration.⁹⁸ Against the background of facilitating foreign investment and trade in the FTZs, and given FTZs' special status as a pilot project for innovative law making and practicing, judicial review over arbitration may be raised to a more international level.

4.4 Severability doctrine

Most recently, in 2019, the CICC rendered its very first ruling which concerned a judicial review over arbitral jurisdiction. In *Luck Treat Limited v Zhong Yuan Cheng Commercial Investment Holdings* ("*Luck Treat*"), an arbitration clause included in a seemingly non-existing share transfer agreement was held as existent and valid.⁹⁹ For the first time, the CICC (and the SPC)

---

96 Supreme People's Court, *Zuigao renmin fayuan guanyu beijing chaolai xinsheng tiyu xiuxian youxiangongsi shenqing chengren dahan shangshi zhongcaiyuan zuozhu de di 12113–0011 hao, di 12112–0012 hao zhongcai caijue anjian qingshi de fuhan* 最高人民法院关于北京潮来新生体育休闲有限公司申请承认大韩商事仲裁院作出的第12113-0011号、第12112-0012号仲裁裁决案件请示的复函, December 18, 2013, http://www.uncitral.org/docs/clout/CHN/CHN_181213_FT_1609.pdf.

97 See Section 3.1 of this chapter.

98 Supreme People's Court, *Opinions of the Supreme People's Court on Providing Judicial Guarantee for the Building of Pilot Free Trade Zones*, art. 9.

99 Yunyu youxiangongsi, Shenzhenshi zhongyuancheng shangye touzi konggu youxiangongsi shenqing queren zhongcai xieyi xiaoli minshi caiding shu (运裕有限公司、深圳市中苑城商业投资控股有限公司申请确认仲裁协议效力民事裁定书) [*Luck Treat Limited v Shenzhen Zhongyuancheng Commercial Investment Co Ltd*] (2019) Zui Gao Fa Min Te No. 1, (Supreme People's Court, September 18, 2019) http://www.lawinfochina.com/display.aspx?lib=case&id=3429&EncodingName=big5.

clarified that arbitration clauses are to be severed and treated independently from the main contract, including its governing law.

Luck Treat ("Seller"), a BVI company, intended to sell its equity shares in a third company to Zhong Yuan Cheng ("Buyer"), a Chinese domestic company. The Seller sent to the Buyer a draft of the share transfer agreement ("STA"). The Buyer signed the draft STA and sent it back to the Seller. The draft STA contained an arbitration clause pointing to arbitration under the SCIA in Shenzhen, and stipulated that it would only come into force upon the signatures of legal representatives of both parties. The Seller eventually did not sign the draft STA. The Buyer initiated arbitration against the Seller pursuant to the arbitration clause in the draft STA. The Seller then applied to the Shenzhen Intermediate People's Court (in Guangdong Province) for denouncing the arbitration clause, arguing that the main contract had not been formed and hence the arbitration clause could not bind the Seller. The SPC transferred the case to the CICC, as the case concerned arbitration dispute under the SCIA, a CICC-accredited arbitral institution pursuant to the CICC One-Stop Institution Notice.[100]

In September 2019, in its ruling on *Luck Treat*, the CICC gave three important jurisprudences. First, it confirmed that the severability of the arbitration clause is a widely recognized international legal doctrine. The existence, validity, and governing law of the arbitration clause should all be severed from that of the main contract. Second, in deciding the effect of an arbitration clause, emphasis should be given to whether there is mutual consent reached between the parties on arbitration. The mutual consent here refers to the offer and acceptance between the parties to bring the disputes to arbitration. Third, once the effect of the arbitration clause is confirmed, the issue of whether the main contract is existent or valid should be left to the arbitral tribunal to decide.

Luck Treat reflects the latest Chinese judicial approach toward arbitration. This is the first judgment of the CICC, and because of CICC's special connection with the SPC, it is the first time that China's highest court clearly defines the severability doctrine in detail, and such clarification clearly reflects a pro-arbitration judicial stance. In the Chinese official press release, CICC's *Luck Treat* judgment was commented as SPC's rigorous support toward the arbitration system in Shenzhen, which is a key indicator of China's ambition in further reform and opening up such as the BRI and the Great Bay Area ("GBA") development, as well as in perfecting the Chinese investment environment.[101]

---

100 See Section 3.3 of this chapter.
101 Shenzhen Court of International Arbitration, "Zuigao guoji shangshi fating diyian zai Shenzhen shenjie Queren dangshiren xuanze Shenzhen guoji zhongcaiyuan guanxia de zhongcai xieyi xiaoli" 最高院国际商事法庭第一案在深圳审结 确认当事人选择深圳国际仲裁院管辖的仲裁协议效力, September 30, 2019, http://www.sohu.com/a/344441888_120054630.

5 Development analyses

5.1 Penetrating factors

It is commonplace today for jurisdictions to market themselves as "arbitration-friendly." As argued, whether a jurisdiction could be termed as "pro-arbitration" or "arbitration-friendly" is usually tested on its infrastructure to enable effective arbitral enforcement. The infrastructure refers to the judicial support toward arbitration, to ensure that courts do not unduly interfere with the conduct of arbitrations, and enforce arbitral awards in accordance with best practices under the New York Convention.

A comparative analysis of Asia-Pacific arbitration reforms shows that among the penetrating factors, in China, such a reform of the infrastructure is typically motivated by economic factors, such as the desire to attract greater foreign investment with the expectation that the latter will in turn lead to the enhancement of economic growth,[102] given that outside investors may be wary of the impartiality of Chinese domestic courts in resolving cross-border commercial disputes. This is especially so as Chinese economy continues to expand in scale and grow in volume globally. Between 2013 and 2019, 18 FTZs have been established in China in five rounds, starting with Shanghai. The Shanghai FTZ was designated as the first BRI-related FTZ to pioneer domestic economic and investment reforms.[103] All these 18 FTZs are then altogether tasked to experiment with various levels of trade and investment liberalization to facilitate the BRI development.[104] China may see the merit in promoting herself as an international or regional arbitration hub. In light of her ambitious BRI development, China's hope of reform in such instance would be to make the court system more "pro-arbitration." Whether it is by way of adjudication of individual cases or issuance of more general judicial interpretations, where existing legislation fails to provide clear or satisfactory solutions, the judiciaries step in to bring along reforms which tend to reflect strong support toward arbitration in consideration of China's economic and investment interests. Hence, judicial efforts from both the central and local levels help ensure a smooth operation of the arbitration system to facilitate China's trade and investment.

In its interpretative function, the 2016 FTZ Opinion and the 2018 CICC Provisions transmit a clear signal to enhance China's out-going economy. Meanwhile, the extension of the pre-reporting system to domestic arbitral awards shows SPC's commitment to support the domestic investment environment.

---

102 See Reyes and Gu, *The Developing World of Arbitration*.
103 "Zimaoqu mingdan kuorong zhi 18 ge shifang liuda jiji xinhao" 自贸区名单扩容至18个释放六大积极信号, *Sina Caijing* 新浪财经, August 27, 2019, http://finance.sina.com.cn/china/2019-08-27/doc-ihytcitn2159462.shtml.
104 Ibid.

There are also evident examples in the adjudication side. In *Duferco* (2009) and *Longlide* (2013), both the central and local judiciaries exhibited judicial leniency toward selecting ICC arbitration seated in China, a move echoing the Chinese government's recent policy to invite some foreign arbitration institutions to open up business representation at the Shanghai FTZ.[105] Likewise, in *Golden Landmark* (2015), both the presiding judge and vice president of the local judiciary in Shanghai expressed that the decision was heavily influenced by the macroeconomic policies—the Shanghai FTZ and the BRI—which aimed at encouraging more foreign investment and transactions with foreign entities.[106] Most recently, in *Luck Treat* (2019), the newly established CICC showed vigorous support toward arbitration in Shenzhen, which was obviously a reflection of the important economic role Shenzhen plays in the BRI and GBA national economic strategies of "going out" (*zouchuqu* 走出去).

5.2 Patterns of reform

On patterns of the reform, SPC's top-down approach has a wide and direct impact that its interpretations (regulatory side) or judgments (adjudicative side) would be binding (or highly influential) on future arbitration practices pertaining to the same (or similar) types of issues in China. In contrast, bottom-up initiatives, such as judgments rendered by individual local judiciaries, are *prima facie* limited to that particular local jurisdiction. Despite indirect in impact, local judiciaries are at the forefront of Chinese judicial practice in supporting arbitration. They are able to identify the limitations and defects of the infrastructure more aptly and follow recent commercial trends more closely.

The regulatory side is clearly a pattern of top-down where the SPC interpretations on the pre-reporting system, *ad hoc* arbitration, and CICC-related arbitral review, clarify the procedure and substance on some of the most controversial scenarios when courts are asked to rule on the validity of arbitral awards.

In contrast, the adjudication side is a mixed pattern with both top-down and bottom-up and shows an interesting trajectory of the two being complementary to each other, where top-down responds to bottom-up by central judiciaries affirming local judicial practices. For example, in *Longlide* (2013), the SPC followed the liberal footsteps of *Duferco* (2009) of the local judiciary several years ago to give effect to the potential of ICC arbitration

---

105 So far, ICC, HKIAC, and SIAC have set up their Chinese representative offices in the Shanghai FTZ. See Gu Weixia, "The Developing Nature of Arbitration in Mainland China and Its Correlation with the Market: Institutional, Ad Hoc, and Foreign Institutions Seated in Mainland China," *Contemporary Asia Arbitration Journal* 10, no. 2 (2017): 257–291.

106 See Gu, "Arbitration outside China without Foreign-related Elements."

seated in China and its resulting arbitral award. In *Castel* (2013) and *Starr Investments* (2014), through the pre-reporting system, the SPC responded to the local judiciaries by delineating "public policy" in China and ruling out Chinese judgments and mandatory administrative regulations from China's public policy. In *Golden Landmark* (2015), the local judiciary in Shanghai exercised judicial discretion in finding unconventional foreign elements for the first time, which was subsequently confirmed in SPC's judicial interpretation in the 2016 FTZ Opinion. As a result, the Chinese judiciary in the past decade, at both the central and local levels, has generally exhibited judicial support and leniency with respect to controversial cases of arbitral enforcement.

6 The future

Top-down legislative revision to the 1994 AL by the central legislature is anticipated as the next direction for reform, given the limitations to the extent in which the SPC may push the boundaries of arbitration practice. In *Longlide* (2013), the SPC attracted criticism after failing to respond to the issues of the scope and application of the New York Convention in China in controversial cases.[107] It remains unclear whether arbitral awards rendered by foreign institutional arbitrations seated in China are considered "non-domestic" awards in China, and whether such awards are enforceable by Chinese courts pursuant to the New York Convention. The reluctance of the SPC to address these issues may stem from a suspicion of judicial activism where the legislation is silent, and where the consequences would be significant. A legal recognition of the outcome flowing from foreign institutional arbitrations seated in China would have a sizable impact on the freedom and openness of arbitration and legal markets as allowed by the Chinese government. Thus, while the SPC inclines toward recognizing the growing phenomena in arbitral practice and toward granting the parties more autonomy in drafting, it is cautious not to bring reforms too swiftly and radically. Only with the passage of time could the SPC gradually introduce more changes. For example, with respect to public policy, the SPC generally displayed a sympathetic and liberal, but "safe," attitude, from *Yongning* (2009) to *Castel* (2013), to discern the proper approach as to how to deal with the jurisdictional conflict between the Chinese court and the foreign arbitral tribunal. All these more controversial questions and issues require legislative efforts. The lack of official legislative support has left the judicial initiatives, whether top-down or bottom-up, as transitional and informal ways of reform with many uncertainties, incapable of inducing systematic breakthroughs. This is especially so in light of China's expanding economic prominence. Relatedly, China may lose its

---

107 *Longlide Packaging Co Ltd v BP Agnati SRL.* See also Section 4.1 of this chapter.

competitiveness value in the international arbitration market because of its overly slow progress in legislative development, despite its strong vigor in economic competitiveness.

Judicial support of good quality is also critical in ensuring the success of the reform. It is encouraging to note that, over the past decade, in addition to issuing very impressive regulatory interpretations to reform the infrastructure, the SPC has been generally supportive of arbitration in practice in controversial matters. In *Longlide* (2013), *Castel* (2013), *Starr Investments* (2014), *Luck Treat* (2019), and the treatment of the jurisdictional incident following the CIETAC split episode (2015),[108] the central-level judiciary has exhibited judicial liberalism and made great efforts to give effect to controversial arbitral awards as much as possible. Lower-level Chinese judiciaries are also gradually more and more supportive of arbitration in unconventional cases. In *Duferco* (2009) and *Golden Landmark* (2015), local judiciaries are seen to push the boundaries of the knowledge by emulating the SPC's pro-arbitration jurisprudence.

Last but not least, the Chinese courts are also advised to change the aspects of what they consider to be a "pro-arbitration" judicial attitude. For the past few years, the Chinese courts have taken a "pro-arbitration" judicial approach to emphasize the number of arbitral awards enforced in China and overseas. The extension of the "pre-reporting" system to even the domestic arbitration regime has become a natural outcome and would make those really defective arbitral awards impossible to be set aside. But equally important is the quality of the supervision of the arbitration system. The role of judicial review over the arbitration process should be emphasized inasmuch as being an essential component of the "pro-arbitration" judicial attitude.

7 Conclusion

The Chinese judiciary, at both the central and local levels, has been generally more proactive in respecting arbitration in the past decade. In an active manner, the SPC has promulgated a series of judicial interpretations to establish a pro-arbitration judiciary in China, such as limitedly granting recognition to *ad hoc* arbitration and extending the pre-reporting system to the domestic arbitration regime. The pace has been impressively rapid in the past several years, responding well to the dispute resolution needs arising out of the FTZ, BRI, and GBA national macroeconomic development strategies. In adjudicative manner, the central and local judiciaries have jointly exhibited judicial support and issued liberal rulings in some of the most controversial arbitral enforcement cases in China, such as the role of foreign institutional arbitrations seated in China, the limits of public policy, the introduction of

108   See discussions in Section 3.3.1 of Chapter 4.

unconventional "foreign-related" element, and the scope and effect of CICC-related arbitration.

The development trajectory shows that arbitration is vital to China's economic and investment interests. This is particularly so in light of China's expansive economic strategies. While the inbound investment associated with the FTZ and GBA initiatives requires a trustworthy alternative to the litigation regime to resolve foreign-related commercial disputes in China, the outbound investment with more Chinese companies "going out" under the BRI development calls for a reliable and out-going dispute resolution mechanism. In both cases, arbitration seems to be the most desirable option.

Bibliography

Anhui Longlide Baozhuang Yinshua Youxian Gongsi yu BP Agnati SRL [*Longlide Packaging Co Ltd v. BP Agnati SRL*] (Anhui Higher People's Court, January 30, 2013).

Bermann, George A. "The Role of National Courts at The Threshold of Arbitration." *American Review of International Arbitration* 28, no. 3 (2018): 219–308.

Cao, Yajing, "*Fahui Shenpan Zhineng Zuoyong: Cujin Zi Mao Shiyan Qu Jiankang Fazhan*" 发挥审判智能作用：促进自贸区健康发展. *People's Court Daily* 人民法院报, January 10, 2017. http://rmfyb.chinacourt.org/paper/html/2017-01/10/content_120669.htm?div=-1.

Carbonneau, Thomas. "Judicial Approbation in Building the Civilization of Arbitration." In *Building the Civilization of Arbitration*, edited by Thomas Carbonneau and Angelica M. Sinopole, 333–365. London: Wildy, Simmonds & Hill Publishing, 2010.

Carbonneau, Thomas. "Judicial Approbation in Building the Civilization of Arbitration." *Penn State Law Review* 113, no. 4 (2009): 1343–1368.

Chinalawinfo.com. Accessed July 16, 2020. http://www.chinalawinfo.com/.

De Gao Gang Tie Gong Si Yu Ning Bo Shi Gong Yi Pin Jin Chu Kou You Xian Gong Si [*Duferco SA v Ningbo Art & Craft Import & Export Corp*] (Ningbo Intermediate People's Court, April 22, 2009).

Freshfields Bruckhaus Deringer. *First Reported Case of a China ICC Award Being Enforced in China*, October 2009. https://www.lexology.com/library/document.ashx?g=b989a013-d798-4784-b1fe-3767336de095.

Gu, Weixia 顾维遐. "Arbitration outside China without Foreign-related Elements" 无涉外因素争议的域外仲裁问题. *Peking University Law Journal* 中外法学 30, no. 3 (2018): 651–670.

Gu, Weixia. "Arbitration in China." In *International Commercial Arbitration in Asia*, 2nd ed., edited by Thomas Ginsburg and Shahla Ali, 77–132. New York: Juris Publishing, 2013.

Gu, Weixia. "Piercing the Veil of Arbitration Reform in China: Promises, Pitfalls, Patterns, Prognoses and Prospects." *American Journal of Comparative Law* 65, no. 4 (2017): 799–840.

Gu, Weixia. "The Developing Nature of Arbitration in Mainland China and Its Correlation with the Market: Institutional, Ad Hoc, and Foreign Institutions Seated in Mainland China." *Contemporary Asia Arbitration Journal* 10, no. 2 (2017): 257–291.

He, Qisheng. "Public Policy in Enforcement of Foreign Arbitral Awards in the Supreme People's Court of China." *Hong Kong Law Journal* 43, no. 1 (2013): 1037–1060.

Hemofarm DD et al v Jinan Yongning Pharmaceutical Co Ltd, Reply of the SPC Concerning the Request for Refusal to Recognize and Enforce the Arbitral Award of the International Court of Arbitration of ICC (2009) Min Si Ta Zi No. 11.

"Judges." China International Commercial Court. Accessed July 14, 2020. http://cicc. court.gov.cn/html/1/218/19/151/index.html.

Ministry of Commerce, National Bureau of Statistics and State Administration of Foreign Exchange. *2016 Statistical Bulletin of China's Outward Foreign Direct Investment*. Beijing: China Statistical Press, 2016. http://cdi.cnki.net/Titles/ SingleNJ?NJCode=N2017120333.

Minshi Susong Fa (民事诉讼法) [Civil Procedure Law] (promulgated by the National People's Congress Standing Committee, June 27, 2017, effective July 1, 2017). http:// en.pkulaw.cn/display.aspx?id=6d9ce94e57cee7afbdfb&lib=law.

Minshi Susong Fa (民事诉讼法) [Civil Procedure Law] (promulgated by the National People's Congress, August 31, 2012, effective January 1, 2013. http://www.lawinfo-china.com/display.aspx?id=11161&lib=law.

National Development and Reform Commission. *Visions and Actions on Jointly Building Silk Road Economic Belt and 21st-Century Maritime Silk Road*. March 28, 2015. http://en.ndrc.gov.cn/newsrelease/201503/t20150330_669367.html.

Qiao, Wenxin 乔文心. "Zuigao renmin fayuan diyi guoji shangshi fating gaoxiao shen-jie shoupi wujian anjian" 最高人民法院第一国际商事法庭高效审结首批五件案件. December 30, 2019. http://cicc.court.gov.cn/html/1/218/149/156/1545.html.

Reyes, Anselmo and Gu Weixia. *The Developing World of Arbitration: A Comparative Study of Arbitration Reform in the Asia Pacific*. Oxford: Hart Publishing, 2018.

Sauvant, Karl P. and Michael Nolan. "China's Outward Foreign Direct Investment and International Investment Law." *Journal of International Economic Law* 36, no. 1 (2015): 1–42.

"Secretary for Justice Promotes Hong Kong's Legal and Dispute Resolution Service in Beijing (with Photos)." Department of Justice, August 18, 2015. https://www.info. gov.hk/gia/general/201508/18/P201508180765.htm.

Shen, Wei and Shang Shu. "Tackling Local Protectionism in Enforcing Foreign Arbitral Awards in China: An Empirical Study of the Supreme People's Court's Review Decisions, 1995–2015." *The China Quarterly* 241, no. 1 (2019): 1–25.

Shenzhen Court of International Arbitration. "Zuigao guoji shangshi fating diyian zai Shenzhen shenjie queren dangshiren xuanze Shenzhen guoji zhongcaiyuan guanxia de zhongcai xieyi xiaoli" 最高院国际商事法庭第一案在深圳审结确认当事人选择深圳国际仲裁院管辖的仲裁协议效力. September 30, 2019. http://www.sohu. com/a/344441888_120054630.

Starr Investments Cayman II Inc v Fujian Zongheng MediaExpress Technology Inc, Fujian Fenzhong Media Inc, Zheng Cheng (2014) Rong Zhi Jian Zi No. 51 (Fuzhou Intermediate People's Court, November 5, 2014).

Supreme People's Court. *Circular of Supreme People's Court on Implementing Convention on the Recognition and Enforcement of Foreign Arbitral Awards Entered by China*. December 31, 1986. http://www.cietac.org/index.php?m=Article&a= show&id=2413&l=en.

Supreme People's Court. *Letter of Reply of the Supreme People's Court to a Request for Instructions on the Non-Recognition and Non-Enforcement of an Arbitration Award of the ICC International Court of Arbitration*. June 2, 2008. http://www. lawinfochina.com/display.aspx?lib=law&id=14615&CGid=.

Supreme People's Court. *Notice of the Supreme People's Court on Inclusion of the First Group of International Commercial Arbitration and Mediation Institutions in the "One-stop" Diversified International Commercial Dispute Resolution Mechanism.* December 5, 2018. http://cicc.court.gov.cn/html/1/219/208/210/1144.html.

Supreme People's Court. *Opinions of the Supreme People's Court on Providing Judicial Guarantee for the Building of Pilot Free Trade Zones.* December 30, 2016. http://en.pkulaw.cn/display.aspx?cgid=441e185f12e602a2bdfb&lib=law.

Supreme People's Court. *Provisions of the Supreme People's Court on Several Issues concerning Trying Cases of Arbitration-Related Judicial Review.* December 26, 2017. http://www.lawinfochina.com/display.aspx?id=27178&lib=law.

Supreme People's Court. *Provisions of the Supreme People's Court on Several Issues concerning the Handling of Cases regarding Enforcement of Arbitral Awards by the People's Courts.* February 22, 2018. http://www.lawinfochina.com/display.aspx?id=30284&lib=law.

Supreme People's Court. *Provisions of the Supreme People's Court on Several Issues Concerning the Establishment of the International Commercial Courts.* July 1, 2018. https://cgc.law.stanford.edu/belt-and-road/b-and-r-texts/20180701-provisions-re-intl-commercial-courts/.

Supreme People's Court. *Relevant Provisions of the Supreme People's Court on Issues Concerning Applications for Verification of Arbitration Cases under Judicial Review.* December 26, 2017. http://www.lawinfochina.com/display.aspx?id=27182&lib=law.

Supreme People's Court. *Reply of the SPC to Application of Castel Electronics Pty Ltd for Recognition and Enforcement of a Foreign Arbitral Award* (2013) Min Si Ta Zi No. 46.

Supreme People's Court. *Reply of the Supreme People's Court to the Request for Instructions on Application for Confirming the Validity of an Arbitration Agreement in the Case of Anhui Long Li De Packaging and Printing Co., Ltd. v. BP Agnati S. R. L.* March 25, 2013. http://en.pkulaw.cn/display.aspx?cgid=233828&lib=law.

Supreme People's Court. *Zuigao renmin fayuan guanyu beijing chaolai xinsheng tiyu xiuxian youxiangongsi shenqing chengren dahan shangshi zhongcaiyuan zuozhu de di 12113–0011 hao, di 12112–0012 hao zhongcai caijue anjian qingshi de fuhan* 最高人民法院关于北京潮来新生体育休闲有限公司申请承认大韩商事仲裁院作出的第12113–0011号、第12112–0012号仲裁裁决案件请示的复函. December 18, 2013. http://www.uncitral.org/docs/clout/CHN/CHN_181213_FT_1609.pdf.

UNCITRAL Secretariat, Emmanuel Gaillard and George A. Bermann, eds. *Guide on the Convention on the Recognition and Enforcement of Foreign Arbitral Awards: New York, 1958.* The Hague: Brill Nijhoff, 2017.

"Weishenme zai Shenzhen, Xian she guoji shangshi fating? Zuigaofa huiying" 为什么在深圳、西安设国际商事法庭？最高法回应. *Zhongguo Xinwen Wang* 中国新闻网, June 28, 2018. http://www.chinanews.com/gn/2018/06-28/8549700.shtml.

Ximenzi guoji maoyi (Shanghai) youxian gongsi yu Shanghai huangjin zhidi youxian gongsi shenqing chengren he zhixing waiguo zhongcai caijue an (西门子国际贸易(上海)有限公司与上海黄金置地有限公司申请承认和执行外国仲裁裁决案) [*Siemens International Trading (Shanghai) Co Ltd v Shanghai Golden Landmark Co Ltd*] (Shanghai Intermediate People's Court, November 27, 2015).

Yao, Daqing. "The China (Shanghai) Pilot Free Trade Zone: Background, Developments and Preliminary Assessment of Initial Impacts." *National Bureau of Economic Research (NBER) Working Paper Series* (2015). https://www.nber.org/papers/w20924.pdf.

Yunyu youxiangongsi, Shenzhenshi zhongyuancheng shangye touzi konggu youxiangongsi shenqing queren zhongcai xieyi xiaoli minshi caiding shu (运裕有限公司、深圳市中苑城商业投资控股有限公司申请确认仲裁协议效力民事裁定书) [*Luck Treat Limited v Shenzhen Zhongyuancheng Commercial Investment Co Ltd*] (2019) Zui Gao Fa Min Te No. 1 (Supreme People's Court, September 18, 2019), http://www.lawinfochina.com/display.aspx?lib=case&id=3429&EncodingName=big5.

Zhao, Xiuwen 赵秀文. "Refusing Recognition and Enforcement of Foreign Arbitral Awards on the Ground of Public Policy from the Case of Yongning Corporation" 从永宁公司案看公共政策作为我国法院拒绝执行外国仲裁裁决的理由. *The Jurist* 法学家 no. 4 (2009): 98–105.

Zhongcai Fa (仲裁法) [Arbitration Law] (promulgated by the Standing Committee of the National People's Congress, August 31, 1994, effective September 1, 1995), http://www.npc.gov.cn/wxzl/wxzl/2000-12/05/content_4624.htm.

"Zhonggong zhongyang bangongting, guowuyuan bangongting yinfa <guanyu jianli 'yidai yilu' guoji shangshi zhengduan jiejue jizhi he jigou de yijian>" 中共中央办公厅、国务院办公厅印发《关于建立"一带一路"国际商事争端解决机制和机构的意见》. *Xinhua She* 新华社, June 27, 2018. http://www.gov.cn/zhengce/2018-06/27/content_5301657.htm.

Zhu, Huafang 朱华芳. "Yu Wai Zhongcai yu Linshi Zhongcai Liang Da Tupo — Zui Gao Fayuan She Zi Mao Qu Zhongcai Sifa Shencha Xin Gui Guancha" 域外仲裁与临时仲裁两大突破——最高法院涉自贸区仲裁司法审查新规观察. *Tiantong Susong Quan* 天同诉讼圈, February 23, 2017. https://mp.weixin.qq.com/s?__biz=MjM5NjA3NDc5MA==&mid=2654696850&idx=1&sn=c864902c091fffc287073604c5fabbb3&chksm=bd2111db8a5698c-d06709e175fb79f4a0191a77fbf5470ac148713f9df348399fa6f6571b4c0#rd.

Zhuhai Arbitration Commission, *Hengqin ziyou maoyi qu linshi zhongcai guize* 横琴自由贸易试验区临时仲裁规则. April 15, 2017. http://cn.oversea.cnki.net/law/detail/detail.aspx?filename=la202001020059&dbcode=CLKLP&dbname=CLKLP.

"Zimaoqu mingdan kuorong zhi 18 ge shifang liuda jiji xinhao" 自贸区名单扩容至18个 释放六大积极信号. *Sina Caijing* 新浪财经, August 27, 2019. http://finance.sina.com.cn/china/2019-08-27/doc-ihytcitn2159462.shtml.

8   Med-arb

When local practices meet (or do not meet) international expectations

1 Introduction

1.1 Preliminaries

Med-arb is a form of hybrid dispute resolution that combines an adjudicative approach (i.e., arbitration) with a non-adjudicative approach (i.e., mediation).[1] During med-arb, the mediation and arbitration stages are carried out by the same person in sequence. A typical med-arb proceeding arises when the parties have entered into arbitration and within that arbitration procedure decide to mediate. If and when mediation fails, arbitration resumes under the same mediator(s)-turned-arbitrator(s), and an award is rendered. Although this process is more accurately known as "arb-med-arb," for ease of reference, the term "med-arb" is used throughout this chapter. A more internationally recognized med-arb system refers to the hybrid dispute resolution mechanism when the mediator(s) and arbitrator(s) are independent, and the mediation and arbitration proceedings operated independently.[2] However, a more Chinese oriented med-arb (*tiaozhong* 调仲) system refers to any hybrid process combining the two. It does not matter if an arbitrator plays a dual and often conflicting role also of a mediator.[3]

This chapter examines the med-arb system, which is a popular commercial dispute resolution system in China.[4] The Chinese-styled med-arb stands odd with the due process standards in international arbitration when its resulting awards seek overseas enforcement. In the past decade, med-arb reforms in

---

1 See Carlos de Vera, "Arbitrating Harmony: Med-Arb and the Confluence of Culture and Rule of Law in the Resolution of International Commercial Disputes in China," *Columbia Journal of Asian Law* 18, no. 1 (2004): 149, 152.

2 Gu Weixia, "When Local Meets International: Mediation Combined with Arbitration in China and Its Prospective Reform in a Comparative Context," *The Journal of Comparative Law* 10, no. 2 (2016): 84–105.

3 Ibid.

4 See China International Economic and Trade Arbitration Commission, *Zhong guo guo ji shang shi zhong cai nian du bao gao (2017)* 中国国际商事仲裁年度报告 (2017), 13, http://www.cietac.org/Uploads/201810/5bd6d2e9b333e.pdf.

China are mainly propelled by the leading Chinese arbitration commissions. The major driving forces of this hybrid dispute resolution reform include the regulatory competition in the Chinese domestic arbitration market, as well as SPC's heightened due process concerns in light of the adjudication business from the Belt and Road Initiative. This chapter argues that China should further regulate med-arb in a way to reconcile local practices (mediation) with international expectations (arbitration) in the context of the Belt and Road Initiative.

1.2 Empirical evidence

In China, med-arb is popular in both domestic as well as international arbitrations. In the early days, for instance, as of 2001, about 20–30% of the CIETAC arbitration cases were withdrawn after settlement, or concluded on the basis of a settlement agreement.[5] CIETAC reported in 2014 that 21.61% of its foreign-related cases were resolved through mediation.[6]

Empirical evidence on med-arb adoption in China in general is lacking. However, as previously discussed in Chapter 4, since September 2015, China International Economic and Trade Arbitration Commission ("CIETAC") and the China Academy of Arbitration Law have been collaboratively compiling and publishing arbitration statistics on a national basis.[7] These statistics include arbitration cases which are concluded by mediation in the preceding year, that is, cases where mediation efforts are successful in leading to consent awards.[8] Table 8.1 tracks the annual and cumulative data since they become available, that is, between the period of 2014 and 2018. Chart 8.1 demonstrates the data by columns and trend lines.

In 2018, 26% of the arbitration cases in China were concluded through mediation (i.e., 26% of the awards rendered in China in 2018 were consent awards). Despite the steady increase of the overall number of the arbitration cases concluded through mediation, its ratio among all arbitration cases was down from 29% in 2017, 58% in 2016, 41% in 2015, and 65% in 2014.

Although the caseload data of Chinese arbitration concluded through mediation are more available recently, there are insufficient data to demonstrate the overall adoption of med-arb in China. However, the average percentage of cases in which consent awards were given (i.e., the overall ratio of

---

5 Wang Shengchang 王生长, *Zhongcai yu tiaojie xiang jiehe de lilun yu shiwu* 仲裁与调解相结合的理论与实务 (Beijing: Falv chubanshe 法律出版社, 2001), 83.

6 See China International Economic and Trade Arbitration Commission, *Annual Report on International Commercial Arbitration in China (2014)*, September 22, 2015, 50, http://www.cietac.org/Uploads/201610/57fc0d50a1742.pdf.

7 See Section 1.2 of Chapter 4 on "Annual Report on International Commercial Arbitration in China."

8 The data of the previous year are only available in the September publication of the current year. At the time when the book manuscript is submitted, the 2019 data are not yet available.

Table 8.1 Med-arb adoption in China (2014–2018)

Year	2014	2015	2016	2017	2018	*Average*
Total number of arbitration cases	113,660	136,924	208,545	239,360	539,542	**247,606**
Number of arbitration cases concluded by mediation (i.e., by consent award)	74,200	56,659	121,527	69,450	140,281	**92,441**
Percentage of arbitration cases concluded by successful mediation (i.e., percentage of consent award)	65%	41%	58%	29%	26%	**47.07%**

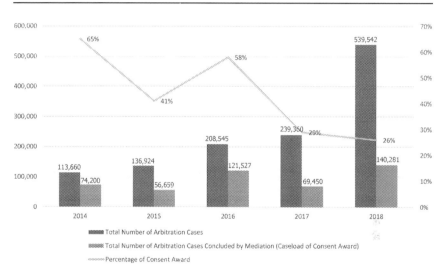

Chart 8.1 Med-arb adoption in China (2014–2018)

successful med-arb) could be as high as 47.07% (see Table 8.1, highlighted).[9] The data do not include those cases where mediation attempts were futile, that is, where mediation was adopted in the arbitration process but, for various reasons, did not lead to a consent award. As such, the overall adoption rate of med-arb in China could only be higher than 47.07%.[10] This finding is important, as it empirically shows the popularity of med-arb as a hybrid dispute resolution mechanism in resolving commercial disputes in China, and reflects the importance in studying and improving the system.

9 China International Economic and Trade Arbitration Commission, *Annual Report on International Commercial Arbitration in China (2015–2019)*.
10 Ibid.

2 Regulatory framework

2.1 The arbitration law

China's Arbitration Law ("AL"), promulgated in 1994 (effective in 1995), spells out the basic procedural rules on arbitration. However, there is an absence of regulation in providing, in particular, procedural safeguards directed at the med-arb process, leading to concerns on due process in Chinese med-arb practices.

The AL strongly encourages the practice of mediation during arbitration proceedings. Under Article 51 of the AL, where parties submit their dispute to arbitration, the arbitral tribunal may take the initiative to conduct mediation even without any specific requests from parties.[11] If the parties indicate their willingness to go through mediation, the arbitral tribunal is obligated to conduct mediation.[12] To ease concerns over the enforceability of a settlement agreement following the hybrid procedure, the AL provides that the tribunal may render an award in accordance with the terms of the mediation settlement agreement and such award can be enforceable across the globe under the New York Convention.[13] The strong emphasis on med-arb in the AL has contributed to the frequent incorporation of mediation into arbitration proceedings in the Chinese arbitral practice.

Article 51 empowers all arbitration institutions in China to conduct med-arb, and all the Chinese arbitration commissions include med-arb clauses in their arbitration rules that largely resemble the statutory language. While the AL has successfully contributed to the thriving of med-arb, it has failed to create a proper environment for med-arb to develop in accordance with internationally recognized due process standards. The AL provides little guidance on the manner in which med-arb should be conducted. Neither the relevant administrative regulations issued by the State Council nor judicial interpretations issued by the SPC address the med-arb process. Questions of whether parties' consent is required for the conduct of med-arb, and who is eligible to act as a mediator, remain unanswered, as are questions about procedural safeguards against bias.

In light of the absence of detailed operational provisions on how the med-arb process should be conducted, med-arb practices in China are highly disparate. The manner in which med-arb is conducted depends very much on the personal style of the arbitrators, and the local customs or practices of the relevant arbitration commission chosen by the parties.

---

11 Zhongcai Fa (仲裁法) [Arbitration Law] (promulgated by the Standing Committee of the National People's Congress, August 31, 1994, effective September 1, 1995), art. 51, http://www.npc.gov.cn/wxzl/wxzl/2000-12/05/content_4624.htm.

12 Ibid.

13 Arbitration Law, art. 49. China became a member of the New York Convention in 1986, making Chinese arbitral awards enforceable overseas.

The recent case of *Gao Haiyan v Keeneye Holdings Ltd* (the "*Keeneye* case") in 2010, where a med-arb award delivered in mainland China was challenged in the Hong Kong High Court in enforcement proceedings, is a typical example of how the usual med-arb practice in China does not meet procedural safeguards. In this case, the Hong Kong Court of Appeal reversed the Hong Kong Court of First Instance's decision which refused the enforcement of an award rendered following med-arb proceedings in Xi'an in the Shaanxi province. The arbitration occurred over two settings, between which mediation took place as agreed by the parties, and upon the suggestion of the arbitral tribunal, over a dinner at the five-star Shangri-La hotel in Xi'an.[14] Following an unsuccessful mediation, the tribunal resumed the arbitration proceedings and rendered an arbitral award, the amount of which was much less lower than that proposed at the mediation. The Court of First Instance refused the enforcement of the award on the ground that the award was tainted by an appearance of bias.[15] This decision was subsequently reversed by the Court of Appeal which held that there was no apparent bias.[16] The case highlights the difficulties inherent in Chinese-styled med-arb proceedings, especially with regard to the more informal modes of mediation in China. This is a crucial concern as parties who opt for arbitration in China are decidedly encouraged to adopt mediation within the arbitration process. Yet, at the same time, outcomes flowing from the med-arb proceedings might run the risk of non-enforcement, thus rendering the arbitral award ineffective.

While the New York Convention stipulates the enforcement standard regarding foreign arbitral awards, it remains silent on the enforcement of arbitral awards derived from hybrid procedures such as med-arb. In one sense, med-arb is a form of dispute resolution which fuses "local" senses and practices with "international" standards. Accordingly, when the Chinese "local" senses and practices of mediation are amalgamated with arbitration, med-arb becomes an "international" product with its outcome being enforceable overseas subject to "international" standards.[17] Hence, if the "local" product is over-infused with informal practices, as the med-arb procedure in the *Keeneye* case reflects, it could be viewed with distrust and even alarm by the international dispute resolution community, due to their concerns that due process might be compromised, and thus bear adverse implications on the neutrality and sanctity of Chinese arbitration and dispute resolution as a whole. The main procedural defects of Chinese-styled med-arb are discussed as follows.

---

14 *Gao Haiyan* v *Keeneye Holdings Ltd* (2010) HKCFI 980 (Hong Kong), paras. 5, 17.
15 Ibid., paras. 100, 102.
16 Ibid., paras. 104–106.
17 Articles 49 and 51 of the Arbitration Law authorize the arbitral tribunal to recognize settlement agreements between the parties through an arbitral award in accordance with the agreement.

2.2 Procedural criticisms

2.2.1 Conflicting roles of arbitrator and mediator

The main criticism of med-arb is the conflict of interest between the arbitral and mediatory roles assumed by the neutral. It is the norm in China for the arbitrator to "switch hats" and become the mediator when mediation occurs within the arbitration proceedings. In such a case, arbitration is stayed and is resumed only when mediation fails.

In order to enhance efficiency, the mediation process in China is often conducted by the very same arbitrator(s) of the case. This is because, according to official discourse, the arbitrator who participated in the mediation will become familiar with the details of the case in the course of mediation. Even if mediation fails, the decision-making process will be speeded up, and the dispute can thereby be resolved within a shorter timeframe. In the absence of proper procedural safeguards, however, the impartiality of the arbitrator may be affected by reason of the arbitrator's participation in the mediation process. The concern is whether the neutral can remain impartial, given the different approaches and attitudes required for the two dispute resolution methods. The arbitrator takes on the role that decides on an appropriate award based on the merits of the submissions from both parties. It is a legal process in which the arbitrator must interpret relevant laws and apply them to facts, just as a judge would do in a court.[18] The mediator, by contrast, does not inquire into the appropriateness of a settlement reached by the parties; rather, the mediator is more interested in the parties reaching a settlement agreement developed on their own.

Because of the very different aims of the two forms of dispute resolution, the approach required of the neutral must not be the same across all stages of the med-arb process. A competent arbitrator should be disinterested and display a "judicial temperament."[19] She must observe the requirements of impartiality and general legal competence from which she draws respect from the parties.[20] A good mediator, by contrast, should be sensitive to inter-party relationships and discover the needs of the parties that might hide behind mediatory exchanges (the so-called "bottom lines"). In facilitating communication between the parties and eventually a settlement, the mediator may take a more involved, personal approach. When practiced separately as single-tier dispute resolution methods, each of the dispute resolution processes generally has no due process concerns, even if they concern with the same subject matter. Theoretically, an arbitration proceeding will not suffer from irregularities or biases, actual or apparent, even when

18 Paul E. Mason, "The Arbitrator as Mediator, and Mediator as Arbitrator," *Journal of International Arbitration* 28, no. 6 (2011): 541–552.
19 Ibid., 543.
20 Ibid.

the same person switches hats between an arbitrator and a mediator, as long as she can maintain the standards required of her in arbitration and mediation, respectively. Due process concerns do not arise from the adoption of hybrid or multi-tier dispute resolution processes *per se*, but from the very human difficulty to partition information obtained in the two stages to ensure impartiality.

2.2.2 Confidentiality

A related procedural concern has to do with confidentiality of information. The issue of due process arises when the neutral, as the mediator, reverts to becoming an arbitrator. In this process, the information obtained by the neutral during the mediation stage might, consciously or otherwise, rely on information provided by the parties during mediation.[21] Such information would not normally be communicated to the arbitrator in arbitration when practiced alone. Mediators who practice evaluative mediation might also reveal to the parties the merits of their respective cases, which would not be known to the parties in arbitration until the award is rendered.[22]

Distinct from arbitration, mediation allows *ex parte* communication, or private caucuses. Information given by a party to the neutral during caucuses is not known to the other party. The other party has no opportunity to defend against such confidential information.[23] It is for the mediator to determine the truthfulness of the information, and the extent to which that information should influence her decision in the arbitration stage shall mediation fail. Parties might also use caucuses to privately influence the neutral in their own favor in the subsequent arbitration. Because mediation may involve discussions into personal and emotional issues between the respective parties and the mediator, the neutral may become more sympathetic toward a particular party.[24] Admittedly, whether the parties will create a bias through these interactions is dependent on the conduct of the individual neutral, but the fact that it cannot be certain that the neutral will not be biased indicates a gap in the regulation of med-arb. Indeed, partiality might only be known or is apparent to parties when mediation fails, at which point it is too late to remedy the proceedings.[25]

---

21 Gu Weixia, "When Local Meets International: Mediation Combined with Arbitration in China and its Prospective Reform in a Comparative Context," *Journal of Comparative Law* 10, no. 2 (2016): 90.
22 James T. Peter, "Med-Arb in International Arbitration," *American Review of International Arbitration* 8, no. 1 (1997): 83–116.
23 Gabrielle Kaufmann-Kohler, "When Arbitrators Facilitate Settlement: Towards a Transnational Standard," *Arbitration International* 25, no. 2 (2009): 198.
24 Peter, "Med-Arb in International Arbitration," 93.
25 Gu, "When Local Meets International," 89–90.

The *Keeneye* case shows the potential dangers of caucusing in creating bias, actual or apparent. The dispute was related to a share transfer agreement. The tribunal, at the Xi'an Arbitration Commission ("XAC") in China, was composed of a presiding arbitrator, and two arbitrators nominated, respectively, by each side. After the first hearing, the tribunal suggested mediation to the parties and both sides expressed their consent. The tribunal also, on its own initiative, proposed that the respondents pay the applicants RMB 250 million as settlement. The tribunal then appointed XAC's Secretary-General and the arbitrator nominated by the applicants as mediators, and to inform the parties of this proposal. The mediators contacted a person affiliated with the respondents. The person described himself to be "a person related to (or affiliated with)"[26] (*guanxiren* 关系人) the respondents. According to the XAC Rules, "[w]ith the approval of the parties, any third party may be invited to assist the mediation, or they may act as the mediator."[27] The mediators asked the respondents to a private dinner meeting at a restaurant in the Xi'an Shangri-La hotel. At the meeting, the Secretary-General asked the respondents' affiliate to "work on" (*zuogongzuo* 做工作) the respondents to get them to accept the settlement proposal. The respondents nonetheless rejected the settlement proposal. The arbitration tribunal reconvened after the failed mediation and decided to award the respondents RMB 50 million. The respondents challenged the award before the Xi'an Intermediate People's Court. The Xi'an Court upheld the award.

The enforcement of the award was then challenged in the Hong Kong Court of First Instance. The Hong Kong Court refused enforcement on several grounds; among others, that the meeting over some "wining and dining"[28] would "cause a fair-minded observer to apprehend a real possibility of bias on the part of the Arbitration Tribunal."[29] Although the evidence showing actual bias was insufficient, the interactions during the Shangri-La dinner, and the contrast between the proposed settlement and the award at the end were held sufficient to constitute apparent bias.[30] This apprehension of bias was enough to render the enforcement of such award a contravention of Hong Kong's public policy, that is, "the most basic notions of justice and morality of the Hong Kong system."[31] The Court of First Instance opined that "[t]he risk of a mediator turned arbitrator appearing to be biased will

---

26 *Gao Haiyan v Keeneye Holdings Ltd*, para. 22.
27 Ibid., para. 21.
28 Ibid., para. 67.
29 Ibid., para. 3.
30 Gu Weixia and Zhang Xianchu, "The Keeneye Case: Rethinking the Content of Public Policy in Cross-Border Arbitration between Hong Kong and Mainland China," *Hong Kong Law Journal* 42, no. 3 (2012): 1006.
31 *Hebei Import & Export Corp v Polytek Engineering Co Ltd* (1998) 1 HKLRD 287 (Hong Kong), para. 47.

always be great."[32] The party seeking enforcement appealed, and the Court of First Instance's decision was reversed. The appellate court decided to allow enforcement on the basis that the enforcement court should have given greater weight to the decision handed down by the supervisory court, the Xi'an Intermediate People's Court, which found no apparent bias, and that the med-arb was properly conducted.[33]

It cannot be assumed that the same standard of apparent bias and deference applied by the Hong Kong Court of Appeal will be replicated by foreign courts. The appellate judgment questions whether the balancing exercise between promoting arbitration and ensuring due process is observed is done right.[34] If deference for the supervisory court is too readily relied on, then the public policy ground to refuse award enforcement can only be applied in very (and sometimes excessively) narrow circumstances.

Unlike those in other jurisdictions, a typical set of arbitration rules in China does not contain provisions specifically on the use of information arisen out of mediation. At most, the rules will only provide some safeguards that prohibit the parties from relying on any statement expressed during the mediation stage by the other party or the tribunal to support their case.[35] Generally, no provision will prevent the tribunal from relying on any information provided to them during the mediation stage to decide on an award subsequently. Even if such rules exist, it might be difficulty to practice, since it amounts to keeping secrets from oneself.

In addition, no statutory safeguards targeting caucusing are available in Chinese law. This sets the Chinese statutory regime aside from other jurisdictions. Hong Kong, for example, has the Arbitration Ordinance that is based upon the UNCITRAL Model Law. The Ordinance allows for arbitrators to assume the role of mediators so long as the parties consent and have not withdrawn their consent in writing.[36] Hong Kong's Arbitration Ordinance expressly provides for a disclosure safeguard. If and when mediation fails and the neutral has obtained confidential information from a party, they "must, before resuming the arbitral proceedings, disclose to all other parties as much of that information as the arbitrator considers is material to the arbitral proceedings."[37] Singapore's International Arbitration Act has a similar safeguard provision.[38] This safeguard allows both parties to know what information was given to the arbitrator and prompts the parties to defend against such information during the arbitral proceedings.

---

32 *Gao Haiyan v Keeneye Holdings Ltd*, para. 72.

33 *Gao Haiyan v Keeneye Holdings Ltd* (2012) 1 HKLRD 627 (Hong Kong), para. 68.

34 Gu and Zhang, "The Keeneye Case," 1023.

35 See, for example, Beijing Arbitration Commission, *Arbitration Rules*, April 1, 2015, art. 42(5), https://www.bjac.org.cn/english/page/data_dl/zcgz_en.pdf.

36 Arbitration Ordinance (Cap. 609) (Hong Kong), s. 33(1).

37 Ibid., s. 33(4).

38 International Arbitration Act (Cap. 143A) (Singapore), s. 17(3).

2.3 Culture and tradition

Attributing the popularity of med-arb to the culture influence is a trope in the Chinese arbitration scholarship. Compared to arbitration, mediation is more culture-laden and less judicialized. The dependency of mediation on culture is a result of the aim to induce voluntary settlement by the parties, and appealing to the cultural background of the parties is a way of inducing that settlement. Arbitration, by contrast, is governed by rules and norms created by the deliberations between potential users of various jurisdictions. It is designed to be an international dispute resolution method.

This mediation approach translates into a more active med-arb management by the Chinese arbitrators. An empirical study on the arbitrators' attitudes toward med-arb between 2011 and 2012 shows that among the 36 active arbitrators interviewed from CIETAC, Beijing Arbitration Commission ("BAC") and Wuhan Arbitration Commission ("WAC"), 50% of the respondents have recommended the parties to mediate in more than 90% of the cases in which they acted as an arbitrator;[39] more than 10% of the respondents recommended mediation in more than 70–90% of the cases they arbitrated.[40] As to parties, mutual consent for med-arb is far more likely to be given when both parties are Chinese.[41] The study also shows the arbitrator respondents who believe med-arb to be appropriate (88.1% of all respondents) have mostly given the following as the primary reasons for conducting med-arb: ease of enforcement of consent award compared to pure award, advantages in costs and efficiency, respect to party's free will, and voluntariness.[42] These reasons are mostly technical and related to the efficiency of dispute resolution, rather than cultural factors. Only a handful of such respondents (6 out of 32) have stated that traditional Chinese culture influenced them to conduct med-arb,[43] among whom one respondent said "mediation reflects the local culture in China and therefore is more easily accepted by the Chinese."[44] Though not representative, this response reflects how culture can manifest itself through the advantage of dispute resolution efficiency without being an influence to med-arb practices in China *per se*.

The original design of the AL, including the requirement that all arbitration institutions must offer mediation within the arbitration process, could be influenced by the Chinese culture and traditions of social harmony. But there is no indication of this from the legislative comments on the draft of the

---

39 Fan Kun, "An Empirical Study of Arbitrators Acting as Mediators in China," *Cardozo Journal of Conflict Resolution* 15, no. 3 (2014): 791.
40 Ibid.
41 Ibid., 792.
42 Ibid., 805.
43 Ibid.
44 Ibid.

AL in 1994.[45] Instead, the comments focused on attributes of arbitration as a feature of "Western law"[46] and "socialist market economic system."[47] The documented legislative intention does not indicate any need to base China's arbitration rules (including med-arb) on Confucian values. Even when one argues that social harmony is an embedded feature of a socialist market system, the comments manifested social harmony through economic language.

Presumably, Chinese parties are more familiar with the med-arb process embedded in their dispute resolution culture and tradition, while foreign parties are less trusting of the process. Foreign parties might also expect an award rather than a settlement agreement at the end.[48] In most of the cases, the Chinese parties choose their arbitrator(s) to conduct mediation because they are already familiar with the arbitrator(s), and the arbitrator is familiar with the facts and background of the dispute.[49] Such an arbitrator also allows quicker arbitration and award rendering if and when mediation fails. Although the behavior of Chinese parties and practices of Chinese arbitration institutions involved in cross-border arbitration can be seen as products of multiple legal cultures and traditions, the practices of med-arb promoted by the Chinese government are distinctively Chinese dispute resolution governance. As due process protection is more dependent on standards and not on safeguards, while weak due process safeguards in med-arb are a pervasive problem, the popularity of med-arb in China is not undermined. Thus, contemporary med-arb reform is primarily shaped by the need to attract foreign parties to use Chinese arbitration services. Where there is no such demand, as in domestic arbitration, developments lag behind. It is those Chinese leading arbitration institutions who need to attract foreign parties that are motivated to reform med-arb due process standards. The pressure is not by the Chinese government from the top, but by the market from the bottom, as will be discussed later in this chapter.

3 Reform

3.1 Legislative reform

As discussed in Chapter 4, China's AL was only very slightly revised in 2017[50] after its promulgation in 1994, and med-arb reform was never mentioned in the proposed revision. Nor has the hybrid system been addressed

---

45 Gu Angran 顾昂然, "Guanyu <Zhonghua renmin gongheguo zhongcaifa (caoan)> de shuoming" 关于《中华人民共和国仲裁法（草案）》的说明, *Renda gongbao* 人大公报, June 28, 1994, http://www.npc.gov.cn/wxzl/gongbao/2001-01/02/content_5003212.htm.

46 Ibid.

47 Ibid.

48 Ibid.

49 Gu, "When Local Meets International," 89.

50 Arbitration Law's first amendment in 2009 changed two article number referencing the Civil Procedure Law (2007). Its second amendment in 2017 concerned a minor change to the qualification of arbitrators.

in the judicial interpretations on arbitration in the SPC-led arbitration reform in the past two decades. Med-arb processes and development has hence lingered in the rules of Chinese arbitration institutions.

3.2 Regulatory competition in the Chinese arbitration market

As an "institutional arbitration dominant" jurisdiction,[51] China has indirectly delegated the regulation of arbitration practices to the market through more than 250 arbitration commissions that have mushroomed over the past two decades. A danger in this regulatory approach is the inconsistency of standards practiced by arbitrators and of safeguards available to the parties among different Chinese arbitration institutions. This is one of the reasons that the procedural defects discussed earlier in this chapter are still a pervasive problem when practicing med-arb in China and why parties, especially foreign parties, remain suspicious of med-arb in China. Foreign investors are unlikely to arbitrate in local arbitration institutions that do not have much experience with cross-border disputes, and it is the arbitration institutions that focus on cross-border disputes in the Chinese arbitration market (i.e., those leading institutions) that are paving the way in modernizing the med-arb regime with a bottom-up approach.

For example, as has often been pointed out, although the AL requires the tribunal to conduct mediation when the parties so request, it does not forbid the tribunal from conducting mediation even when a party decides against mediation. The issue of party consent is dealt with most recently by CIETAC's revised Arbitration Rules, effective since January 2015 (the "2015 CIETAC Rules"), which expressly state that med-arb can only proceed with the consent of both parties, and that mediation must end when either party so requests.[52] BAC, the post-CIETAC-split Shenzhen Court of International Arbitration ("SCIA"), and Shanghai International Arbitration Center ("SHIAC") have their most recently revised rules that stipulate the same.[53] In practice, according to Fan's survey, 77.8% of the arbitrator respondents take the initiative to propose med-arb without being prompted by the party,[54] suggesting med-arb

---

51 See discussions in Chapter 4.
52 China Council for the Promotion of International Trade, *China International Economic and Trade Arbitration Commission (CIETAC) Arbitration Rules*, November 4, 2014, art. 47, http://www.cietac.org/index.php?m=Page&a=index&id=106&l=en.
53 Beijing Arbitration Commission, *Arbitration Rules*, July 4, 2019, arts. 43–44, 67, https://www.bjac.org.cn/english/page/zc/guize_en2019.html; Shenzhen Court of International Arbitration, February 21, 2019, art. 48, http://www.sccietac.org/index.php/Home/index/rule/id/791.html; Shanghai International Arbitration Center, *Shanghai International Economic and Trade Arbitration Commission (Shanghai International Arbitration Center Arbitration Rules*, January 1, 2015, art. 41, http://www.shiac.org/upload/day_141230/SHIAC_ARBITRATION_RULES_2015_141222.pdf.
54 Fan, "An Empirical Study of Arbitrators Acting as Mediators in China," 791.

is just a "matter of good practice."[55] However, the survey also found these initiatives mainly take place during or after the main hearing.[56] Thus, parties are likely to have the opportunity to argue their case without entering the mediation stage.

The AL empowers the tribunal to conduct mediation, but is silent on whether third parties can also mediate. As the arbitrators generally assumed the role of mediators as a matter of practice, another major reform on med-arb in the past several years concerns whether parties can request third-party mediation from an independent mediator. After the initial refusal to enforce the award in the *Keeneye* case, Chinese arbitration institutions have taken some steps to mitigate potential procedural irregularities. The 2015 CIETAC Rules expressly state that with the parties' consent, CIETAC may assist the parties to mediate the dispute if the parties do not wish mediation to be conducted by the arbitral tribunal.[57] The previous CIETAC Rules (2012 and 2005 versions) did not suggest that med-arb can be conducted other than by the tribunal. The change in the CIETAC Rules allows the parties to understand that mediation by the arbitral tribunal is not the only option available.

The most recently revised BAC Rules, taking effect in September 2019 (the "2019 BAC Rules"), are more explicit with alternative arrangements. They provide for "independent mediation" at BAC's Mediation Center in accordance with the BAC Mediation Center Mediation Rules.[58] But such mediation is separate from the arbitral proceedings and strictly speaking, is not a form of traditional med-arb. As with self-settlement, parties who have reached a settlement agreement through the Mediation Center can request the arbitral tribunal to render an award based on that agreement,[59] allowing the agreement to be enforced overseas under the New York Convention. With the approval of the BAC Chairperson and additional costs borne by the parties, the BAC Rules also allow international arbitrations to replace the arbitrator after mediation fails.[60] The explicit arrangements for a separate mediation mechanism and for allowing arbitrator replacement are rare among arbitration rules in China. Similar to other rules, though, the language of the most recent CIETAC rules still does not expressly allow the possibility of mediation by independent mediators. The 2015 CIETAC Rules attempted to provide non-CIETAC mediation, but it only vaguely provided that CIETAC may, with the consent of both parties, assist the parties to conciliate the dispute "in a manner and procedure it

---

55 Ibid.
56 Ibid., 795–796.
57 China Council for the Promotion of International Trade, *CIETAC Arbitration Rules 2015*, art. 47(8).
58 Beijing Arbitration Commission, *BAC Arbitration Rules 2019*, art. 44.
59 Ibid., art. 43(2).
60 Ibid., art. 67(2).

considers appropriate."[61] It is unclear how the parties may be "assisted" under this rule, or what arrangements have been made under the rule.

Of all the leading Chinese arbitration institutions, SCIA is the most innovative in dealing with med-arb. When SCIA split from CIETAC in 2012, its updated rules allowed parties involved in international commercial disputes relating to Hong Kong, Macau, and Taiwan to submit their disputes to the SCIA using UNCITRAL Rules in lieu of SCIA Rules.[62] Although this change was in line with CIETAC's 2015 Rules, which allows hybrid arbitration clauses specifying CIETAC arbitration using non-CIETAC arbitration rules, such as the UNCITRAL Rules,[63] it is the first set of Chinese arbitration rules that explicitly referred to the application of the UNCITRAL rules. Since 2016, SCIA introduced the "Guidelines for the Administration of Arbitration under the UNCITRAL Arbitration Rules" (the "SCIA UNCITRAL Guidelines"), which further regulates how SCIA is to apply the UNCITRAL Rules. This means that foreign parties might opt for the UNCITRAL Rules with which they might be more familiar with rather than the SCIA Rules. This approach was confirmed in SCIA's latest revision to its rules in February 2019.[64]

Moreover, both SCIA and CIETAC recently created mediation centers, or set up schemes to allow for mediation by mediators other than the arbitral tribunal. In 2008, SCIA created its mediation center to encourage mediation before and outside existing arbitration proceedings.[65] SCIA further promoted what it called the "Diversified Harmonious Dispute Resolution" to echo China's Fourth Five-Year Court Reform Outline (2014–2018).[66] Moreover, SCIA advertised a combination of Hong Kong mediation and Shenzhen arbitration, as well as alternative arrangements under the Guangdong–Hong Kong–Macau Mediation Alliance.[67] In a similar vein, in May 2018, CIETAC established its own mediation center.

---

61 China Council for the Promotion of International Trade, *CIETAC Arbitration Rules 2015*, art. 47(8) (emphasis added).

62 Shenzhen Court of International Arbitration, November 4, 2016, art. 3(4), https://uk.practicallaw.thomsonreuters.com/w-005-1124?transitionType=Default&contextData=(sc. Default).

63 China Council for the Promotion of International Trade, *CIETAC Arbitration Rules 2015*, art. 4(3).

64 Shenzhen Court of International Arbitration, *Shenzhen guoji zhongcai yuan zhongcai guize 2019*, art. 3(4).

65 Shenzhen Court of International Arbitration, "Huanan guozhong tiaojie zhongxin jieshao" 华南国仲调解中心介绍, July 30, 2014, http://www.cnarb.com/Item/1245.aspx.

66 Supreme People's Court, *Opinions of the Supreme People's Court on People's Courts Further Deepening the Reform of Diversified Dispute Resolution Mechanism*, June 28, 2016, https://www.pkulaw.com/en_law/1418572db3297a30bdfb.html.

67 Liu Xiaochun, "Innovations of Chinese International Arbitration–From the Perspective of SCIA," (PowerPoint presentation, Seoul, November 8, 2017), http://uncitralrcap.org/wp-content/uploads/2017/12/1-4.-SCIA-President_Liu-ADR_Conference.pdf.

Larger, more advanced and outward-facing institutions, such as CIETAC, BAC, and SCIA, are motivated to conduct impartial arbitration not by laws and regulations, but by the pressure from the market, both internally and externally. As long as market pressures continue to propel Chinese leading arbitration institutions in aligning the Chinese sense of mediation with international standards, the prospect of the reform is promising. Yet, it remains to be seen whether foreign enterprises and investors would prefer a seat of arbitration with greater due process safeguards in the region (such as Hong Kong and Singapore), given the increased competition the Belt and Road Initiative brings.

3.3 Judicial promotion at the China international commercial court

As discussed in Chapter 7, recently, the SPC established the China International Commercial Court ("CICC") in light of dispute resolution needs out of China's Belt and Road Initiative ("BRI") development.[68] Considering the traditional distrust and reluctance of investors to resolve business disputes through foreign courts, with which they may not be familiar, as well as its potential for offering commercially flexible solutions and particular suitability for mitigating conflicts among different legal systems, international commercial arbitration will under market forces form a preferred, indeed optimal, primary vehicle for commercial dispute resolution under the BRI.[69]

For hybrid system of med-arb, the most important provision is Article 11 of the CICC Provisions, which formulated a new "one-stop" international commercial dispute resolution mechanism:

> The Supreme People's Court will set up an International Commercial Expert Committee and select international commercial mediation institutions and international commercial arbitration institutions that meet certain conditions to build up together with the International Commercial Court a dispute resolution platform on which mediation, arbitration, and litigation are efficiently linked, thereby creating a "one-stop" international commercial dispute resolution mechanism.
>
> The International Commercial Court supports parties to settle their international commercial disputes by choosing the approach they consider appropriate through the dispute resolution platform on which mediation, arbitration and litigation are efficiently linked.

---

68 See discussions in Section 3.3 of Chapter 7.
69 Hong Kong's former Secretary for Justice Rimsky Yuen envisioned that opportunities for outward expansion of the local legal and arbitration sectors lay in providing services to alleviating the "legal uncertainties" along "One Belt, One Road" countries. See "Secretary for Justice Promotes Hong Kong's Legal and Dispute Resolution Service in Beijing (with Photos)," Department of Justice, August 18, 2015, https://www.info.gov.hk/gia/general/201508/18/P201508180765.htm.

As such, CICC now allows the establishment of an International Commercial Experts Committee ("ICEC") that consists of both Chinese and foreign experts on international law to mediate disputes at parties' request.[70] As of May 2020, 31 Chinese and foreign experts have been appointed as the first batch of the members of the ICEC, out of whom ten are from mainland China.[71]

Moreover, CICC allows international commercial disputes to be mediated and arbitrated in a single platform. The single platform does not imply that mediation and arbitration is to be conducted by the same personnel or institution. Rather, Article 11 seems to suggest that mediation and arbitration in med-arb procedures are to be conducted by separate mediation and arbitration institutions, which is different from the traditional Chinese-styled med-arb. This creation of the integrated mediation and arbitration platform but with separate institutions is an important feature of the CICC, and indicates China's reform to provide a "one-stop" hybrid dispute resolution platform that aims to alleviate due process concerns in cross-border med-arb, particularly in the context of dispute resolution under the BRI.

This approach echoes with SPC's 2016 ADR Opinion, which started to explore the linkage between Chinese courts and Chinese arbitration and mediation.[72] In a similar vein, SPC's BRI Mechanism and Institutions Opinion stressed the need to build dispute resolution mechanisms and institutions that can account for the inconsistencies of law and legal culture across the BRI jurisdictions.[73] The solution suggested is a "diversified" dispute resolution system to satisfy the range of disputes that the BRI will produce. "Diversification" here is taken to mean the use of mediation, arbitration, and litigation altogether to resolve disputes.[74]

While detailed implementation rules are still under preparation, in December 2018, the CICC designated five Chinese arbitration institutions and two mediation institutions to be part of its "one-stop" integrated mediation and arbitration platform under the CICC One-Stop Institution Notice. As discussed in Chapter 7, the five arbitration institutions linked with the CICC are CIETAC, BAC, SCIA, Shanghai International Arbitration Center ("SHIAC"), and China Maritime Arbitration Center

---

70 Supreme People's Court, *Provisions of the Supreme People's Court on Several Issues Concerning the Establishment of the International Commercial Courts*, July 1, 2018, art. 11, https://cgc.law.stanford.edu/belt-and-road/b-and-r-texts/20180701-provisions-re-intl-commercial-courts/.

71 See "Judges," China International Commercial Court, accessed July 14, 2020, http://cicc.court.gov.cn/html/1/218/19/151/index.html.

72 See discussions in Section 3.2 of Chapter 6.

73 See discussions in Section 3.3 of Chapter 7.

74 Supreme People's Court, *Provisions of the Supreme People's Court on Several Issues Concerning the Establishment of the International Commercial Courts*, art. 11,

("CMAC").[75] Arbitration cases under these five designated institutions are subject to judicial support and supervision directly under the CICC.[76]

Likewise, CICC has designated two most experienced international institutional mediation providers in China[77] to link with its "one-stop" hybrid dispute resolution platform.[78] The two specialized international mediation institutions are China Council for the Promotion of International Trade ("CCPIT") Mediation Center[79] and Shanghai Commercial Mediation Center ("SCMC").[80] If all the Chinese legislative requirements on mediation are satisfied, mediation settlement agreements reached at the two designated Chinese mediation centers can be converted into CICC judicial settlement agreements.[81]

4 Development analyses

4.1 Penetrating factors

As previously analyzed in Chapter 4, the Chinese arbitration market has been formed. The rising competition among Chinese arbitration commissions represents a push toward professionalism and internationalization of the latest Chinese arbitration landscape. Foreign investors are unlikely to arbitrate in Chinese local arbitration institutions that do not have much experience with international disputes. In the absence of legislative development and judicial interpretation development, it is the institutions which focus on international disputes that are paving the way in modernizing and standardizing Chinese med-arb system from a bottom-up approach. These leading arbitration institutions, in order to win clients and reputation, compete not only within the Chinese arbitration market but also with overseas competitors in the regional and international market.

These Chinese leading arbitral institutions are not high in numbers, and are concentrated in first-tier Chinese cities. According to the Annual Report on International Commercial Arbitration in China (the "Annual Report")

---

75 Supreme People's Court, *Notice of the Supreme People's Court on Inclusion of the First Group of International Commercial Arbitration and Mediation Institutions in the "One-stop" Diversified International Commercial Dispute Resolution Mechanism*, December 5, 2018, art. 2, http://cicc.court.gov.cn/html/1/219/208/210/1144.html. See also discussions in Chapter 7.
76 Supreme People's Court, *Provisions of the Supreme People's Court on Several Issues Concerning the Establishment of the International Commercial Courts*, art. 14.
77 See also discussions in Section 1.1 of Chapter 5 on different types of mediation in China.
78 Supreme People's Court, *Notice of the Supreme People's Court on Inclusion of the First Group of International Commercial Arbitration and Mediation Institutions in the "One-stop" Diversified International Commercial Dispute Resolution Mechanism*, art. 2.
79 CCPIT Mediation Center is accessible at http://adr.ccpit.org/EN/Index/index.html.
80 SCMC is accessible at http://www.scmc.org.cn/.
81 Supreme People's Court, *Provisions of the Supreme People's Court on Several Issues Concerning the Establishment of the International Commercial Courts*, art. 3.

compiled by CIETAC, in late 2018, of the 253 institutions, only 60 handled "foreign-related" arbitration cases in 2017.[82] This number remained stable from that in 2016, where 62 institutions handled "foreign-related" cases.[83] The 2017 Annual Report further showed that, only CIETAC, Guangzhou Arbitration Commission ("GAC") and SHIAC handled more than 100 "foreign-related" cases in 2017.[84] This statistic is however missing from the 2016 Annual Report. Another set of statistics shows the Chinese leading arbitration institutions which handle the largest disputed amount in "foreign-related" arbitration cases. The Report shows that in 2017, CIETAC, BAC, SCIA, and SHIAC are the top four institutions.[85] The vast majority of Chinese arbitration institutions do not concern themselves with cases involving a foreign party, a foreign subject matter, or a performance of obligations outside China. Therefore, market regulation of med-arb and of arbitration more generally in China are shaped by only a handful of Chinese leading arbitration institutions.

Indeed, market regulation in this sense is not a purposive exercise to control how parties and practitioners are to utilize med-arb in their conflicts. Rather, the leading institutions are constantly reviewing and revising their arbitration rules to remain competitive in the market, by which they are also indirectly promoting the standard of procedural fairness in domestic, and more importantly, cross-border med-arb procedures. Market forces and institutional competition remain a major driver of med-arb reform in China.

On the other hand, the Chinese government is aware that arbitration serves China's foreign investment interests, and med-arb bears special meaning to China's dispute resolution interests in "going out" (*zouchuqu* 走出去), particularly in light of her BRI development. In China, the "design from the top" (*dingceng sheji* 顶层设计)—to use a policy buzzword used by the Chinese government to promote judicial and dispute resolution reform—may be inspired by foreign trends, but legal reformers are very clear that such trends are specifically selected to reflect the needs of China. The exercise of selecting the international arbitration norms to be followed in China reflects the fact that Chinese top-down reformers cannot breach certain entrenched socio-political norms. Indeed, one of the five basic principles expressed in the SPC's Diversified Dispute Resolution Opinion in 2016 is the "diversified dispute resolution system with Chinese characteristics."[86] In the meantime, however, as more Chinese companies are investing in

---

82 China International Economic and Trade Arbitration Commission, *Annual Report on International Commercial Arbitration in China (2018)*, 14.

83 China International Economic and Trade Arbitration Commission, *Annual Report on International Commercial Arbitration in China (2017)*, 14.

84 Ibid., 73.

85 Ibid., 74.

86 Supreme People's Court, *Opinions of the Supreme People's Court on People's Courts Further Deepening the Reform of Diversified Dispute Resolution Mechanism*, June 28, 2016, http://en.pkulaw.cn/display.aspx?cgid=1418572db3297a30bdfb&lib=law.

foreign countries, China is obliged to take reference from other jurisdictions when designing her own hybrid dispute resolution systems when "going out." The CICC established in 2018 and the "one-stop" hybrid dispute resolution platform put forward by the CICC is a typical example that the SPC's top-down promotion efforts on med-arb is driven by the dispute resolution needs arising out of China's BRI development.

4.2 Patterns of reform

The pattern of med-arb reform in China, as with the development path of Chinese arbitration, is predominantly shaped by the fast-developing economy. The market forces driving competitions among Chinese arbitration institutions are bottom-up. The regulatory reform initiatives spearheaded by CIETAC, BAC, and SCIA lie in their intent to enhance their competitiveness and to be able to attract international clients. As argued, this intent does not come from the pressure of the Chinese government, but from their own motivation. Perhaps what is different between the trajectory of arbitration development and med-arb development is about the nature of reform the arbitration market is leading. While Chinese leading arbitration institutions are pushing forward institutional reforms to form an arbitration market in the Chinese arbitration landscape, the med-arb reforms led by them are largely regulatory, instead of institutional, in nature, as there is a huge regulatory gap in the med-arb system in China.

In opposite, the most recent med-arb reform led by the SPC's CICC and its associated "one-stop" hybrid dispute resolution platform is top-down in pattern. As both the initiator and the largest economy in the BRI, China is on the one hand pressured, but on the other hand in a unique position to shape future BRI dispute resolution norms. Given the inconsistencies of laws and legal cultures across the BRI jurisdictions, China is expected to build dispute resolution mechanisms and institutions that could accommodate BRI's demands and realities. The solution suggested is a "diversified (hybrid)" dispute resolution proposal to satisfy the range of disputes that the BRI will produce. Therefore, besides the need to attract foreign parties to compete with regional institutions, China is motivated to establish hybrid dispute resolution norms, such as med-arb, which is particularly fit for the varied cultural and socio-economic contexts under the BRI. These needs are the leading factors in allowing China to look beyond cultural and socio-political factors, and to initiate reforms from a top-down vantage point.

5 The future

5.1 The credibility of cross-border med-arb in future

Before asking how China could promote med-arb under the BRI context, we need to consider what the most valuable and least desirable features of cross-border med-arb are to arbitration users. Then, we can look at what

China could do to mitigate the shortcomings of med-arb, and in the meantime, to amplify its advantages as perceived by potential parties—not only Chinese parties, but also foreign parties alongside the BRI roadmap.

In a recent survey conducted by Queen Mary University of London with respect to mainly European private practitioners, in-house counsels and arbitrators, the least valuable characteristic of cross-border arbitration is the cost involved.[87] Only 3% of 922 respondents regarded it as one of the "three most valuable characteristics of international arbitration," and 67% regarded it as one of the "three worst characteristics of international arbitration."[88] "Confidentiality and privacy" (36%) and "neutrality" (25%) stood in the middle, while the "enforceability of awards" (64%), and "avoiding specific legal systems/national courts" (60%) are the most valued characteristics.[89]

The survey also asked respondents the factors they contemplate when choosing a seat. The "general reputation and recognition of the seat" is considered the most important factor, followed by "neutrality and impartiality of the local legal system," "national arbitration law," and "track record of enforcing agreements to arbitrate and arbitral awards."[90] Despite being considered as one of the worst qualities of cross-border arbitration, cost is only regarded by about 5% of the respondents to be one of top four factors in choosing a seat.[91]

Compared to the leading arbitral seats and arbitration institutions in the Asian region, that is, the Hong Kong International Arbitration Centre ("HKIAC") in Hong Kong and Singapore International Arbitration Center ("SIAC") in Singapore, leading Chinese arbitration institutions such as CIETAC, BAC, and SCIA are probably less attractive to foreign parties than HKIAC and SIAC. As learned from the Queen Mary survey results, Chinese arbitration institutions should improve on the aspect of neutrality and impartiality in med-arb processes, and the enforceability of the med-arb-led consent awards in future. Although the outcome of the *Keeneye* case could be an isolated one, the fact pattern has not been tested in courts other than those in Hong Kong. BRI jurisdictions may not give as much weight to the deference to the Chinese supervisory court as what the Hong Kong Court of Appeal had done.

One suggestion is perhaps that Chinese courts should adopt stricter standards when exercising their supervisory powers over med-arb awards

---

87 Queen Mary University of London School of International Arbitration and White & Case LLP, *2018 International Arbitration Survey: The Evolution of International Arbitration*, May 9, 2018, 7, https://www.whitecase.com/publications/insight/2018-international-arbitration-survey-evolution-international-arbitration.

88 Ibid., 7–8.

89 Ibid., 7.

90 Ibid., 11.

91 Ibid.

that manifest due process issues. This would make med-arb more credible to potential users. In this respect, starting from 2018, the SPC has made arbitral awards more difficult to be set aside by lower-level courts, even in domestic arbitrations. As discussed in Chapter 7, the "pre-reporting system," which used to be exclusively applied to "foreign-related cases," is now also applied to domestic cases, that is, arbitrations conducted within mainland China without any foreign elements.[92] This new judicial policy prevents lower-level courts from being subject to local protectionism and corruption, and it allows the SPC and provincial-level High People's Courts to harmonize the standards for setting aside arbitral awards nationally. For med-arb, however, the comprehensive pre-reporting system will make Chinese courts more difficult in setting aside awards for procedural irregularities that might emerge in Chinese-styled med-arb procedures.

While unanimously applying the pre-reporting system would benefit Chinese overall arbitration enforcement records, Chinese courts are not injecting confidence in foreign parties by alleviating the due process concerns in the Chinese-styled med-arb. Arbitration users are still not seeing Chinese courts as competent reviewers of the arbitrator's partiality when the arbitrator also acts as the mediator in the same case. Perception is important, as the Queen Mary survey shows that "general reputation and recognition," "neutrality and impartiality of the local legal system," and "national arbitration laws" are the most important factors considered when selecting an arbitration seat regionally or internationally.[93] The survey suggests that arbitration users would prefer a seat if its formal arbitration legal structure is seen to be treating users impartially, that is, being "perceived" to be impartial.[94]

5.2 Singapore's experience and the impact on CICC's "one-stop" platform

Promoting efforts on med-arb are similarly found in Singapore recently. The Singapore International Arbitration Center ("SIAC") implements the separation of arbitration and mediation by design. In 2014, the SIAC and Singapore International Mediation Centre ("SIMC") launched an Arb-Med-Arb Protocol (the "AMA Protocol"), where parties entering into an arbitration agreement can settle by both arbitration and mediation. If mediation succeeds, the mediation settlement is considered a consent

---

92 Supreme People's Court, *Relevant Provisions of the Supreme People's Court on Issues concerning Applications for Verification of Arbitration Cases under Judicial Review*, December 26, 2017, art. 2(2), http://www.lawinfochina.com/display.aspx?id=27182&lib=law.

93 Queen Mary University of London School of International Arbitration and White & Case LLP, *2018 International Arbitration Survey: The Evolution of International Arbitration*, 10.

94 Ibid.

award, and is capable of being enforced under the New York Convention.[95] If mediation fails, the parties resume arbitration.[96] Pursuant to the AMA Protocol, arbitration and mediation are conducted independently by the SIAC and SIMC, with arbitrators and mediators appointed by the two institutions separately. The institutional partitioning provides parties with a chance at amicable settlement without the risk of being subject to the same neutral with potentially conflicting roles. The drawback of institutional partitioning is the additional time and resources needed. When med-arb is performed under one roof, the time and resources needed to appoint mediators (or rather, to turn arbitrators into mediators and back) are less demanding.

Singapore's AMA approach quite rightfully rejects the integrated approach to med-arb, which, as demonstrated by how med-arb is conducted in China, has serious defects in due process. But the question turns now to whether Chinese parties, which contribute most of the caseload of Chinese arbitration institutions, are receptive to such an institutional arrangement. Another question is whether Chinese parties are aware of the due process standards required. The *Keeneye* case might have given Chinese arbitrators a false sense of security.

Nevertheless, the attempt by the CICC to move away from conducting arbitration (or litigation) and mediation under one roof and by the same neutral is encouraging, the practice of which has concerned foreign parties due to procedural irregularities. The CICC's new efforts in 2018 bear some resemblance to Singapore's AMA Protocol in 2014. This is particularly pressing in light of the BRI development, as hybrid approaches to disputes such as mediation combined with arbitration (or litigation) is expected to rise exponentially where China is expected to take the lead in streamlining BRI-related dispute resolution processes.

The most recent efforts by the CICC, that is, the shift to separate mediation and arbitration by different institutions rather than med-arb under one roof by the same neutral(s), may indicate that where Chinese parties are not involved exclusively such as those under a cross-border commercial arbitration regime, China is willing to explore due-process-valued hybrid dispute resolution processes. While mediation is an essential part of the Chinese cultural legacy, med-arb might not be required to manifest itself at the sacrifice of justice and impartiality. What the CICC "one-stop" platform sacrifices as compared to traditional Chinese-styled med-arb is the efficiency and lower costs that med-arb conducted by the same neutral is seen to provide.

---

95 "The Singapore Arb-Med-Arb Clause," Singapore International Mediation Centre, accessed July 14, 2020, https://www.siac.org.sg/model-clauses/the-singapore-arb-med-arb-clause/71-resources/frequently-asked-questions.
96 Ibid.

However, as argued earlier in this chapter, the need to attract foreign parties in addition to merely Chinese ones, and the pressure to compete in the BRI arbitration market might be the primary factors in diminishing a Chinese characteristic divide in med-arb practices. As both the initiator and the largest economy in the BRI development, China is in the unique position to shape regional arbitration norms with respect to the BRI. These needs are the leading factors in allowing China to look beyond cultural and socio-political factors.

6 Conclusion

China should regulate med-arb in a better way in order to reconcile local practices (emphasizing mediation) with international expectations (which see arbitration primarily as a form of umpiring). By exporting Chinese-styled med-arb of cultural harmony, procedural looseness, outcome-orientation, and emphasis on efficiency, the problem arises that it might not be compatible with the international compliance of due process under the New York Convention when consequent awards seek recognition and enforcement overseas.

Interestingly, the development of med-arb in China over the past decade does not seem to indicate that due process issues are so pressing such that party familiarity and dispute resolution efficiency are to be subverted for higher standards of impartiality, especially for Chinese domestic parties. While it is still too early to make conclusions on whether Chinese-styled med-arb with due process concerns will impede cross-border adjudication business under the BRI, judging from the most recent efforts of those leading Chinese arbitration institution such as CIETAC, BAC, and SCIA, it is evident that the regulation of med-arb to detach the two processes from being under one roof has become the pressing trend, when they are facing international clients and have to compete with international institutional arbitration service providers in the BRI dispute resolution market.

The establishment of the CICC and its publication of the "One-Stop" Platform proposal shows an enhanced awareness of procedural justice issues in hybrid dispute resolution processes, and the embrace of more practices in med-arb under the BRI dispute resolution context in which China is expected to spearhead. The most recent attempt by the CICC shows that the need to attract foreign parties in addition to merely Chinese ones and the pressure to compete in the BRI dispute resolution market are the leading factors in driving Chinese regulators to look beyond socio-political governance imperatives and cultural boundaries. Moreover, as China is anticipated to propel the BRI dispute resolution system, med-arb as a preference of China will remain a fluid area of localized globalism vis-à-vis globalized localism.

Bibliography

Arbitration Ordinance (Cap. 609) (Hong Kong).

Beijing Arbitration Commission. *Arbitration Rules*, April 1, 2015. https://www.bjac. org.cn/english/page/data_dl/zcgz_en.pdf.

Beijing Arbitration Commission. *Arbitration Rules*, July 4, 2019. https://www.bjac. org.cn/english/page/zc/guize_en2019.html.

China Council for the Promotion of International Trade. *China International Economic and Trade Arbitration Commission (CIETAC) Arbitration Rules*, November 4, 2014. http://www.cietac.org/index.php?m=Page&a=index&id=106&l=en.

China Council for the Promotion of International Trade. *China International Economic and Trade Arbitration Commission International Investment Arbitration Rules (For Trial Implementation)*, September 12, 2017. http://www.cietac.org/index. php?m=Page&a=index&id=390&l=en.

China International Economic and Trade Arbitration Commission. *Annual Report on International Commercial Arbitration in China (2014)*. http://www.cietac.org/ Uploads/201610/57fc0d50a1742.pdf.

China International Economic and Trade Arbitration Commission. *Annual Report on International Commercial Arbitration in China (2015)*.

China International Economic and Trade Arbitration Commission. *Annual Report on International Commercial Arbitration in China (2016)*.

China International Economic and Trade Arbitration Commission. *Annual Report on International Commercial Arbitration in China (2017)*.

China International Economic and Trade Arbitration Commission. *Annual Report on International Commercial Arbitration in China (2018)*.

China International Economic and Trade Arbitration Commission. *Annual Report on International Commercial Arbitration in China (2019)*.

De Vera, Carlos. "Arbitrating Harmony: Med-Arb and the Confluence of Culture and Rule of Law in the Resolution of International Commercial Disputes in China." *Columbia Journal of Asian Law* 18, no. 1 (2004): 149–194.

Fan, Kun. "An Empirical Study of Arbitrators Acting as Mediators in China." *Cardozo Journal of Conflict Resolution* 15, no. 3 (2014): 777–811.

Gao Haiyan v Keeneye Holdings Ltd (2010) HKCFI 980 (Hong Kong).

Gao Haiyan v Keeneye Holdings Ltd (2012) 1 HKLRD 627 (Hong Kong).

Gu, Angran 顾昂然. "Guanyu Zhonghua renmin gongheguo zhongcaifa (caoan) de shuoming" 关于《中华人民共和国仲裁法（草案）》的说明. *Renda gongbao* 人大公报, June 28, 1994. http://www.npc.gov.cn/wxzl/gongbao/2001-01/02/content_5003212.htm.

Gu, Weixia. "Hybrid Dispute Resolution Beyond the Belt and Road: Toward a New Design of Chinese Arb-Med(-Arb) and Its Global Implications." *Washington International Law Journal* 29, no. 1 (2019): 117–171.

Gu, Weixia. "When Local Meets International: Mediation Combined with Arbitration in China and its Prospective Reform in a Comparative Context." *Journal of Comparative Law* 10, no. 2 (2016): 84–105.

Gu, Weixia and Xianchu Zhang. "The Keeneye Case: Rethinking the Content of Public Policy in Cross-Border Arbitration between Hong Kong and Mainland China." *Hong Kong Law Journal* 42, no. 3 (2012): 1001–1029.

Hebei Import & Export Corp v Polytek Engineering Co Ltd (1998) 1 HKLRD 287 (Hong Kong).

International Arbitration Act (Cap. 143A) (Singapore).

"Judges." *China International Commercial Court.* Accessed July 14, 2020. http://cicc.court.gov.cn/html/1/218/19/151/index.html.

Kaufmann-Kohler, Gabrielle. "When Arbitrators Facilitate Settlement: Towards a Transnational Standard." *Arbitration International* 25, no. 2 (2009): 187–206.

Liu, Xiaochun. "Innovations of Chinese International Arbitration–From the Perspective of SCIA." PowerPoint presentation, Seoul, November 8, 2017. http://uncitralrcap.org/wp-content/uploads/2017/12/1-4.-SCIA-President_Liu-ADR_Conference.pdf.

Mason, Paul E. "The Arbitrator as Mediator, and Mediator as Arbitrator." *Journal of International Arbitration* 28, no. 6 (2011): 541–552.

Peter, James T. "Med-Arb in International Arbitration." *American Review of International Arbitration* 8, no. 1 (1997): 83–116.

Queen Mary University of London School of International Arbitration and White & Case LLP. *2018 International Arbitration Survey: The Evolution of International Arbitration*, May 9, 2018. https://www.whitecase.com/publications/insight/2018-international-arbitration-survey-evolution-international-arbitration.

"Secretary for Justice Promotes Hong Kong's Legal and Dispute Resolution Service in Beijing (with Photos)." Department of Justice, August 18, 2015. https://www.info.gov.hk/gia/general/201508/18/P201508180765.htm.

Shanghai International Arbitration Center. *Shanghai International Economic and Trade Arbitration Commission (Shanghai International Arbitration Center Arbitration Rules*, January 1, 2015. http://www.shiac.org/upload/day_141230/SHIAC_ARBITRATION_RULES_2015_141222.pdf.

Shenzhen Court of International Arbitration. "Huanan guozhong tiaojie zhongxin jieshao" 华南国仲调解中心介绍, July 30, 2014. http://www.cnarb.com/Item/1245.aspx.

Shenzhen Court of International Arbitration. *Shenzhen guoji zhongcai yuan zhongcai guize* 深圳国际仲裁院仲裁规则, November 4, 2016. https://uk.practicallaw.thomsonreuters.com/w-005-1124?transitionType=Default&contextData=(sc.Default).

Shenzhen Court of International Arbitration. *Shenzhen guoji zhongcai yuan zhongcai guize* 深圳国际仲裁院仲裁规则, February 21, 2019. http://www.sccietac.org/index.php/Home/index/rule/id/791.html.

Supreme People's Court. *Notice of the Supreme People's Court on Inclusion of the First Group of International Commercial Arbitration and Mediation Institutions in the "One-stop" Diversified International Commercial Dispute Resolution Mechanism*, December 5, 2018. http://cicc.court.gov.cn/html/1/219/208/210/1144.html.

Supreme People's Court. *Opinions of the Supreme People's Court on People's Courts Further Deepening the Reform of Diversified Dispute Resolution Mechanism*, June 28, 2016. https://www.pkulaw.com/en_law/1418572db3297a30bdfb.html.

Supreme People's Court. *Provisions of the Supreme People's Court on Several Issues Concerning the Establishment of the International Commercial Courts*, July 1, 2018. https://cgc.law.stanford.edu/belt-and-road/b-and-r-texts/20180701-provisions-re-intl-commercial-courts/.

Supreme People's Court. *Relevant Provisions of the Supreme People's Court on Issues concerning Applications for Verification of Arbitration Cases under Judicial Review*, December 26, 2017. http://www.lawinfochina.com/display.aspx?id=27182&lib=law.

"The Singapore Arb-Med-Arb Clause." *Singapore International Mediation Centre.* Accessed July 14, 2020. https://www.siac.org.sg/model-clauses/the-singapore-arb-med-arb-clause/71-resources/frequently-asked-questions.

Wang, Shengchang 王生长. *Zhongcai yu tiaojie xiang jiehe de lilun yu shiwu* 仲裁与调解相结合的理论与实务. Beijing: Falv chubanshe 法律出版社, 2001.

Zhongcai Fa (仲裁法) [Arbitration Law] (promulgated by the Standing Committee of the National People's Congress, August 31, 1994, effective September 1, 1995). http://www.npc.gov.cn/wxzl/wxzl/2000-12/05/content_4624.htm.

Part IV
Conclusion

9 Conclusions
China's civil justice reform

1 Introduction

Chapter 1 of this book promised five deliverables. The first, an up-to-date account of the three major civil dispute resolution systems and their hybrid systems, including their actual adoption, procedural rules, and institutional designs, has been provided in the previous chapters. The second, third, and fourth aims, an analytical exploration of the law and development (reform) of the three major civil dispute resolution systems and their hybrid systems, have also been covered in the "Development Analyses" sections in the preceding six chapters.

This chapter will first reflect on China's dispute resolution law and development in the most recent decade. This concluding chapter will further address the fifth aim of the book, that is, to study contemporary civil justice reforms elsewhere in the world so as to provide a comparative framework for thinking about likely trajectories of civil justice reform in China in the years to come.

2 China's dispute resolution reform

This part will deal with the empirical and "law and development" queries posed in the introductory chapter of the book, and pull together various strands in those previous chapters to conclude on China's dispute resolution reform in the most recent decade.

2.1 Conclusions on empirical study

There are two empirical queries raised in Chapter 1 of this book. First, as regards primary (and established) civil dispute resolution systems—civil litigation, arbitration, and mediation—whether legalization and formalization (such as legislative enactment or amendment) have brought about significant increases in the caseload and the number of handling institutions of the relevant civil dispute resolution system. Second, as regards hybrid (and emerging) civil dispute resolution systems—judicial mediation, judicial enforcement of arbitration, and med-arb—whether a particular hybrid dispute resolution mechanism has been widely adopted in resolving civil and commercial disputes in China and how they have been regulated and reformed.

On the first empirical query, through careful analyses of the empirical data over the most recent decade, the book concludes that the promulgation of formal dispute resolution laws or amendment of the same have led to significant increases in the caseload handled by the pertinent dispute resolution system. This conclusion has been empirically tested from Chapters 3 to 5 in the systems of civil litigation, arbitration, and mediation.

On civil litigation, amendments of the Civil Procedure Law (in 2012 and 2017) to include public interest litigations in the civil causes of action have led to an overall increase in both environmental and consumer public interest litigation cases. However, there are more significant increases in environmental cases than in consumer cases. The empirical findings show that when the "administrative level" benchmark of social organizations to sue is more relaxed, there is a corresponding increase in the caseload in civil public interest litigation cases.[1]

On arbitration and mediation, the promulgation of the Arbitration Law (in 1994) has led to significant increases in the caseload of arbitration and growing numbers of the Chinese arbitration commissions.[2] The empirical results, however, stand in stark contrast with those found in the mediation regime where the promulgation of the People's Mediation Law (in 2010) has only led to a growth of the cases handled by the people's mediation system, but not an increase in the overall number of the people's mediation committees in China.[3] The empirical findings show that although mediation and arbitration are both treated as important ADR mechanisms in China to handle civil and commercial disputes, with arbitration focused on pure commercial cases and its dispute resolution outcomes having the benefit of international enforcement, the nature and feature of the Chinese arbitration system vis-à-vis the Chinese mediation system, as well as those of the Chinese arbitration commissions vis-à-vis the Chinese people's mediation committees, are very different.

On the second empirical query, through closely following the statistics of the most recent decade, this book concludes that the three hybrid dispute resolution mechanisms under investigation are widely utilized in resolving civil and commercial disputes in China, and some are over-regulated whilst others are under-regulated, so that reforms are in demand. This conclusion has been empirically tested from Chapters 6 to 8 in the systems of judicial mediation, judicial enforcement of arbitration (with particular focus on the pre-reporting system), as well as med-arb.

---

1 See discussions in Chapter 3.
2 See discussions in Chapter 4.
3 See discussions in Chapter 5.

On judicial mediation, the data show that Chinese courts commonly adopt judicial mediation to resolve various types of civil disputes. The data empirically show judicial mediation's high popularity in civil litigation in China, and reflects the high importance attached to the study and improvement of the system. The empirical findings further demonstrate the heavier reliance on judicial mediation in pure civil disputes in which relationship-keeping (family, torts, and labor) is important than in commercial disputes,[4] reflecting the social function of mediation in building harmonious relations.

On judicial enforcement over arbitration, the data reveal the heavy reliance of the pre-reporting system in arbitration enforcement by foreign investors and the more balanced regulatory approach to extend the system to domestic investors since 2017. The enforcement data also empirically test the investment-sensitiveness of judicial enforcement over arbitration, whose records have followed closely China's national investment strategies such as the Belt and Road Initiative and Free Trade Zone development.[5] The empirical study shows the importance of efforts to improve the system to contribute to China's overall investment environment.

On med-arb, the data empirically show its popularity in the Chinese arbitration setting and the lack of regulation thereof, as a hybrid dispute resolution mechanism gaining increasing importance and recognition in commercial dispute resolution in China.[6]

2.2 Conclusions on law and development studies

Chapter 1 has further raised the issue of how unique China's civil dispute resolution landscape has been reformed in the most recent decade. As discussed in this book, the civil dispute resolution landscape of China works as an ecology, which comprises of several tranches of dispute resolution systems and pertinent systems. Each of these systems has their own institutions and procedures and they interact with one another. By adopting social science contextual studies and law and development analyses, the following section will conclude with the features of the reform discourse and substantiate its uniqueness, summarized by the author as: (a) contextualized in reform contents; (b) hybrid in reform patterns; and (c) fragmented in reform process.

2.2.1 Contextualized in reform contents

First, the details of the civil dispute resolution reforms have been shaped by China's wider political, economic, societal, cultural, and international factors.

---

4 See discussions in Chapter 6.
5 See discussions in Chapter 7.
6 See discussions in Chapter 8.

Fu and Palmer have argued that dispute resolution runs the danger of being a politicized process in authoritarian states.[7] Among the civil dispute resolution systems in China, arbitration as a pure commercial dispute resolution system is comparatively less politicized. China's arbitration reform has been largely influenced by Chinese market forces and investment strategy.[8] The reforms are seen as attempts to contextualize a unique socio-economic dynamic in the Chinese arbitration landscape, with both elements of control and market competition. Unlike the judiciary and mediation committees, arbitration commissions are "private institutions" (*minjian jigou* 民间机构), or at least seek to be non-governmental in nature (*minjianxing* 民间性). In the most recent decade, the free market features have become an even more important force driving the arbitration reform, which has also had positive impacts on the reform of the associated judicial enforcement of the arbitration system in China.

While arbitration is more rule-based and internationalized, mediation is more culture-laden, jurisdiction-specific, and socio-politically embedded.[9] Socio-political orientations prevail in mediation regimes, both in-court (such as the judicial mediation system) and out-of-court (such as the people's mediation system and labor mediation system), making the mediation reforms highly socio-politicized in reform contents. China has consistently been "taking advantage of" mediation's cultural legacy of harmony for enhancing social stability and governance legitimacy.[10] China's distinctive "priority of mediation" national policy throughout the majority part of the 2000s and early 2010s has been strongly infused with China's socio-political contexts, with a felt need by the Chinese leadership to impose instrumentalist promotion and imposition of mediation, justified by a responsibility to maintain social stability and leadership legitimacy, until the trajectory was gradually pulled back to normalization since the mid-2010s. On the other hand, the med-arb system, due to arbitration's commercial and international nature, has developed in a less politicized context but has been influenced by a combination of Chinese local culture (more active mediatory intervention) and international expectations (due-process-driven arbitration).[11]

The arbitration regime is more closely contextualized in the market (both domestic and international) and emphasizes commercial certainty, whereas the mediation regime is prone to the influence of socio-political forces and constraints, and is less certain in the dispute resolution outcome. Compared

---

7 Fu Hualing and Michael Palmer, "Introduction," in *Mediation in Contemporary China: Continuity and Change*, eds. Fu Hualing and Michael Palmer (London: Wildy, Simmonds & Hill Publishing, 2017), 2.

8 See discussions in Section 4.1 of Chapter 4 and Section 5.1 of Chapter 7.

9 Jacqueline Nolan-Haley, "Mediation: The New Arbitration," *Harvard Negotiation Law Review* 17, no. 1 (2012): 86.

10 See discussions in Chapters 5 and 6.

11 See discussions in Chapter 8.

to arbitration and mediation, civil litigation is arguably somewhere in the middle, comparatively more socio-politicized than commercial arbitration but less so than mediation. China's civil litigation reform in the past decade was largely triggered by bottom-up societal grievances. The reform contents account for socio-economic factors such as urbanization and industrialization waves (with environment problems as a key example), but are primarily shaped by socio-political factors such as how to accommodate civil activism in certain civil torts that might be considered litigiously sensitive.[12] Together with the subsequently amended Consumer Protection Law and Environment Protection Law in the mid-2010s, civil public interest litigations have pushed the conventional boundaries of access to civil justice by certain mass tort claims in China.

2.2.2 Hybrid in reform patterns

Second, the reform paths are hybrid in that they have been pushed by the bottom-up demand, followed by top-down responses, and then complemented by bottom-up societal or market initiatives.

As shown in this book, the reform patterns are largely hybrid and dynamic in nature. The reform path of civil litigation began with the demands from the societal grievances at the bottom, identifying inadequacies of the existing civil litigation system, and then pushing for civil public interest litigation as a reform.[13] Similar to the reform path of civil litigation, the development of the mediation regimes (both judicial and extra-judicial) also started with bottom-up societal conflicts, before receiving top-down responses, on the role of mediation in China's dispute resolution governance.[14] In both the cases of civil litigation and mediation, the bottom-up demands are often triggered by changing socio-political contexts in China, and the top-down responses usually take the following forms—legal, judicial, institutional, or even political. For example, the civil litigation system has experienced two rounds of legislative amendments to the Civil Procedure Law in the past decade. The people's mediation and labor mediation systems have seen the promulgation of new laws, setting up of new mediation committees or consolidation of existing mediation committees. For judicial mediation, there have been numerous rounds of court reform, judicial interpretations, and moreover, political policies regarding the changing tone toward judicial mediation, both at the institutional and procedural levels. These top-down responses legalize, institutionalize, and more delicately, instrumentalize the relevant civil dispute resolution systems. In the meantime, there are patterns of bottom-up local initiatives if the top-down responses are not satisfactory.

12 See discussions in Chapter 3.
13 See discussions in Section 4.2 of Chapter 3.
14 See discussions in Section 4.2 of Chapter 5 and Section 4 of Chapter 6.

The mediation development trajectories, both judicial and extra-judicial, have seen significant patterns of bottom-up local initiatives.[15]

On the other hand, the development path of arbitration in China is distinct from that of civil litigation and mediation in the sense that the Arbitration Law has not been substantially amended for more than two decades, despite arbitration's close connection with the market economy and investment environment. China's arbitration regime has seen a simultaneous combination of developments of both top-down regulatory reform led by SPC's judicial interpretations, and bottom-up formation and expansion of the Chinese institutional arbitration market pushed by the market forces. At the bottom level, in the past decade, there have been vibrant competitions among more than 250 Chinese arbitration commissions to attract cases, which have led to a rapid development of these arbitration institutions and their rules to cater to market needs. It seems that the Chinese central government has indirectly "authorized" the reform role to the Chinese arbitration institutions that should otherwise been taken up by top-down legislative amendments to the Arbitration Law. As an "institutional arbitration dominant" jurisdiction, it turns out that China has indirectly delegated the regulation of arbitration to the market of the Chinese arbitration commissions that have mushroomed over the past two decades, which propelled arbitration to become the most vibrant and competitive dispute resolution system in China. The successes of the Beijing Arbitration Commission and Shenzhen Court of International Arbitration after the CIETAC split incident have re-affirmed this dynamic.[16]

2.2.3 Fragmentation in reform process

Third, the reform process has been piecemeal or fragmented. There is a lack of desirable central planning by the Chinese leadership that could direct the overall development of the civil dispute resolution landscape. The state has so far failed to set out and ultimately carry out a comprehensive, coherent, consistent, and methodical scheme that accounts for all existing forms of civil dispute resolution. The reform of the dispute resolution procedures is often not well coordinated with the reform of the pertinent dispute resolution institutions. In a similar vein, the reform of the civil litigation system has not been well coordinated with the reform of the arbitration system, though it touches on the judicial confirmation of mediation settlement agreements that resulted from the people's mediation system.

While procedural reforms of the civil dispute resolution systems largely involved procedural law reforms (such as the amendment of existing laws, promulgation of new laws, publication of new judicial interpretations, etc.),

---

15 Ibid.
16 See discussion in Section 4.2 of Chapter 4, Section 5.2 of Chapter 7, and Section 3.2 of Chapter 8.

institutional reforms of the pertinent civil dispute resolution institutions—courts (for civil litigation and judicial mediation), arbitration commissions (for arbitration and med-arb), and mediation committees (for extra-judicial civil mediations such as people's mediation and labor mediation)—have been promoted by various regulatory branches and sources, and driven by different motivations.

The five rounds of China's court reform over more than three decades, led by different SPC Presidents (Chief Justices) who had very different professional backgrounds and career experiences, have seen waxes and wanes of the role of courts in China's societal governance, as well as pendulum swings between adjudicatory and mediatory justice.[17]

With its strong focus on stability and harmonious society building, the institutional developments of the people's mediation committees and labor dispute mediation committees have largely been motivated by the policy to use mediatory intervention to control disagreements so that social stability could be maintained.[18] The institutional reforms of Chinese arbitration commissions are more optimistic. With free market features being the primary force driving the arbitration institutional reform, while some elements of the system are still under-developed, there are several Chinese arbitration commissions growing and becoming outstanding enough to be advanced institutional players that have the capacity to compete with regional and international institutional arbitration players in light of the dispute resolution competition along the Belt and Road.[19]

The Chinese approach to the reform is different from those contemporary civil justice reforms in developed rule-of-law jurisdictions, which are more often approached holistically in the reform processes, focused on enhancement of procedural justice in the reform contents, and showing a legally top-down pattern in the reform paths. The Chinese approach to civil justice reform is, however, seen as a social project to adapt and respond to China's unique socio-political and socio-economic contextual environment. This will be further examined in this chapter in providing comparative insights and ideas regarding China's civil justice reform in the future.

3 China's civil justice reform in the future

This book finally places the law and development of Chinese dispute resolution in the context of the wider international trends of civil justice reform. The final part of this conclusion will refer to contemporary civil justice movements elsewhere to provide a comparative framework for thinking about civil justice reform in China in the future.

17 See discussions in Section 3 of Chapter 2 and Sections 2.2, 2.3, and 3.2 of Chapter 6.
18 See discussions in Sections 4 and 5 of Chapter 5.
19 See discussions in Section 3.3 of Chapter 4 and Section 3.2 of Chapter 8.

3.1 Civil justice movement elsewhere

Many established rule-of-law jurisdictions, such as the United Kingdom ("UK"), the United States ("US"), Australia and Hong Kong, faced a similar kind of civil justice crises in the past several decades, and they have gone through significant revisions of their civil justice systems in recent decades. Although their relative weight and exact formulation varied, these contemporary civil justice reforms all shared a common set of principles that underlined the reform which emphasized procedural concerns in civil trials, such as cost effectiveness, expeditiousness, and the use of ADRs.[20]

The UK is one of the first contemporary movers of civil justice reform in the common law world. Hong Kong has followed the UK's footsteps closely in civil justice reform, but also shares close connection with China in economic exchange and culture proximity. These two jurisdictions are chosen here for study, and their civil justice reforms are discussed, so as to suggest comparative insights that China might gain from their experiences.

Both the UK and Hong Kong have a common-law type adversarial procedure in civil trials. However, the passive role of the judge led to procedural inefficiency and undue delay, which called for respective reforms. In the UK, the major reforms to the civil justice landscape took place in 1998, following the Access to Justice Reports by Lord Woolf in 1995 and 1996, respectively. In the two reports, Lord Woolf concluded that while the problems of cost, delay, and complexity in civil justice were interlinked, the principal cause of the shortcomings of the civil justice system was found in the behavior of lawyers and their adversarial tactics. Lord Woolf proposed an increased judicial power to be exercised by judges in case management and promotion of earlier settlement through the introduction of a new civil procedural code, the Civil Procedural Rules (the "CPR").[21] Lord Woolf believed that the role of the court in the UK was not merely to deliver justice on the merits, but also to do so at proportionate cost and in a timely manner.[22] These "overriding objectives" aimed to increase access to civil justice by the general public and rectify procedural inefficiency, and they were enthusiastically embraced by judges when interpreting the rules.[23] In Hong Kong, the civil justice reform ("CJR") came into force in 2009, more than ten years after the Woolf Reform in the UK. Similar to the "overriding objectives"

---

20 Michael Legg and Andrew Higgins, "Responding to Cost and Delay Through Overriding Objectives—Successful Innovation?," in *The Dynamism of Civil Procedure—Global Trends and Development*, eds. Colin B. Picker and Guy I. Seidman (New York: Springer, 2016), 157–159.

21 The Civil Procedural Rules 1998 (United Kingdom), http://www.legislation.gov.uk/uksi/1998/3132/contents/made.

22 Ibid., rule 1.1.

23 Ibid., rule 1.2(b) states the court must seek to give effect to the overriding objective when it interprets any rule, while rule 1.3 imposes a duty on the parties to help the court further the overriding objective.

in the UK, the CJR in Hong Kong introduced the "underlying objectives" in the Rules of the High Court, conferring case management powers on the courts, under the principles of efficiency, expedition, and equality of arms.[24]

Moreover, the civil justice reforms in the UK and Hong Kong both identified the need to devote more resources to ADR services and developments in order to relieve the court burden, increase access to justice, and eliminate undue delays and other procedural inefficiencies. Specifically, the reforms called for mediation mechanisms to be integrated into the civil litigation process as a standard alternative to the traditional adversarial trial process. ADR services such as arbitration were also promoted as they were deemed to have the advantage of saving scarce judicial resources and producing quicker results, so as to ultimately relegate trial to a mechanism of last resort. Under the new landscape of civil justice systems in the UK and Hong Kong, ADR, in particular mediation, is required to be attempted before court proceedings in order to achieve earlier settlement. Lord Woolf further enhanced the role of ADR within the court processes by conferring on the court discretionary powers of case management to facilitate ADR procedures.[25] If a party refuses to consider ADR options at an appropriate point, it could well end up facing adverse cost implications.[26] In a similar vein, in Hong Kong, if the court is of the view that a party has unreasonably refused an offer of mediation, the court might deprive the party of legal costs. The cost sanction exerts pressures on parties to at least attempt settlement in court processes.[27]

The ADR movement, including such innovations as the encouragement of settlements in civil trials, has also been absorbed in other established jurisdictions in the world. Nolan-Haley argues for a renewed appreciation of mediation in the US, given the high cost of litigation and adversarial gain dominated by lawyers.[28] Menkel-Meadow traces the increasing institutionalization and formalization of ADR services as part of the overall pattern in

---

24 The Rules of the High Court (Cap. 4A) (Hong Kong), Order 1A, rule 1.
25 For example, rule 1.4(e) of the Civil Procedural Rules provides that the court must encourage and facilitate parties to use an ADR procedure if it considers that appropriate. Additionally, during the litigation process the parties may request a stay of proceedings under rule 26.4 in order to attempt settlement.
26 The CPR has a number of pre-action protocols. In the Practice Direction to these protocols, one of the objectives is to enable parties to avoid litigation by agreeing to a settlement of the claim before the commencement of proceedings. Under the Practice Direction, the court can make significant costs sanctions if it believes that the non-compliance by parties has led to the commencement of proceedings that should not have needed to be commenced.
27 Gu Weixia, "Civil Justice Reform in Hong Kong: Challenges and Opportunities for Development of Alternative Dispute Resolution," *Hong Kong Law Journal* 40, no. 1 (2010): 43–64.
28 Jacqueline Nolan-Haley, "Mediation: The Best and Worst of Times," *Cardozo Journal of Conflict Resolution* 16, no. 1 (2014): 731–740.

the US civil litigation system in recent decades.[29] Likewise, in the UK, Genn has researched extensively the decline in trials in English civil courts in the past decade. She argues that private settlement often secured by means of meditation under court's case management powers has become a popular trend to process civil disputes in the UK.[30]

These contemporary civil justice reforms have been viewed to be successful where the court's case management powers were promoted, and the use of ADR services became more institutionalized. There has also been an increasing need for high quality and integrity in the use of ADR methods (such as mediation) in civil trials, as renewed aims for civil justice reforms.[31]

3.2 Comparative insights for China

Contemporary civil justice reforms in the established rule-of-law jurisdictions have transcended the court's role from purely searching for substantive justice to embracing a multi-faceted agenda to make legal proceedings cheaper, quicker, and more accessible. This was achieved through instructing the judges to act also as case managers responsible for rationing and proportioning civil procedures, as well as encouraging the use of ADR and settlement in the civil litigation. The ultimate objectives were to resolve procedural concerns on civil justice. The following discussion shows, however, that there are some fundamental differences that distinguish the Chinese approach to civil justice reform from those outlined earlier in this chapter.

To begin with, in the established rule-of-law jurisdictions, civil justice reforms were primarily procedural reforms that targeted at how the judiciary and legal profession could operate more economically in procedure so as to reduce the financial burden of the disputants and the length of the judicial processes. The reforms did not aim to solve social problems and issues, and even if they did, that was not directly intended.

By contrast, China's civil justice reform in the most recent decades is part of a much larger social project of which the principal aims have been to adapt and respond to a bundle of socio-economic and socio-political transformations in China.[32] It is an ambitious task to resolve social issues through reforming civil dispute resolution and related institutions. Economic growth, a stable society, and above all, the Party's governance legitimacy,

---

29 Carrie Menkel-Meadow, "Regulation of Dispute Resolution in the United States of America: From the Formal to Informal to the 'Semi-Formal'," in *Regulating Dispute Resolution: ADR and Access to Justice at the Crossroads*, eds. Felix Steffek, Hannes Unberath, Hazel Genn, Reinhard Greger and Carrie Menkel-Meadow (Oxford: Hart, 2013), 419–454.

30 Hazel Genn, "Why the Privatization of Civil Justice is A Rule of Law Issue," (lecture, London, November 19, 2012), https://www.ucl.ac.uk/laws/sites/laws/files/36th-f-a-mann-lecture-19.11.12-professor-hazel-genn.pdf.

31 Carrie Menkel-Meadow, "Maintaining ADR Integrity," *Alternatives to the High Cost of Litigation* 27, no. 1 (2009): 7–9.

32 See Section 2 of this chapter.

remain motivations for China's civil justice reform. This also reminds us that civil justice in China is more of an instrument, but not an end, of pursuing those substantive goals above. The many challenges that China's civil dispute resolution reforms have endured, as examined by previous chapters of this book, prove this. This is the core reason that sets China's civil justice reform in the past one to two decades and in the foreseeable future apart from other jurisdictions.

As already noted, in jurisdictions of established rule-of-law systems and traditions, civil justice reforms were mainly brought about by concerns over procedural justice. In a huge developing rule-of-law jurisdiction such as China, however, while the amended Civil Procedural Law might have solved the problems of due process and court efficiency in part, the reforms were ultimately shaped by the socio-economic and socio-political contextual factors of China. Procedurally, civil public interest litigation was introduced in 2012 and expanded in 2017 in the amendments to the Civil Procedure Law as a result of the rapid economic transformation (such as industrialization and urbanization) in China and the resulting societal problems involving devastating product liability and environmental pollution.[33] By adding a new cause of action with respect to serious mass torts, although the reform might have enhanced the access to civil justice by the general Chinese public, the underlying rationale was still to propose a mechanism for the public to air their grievances on socio-economic and socio-political issues.

Institutionally, the first two rounds of the Chinese court reform (1999–2008) exhibited ambitions of the modernization of the judiciary and aspirations of procedural justice according to internationally established norms.[34] The reforms that enabled the judiciary to provide for more procedural safeguards in civil litigation were also motivated by economic development. At the time, China was taking major steps toward opening up its economy to the international market. One development was China's accession to the World Trade Organization ("WTO") in late 2001, and in association with the accession, China needed to learn to become a WTO player in the initial years. By introducing a professional judiciary, China hoped to attract more foreign investments. However, once economic development was no longer the priority or imperative consideration that would inform the civil justice reform, the socio-political contextual environment became the primary consideration of top-down reforms. By the third round of the court reform (2009–2013), litigation was seen to be a barrier to a harmonious society, which the Chinese government aimed to construct at the time. Civil litigation was sidelined as a last resort mechanism to resolve disputes, not because of cost and efficiency as other jurisdictions might have considered, but for the sake of stability maintenance of Chinese governance legitimacy in China's unique

---

33 See discussions in Chapter 3.
34 See discussions in Chapter 2.

circumstances. Mediation was heavily promoted as the principal method in civil dispute resolution, even at the expense of procedural justice, focusing on the substantive outcome of the dispute resolution process. One of the then main tensions in the Chinese civil dispute resolution landscape was between adjudicatory justice and mediatory justice. There was significant overlap of which disputes ought to be resolved through litigation and which by mediation. With maintenance of harmonious society as the prevailing socio-political philosophy at the time, mediation was perceived as having encroached into civil litigation's empire of dispute resolution.[35] The most recent court reform after 2013 saw a decline of the "mediation first" policy and a switch to normalized approach of "mediation as appropriate" where litigation and mediation are required to be adopted to serve different purposes.

In addition, although civil justice reforms or civil procedural reforms in other jurisdictions might have relied on the top-down pattern in reform as part of their responsive governance, in the sense that their judicial institutions initiated the reforms and legislative authorities promulgated legislative amendments to the civil procedural laws and rules, the judicial institutional contexts of those jurisdictions and China are entirely different. The Chinese judiciary operates under the Party. This means that the Chinese courts are integrated into the Party governance structure, and do not constitute a separate branch of the state power whose primary constitutional function is to resolve disputes through adjudication. Thus, not only are the courts instrumentally used to promote substantive Party-State policies, as in the case of the consistent promotion, and even prioritization, of judicial mediation in Chinese civil trials, the performance of the courts and judges is also evaluated with respect to their ability to promote the Party-State governance policies. Courts in China carry an implicit duty to promote state legitimacy both in their operation and adjudicatory outcomes.[36]

Moreover, there is the relative unimportance of procedural justice in the Chinese approach to the dispute resolution reform. Due to the reasons explained earlier in this chapter, the foremost consideration in China's policy of civil justice reform is whether the reform could promote state legitimacy, concertized by economic development and social stability. Improvements to civil and commercial dispute resolution procedures as part of the civil justice reform are considered ancillary, and only happen to emerge when state legitimacy is in the first place improved. The top-down responses, informed by socio-economic and socio-political contexts from bottom-up, will actively seek to promote improvements to procedural justice only if they promote state legitimacy. One example of this would be the latest developments in arbitration such as the formation of the Chinese arbitration market and the rise of several leading Chinese arbitration institutions to compete in

---

35 See discussions in Chapter 6.
36 See discussions in Chapter 2.

the Belt and Road dispute resolution market on behalf of China.[37] Another example would be the recent "judgments online" project promoted in China to enhance judicial transparency and judge's accountability.[38]

The respective theoretical perceptions of civil justice in China could also explain their differences in the extent of institutionalization. Contemporary civil justice reforms in established rule-of-law jurisdictions are considered both a public and private good. It was believed that when private disputes could be settled in a timely, cost-efficient manner, the public could also be benefitted by the resulting improvement in access to justice and removal of the procedural bars for the public to bring their disputes for resolution.[39] On the other hand, in China, as a huge developing rule-of-law nation, the civil justice reform is taken as a social project which has all along aimed to respond to the changes according to the socio-political and socio-economic contexts in China. Social stability and societal harmony were prioritized over procedural justice and due process, as shown in the massive mediation campaigns both inside and outside the Chinese courts.[40] Accordingly, while civil justice reforms in the UK and in Hong Kong were more holistic because they aimed to achieve merely procedural objectives, the reforms in China were rather multi-directional and fragmented because they targeted at more variables, political, social, economic, legal, etc.

Last but not least, in the experiences of the UK and Hong Kong, arbitration, mediation, and other ADR systems are regulated and institutionalized more systematically as part of the whole package of the civil justice reform, suggesting that efforts to reform the civil litigation system must also involve concerted changes to the arbitration, mediation, and other ADR systems. However, in China, arbitration, mediation, and their hybrid dispute resolution mechanisms developed more on their own. China's ADR regimes in general have grown in a more piecemeal, fragmented, and ad hoc manner, rather than having the entire civil justice project taken holistically. The strong social function of mediation in China presents additional difficulty to it being taken as part of the Chinese civil justice reform. Hence, China's civil justice reform journey did not bring about the expected outcomes like the reforms that happened in the UK and Hong Kong.

3.3 Concluding remarks and the future of China's civil justice reform

China's civil justice reform journey thus far has not been easy—and it should not be expected to be so. The transformation of Chinese society took off since the early days of China's economic reform in the late 1970s and 1980s,

37 See discussions in Chapters 4 and 8.
38 See discussions in Chapter 2.
39 Hazel Genn, "What Is Civil Justice For? Reform, ADR, and Access to Justice," *Yale Journal of Law & Humanities* 24, no. 1 (2012): 397–417.
40 See discussions in Chapters 5 and 6.

and the country is still very much in a state of transition. If those early days were contemporary China's infancy, then the 2000s, 2010s, and the days to come would be China's adolescence. China is still learning to adapt to and resolve the many challenges of social transformation, using the limited legal tools under China's unique governance structure that may not be suited for such a tremendous task.

By contrast, addressing the issues pertaining to social transformation is never the objective of civil justice reforms in Western jurisdictions or Asian jurisdictions with established legal systems. In those jurisdictions, reforms are designed to target shortcomings of the civil procedure, and in particular, to improve the procedural access to justice. Procedural reforms aim at reducing parties' financial burden and increasing judges' handling efficiency through case management, while institutional reforms work toward promoting and integrating more ADR services to reduce the judicial workload and resources. Thus, civil justice reforms of this kind only concern with the fine-tuning of procedures and the consolidation of dispute resolution services.

China's civil justice reform is a social project of a much larger scale. It is more concerned with handling socio-political and socio-economic problems than with issues such as improvement of the procedure and consolidation of dispute resolution services. Civil dispute resolution procedural mechanisms and their counterpart institutions only come into play as instruments for social transformation and to resolve the disputes arising from such a transformation. The instrumentalist nature which sets China's civil justice reform apart from those in other jurisdictions has several implications.

To begin with, the success of China's civil justice reform is measured not by easily quantifiable measures of lowering down judicial costs, caseloads, and average length of proceedings, but the extent to which social conflicts are alleviated. This measure of success is problematically unique to China's socio-political and socio-economic contextual settings. When civil justice reform is tasked with dealing with such persistent issues, then the "reform" becomes an aspect of social development project, rather than a purely legal project leading to structured legal changes such as the enhancement of procedural justice, which had occurred in general civil justice reforms elsewhere. As a result, it would be difficult to define a state where civil justice reform in China could be "complete."

This implies further that China's civil justice reform was not designed from the outset to meet a certain legal objective. Rather, as demonstrated by developments in all three major civil dispute resolution systems and their hybrid systems explored in previous chapters, in most of the cases, reforms tend to address socio-political and socio-economic issues and are piecemeal or fragmented in the reform process. They are driven by the expected instrumentalist outcomes of state legitimacy, which are then concretized by outcomes of social stability and economic development; any improvements to the access to civil justice are ancillary to give effect to these outcomes.

When thinking about civil justice reform in China, it is perhaps inaccurate to conceive it as a self-contained, systematic revamping of civil procedures and pertaining dispute resolution institutions. It is more accurately a collection of fragmented, ad hoc, and incremental social responses, rather than a series of sweeping and foundational legal reforms. There has been little effort by the Chinese leadership to organize civil litigation, arbitration, mediation, and the hybrid dispute resolution mechanisms arising out of their interactions and procedures into a grand, institutionalized, coherent, and consistent civil justice mega-scheme as what contemporary civil justice movements elsewhere have aimed at. This socio-legal-driven and piecemeal approach might have served its purpose before the emergence of the "strangers' society" in China with the litigation explosion, and before China opened up its market completely to foreign investments. But, as the sphere of application of the civil dispute resolution systems collides with the transitions of the wider Chinese society in which they are placed, the functions of each of these mechanisms and their interactions become elusive, and their respective limitations in their social settings begin to emerge.

What about the future of China's civil dispute resolution landscape and civil justice reform in general? Prediction is sometimes perilous, particularly as the subject is complexly embedded in China's wider socio-economic and socio-political transitions. For readers who have followed the arguments in the previous chapters, as well as those already discussed in this concluding chapter, they may appreciate China's distinctive social contextual constraints on the entire civil dispute resolution landscape and its development. As such, skepticism will continue to be the watchword on the effect of future reform, based on the implications of the contextual constraints' thesis presented in this book. In addition, while the procedures of civil litigation, arbitration, mediation, and their hybrid dispute resolution mechanisms may be more technically improved and further fine-tuned in the foreseeable future, pertaining institutional reforms are more politically sensitive and difficult.

As the world's most populous country and largest developing rule-of-law jurisdiction with an authoritarian political system, at present, the political priority of social stability maintenance may still loom large in all dispute resolution institutions, including Chinese courts, mediation committees, and arbitration commissions. But, the proportion of cases perceived to be politically sensitive is much lower in the arbitration setting. It does seem that socio-political embeddedness is less of a tangled web in arbitration institutions, although they are subject to the socio-economic environment such as China's market orientation and investment policies. The development path of Chinese arbitration has seen the establishment of the Chinese institutional arbitration market and the flourishing of some leading Chinese arbitration commissions in a unique synthesis of socio-economic dynamics. As this book emphasizes, the arbitration regime is relatively more rule-based, commercialized, and internationalized. The arbitration regime has seen the success of institutional reform, but the experience of market-driven institutional reform of Chinese arbitration commissions may not be easily transplanted to the Chinese courts and mediation committees. As pointed out earlier, the civil litigation and mediation regimes are more instrumentalist in nature and socio-politically embedded.

Then what is the likely future of China's civil litigation and mediation regimes? Fortunately, the situation is not without hope, at least from an academic point of view. There are some promising signs that favor the gradual "evolution" toward more structured change and progress in China's civil litigation and mediation regimes.

If we look at the grand dispute resolution policies developed by China in the most recent years, the central government has been pushing for greater legitimacy of law both within the instrumentalist framework of the Chinese state, and to expand China's influence in the international legal order in the context of her ambitious development of the Belt and Road Initiative.[41] To accomplish this, central policies have been adjusted to move back again toward court professionalization and judicial identity in China,[42] and toward upgrading the Chinese mediation system toward professionalism-building to facilitate the "one-stop" platform created by the China International Commercial Court.[43] In Ng and He's recently published empirical studies on Chinese courts, many of the young Chinese judges they interviewed expressed their professional aspiration to develop a rule-based culture in civil litigation that will put more emphasis on procedural justice. Meanwhile, newer law graduates see a civil judge's primary responsibility as adjudication rather than judicial mediation. They want to use the law more, and are more reluctant to yield to external and internal extralegal demands in trials.[44]

As to mediation, it has been revealed in previous chapters that Chinese mediators do not enjoy occupational security. Their incentive of involvement in the mediation work is largely derived from their sense of social responsibility in contributing toward a harmonious society.[45] Scholars have now published works to strengthen the mediators' identity in China, and they have also introduced rule-of-law-based mediation theories and practices to the Chinese community.[46] Chinese law schools are also promoting the professionalization of mediators and arbitrators. Mediation, arbitration, and ADR courses are now taught in some of China's leading law schools as legal

41 Matthew Erie, "Chinese Law and Development," *Harvard International Law Journal* 62, no. 1 (2021), https://ssrn.com/abstract=3552044.

42 See discussions in Section 3.4 of Chapter 2 and Section 3.2 of Chapter 6.

43 See discussions in Section 3.3 of Chapter 8.

44 Ng Kwai Hang and He Xin, *Embedded Courts: Judicial Decision-Making in China* (Cambridge: Cambridge University Press, 2017), 197–198.

45 See discussions in Section 5.1 of Chapter 5.

46 Peter Chan, *Mediation in Contemporary Chinese Civil Justice* (Leiden: Brill, 2017); see also Zhao Yun, *Mediation Practice and Skills* 调解实务与技能, (Beijing: Tsinghua University Press 北京: 清华大学出版社, 2015).

subjects separate from civil litigation.[47] China's recent accession to the United Nations Convention on International Settlement Agreements Resulting from Mediation (also referred to as the "Singapore Mediation Convention") has further exerted pressure on Chinese mediation to live up to at least some international standards.[48] It would therefore be likely that this new generation of college-trained mediators will develop professionalism and a greater affinity with procedural justice in the Chinese mediation system.

To conclude, this is an academic work which seeks to provide comprehensive insights into the status quo and reform of the entire civil dispute resolution landscape (civil litigation, arbitration, mediation, and hybrid dispute resolution systems arising out of their interactions) in recent decades in China. While this book has identified the uniqueness of the landscape through empirical, contextual, and comparative research, as well as the law and development analytical framework, the book has also pointed out that some of the constraints and pitfalls are rooted in some systemic problems in China.[49] In essence, China's civil dispute resolution landscape is a social development project rather than a purely legal project, conditioned by China's political considerations, in various forms and varying degrees that distinguish the Chinese approach to civil justice reform from contemporary civil justice reform elsewhere. The political priority of social stability maintenance still looms large in all dispute resolution institutions, including Chinese courts, mediation committees, and arbitration commissions, although arbitration is comparatively less politicized. In the end, China's civil justice reform, as with reforms of other legal areas, would be part of an ongoing project to achieve overall progress in the rule of law. As this book makes clear, the arbitration system in China and its associated hybrid dispute resolution mechanisms, such as judicial enforcement of arbitration and med-arb, have already seen some hopeful developments. Chinese arbitration reform in the most recent years has won trust at both institutional and procedural levels. China's civil litigation and mediation regimes, particularly their operational institutions, though entangled by more socio-political constraints and less influenced by market forces and international norms, are far from hopeless. Younger generations of dispute resolution scholars and practitioners in China, who aspire to higher standards of dispute resolution professionalism, are expected to grow to become the pacesetters in implementing necessary civil justice reforms as a legal or

---

47 For example, Renmin University Law School runs the famous research center on dispute resolution where mediation, arbitration, and ADR courses are all separately offered in Renmin University Law School.

48 On August 7, 2019, China joined the Singapore Mediation Convention. See "China Signs the United Nations Convention on International Settlement Agreements Resulting from Mediation," Ministry of Commerce, August 8, 2019, http://english.mofcom.gov.cn/article/newsrelease/significantnews/201908/20190802891357.shtml.

49 See discussions in Chapters 3 to 8 on the sections entitled "The Future."

rule-of-law project in China in the future. Such a project is likely to focus on enhancement of procedural justice in its reform contents, to adopt a holistic and coherent approach in its reform process, and to follow mainly a legally top-down reform pattern.

Bibliography

Chan, Peter. *Mediation in Contemporary Chinese Civil Justice*. Leiden: Brill, 2017.

"China Signs the United Nations Convention on International Settlement Agreements Resulting from Mediation." Ministry of Commerce, August 8, 2019. http://english.mofcom.gov.cn/article/newsrelease/significantnews/201908/20190802891357.shtml.

Erie, Matthew. "Chinese Law and Development." *Harvard International Law Journal* 62, no. 1 (2021). https://ssrn.com/abstract=3552044.

Fu, Hualing and Michael Palmer. "Introduction." In *Mediation in Contemporary China: Continuity and Change*, edited by Fu Hualing and Michael Palmer, 1–33. London: Wildy, Simmonds & Hill Publishing, 2017.

Genn, Hazel. "What Is Civil Justice For? Reform, ADR, and Access to Justice." *Yale Journal of Law & Humanities* 24, no. 1 (2012): 397–417.

Genn, Hazel. "Why the Privatization of Civil Justice is A Rule of Law Issue." Lecture, London, November 19, 2012. https://www.ucl.ac.uk/laws/sites/laws/files/36th-f-a-mann-lecture-19.11.12-professor-hazel-genn.pdf.

Gu, Weixia, "Civil Justice Reform in Hong Kong: Challenges and Opportunities for Development of Alternative Dispute Resolution." *Hong Kong Law Journal* 40, no. 1 (2010): 43–64.

Legg, Michael. and Andrew Higgins, "Responding to Cost and Delay Through Overriding Objectives—Successful Innovation?." In *The Dynamism of Civil Procedure—Global Trends and Development*, edited by Colin B. Picker and Guy I. Seidman, 157–181. New York: Springer, 2016.

Menkel-Meadow, Carrie. "Maintaining ADR Integrity." *Alternatives to the High Cost of Litigation* 27, no. 1 (2009): 7–9.

Menkel-Meadow, Carrie. "Regulation of Dispute Resolution in the United States of America: From the Formal to Informal to the 'Semi-Formal'." In *Regulating Dispute Resolution: ADR and Access to Justice at the Crossroads*, edited by Felix Steffek, Hannes Unberath, Hazel Genn, Reinhard Greger and Carrie Menkel-Meadow, 419–454. Oxford: Hart, 2013.

Ng, Kwai Hang and He Xin, *Embedded Courts: Judicial Decision-Making in China*. Cambridge: Cambridge University Press, 2017.

Nolan-Haley, Jacqueline. "Mediation: The Best and Worst of Times." *Cardozo Journal of Conflict Resolution* 16, no. 1 (2014): 731–740.

Nolan-Haley, Jacqueline. "Mediation: The New Arbitration." *Harvard Negotiation Law Review* 17, no, 1 (2012): 61–95.

The Civil Procedural Rules 1998 (United Kingdom). http://www.legislation.gov.uk/uksi/1998/3132/contents/made.

The Rules of the High Court (Cap. 4A) (Hong Kong).

Zhao, Yun. *Mediation Practice and Skills* 北京: 清华大学出版社 Beijing: Tsinghua University Press 调解实务与技能, 2015.

Index

Printed in the United States
By Bookmasters